Vauxhall Carlton Owners Workshop Manual

John S Mead

Models covered

Vauxhall Carlton Saloon and Estate
Base, L, GL, iCD and iGL
1796 cc, 1979 cc & 2197 cc petrol engines

Does not cover Diesel engine or 'new' Carlton introduced November 1986

(480-8S6)

ABCDE
FGHIJ
KLMN

2

THE BOOK

Haynes Publishing Group
Sparkford Nr Yeovil
Somerset BA22 7JJ England

Haynes Publications, Inc
861 Lawrence Drive
Newbury Park
California 91320 USA

Acknowledgements

Thanks are due to the Champion Sparking Plug Company Limited who supplied the illustrations showing spark plug conditions, to Holt Lloyd Limited who supplied the illustrations showing bodywork repair, and to Duckhams Oils who provided lubrication data. Thanks are also due to Vauxhall Motors Limited for the supply of technical information and certain illustrations and to all those people at Sparkford who helped in the production of this manual.

A book in the **Haynes Owners Workshop Manual Series**

Printed by J. H. Haynes & Co. Ltd, Sparkford, Nr Yeovil, Somerset BA22 7JJ, England

ISBN 1 85010 329 1

British Library Cataloguing in Publication Data
Mead, John S.
   Vauxhall Carlton ('78 to '86) owners workshop manual.
   -3rd ed- (Owners Workshop Manuals/Haynes).
   1. Carlton automobile
   I. Title   II. Series
   629.28'722   TL215.C3/
   ISBN 1-85010-329-1

Restoring and Preserving our Motoring Heritage

Few people can have had the luck to realise their dreams to quite the same extent and in such a remarkable fashion as John Haynes, Founder and Chairman of the Haynes Publishing Group.

Since 1965 his unique approach to workshop manual publishing has proved so successful that millions of Haynes Manuals are now sold every year throughout the world, covering literally thousands of different makes and models of cars, vans and motorcycles.

A continuing passion for cars and motoring led to the founding in 1985 of a Charitable Trust dedicated to the restoration and preservation of our motoring heritage. To inaugurate the new Museum, John Haynes donated virtually his entire private collection of 52 cars.

Now with an unrivalled international collection of over 210 veteran, vintage and classic cars and motorcycles, the Haynes Motor Museum in Somerset is well on the way to becoming one of the most interesting Motor Museums in the world.

A 70 seat video cinema, a cafe and an extensive motoring bookshop, together with a specially constructed one kilometre motor circuit, make a visit to the Haynes Motor Museum a truly unforgettable experience.

Every vehicle in the museum is preserved in as near as possible mint condition and each car is run every six months on the motor circuit.

Enjoy the picnic area set amongst the rolling Somerset hills. Peer through the William Morris workshop windows at cars being restored, and browse through the extensive displays of fascinating motoring memorabilia.

From the 1903 Oldsmobile through such classics as an MG Midget to the mighty 'E' Type Jaguar, Lamborghini, Ferrari Berlinetta Boxer, and Graham Hill's Lola Cosworth, there is something for everyone, young and old alike, at this Somerset Museum.

Haynes Motor Museum

Situated mid-way between London and Penzance, the Haynes Motor Museum is located just off the A303 at Sparkford, Somerset (home of the Haynes Manual) and is open to the public 7 days a week all year round, except Christmas Day and Boxing Day.

Contents

Spark plug condition and bodywork repair colour pages between pages 32 and 33

About this manual

Its aim

The aim of this manual is to help you get the best value from your car. It can do so in several ways. It can help you decide what work must be done (even should you choose to get it done by a garage), provide information on routine maintenance and servicing, and give a logical course of action and diagnosis when random faults occur. However, it is hoped that you will use the manual by tackling the work yourself. On simpler jobs it may even be quicker than booking the car into a garage and going there twice to leave and collect it. Perhaps most important, a lot of money can be saved by avoiding the costs the garage must charge to cover its labour and overheads.

The manual has drawings and descriptions to show the function of the various components so that their layout can be understood. Then the tasks are described and photographed in a step-by-step sequence so that even a novice can do the work.

Its arrangement

The manual is divided into thirteen Chapters, each covering a logical sub-division of the vehicle. The Chapters are each divided into Sections, numbered with single figures, eg 5; and the Sections into paragraphs (or sub-sections), with decimal numbers following on from the Section they are in, eg 5.1, 5.2, 5.3 etc.

It is freely illustrated, especially in those parts where there is a detailed sequence of operations to be carried out. There are two forms of illustration: figures and photographs. The figures are numbered in sequence with decimal numbers, according to their position in the Chapter – eg Fig. 6.4 is the fourth drawing/illustration in Chapter 6. Photographs carry the same number (either individually or in related groups) as the Section or sub-section to which they relate.

There is an alphabetical index at the back of the manual as well as a contents list at the front. Each Chapter is also preceded by its own individual contents list.

References to the 'left' or 'right' of the vehicle are in the sense of a person in the driver's seat facing forwards.

Unless otherwise stated, nuts and bolts are removed by turning anti-clockwise, and tightened by turning clockwise.

Vehicle manufacturers continually make changes to specifications and recommendations, and these, when notified, are incorporated into our manuals at the earliest opportunity.

Whilst every care is taken to ensure that the information in this manual is correct, no liability can be accepted by the authors or publishers for loss, damage or injury caused by any errors in, or omissions from, the information given.

Introduction to the Vauxhall Carlton

The new Vauxhall Carlton 2000, introduced in October 1978, has been completely styled and engineered around a proven formula which offers spacious and comfortable accommodation, lively performance and excellent handling.

The models covered by this manual comprise the four-door Saloons and five-door Estate car, available with either a 2 litre or 2.2 litre cam-in-head engine, or a 1.8 litre overhead camshaft engine.

All models are equipped with servo-assisted brakes, disc on the front wheels and drum at the rear. For safety, the system is dual line with a special anti-locking valve fitted in the hydraulic line to the rear brakes.

Front suspension is independent by MacPherson struts, a departure from the traditional Vauxhall wishbone type, while the live rear axle is located by trailing arms and a Panhard rod and is supported by coil springs and telescopic shock absorbers. Anti-roll bars are fitted at the front and rear.

The steering gear is of the recirculating ball type, incorporating a collapsible mesh, energy absorbing steering column.

These models have been available with a four-speed manual gearbox (with an optional overdrive unit for a short period), five-speed manual gearbox and three-speed automatic transmission.

Vauxhall Carlton Saloon

Vauxhall Carlton Estate

General weights and dimensions

For information applicable to later models, see Supplement at end of manual

Dimensions

	Saloon	Estate
Overall length	4743 mm (186.7 in)	4731 mm (186.3 in)
Overall width	1734 mm (68.3 in)	1734 mm (68.3 in)
Overall height (unladen)	1361 mm (53.6 in)	1428 mm (56.2 in)
Wheelbase	2668 mm (105 in)	2668 mm (105 in)
Front track	1435 mm (56 in)	1435 mm (56 in)
Rear track	1412 mm (55 in)	1432 mm (56 in)

Kerb weights

	Saloon	Estate
Manual transmission models	1130 kg (2491 lb)	1180 kg (2601 lb)
Automatic transmission models	1150 kg (2535 lb)	1200 kg (2646 lb)

Permissible trailer weights

	Saloon	Estate
With brakes	1500 kg (3307 lb)	1500 kg (3307 lb)
Without brakes	570 kg (1257 lb)	585 kg (1290 lb)

Permissible roof rack load

	Saloon	Estate
Permissible roof rack load	80 kg (176 lb)	80 kg (176 lb)

Buying spare parts and vehicle identification numbers

Buying spare parts

Spare parts are available from many sources, for example: Vauxhall garages, other garages and accessory shops, and motor factors. Our advice regarding spare part sources is as follows:

Officially appointed Vauxhall garages – This is the best source of parts which are peculiar to your car and are otherwise not generally available (eg complete cylinder heads, internal gearbox components, badges, interior trim etc). It is also the only place at which you should buy parts if your car is still under warranty – non-Vauxhall components may invalidate the warranty. To be sure of obtaining the correct parts it will always be necessary to give the storeman your car's engine and chassis number, and if possible, to take the 'old' part along for positive identification. Remember that many parts are available on a factory exchange scheme – any parts returned should always be clean! It obviously makes good sense to go straight to the specialists on your car for this type of part for they are best equipped to supply you.

Other garages and accessory shops – These are often very good places to buy materials and components needed for the maintenance of your car (eg oil filters, spark plugs, bulbs, fan belts, oils and greases, touch-up paint, filler paste etc). They also sell general accessories, usually have convenient opening hours, charge lower prices and can often be found not far from home.

Motor factors – Good factors will stock all of the more important components which wear out relatively quickly (eg clutch components, pistons, valves, exhaust systems, brake cylinders/pipes/ hoses/seals/ shoes and pads etc). Motor factors will often provide new or reconditioned components on a part exchange basis – this can save a considerable amount of money.

Vehicle identification numbers

The *vehicle identification number plate* is located inside the engine compartment on top of the front end panel. The plate is marked with the vehicle chassis and designation number and the colour code. Also shown is the maximum gross weight for the car.

The *engine number* is stamped on a machined flat located on the left-hand side of the cylinder block.

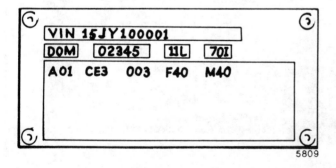

Vehicle identification plate

Location of engine number

Tools and working facilities

Introduction

A selection of good tools is a fundamental requirement for anyone contemplating the maintenance and repair of a motor vehicle. For the owner who does not possess any, their purchase will prove a considerable expense, offsetting some of the savings made by doing-it-yourself. However, provided that the tools purchased meet the relevant national safety standards and are of good quality, they will last for many years and prove an extremely worthwhile investment.

To help the average owner to decide which tools are needed to carry out the various tasks detailed in this manual, we have compiled three lists of tools under the following headings: *Maintenance and minor repair*, *Repair and overhaul*, and *Special*. The newcomer to practical mechanics should start off with the *Maintenance and minor repair* tool kit and confine himself to the simpler jobs around the vehicle. Then, as his confidence and experience grows, he can undertake more difficult tasks, buying extra tools as, and when, they are needed. In this way, a *Maintenance and minor repair* tool kit can be built-up into a *Repair and overhaul* tool kit over a considerable period of time without any major cash outlays. The experienced do-it-yourselfer will have a tool kit good enough for most repair and overhaul procedures and will add tools from the *Special* category when he feels the expense is justified by the amount of use these tools will be put to.

It is obviously not possible to cover the subject of tools fully here. For those who wish to learn more about tools and their use there is a book entitled *How to Choose and Use Car Tools* available from the publishers of this manual.

Maintenance and minor repair tool kit

The tools given in this list should be considered as a minimum requirement if routine maintenance, servicing and minor repair operations are to be undertaken. We recommend the purchase of combination wrenches (ring one end, open-ended the other); although more expensive than open-ended ones, they do give the advantages of both types of wrench.

Combination spanners - 10, 11, 12, 13, 14, 17 mm
Adjustable wrench - 9 inch
Spark plug spanner (with rubber insert)
Spark plug gap adjustment tool
Set of feeler gauges
Gearbox and rear axle filler plug key
Brake bleed nipple spanner
Screwdriver - 4 in long x $\frac{1}{4}$ in dia (flat blade)
Screwdriver - 4 in long x $\frac{1}{4}$ in dia (cross blade)
Combination pliers - 6 inch
Hacksaw, junior
Tyre pump
Tyre pressure gauge
Grease gun
Oil can
Fine emery cloth (1 sheet)
Wire brush (small)
Funnel (medium size)

Repair and overhaul tool kit

These tools are virtually essential for anyone undertaking any major repairs to a motor vehicle, and are additional to those given in the *Maintenance and minor repair* list. Included in this list is a comprehensive set of sockets. Although these are expensive they will be found invaluable as they are so versatile - particularly if various drives are included in the set. We recommend the $\frac{1}{2}$ in square-drive type, as this can be used with most proprietary torque wrenches. If you cannot afford a socket set, even bought piecemeal, then inexpensive tubular box wrenches are a useful alternative.

The tools in this list will occasionally need to be supplemented by tools from the *Special* list.

Sockets (or box spanners) to cover range in previous list
Reversible ratchet drive (for use with sockets)
Extension piece, 10 inch (for use with sockets)
Universal joint (for use with sockets)

Torque wrench (for use with sockets)
Mole wrench - 8 inch
Ball pein hammer
Soft-faced hammer, plastic or rubber
Screwdriver - 6 in long x $\frac{5}{16}$ in dia (flat blade)
Screwdriver - 2 in long x $\frac{5}{16}$ in square (flat blade)
Screwdriver - 1$\frac{1}{2}$ in long x $\frac{1}{4}$ in dia (cross blade)
Screwdriver - 3 in long x $\frac{1}{8}$ in dia (electricians)
Pliers - electricians side cutters
Pliers - needle nosed
Pliers - circlip (internal and external)
Cold chisel - $\frac{1}{2}$ inch
Scriber
Scraper
Center punch
Pin punch
Hacksaw
Valve grinding tool
Steel rule/straight edge
Allen keys
Selection of files
Wire brush (large)
Axle-stands
Jack (strong scissor or hydraulic type)

Special tools

The tools in this list are those which are not used regularly, are expensive to buy, or which need to be used in accordance with their manufacturers' instructions. Unless relatively difficult mechanical jobs are undertaken frequently, it will not be economic to buy many of these tools. Where this is the case, you could consider clubbing together with friends (or a motorists' club) to make a joint purchase, or borrowing the tools against a deposit from a local garage or tool hire specialist.

The following list contains only those tools and instruments freely available to the public, and not those special tools produced by the vehicle manufacturer specifically for its dealer network. You will find occasional references to these manufacturers' special tools in the text of this manual. Generally, an alternative method of doing the job without the vehicle manufacturers' special tool is given. However, sometimes, there is no alternative to using them. Where this is the case and the relevant tool cannot be bought or borrowed you will have to entrust the work to a franchised garage.

Valve spring compressor (where applicable)
Piston ring compressor
Balljoint separator
Universal hub/bearing puller
Impact screwdriver
Micrometer and/or vernier gauge
Dial gauge
Stroboscopic timing light
Dwell angle meter/tachometer
Universal electrical multi-meter
Cylinder compression gauge
Lifting tackle
Trolley jack
Light with extension lead

Buying tools

For practically all tools, a tool factor is the best source since he will have a very comprehensive range compared with the average garage or accessory shop. Having said that, accessory shops often offer excellent quality tools at discount prices, so it pays to shop around.

There are plenty of good tools around at reasonable prices, but always aim to purchase items which meet the relevant national safety standards. If in doubt, ask the proprietor or manager of the shop for advice before making a purchase.

Care and maintenance of tools

Having purchased a reasonable tool kit, it is necessary to keep the tools in a clean serviceable condition. After use, always wipe off any dirt, grease and metal particles using a clean, dry cloth, before putting the tools away. Never leave them lying around after they have been used. A simple tool rack on the garage or workshop wall, for items such as screwdrivers and pliers is a good idea. Store all normal wrenches and sockets in a metal box. Any measuring instruments, gauges, meters, etc, must be carefully stored where they cannot be damaged or become rusty.

Take a little care when tools are used. Hammer heads inevitably become marked and screwdrivers lose the keen edge on their blades from time to time. A little timely attention with emery cloth or a file will soon restore items like this to a good serviceable finish.

Working facilities

Not to be forgotten when discussing tools, is the workshop itself. If anything more than routine maintenance is to be carried out, some form of suitable working area becomes essential.

It is appreciated that many an owner mechanic is forced by circumstances to remove an engine or similar item, without the benefit of a garage or workshop. Having done this, any repairs should always be done under the cover of a roof.

Wherever possible, any dismantling should be done on a clean flat workbench or table at a suitable working height.

Any workbench needs a vice: one with a jaw opening of 4 in (100 mm) is suitable for most jobs. As mentioned previously, some clean dry storage space is also required for tools, as well as the lubricants, cleaning fluids, touch-up paints and so on which become necessary.

Another item which may be required, and which has a much more general usage, is an electric drill with a chuck capacity of at least $\frac{5}{16}$ in (8 mm). This, together with a good range of twist drills, is virtually essential for fitting accessories such as wing mirrors and reversing lights.

Last, but not least, always keep a supply of old newspapers and clean, lint-free rags available, and try to keep any working area as clean as possible.

Spanner jaw gap comparison table

Jaw gap (in)	Spanner size
0·250	$\frac{1}{4}$ in AF
0·276	7 mm
0·313	$\frac{5}{16}$ in AF
0·315	8 mm
0·344	$\frac{11}{32}$ in AF; $\frac{1}{8}$ in Whitworth
0·354	9 mm
0·375	$\frac{3}{8}$ in AF
0·394	10 mm
0·433	11 mm
0·438	$\frac{7}{16}$ in AF
0·445	$\frac{3}{16}$ in Whitworth; $\frac{1}{4}$ in BSF
0·472	12 mm
0·500	$\frac{1}{2}$ in AF
0·512	13 mm
0·525	$\frac{1}{4}$ in Whitworth; $\frac{5}{16}$ in BSF
0·551	14 mm
0·563	$\frac{9}{16}$ in AF
0·591	15 mm
0·600	$\frac{5}{16}$ in Whitworth; $\frac{3}{8}$ in BSF
0·625	$\frac{5}{8}$ in AF
0·630	16 mm
0·669	17 mm
0·686	$\frac{11}{16}$ in AF
0·709	18 mm
0·710	$\frac{3}{8}$ in Whitworth; $\frac{7}{16}$ in BSF
0·748	19 mm
0·750	$\frac{3}{4}$ in AF
0·813	$\frac{13}{16}$ in AF
0·820	$\frac{7}{16}$ in Whitworth; $\frac{1}{2}$ in BSF
0·866	22 mm
0·875	$\frac{7}{8}$ in AF
0·920	$\frac{1}{2}$ in Whitworth; $\frac{9}{16}$ in BSF
0·938	$\frac{15}{16}$ in AF
0·945	24 mm
1·000	1 in AF
1·010	$\frac{9}{16}$ in Whitworth; $\frac{5}{8}$ in BSF
1·024	26 mm
1·063	$1\frac{1}{16}$ in AF; 27 mm
1·100	$\frac{5}{8}$ in Whitworth; $\frac{11}{16}$ in BSF
1·125	$1\frac{1}{8}$ in AF
1·181	30 mm
1·200	$\frac{11}{16}$ in Whitworth; $\frac{3}{4}$ in BSF
1·250	$1\frac{1}{4}$ in AF
1·260	32 mm
1·300	$\frac{3}{4}$ in Whitworth; $\frac{7}{8}$ in BSF
1·313	$1\frac{5}{16}$ in AF
1·390	$\frac{13}{16}$ in Whitworth; $\frac{15}{16}$ in BSF
1·417	36 mm
1·438	$1\frac{7}{16}$ in AF
1·480	$\frac{7}{8}$ in Whitworth; 1 in BSF
1·500	$1\frac{1}{2}$ in AF
1·575	40 mm; $\frac{15}{16}$ in Whitworth
1·614	41 mm
1·625	$1\frac{5}{8}$ in AF
1·670	1 in Whitworth; $1\frac{1}{8}$ in BSF
1·688	$1\frac{11}{16}$ in AF
1·811	46 mm
1·813	$1\frac{13}{16}$ in AF
1·860	$1\frac{1}{8}$ in Whitworth; $1\frac{1}{4}$ in BSF
1·875	$1\frac{7}{8}$ in AF
1·969	50 mm
2·000	2 in AF
2·050	$1\frac{1}{4}$ in Whitworth; $1\frac{3}{8}$ in BSF
2·165	55 mm
2·362	60 mm

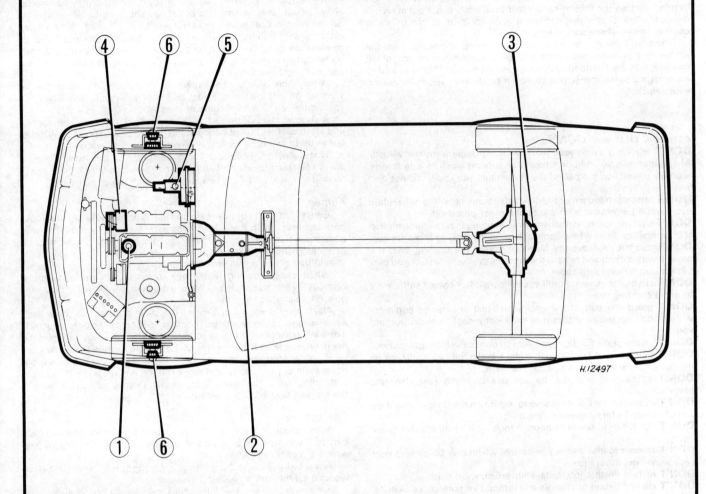

H.12497

Recommended lubricants and fluids

Component or system	Lubricant type/specification	Duckhams recommendation
1 Engine	Multigrade engine oil, viscosity range SAE 10W/40 to 20W/50	Duckhams QXR, Hypergrade, or 10W/40 Motor Oil
2 Transmission Manual:		
4-speed	Hypoid gear oil, viscosity SAE 80EP	Duckhams Hypoid 80
5-speed	GM special oil 90 006 326	Duckhams Hypoid 75W/90S
Automatic	Dexron II type ATF	Duckhams D-Matic
3 Rear axle	Hypoid gear oil, viscosity SAE 90EP	Duckhams Hypoid 90S
4 Power steering	Dexron II type ATF	Duckhams D-Matic
5 Brake fluid reservoir	Hydraulic fluid to SAE J1703/DOT 3	Duckhams Universal Brake and Clutch Fluid
6 Front wheel bearings	Multi-purpose lithium based grease	Duckhams LB 10

Safety first!

Professional motor mechanics are trained in safe working procedures. However enthusiastic you may be about getting on with the job in hand, do take the time to ensure that your safety is not put at risk. A moment's lack of attention can result in an accident, as can failure to observe certain elementary precautions.

There will always be new ways of having accidents, and the following points do not pretend to be a comprehensive list of all dangers; they are intended rather to make you aware of the risks and to encourage a safety-conscious approach to all work you carry out on your vehicle.

Essential DOs and DON'Ts

DON'T rely on a single jack when working underneath the vehicle. Always use reliable additional means of support, such as axle stands, securely placed under a part of the vehicle that you know will not give way.

DON'T attempt to loosen or tighten high-torque nuts (e.g. wheel hub nuts) while the vehicle is on a jack; it may be pulled off.

DON'T start the engine without first ascertaining that the transmission is in neutral (or 'Park' where applicable) and the parking brake applied.

DON'T suddenly remove the filler cap from a hot cooling system – cover it with a cloth and release the pressure gradually first, or you may get scalded by escaping coolant.

DON'T attempt to drain oil until you are sure it has cooled sufficiently to avoid scalding you.

DON'T grasp any part of the engine, exhaust or catalytic converter without first ascertaining that it is sufficiently cool to avoid burning you.

DON'T allow brake fluid or antifreeze to contact vehicle paintwork.

DON'T syphon toxic liquids such as fuel, brake fluid or antifreeze by mouth, or allow them to remain on your skin.

DON'T inhale dust – it may be injurious to health (see *Asbestos* below).

DON'T allow any spilt oil or grease to remain on the floor – wipe it up straight away, before someone slips on it.

DON'T use ill-fitting spanners or other tools which may slip and cause injury.

DON'T attempt to lift a heavy component which may be beyond your capability – get assistance.

DON'T rush to finish a job, or take unverified short cuts.

DON'T allow children or animals in or around an unattended vehicle.

DO wear eye protection when using power tools such as drill, sander, bench grinder etc, and when working under the vehicle.

DO use a barrier cream on your hands prior to undertaking dirty jobs – it will protect your skin from infection as well as making the dirt easier to remove afterwards; but make sure your hands aren't left slippery. Note that long-term contact with used engine oil can be a health hazard.

DO keep loose clothing (cuffs, tie etc) and long hair well out of the way of moving mechanical parts.

DO remove rings, wristwatch etc, before working on the vehicle – especially the electrical system.

DO ensure that any lifting tackle used has a safe working load rating adequate for the job.

DO keep your work area tidy – it is only too easy to fall over articles left lying around.

DO get someone to check periodically that all is well, when working alone on the vehicle.

DO carry out work in a logical sequence and check that everything is correctly assembled and tightened afterwards.

DO remember that your vehicle's safety affects that of yourself and others. If in doubt on any point, get specialist advice.

IF, in spite of following these precautions, you are unfortunate enough to injure yourself, seek medical attention as soon as possible.

Asbestos

Certain friction, insulating, sealing, and other products – such as brake linings, brake bands, clutch linings, torque converters, gaskets, etc – contain asbestos. *Extreme care must be taken to avoid inhalation of dust from such products since it is hazardous to health.* If in doubt, assume that they *do* contain asbestos.

Fire

Remember at all times that petrol (gasoline) is highly flammable. Never smoke, or have any kind of naked flame around, when working on the vehicle. But the risk does not end there – a spark caused by an electrical short-circuit, by two metal surfaces contacting each other, by careless use of tools, or even by static electricity built up in your body under certain conditions, can ignite petrol vapour, which in a confined space is highly explosive.

Always disconnect the battery earth (ground) terminal before working on any part of the fuel or electrical system, and never risk spilling fuel on to a hot engine or exhaust.

It is recommended that a fire extinguisher of a type suitable for fuel and electrical fires is kept handy in the garage or workplace at all times. Never try to extinguish a fuel or electrical fire with water.

Note: *Any reference to a 'torch' appearing in this manual should always be taken to mean a hand-held battery-operated electric lamp or flashlight. It does NOT mean a welding/gas torch or blowlamp.*

Fumes

Certain fumes are highly toxic and can quickly cause unconsciousness and even death if inhaled to any extent. Petrol (gasoline) vapour comes into this category, as do the vapours from certain solvents such as trichloroethylene. Any draining or pouring of such volatile fluids should be done in a well ventilated area.

When using cleaning fluids and solvents, read the instructions carefully. Never use materials from unmarked containers – they may give off poisonous vapours.

Never run the engine of a motor vehicle in an enclosed space such as a garage. Exhaust fumes contain carbon monoxide which is extremely poisonous; if you need to run the engine, always do so in the open air or at least have the rear of the vehicle outside the workplace.

If you are fortunate enough to have the use of an inspection pit, never drain or pour petrol, and never run the engine, while the vehicle is standing over it; the fumes, being heavier than air, will concentrate in the pit with possibly lethal results.

The battery

Never cause a spark, or allow a naked light, near the vehicle's battery. It will normally be giving off a certain amount of hydrogen gas, which is highly explosive.

Always disconnect the battery earth (ground) terminal before working on the fuel or electrical systems.

If possible, loosen the filler plugs or cover when charging the battery from an external source. Do not charge at an excessive rate or the battery may burst.

Take care when topping up and when carrying the battery. The acid electrolyte, even when diluted, is very corrosive and should not be allowed to contact the eyes or skin.

If you ever need to prepare electrolyte yourself, always add the acid slowly to the water, and never the other way round. Protect against splashes by wearing rubber gloves and goggles.

When jump starting a car using a booster battery, for negative earth (ground) vehicles, connect the jump leads in the following sequence: First connect one jump lead between the positive (+) terminals of the two batteries. Then connect the other jump lead first to the negative (−) terminal of the booster battery, and then to a good earthing (ground) point on the vehicle to be started, at least 18 in (45 cm) from the battery if possible. Ensure that hands and jump leads are clear of any moving parts, and that the two vehicles do not touch. Disconnect the leads in the reverse order.

Mains electricity and electrical equipment

When using an electric power tool, inspection light etc, always ensure that the appliance is correctly connected to its plug and that, where necessary, it is properly earthed (grounded). Do not use such appliances in damp conditions and, again, beware of creating a spark or applying excessive heat in the vicinity of fuel or fuel vapour. Also ensure that the appliances meet the relevant national safety standards.

Ignition HT voltage

A severe electric shock can result from touching certain parts of the ignition system, such as the HT leads, when the engine is running or being cranked, particularly if components are damp or the insulation is defective. Where an electronic ignition system is fitted, the HT voltage is much higher and could prove fatal.

Routine maintenance

For modifications, and information applicable to later models, see Supplement at end of manual

Introduction

The Routine Maintenance instructions listed are basically those recommended by the vehicle manufacturer. They are sometimes supplemented by additional maintenance tasks proven to be necessary.

The following maintenance instructions should always be used in conjunction with the servicing schedule detailed in the owner's handbook or Protection Plan booklet supplied with each new car, as the servicing requirement may be altered by the manufacturer in the course of time.

In the case of a new car the first free service must be carried out within one month or 500 miles (800 km) from date of delivery following by the three month or 3000 miles (5000 km) service check-up. Details of these services will be found in the owner's handbook and should be carried out by the authorised dealer.

Weekly, before a long journey, or every 250 miles (400 km)

Check the level of the engine oil and top-up if necessary.

Check the level of the electrolyte in the battery and top-up with distilled water as necessary. Make sure that the top of the battery is always kept clean and free from moisture.

Check the level of coolant in the radiator. The coolant should be around 40 mm (1.5 in) below the top of the radiator filler neck. Add antifreeze solution or plain water as necessary. Remember, if the engine is hot, only turn the filler cap one-quarter of a turn at first, to allow the system to lose pressure; then press the cap down and turn past the safety notch to remove.

Check the tyre pressures with an accurate gauge and adjust as necessary. *Carefully* inspect the tyre walls (both sides of the tyre) and the treads for damage. The law (UK) requires at least 1 mm deep tread across three-quarters of the width of the tyre around the whole periphery of the tyre.

Check the level of fluid in the brake fluid reservoir and replenish as necessary to the correct level marked on the reservoir. Should the brake system need replenishing weekly, the brake system should be thoroughly checked for leaks. As a matter of routine it is also wise to carefully inspect the flexible brake pipe; use a mirror and torch to view those hidden areas.

Check the fluid level in the power assisted steering fluid reservoir and top-up as necessary.

Check the tightness of the wheel nuts.

Refill the windscreen washer bottle with soft water, adding a screen wash such as Turtle Wax High Tech Screen Wash. Finally, check that the jets operate cleanly and accurately.

Check each electrical system on the vehicle in turn; ensure that all lights work properly and the response of each system is immediate.

Every 3000 miles (5000 km) or 3 months, whichever occurs first

Under extreme operating conditions such as trailer pulling, frequent short trip operations that prevent the engine really warming up, or operating in dusty terrain, the engine oil should be changed at 3000 mile (5000 km) intervals. The weekly checks detailed previously should also be carried out.

Topping up the engine oil

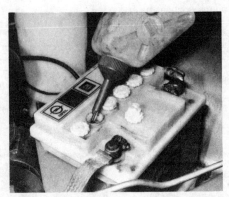
Topping up the battery

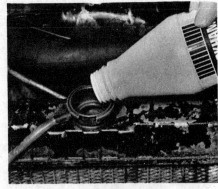
Topping up the radiator

Checking the tyre pressures

Topping up the brake fluid level

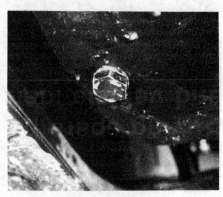
Engine oil drain plug

Every 6000 miles (10 000 km) or 6 months, whichever occurs first

Carry out the 250 miles/weekly checks plus the following:

Oil filter
Renew the oil filter as well as the engine oil every 6000 miles (10 000 km). The filter is of the full-flow cartridge type. It is recommended that the sealing gasket on the new filter be smeared with engine oil before fitting. Once the new filter has been screwed on, tighten the cartridge with hand effort only.

Battery
Remove the battery and clean the terminals and connectors

Gearbox and rear axle
Check the level of oil in the gearbox and rear axle by removing the level/filler plug, and topping-up with gear oil until it begins to flow from each plug hole. Refit the plugs. The oil does not need to be changed within the life of the gearbox or rear axle between overhauls.

Automatic transmission
With the vehicle parked on a level surface and the engine running, select the 'Park' position with the shift lever. Remove and wipe clean the oil reservoir dipstick. Re-insert until the cap is seated, remove and observe the level on the stick. Top-up to the 'FULL' mark on the stick. Do not overfill.

Brake pads and linings
Front disc brakes: The minimum allowable thickness of the pad and friction plate is 7 mm (0.28 in). If any of the four pads has worn below the dimension, all four pads must be renewed. Partial renewal of brake pads will result in unequal braking. Note that the disc brakes are self-adjusting and the only running check is to ensure that the brake pistons are functioning properly. The pistons should retract a little into the caliper block to allow a small running clearance between the pad and disc.

Rear drum brakes: Remove the brake drums and inspect the drum friction surface for scores. If scores are found refer to Chapter 9. Inspect the brake shoes and linings – if the friction material has been worn down to the rivets, it is time to reline the shoes. If bonded linings are used, then renewal is necessary when the friction material has worn to within 1.6 mm (0.06 in) of the shoe. Check the adjustment of the brake shoe position after referring to Chapter 9. Turn the individual shoe adjusters until both shoes bind on the drum, then relax the adjusters until the drum can just be rotated freely.

Handbrake
The handbrake needs adjustment if the brakes are not applied between the 3rd and 5th notches of the lever movement. To adjust, tighten the self-locking nut at the handbrake equalizer bracket until the correct lever movement is obtained.

Suspension and steering
Carefully check the suspension for slackness or damage. It will be useful to jack-up the wheels so that they may be gripped to force them up-and-down, forward-and-back, and in-and-out. If any slackness is detected, investigate, refer to Chapter 11 and repair immediately. Whilst the front wheels are jacked-up, grip the wheels and force them around against the steering linkage. As with suspension, if any sloppiness or uneven movement is detected, investigate, refer to Chapter 11 of this manual and repair immediately.

Exhaust system
The exhaust system should be closely inspected for cracks, holes, broken shackle parts and gross deterioration. Renovate the system appropriately. Remember that faults such as holes or broken shackles should not be tolerated at all; exhaust fumes can leak into the passenger compartment.

Ignition system
Remove the spark plugs and inspect them for colour and electrode gap. The static timing may also be checked using the technique described in Chapter 4.

Cooling system
Check fanbelt tension and adjust if necessary. Examine hoses and clips and tighten/renew where necessary.

General safety checks
Lap and shoulder safety belts: Inspect the belts and renew them if any fabric and material deterioration is found. Check that the anchorage points are in good order, free from corrosion and the various nuts and bolts tight.

Heater: Check that the defroster system is effective by operating occasionally and sensing that sufficient warm air is being blown onto the windscreen.

Horn: Operate the horn occasionally to ensure that it is in working order.

Seats: Inspect the front seat adjustment mechanisms. Ensure that all latch pawls are properly engaged and that no components are excessively worn. Remember to inspect the headrest mountings if fitted, checking that they are complete and in proper order.

Location of gearbox filler plug (arrowed)

Rear axle filler plug

Every 12 000 miles (20 000 km) or 12 months, whichever occurs first

Carry out the tasks listed under the weekly and 6 months service intervals plus the following:

Oil can lubrication

Apply a spot of oil to the door, bonnet and boot hinges. Also lightly oil the door strikers, check links and lock barrels.

Cooling system

Check the strength of the antifreeze in the coolant and top-up if necessary. Inspect the fanbelt for wear and renew if necessary. Adjust the tension of the fanbelt whether it is renewed or not.

Ignition system

Renew all spark plugs. Fit a new set of contact breaker points, set the points to the correct gap and apply a spot of oil to the cam lubrication pad. Check the operation of the distributor advance mechanism and ignition timing (see Chapter 4).

Engine adjustments

Check and if necessary adjust the engine idling settings.

Mechanical linkages

Check the throttle, handbrake and gearchange linkage for wear and adjust/renew where necessary and lubricate.

Wheel bearings

Jack the front wheels off the ground and check for wear in the wheel bearings. Adjust the wheel bearings as necessary. Clean and repack with recommended grease. Chapter 11 details the technique for adjusting and cleaning the bearings.

Fuel filter

Clean out the gauze fuel filter in the top of the fuel pump and also the wire mesh inlet filter at the carburettor fuel pipe union (see Chapter 3).

Carburettor air filter

The air filter element should be renewed yearly, or more frequently if the vehicle is being used in a dusty environment.

Body

Have the headlight alignment checked, preferably by a Vauxhall dealer who will have the correct equipment to do this accurately.

Clutch

Check, and if necessary adjust, the clutch operating arm and pedal height as described in Chapter 5.

Brakes

Drain the brake hydraulic circuit of fluid. Replenish with new fluid and bleed the system of air (see Chapter 9).

Every 24 000 miles (40 000 km) or 2 years, whichever occurs first

Carry out the checks detailed in the weekly, 6 month and yearly service schedules plus the following:

Automatic transmission

Drain, and refill the transmission with the recommended lubricant.

Steering and suspension

Check the steering gear balljoints for wear using the method described in the 6 monthly checklist. Examine all the steering gear rubber boots for splits or perishing, and renew where necessary. Check all shock absorbers for leaks, and the suspension rubber bushes for deterioration: renew if faults are evident.

Engine tune

After two years use, it is a good policy to take the car to a dealer equipped with an electronic engine tuner, or similar and have the engine completely checked over for faults that would not normally be detected (ie low compression, incorrect fuel combustion, high speed engine timing etc).

Jacking and towing

For further information, see Supplement at end of manual

When changing a roadwheel, the jack supplied with the vehicle may be used, inserting it in the jacking points located adjacent to each wheel. For maintenance and repairs, use a jack located beneath the front crossmember or rear axle, and always supplement the jack with axle stands or blocks positioned under the bodyframe members.

When towing another vehicle, attach the tow-rope to the towing eye located on the right-hand side rear underbody. When being towed, attach the tow-rope to one of the eyes locates on the front axle.

Vehicles with automatic transmission should not be towed faster than 30 mph (50 km/h) nor for a distance exceeding 30 miles (50 km).

Where these restrictions are to be exceeded, either disconnect the propeller shaft from the rear axle or raise the rear roadwheels on a towing dolly.

If a vehicle is being towed with its roadwheels in contact with the road, unlock the steering and anticipate the need for greater brake pedal pressures as there will be no servo assistance.

Chapter 1 Engine

For modifications, and information applicable to later models, see Supplement at end of manual

Contents

Specifications

Engine – general

Type	Four cylinder in-line, camshaft-in-head (CIH)
Engine designation	20S
Bore	95 mm (3.740 in)
Stroke	69.8 mm (2.75 in)
Displacement	1979 cc (120.7 cu in)
Max bhp (DIN)	100 at 5200 rpm
Max torque	158 Nm (117 lbf ft) at 3400 to 3800 rpm
Compression ratio	9.0 : 1
Compression pressure at starter speed (hot)	9.7 bar (140 lbf/in^2)
Firing order	1 – 3 – 4 – 2
Lubrication system	Pressure fed by gear type pump, full-flow filter element
Engine oil capacity:	
Dry engine	4.1 litres (7.22 Imp pints)
Refill with filter change	3.8 litres (6.68 Imp pints)
Refill without filter change	3.5 litres (6.16 Imp pints)
Oil pressure (hot)	0.5 bar (7 lbf/in^2) at 800 to 850 rpm

Valves and springs

Valve dimensions (inlet):

Stem diameter:	
Standard	8.987 to 9.000 mm (0.3538 to 0.354 in)
Oversize 1	9.062 to 9.075 mm (0.3568 to 0.357 in)
Oversize 2	9.137 to 9.150 mm (0.3597 to 0.360 in)
Oversize A	9.287 to 9.300 mm (0.3656 to 0.366 in)
Total length	123 mm (4.843 in)

Valve head diameter	42 mm (1.654 in)
Valve dimensions (exhaust):	
Stem diameter:	
Standard	8.952 to 8.965 mm (0.3524 to 0.353 in)
Oversize 1	9.027 to 9.040 mm (0.3554 to 0.356 in)
Oversize 2	9.102 to 9.115 mm (0.3583 to 0.359 in)
Oversize A	9.252 to 9.265 mm (0.3643 to 0.365 in)
Total length	123.70 mm (4.870 in)
Valve head diameter	37 mm (1.457 in)
Valve stem clearance:	
Inlet	0.035 to 0.073 mm (0.0013 to 0.0028 in)
Exhaust	0.045 to 0.083 mm (0.0017 to 0.0032 in)
Valve seat angle (inlet and exhaust)	44°
Valve seat width in cylinder head:	
Inlet	1.25 to 1.50 mm (0.049 to 0.059 in)
Exhaust	1.60 to 1.85 mm (0.063 to 0.073 in)
Valve springs – free length	
Inlet	56.8 mm (2.236 in)
Exhaust	52.0 mm (2.047 in)
Valve timing:	
Inlet opens	32° BTDC
Inlet closes	90° ABDC
Exhaust opens	72° BBDC
Exhaust closes	50° ATDC

Cylinder block and pistons

Maximum cylinder bore oversize (reboring)	0.5 mm (0.020 in)
Permissible cylinder bore ovality after grinding	0.013 mm (0.0005 in)
Permissible cylinder bore taper after grinding	0.013 mm (0.0005 in)
Piston clearance (nominal) after overhaul	0.03 mm (0.001 in)
Piston oversizes	0.5 mm (0.020 in)
Piston ring gaps:	
Compression rings	0.40 to 0.65 mm (0.0157 to 0.0166 in)
Oil control ring	0.38 to 1.40 mm (0.015 to 0.055 in)
Clearance in piston grooves:	
Top ring	0.06 to 0.09 mm (0.002 to 0.003 in)
Centre ring	0.03 to 0.06 mm (0.001 to 0.002 in)

Crankshaft

Crankshaft endfloat	0.04 to 0.16 mm (0.0016 to 0.0063 in)
Connecting rod bearing journal diameter	51.97 to 51.99 mm (2.046 to 2.047 in)
Main bearing journal diameter	57.99 to 58.003 mm (2.282 to 2.283 in)
Connecting rod journal clearance in bearing	0.01 to 0.06 mm (0.0006 to 0.0024 in)
Main bearing journal clearance in bearing	0.02 to 0.06 mm (0.0009 to 0.0025 in)

Camshaft and bearings

Journal diameter (nominal):	
First	48.93 to 48.95 mm (1.926 to 1.927 in)
Second	48.68 to 48.70 mm (1.916 to 1.917 in)
Third	48.56 to 48.57 mm (1.911 to 1.912 in)
Fourth	48.435 to 48.45 mm (1.906 to 1.907 in)
Clearance in bearings	0.07 to 0.11 mm (0.002 to 0.004 in)
Endfloat	0.10 to 0.20 mm (0.004 to 0.008 in)
Permissible dimension (cam peak to base)	40.10 mm (1.576 in)

Engine lubrication

Oil type/specification	Multigrade engine oil, viscosity range SAE 10W/40 to 20W/50 (Duckhams QXR, Hypergrade, or 10W/40 Motor Oil)
Oil pump:	
Protrusion of gears from pump body	0.00 to 0.10 mm (0.000 to 0.004 in)
Radial clearance in body	0.10 to 0.25 mm (0.004 to 0.010 in)
Backlash between teeth	0.10 to 0.20 mm (0.004 to 0.009 in)
Clearance on driven spindle	0.008 to 0.039 mm (0.0003 to 0.0015 in)
Oil pressure relief valve spring free length	35.00 mm (1.38 in)
Oil filter	Champion C103

Torque wrench settings

	Nm	lbf ft
Connecting rod bolts	45	33
Main bearing bolts	110	81
Cylinder head bolts		
Stage 1	60	44
Stage 2	Tighten further 90°	Tighten further 90°
Stage 3 (when warm)	Tighten further 30°	Tighten further 30°
Flywheel or drive disc-to-crankshaft bolts	60	44
Crankshaft pulley bolt	100	74
Camshaft sprocket bolts	25	18
Manifold-to-cylinder head bolts	35	26
Rocker stud in cylinder head	35	26

Torque wrench settings

	Nm	lbf ft
Timing cover bolts	15	11
Water pump bolts	15	11
Transmission-to-engine bolts	45	33
Spark plugs	40	30
Engine mounting bracket bolts	35	26
Engine rubber mounting bolts	40	30
Oil pump cover bolts	6	4
Fuel pump bolts	15	11
Alternator bracket bolts	40	30
Sump bolts	5	4
Cylinder head-to-timing cover bolts	25	18

1 General description

The GM 20S engine is a water cooled, four-cylinder, four-stroke petrol engine of camshaft-in-head configuration, and 1979 cc (120.7 cu in) capacity.

The combined crankcase and cylinder block is of cast iron construction and houses the pistons, connecting rods, and crankshaft. The solid skirt cast aluminium alloy pistons are retained on the connecting rods by offset gudgeon pins, which are an interference fit in the connecting rod small-end bore. The connecting rods are attached to the crankshaft by renewable shell type big-end bearings.

The forged steel crankshaft is carried in five main bearings also of the renewable shell type. Crankshaft endfloat is controlled by thrust washers which are an integral part of the rear main bearing shell.

The camshaft is contained within the cast iron cylinder head, and is supported by four bearings. Camshaft drive is by a duplex timing chain from a sprocket on the crankshaft. To eliminate backlash and prevent slackness of the chain, a chain guide is fitted to the cylinder block, and a spring-loaded hydraulic tensioner is incorporated in the timing cover.

The inclined inlet and exhaust valves operate in guides bored directly in the cylinder head. Valve actuation is via stud mounted rocker arms and hydraulic tappets activated by the camshaft.

The engine oil pump is operated by the distributor shaft which is driven by a helical gear off the front of the crankshaft. Oil is pumped from the sump through a full-flow filter to the crankshaft main oil gallery and then through drillings in the timing cover and cylinder head. The cylinder bores are lubricated by oil from a spray hole in each connecting rod, above the big-end journal.

Crankcase ventilation is via a main breather hose from the rocker cover to the air cleaner and a second, smaller hose from the rocker cover to the inlet manifold.

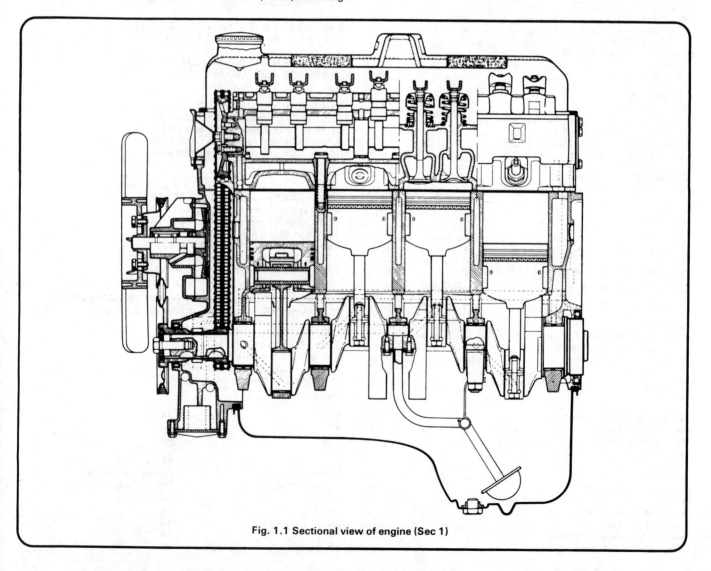

Fig. 1.1 Sectional view of engine (Sec 1)

2 Main operations possible with the engine in the car

The following operations can be carried out with the engine in place:

Removal and refitting of the cylinder head
Removal and refitting of the camshaft (cylinder head removed)
Removal and refitting of the oil pump
Removal and refitting of the sump
Removal and refitting of the big-end bearings
Removal and refitting of the pistons and connecting rods (cylinder head removed)
Removal and refitting of the flywheel (gearbox removed)
Removal and refitting of the front engine mountings
Removal and refitting of the timing gear components (cylinder head and sump removed)

3 Major operations requiring engine removal

The following operations can only be carried out with the engine removed from the car:

Removal and refitting of the main bearings
Removal and refitting of the crankshaft
Removal and refitting of the crankshaft rear oil seal. This is also possible with the engine in place, but a special fitting tool will be required to prevent damage to the seal lips

4 Methods of engine removal

The engine may be lifted out either on its own or in unit with the gearbox. On models fitted with automatic transmission it is recommended that the engine be lifted out on its own, unless a substantial crane or overhead hoist is available, because of the weight factor. If the engine and gearbox are removed as a unit they have to be lifted out at a very steep angle, so make sure there is sufficient lifting height available.

5 Engine – removal (with manual gearbox or automatic transmission)

1   The do-it-yourself owner should be able to remove the power unit fairly easily in about four hours. It is essential to have a sturdy hoist and two axle stands if an inspection pit is not available.
2   The sequence of operations listed in this Section is not critical, as the position of the person carrying out the work, or the tool in his hand will to a certain extent determine the order in which the work is tackled. Obviously, the power unit cannot be removed until everything is disconnected from it and the following sequence will ensure that nothing is forgotten.
3   Open the bonnet and mark the position of the hinge brackets on the bonnet using a soft pencil.
4   Disconnect the bonnet illuminating light electrical lead.
5   With the help of an assistant, undo and remove the bonnet

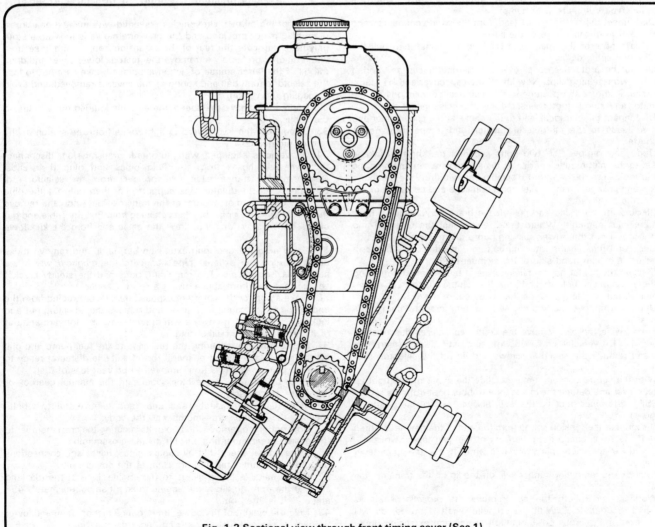

Fig. 1.2 Sectional view through front timing cover (Sec 1)

retaining bolts and lift off the bonnet. Store the bonnet in a safe place where it will not be knocked or scratched.

6   Disconnect the battery terminals, undo and remove the retaining bolt and clamp and finally, lift out the battery.

7   Undo and remove the central bolt securing the air cleaner to the carburettor, pull off the vacuum supply hose, the engine breather hose and the hot air duct, then lift off the air cleaner.

8   Place a container of capacity approximately 6.25 litres (11 pints) beneath the radiator. Release the radiator filler cap and slacken the bottom hose retaining clip at the radiator. Slowly pull off the hose and allow the water to drain into the container.

9   When the radiator has drained, remove the plug at the rear right-hand side of the cylinder block and drain the engine. When empty, refit the plug.

10   Detach the vacuum advance pipe from the distributor and carburettor, but leave it attached to the top hose.

11   Slacken the top hose retaining clip and pull the hose off the thermostat housing.

12   On vehicles equipped with automatic transmission, undo and remove the two fluid cooler pipes at the base of the radiator. Plug the pipes and unions upon removal, to prevent further loss of fluid and dirt ingress.

13   If a radiator fan cowl is fitted, undo and remove the securing scews and position the cowl over the fan blades.

14   Using pliers, compress and withdraw the two radiator retaining clips and then carefully lift out the radiator, complete with top hose and vacuum pipe. Take care not to damage the radiator fins as the unit is removed.

15   Make a note of the wiring connections to the windscreen washer pump, then remove the wires and the water hose. Now lift out the water reservoir complete with pump.

16   Disconnect the distributor LT lead from the wiring connector, and the HT lead from the centre of the coil.

17   Make a note of the spark plug HT lead locations, then pull the leads off the spark plugs.

18   Lift up the protective cover over the distributor cap and spring back the two retaining clips. Now lift off the cap, cover and HT leads.

19   Make a note of the position of the electrical connections on the alternator and starter motor solenoid and then disconnect them.

20   Disconnect the electrical lead to the choke at the cable joiner and the two leads to the oil pressure switch and temperature gauge transmitter.

21   Undo and remove the two bolts securing the throttle linkage bracket to the inlet manifold. Prise up the spring wire clip retaining the throttle rod ball to the carburettor spindle and withdraw the complete bracket and linkage. Position the bracket, linkage and cable out of the way on the bulkhead.

22   Slacken the hose clip and pull off the brake servo vacuum hose from the inlet manifold. Where fitted, disconnect the pressure and return hoses from the power steering pump, then plug their ends.

23   Undo and remove the retaining bolt and lift off the engine earth strap from the right-hand side of the cylinder block.

24   Slacken the heater hose retaining clips at the thermostat housing and water pump and pull off the hoses. Detach the support clip on the thermostat housing and position the hoses out of the way.

25   Undo and remove the two engine mounting upper retaining nuts and washers.

26   From inside the car, remove the centre console as described in Chapter 12. On vehicles equipped with automatic transmission, first undo and remove the securing screws and lift off the selector lever cover.

27   With the centre console removed, slide the upper rubber boot up the gear lever and detach the lower, inner rubber boot from the rubber seal. Slide the inner boot up the lever also, to expose the gearlever linkage.

28   Disconnect the tension spring from the end of the gear lever, then prise off the small circlip from the front of the gear lever pivot pin.

29   Withdraw the pivot pin rearwards and lift out the gear lever assembly.

30   Unhook the remaining rubber seal off the lip on the transmission tunnel.

31   Working underneath the car, remove the propeller shaft as described in Chapter 7. With the propeller shaft removed, oil will escape from the gearbox or automatic transmission extension housing. On vehicles equipped with automatic transmission, the fluid may be drained into a suitable container after removing the drain plug from

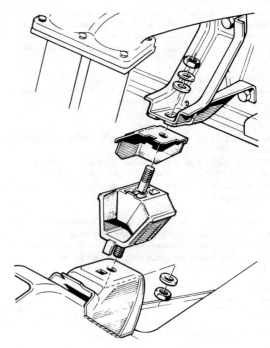

Fig. 1.3 Engine mounting assembly – right-hand side (Sec 5)

the rear of the oil pan. On vehicles equipped with manual gearbox, a drain plug is not provided and the only alternative is to wrap a stout polythene bag over the rear of the extension housing firmly secured with string, or preferably to remove the gearbox lower cover and drain the oil. If the latter course of action is pursued, take care not to lose the selector detent ball and spring as the cover is removed, and avoid damaging the gasket.

32   Undo and remove the speedometer cable knurled nut and lift off the cable.

33   Disconnect the two reversing light wires from the switch at the rear of the gearbox.

34   On vehicles equipped with automatic transmission, disconnect the two fluid hoses from the fluid pipes and plug their ends. Disconnect the transmission selector lever from the selector rod. Disconnect the modulator pipe support clip, then pull out the pipe from the diaphragm at the rear of the transmission. Undo and remove the kickdown cable angle bracket retaining bolt. Pull the cable end out of the transmission and withdraw the cable end from the kickdown valve.

35   Using a socket and long extension bar, undo and remove those bolts securing the exhaust pipe flange to the manifold which are accessible from below. The remaining bolts and the steady bracket can be removed from above, using a short spanner.

36   Make a note of the length of exposed threads protruding from the end of the clutch cable, then undo and remove the adjusting nut and locknut. The cable can now be withdrawn, moving it forward and out of its location in the bellhousing.

37   Slacken the clip securing the fuel pipe to the fuel pump and pull off the pipe. Have a plug or metal rod of suitable diameter ready to plug the pipe as soon as it is removed to prevent loss of fuel.

38   Place a jack or suitable blocks beneath the manual gearbox or automatic transmission.

39   Bend back the locktabs and undo and remove the two bolts securing the gearbox crossmember to the body.

40   Now undo and remove the two bolts securing the crossmember to the gearbox rear mounting and lift off the crossmember.

41   Make a final check that all cables, pipes, hoses and connections have been disconnected and are clear of the power unit.

42   Attach suitable lifting slings to the engine, long at the rear and short at the front, to allow the engine to adopt an approximately 45° angle as it is lifted out.

43   Take the weight of the power unit on the hoist or crane and lower the jack or remove the blocks from under the gearbox.

44   Raise the engine and transmission and at the same time pull it forward until the sump is over the front body panel (photo).

5.44 Removing the engine from the car

45 An assistant should now lift the rear of the transmission over the panel, and when all is clear, lower the power unit to the ground.
46 Thoroughly wash the exterior with paraffin or a water soluble cleaner. Wash off with a strong water jet and dry thoroughly.
47 The gearbox may now be removed from the engine. Undo and remove the two bolts securing the starter motor flange to the bellhousing and the single bolt securing the starter steady bracket to the cylinder block. Lift away the starter motor.
48 Undo and remove the bolts securing the two lower support brackets to the cylinder block and bellhousing, then lift off the brackets.
49 Undo and remove the remaining bolts securing the flywheel lower cover plate to the bellhousing and lift off the plate.
50 If automatic transmission is fitted, turn the engine over using a large socket on the crankshaft pulley nut until the torque converter retaining bolts are visible through the starter motor opening.
51 Continue turning the engine and check that there is a painted white alignment mark between the torque converter and drive disc, adjacent to one of the bolt holes. If an alignment mark is not visible, make your own mark using a dab of paint. It is essential that the torque converter is refitted in the same position on the drive disc to maintain correct balance conditions upon reassembly.
52 Now undo and remove the torque converter to drive disc retaining bolts.
53 Undo and remove the bolts securing the bellhousing to the engine and carefully withdraw the gearbox or automatic transmission. Do not allow the weight of the gearbox to hang on the input shaft. If an automatic transmission unit is being removed, ensure that the torque converter stays on the transmission as the unit is withdrawn. If necessary, push it off the drive disc using a block of wood inserted through the starter motor opening.

6 Engine – removal (without manual gearbox or automatic transmission)

1 Follow the instructions given in Section 5, paragraphs 1 to 25 inclusive.
2 From underneath the car, undo and remove the accessible bolts securing the exhaust pipe flange to the manifold, using a socket and long extension bar. The remaining bolts and the steady bracket can be removed from above, using a short spanner.
3 Slacken the clip securing the fuel pipe to the fuel pump and pull off the pipe. Have a plug or metal rod of suitable diameter ready to plug the pipe as soon as it is removed, to prevent loss of fuel.
4 Undo and remove the bolts securing the two engine lower steady brackets to the engine and bellhousing and lift off the brackets.
5 Now undo and remove the remaining bolts retaining the flywheel cover plate to the bellhousing. Lift away the plate.
6 On vehicles equipped with automatic transmission, turn the

engine over using a large socket on the crankshaft pulley nut, and undo and remove the torque converter to drive disc retaining bolts as they become visible through the opening in the bellhousing. If a white painted alignment mark is not visible between the torque converter and drive disc adjacent to one of the retaining bolts, make a suitable mark using a dab of paint.
7 Place a jack or blocks beneath the bellhousing to support it when the engine is lifted out.
8 Undo and remove the two bolts securing the starter motor flange to the bellhousing and the single bolt securing the support bracket to the engine. Lift out the starter motor.
9 Attach suitable lifting slings to the engine and just take the weight of the unit.
10 Undo and remove the remaining bolts securing the bellhousing to the engine.
11 Now lift the engine slightly on the hoist and pull it forward to disengage the gearbox input shaft. In the case of automatic transmission, ensure that the torque converter stays behind on the transmission as the engine is pulled forward. If necessary, release the torque converter from the drive disc using a block of wood inserted through the starter motor opening.
12 Raise the hoist and lift the engine out of the car.
13 With the engine removed, thoroughly wash the exterior with paraffin or a water soluble cleaner. Wash off with a strong water jet and dry thoroughly.

7 Engine – dismantling (general)

1 It is best to mount the engine on a dismantling stand, but is this is not available, stand the engine on a strong bench at a comfortable working height. Failing this, it will have to be stripped down on the floor.
2 During the dismantling process, the greatest care should be taken to keep the exposed parts free from dirt. As an aid to achieving this, thoroughly clean down the outside of the engine, first removing all traces of oil and congealed dirt.
3 A good grease solvent will make the job much easier, for after the solvent has been applied and allowed to stand for a time, a vigorous jet of water will wash off the solvent and grease with it. If the dirt is thick and deeply embedded, work the solvent into it with a strong stiff brush.
4 Finally wipe down the exterior of the engine with a rag and only then, when it is quite clean, should the dismantling process begin. As the engine is stripped, clean each part in a bath of paraffin or petrol.
5 Never immerse parts with oilways in paraffin eg crankshaft. To clean these parts, wipe down carefully with a petrol dampened rag. Oilways can be cleaned out with wire. If an airline is available, all parts can be blown dry and the oilways blown through as an added precaution.
6 Re-use of old gaskets is false economy. To avoid the possibility of trouble after the engine has been reassembled always use new gaskets throughout.
7 Do not throw away the old gaskets, for sometimes it happens that an immediate replacement cannot be found and the old gasket is then very useful as a template. Hang up the gaskets as they are removed.
8 To strip the engine, it is best to work from the top down. The crankcase provides a firm base on which the engine can be supported in an upright position. When the stage is reached where the crankshaft must be removed, the engine can be turned on its side and all other work carried out with it in this position.
9 Wherever possible, refit nuts, bolts and washers finger tight from wherever they were removed. This helps to avoid loss and muddle. If they cannot be refitted, arrange them in such a fashion that it is clear from whence they came.
10 Before dismantling begins, it is important that two special tools are obtained or certain work cannot be carried out. The tools are 8 and 12 mm splined wrenches and are shown in the photo. They are necessary for removing the cylinder head bolts and camshaft sprocket bolts.

8 Engine ancillary components – removal

Before basic engine dismantling begins it is necessary to remove the engine ancillary components as follows:

7.10 The 8 and 12 mm splined wrenches necessary for timing chain sprocket and cylinder head removal

8.1 Removing the alternator

8.3 Removing the thermostat housing assembly

8.5 Lifting off the manifolds complete with carburettor

8.6a Suitably mark the distributor flange ...

8.6b ... remove the retaining bolt and clamp plate ...

8.6c ... and lift out the distributor

8.7a Remove the fan and pulley ...

8.7b ... and then the water pump

9.10 Withdrawing the timing chain tensioner

9.11 Removing the camshaft thrust plate

9.13 Cylinder head bolts accessible through relieved sections of camshaft

(a) *Alternator*
(b) *Fuel pump*
(c) *Thermostat*
(d) *Oil filter cartridge*
(e) *Inlet and exhaust manifolds with carburettor*
(f) *Distributor*
(g) *Water pump*

It is possible to remove any of these components with the engine in place in the car, if it is merely the individual items which require attention. Assuming the engine to be out of the car and on a bench, and that the items mentioned are still on the engine, follow the procedures described below.

1   *Slacken the alternator* retaining nuts and bolts; move the unit towards the cylinder block, then remove the fan belt. Continue to remove the nuts and bolts retaining the alternator on the rubber mounting bracket, then lift the unit away. Remove the rubber mounting bracket and store with the alternator and its earthing strap (photo).

2   *Fuel pump:* Two bolts secure the fuel pump to the engine block. Once the two have been removed, the pump together with the gasket and asbestos spacer can be removed.

3   *Thermostat:* This item is retained underneath the cylinder head water outlet elbow cap. Again, once two bolts have been removed, the cap can be lifted up to reveal the thermostat, which can then be simply lifted out of the housing (photo).

4   *Oil filter cartridge:* This is of the disposable type, and is simply removed by gripping tightly and unscrewing from the engine block. If the unit is tight, use a strap wrench to release it.

5   *Inlet and exhaust manifolds with carburettor:* The inlet and exhaust manifolds are bolted together to form a single assembly and may be removed from the engine with the carburettor still in position. Undo and remove the retaining bolts and lift off the manifolds (photo). The manifolds may be separated by undoing and removing the long bolts which secure them at the centre of the inlet manifold.

6   *Distributor:* It is necessary to have removed the fuel pump before the distributor can be withdrawn from the cylinder block. Once the pump has been removed, scribe a mark between the distributor and timing cover flanges using a small file (photo). This will ensure refitting in the same position. Now undo and remove the retaining bolt and clamp plate then lift out the distributor (photos).

7   *Water pump:* Begin by removing the four bolts which secure the fan and pulley on the water pump shaft flange. Lift the fan and pulley clear, then undo and remove the six bolts which retain the pump body to the timing cover. Lift off the pump (photos).

9 Cylinder head – removal (engine in car)

1   It should be noted that the cylinder head bolts and camshaft sprocket bolts have splined heads which require the use of two special tools for removal.

2   These tools are 12mm and 8mm splined wrenches and are obtainable from your GM dealer or a good motor accessory or tool factors shop. As no other tool will fit these bolts, it is essential to obtain the right ones before attempting to dismantle the cylinder head.

3   Disconnect the battery earth terminal, then drain the cooling system fully as described in Chapter 2.

4   Slacken the hose clips and remove the radiator top hose and then the heater hose from the thermostat housing.

5   Rotate the engine by means of the fan until No 4 piston in approaching TDC on the firing stroke. This will be the case when the steel ball in the flywheel is in line with the pointer in the housing and the distributor rotor arm is pointing toward No 4 spark plug lead segment in the distributor cap.

6   Remove the air cleaner, referring to Chapter 3 if necessary, then undo and remove the petrol pipe union at the carburettor.

7   Undo and remove the six bolts securing the inlet and exhaust manifolds to the cylinder head and the bolt securing the exhaust flange steady bracket to the cylinder block. The manifolds (complete with carburettor) can now be moved sideways, away from the cylinder head, and tied in this position with a length of string.

8   Undo and remove the retaining screws and lift off the rocker cover and gasket.

9   Disconnect the electrical lead to the temperature gauge sensor unit, then pull off the spark plug HT leads after suitably marking them

for correct refitment.

10   Using a large socket or ring spanner, undo and remove the timing chain tensioner from its location in the lower right-hand side of the timing cover (photo).

11   Undo and remove the three bolts and lift off the camshaft thrust plate from the front of the cylinder head (photo). Now remove the plastic thrust bolt.

12   Using the 8 mm splined wrench described previously, undo and remove the three camshaft sprocket retaining bolts. The sprocket can now be carefully levered off the camshaft. Once detached, the sprocket and chain will rest on the support bracket bolted to the cylinder block.

13   Next, undo and remove the cylinder head retaining bolts, using the 12 mm splined wrench, in the reverse order to the tightening sequence shown in Fig. 1.15. There are two additional bolts at the front of the cylinder head that thread directly into the timing cover. These two bolts should be removed first, using an Allen key to avoid damaging the aluminium threads in the timing cover as the gasket clamping load is released. **Note:** *There are three relieved sections on the camshaft to provide access to the cylinder head bolts located directly beneath it (photo).*

14   The cylinder head should now be free of attachments to the engine and car and ready to be lifted off. It may be necessary to seek the help of a second person at this stage as the cylinder head is heavy.

15   If the cylinder head appears to be stuck on the block, do not try to free it by prising it off with a screwdriver or chisel, but tap the cylinder head firmly with a plastic or wooden-headed mallet. The mild shocks should break the bond between the gasket, head, and block, allowing the cylinder head to be lifted clear.

16   With the cylinder head removed, do not place it face down on the bench as this may damage the protruding valves. Lay it on its side or preferably support it on wooden blocks.

10 Cylinder head – removal (engine out of car)

1   Remove the ancillary components listed in Section 8 and proceed as directed in paragraphs 10 to 16 inclusive of the previous Section.

11 Cylinder head dismantling – camshaft and tappet removal

The cylinder head is of high grade chromium grey cast iron. The camshaft runs on bearings in the cylinder head. The tappet barrels move in bores machined in the cylinder head and the rockers, which transmit the tappet movement to the valves, pivot on special fittings screwed into the cylinder head. These valves move in bores machined directly in the cylinder head and the exhaust valves are seated on special inserts of temperature resistant material. The combustion chamber surface in the cylinder head has been 'aluminised' as well as the seats of the inlet valves. This finish makes for long surface life and inhibits the formation of carbon deposits.

1   Once the cylinder head has been removed, place it on a clean bench and commence the removal of:

(a) *Rockers and pivots*
(b) *Camshaft and tappets*
(c) *Valve assemblies*

2   The rockers are removed by simply undoing and removing the locking nuts which retain the rocker pivot pieces on the mounting stud. Store the rockers and pivots in such a manner as to facilitate the refitting of those items into the exact positions from which they were removed (photos).

3   Having already taken off the front camshaft end cover plate during the cylinder head removal, undo and remove the bolts securing the side and rear camshaft access plates.

4   Turn the cylinder head on its side and extract the tappet barrels and, as with the rockers, store them so that they can be refitted to the bores from which they were taken (photo).

5   The camshaft can now be extracted through the forward end of the cylinder head. Use the access apertures in the cylinder head to support the camshaft and prevent the soft bearing surfaces in the cylinder head being scratched and damaged by the sharp edges of the cam lobes (photo).

6   If the water outlet elbow has not yet been removed, it should be now. It is secured to the cylinder head by three bolts.

11.2a Undo the rocker adjusting nut, ...

11.2b ... lift off the rocker seat, ...

11.2c ... followed by the rocker

11.4 Removing the hydraulic tappet barrels

11.5 Withdraw the camshaft from the front

12 Valves – removal

The valves can be removed from the cylinder head by the following method:

1   With a valve spring compressor, compress each spring in turn until the two halves of the collets can be removed. Release the compressor and remove the valve spring cap, spring, upper and lower spring seating and finally the valve itself (photos).

2   As usual, store all the parts so they may be refitted into the exact position from which they were taken.

3   If when the valve spring compressor is screwed down, the valve spring cap refuses to free and expose the split collets, do not screw the compressor further in, in an effort to force the cap free. Gently tap the top of the tool directly over the cap with a light hammer. This will free the cap. Whilst you are tapping the tool, hold the compressor firmly with your other hand to prevent the tool jumping off the cap when it is released.

4   As mentioned earlier, there are no valve guide inserts as such in this engine. If on inspection the valve stem bores in the cylinder head are found to be excessively worn, they will have to be reamed out to the next oversize. Valves with the appropriate oversize stem will need to be fitted when the engine is reassembled.

13 Flywheel and sump – removal

1   With the clutch removed as described in Chapter 5, lock the flywheel using a screwdriver in mesh with the starter ring and undo the six bolts that secure the flywheel to the camshaft in a diagonal and progressive manner. Note that one of the bolts is marked with a letter P on its head. This is a shouldered locating bolt and its position on the flywheel should be suitably marked with a dab of paint before removal (photo).

2   With the retaining bolts removed, the flywheel can be lifted off the rear of the crankshaft.

3   Undo and remove the bolts that secure the sump to the underside

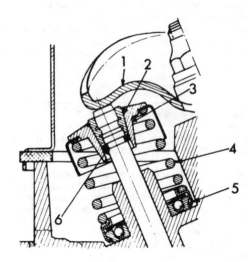

Fig. 1.4 Sectional view of exhaust valve components (Sec 12)

1	Rocker	4	Spring
2	Cotters	5	Spring seat
3	Spring cap	6	Oil seal

of the crankcase.

4   Lift away the sump and gasket.

5   The two bolts securing the oil pick-up tube and strainer can now be undone and the tube lifted off.

6   If the sump is being removed with the engine still in the car, position the crankshaft with No 4 piston at TDC. This will give the clearance necessary to remove the sump.

12.1a Compress the valve spring using a compressor and lift out the collets

12.1b The valve can then be withdrawn

13.1 The shouldered flywheel locating bolt suitably marked before removal

14.2 Removing the crankshaft pulley retaining bolt

14 Timing cover, chain and gears – removal

1   These components may be removed with the engine still in position in the car, providing the following components are removed first by referring to the relevant Chapter and Sections of this manual. (If the engine is out of the car and on the bench, these items will already have been removed as part of the engine dismantling sequence):

(a) Radiator
(b) Cylinder head
(c) Fuel pump
(d) Distributor
(e) Timing chain tensioner
(f) Sump
(g) Water pump
(h) Alternator and mounting bracket

2   Next to be removed is the crankshaft pulley. Place a block of wood between one of the crankshaft throws and the crankcase to prevent it from turning, then undo and remove the retaining bolt. Lever off the pulley using two screwdrivers (photo).

3   The bolts securing the timing cover to the cylinder block can now be undone and removed and the timing cover lifted off.

4   Slide the distributor drivegear off the end of the crankshaft, carefully using two screwdrivers as levers if it is initially tight (photo).

Fig. 1.5 Identification of shouldered flywheel retaining bolt
(Sec 13)

14.4 Withdrawing the distributor drivegear

15.3 Removing the big-end bearing caps

15.5 Refit the caps and shells to their rods upon removal

5   Lift the camshaft sprocket and timing chain off the support bracket and crankshaft drivegear. If required, the gear may be levered off the crankshaft using two screwdrivers. Take care not to lose the Woodruff keys from the nose of the crankshaft. If the timing chain is to be refitted, mark its original direction of rotation before removing it.

15 Pistons, connecting rods and big-end bearings – removal

1   Note that the pistons have a notch on their crown, indicating the forward facing side. Inspect the big-end bearing caps and connecting rods to make sure identification marks are visible. This is to ensure that the correct end caps are fitted to the correct connecting rods and the connecting rods placed in their respective bores. If no marks are visible, suitably mark the caps one to four, using a centre punch.
2   Undo and remove the big-end bearing bolts and place them to one side in the order in which they were removed.
3   Remove the big-end caps, taking care to keep them in the right order and the correct way round (photo). Also ensure that the shell bearings are kept with their correct caps.
4   If the big-end caps are difficult to remove, they may be gently tapped on their sides, using a soft hammer.
5   After removing each big-end cap, the piston and connecting rod assembly should be withdrawn upwards and out of its cylinders. Tap the connecting rods using a length of wood and light hammer until the piston emerges out of the top of the cylinder bore. Now lift out the assembly and refit the correct big-end cap and bolts finger tight (photo). Lay the piston assemblies out in the correct order for refitting in the same bore as they were originally fitted.

16 Crankshaft and main bearings – removal

1   The crankshaft is of forged steel and is supported in five main bearings. The endfloat of the shaft is governed by the rear main bearing shell. The rear crankshaft oil seal is mounted in the rear main bearing cap.
2   In order to be able to remove the crankshaft it will be necessary to have completed the following tasks:

    (a) Removal of engine and gearbox
    (b) Separation of engine and gearbox
    (c) Removal of the cylinder head
    (d) Removal of the sump
    (e) Removal of the timing case and timing chain
    (f) Oil collecting tube and strainer
    (g) The big-end bearings

It is not essential to have extracted the pistons and connecting rods, but it makes for a less cluttered engine block during the crankshaft removal.
3   Check that the main bearing caps have identification numbers marked on them; No 1 should be at the front and No 5 should be the rear main cap. If for some reason identification cannot be found, use a centre punch to identify the caps.
4   Before removing the crankshaft, it is wise to check the existing endfloat. Use feeler gauges or a dial gauge to measure the gap

between the rearmost main bearing journal wall on the crankshaft and the shoulder of the bearing shell in the bearing cap (photo).
5   Move the crankshaft forwards as far as it will go with two tyre levers to obtain a maximum reading. The endfloat should be within the dimensions given in the Specifications. If the endfloat exceeds those figures, then rear bearing shells with oversize side bearing shoulders should be fitted. See the Specification Section at the beginning of this Chapter for thrust and main bearing data.
6   Having ensured that the bearing caps have been marked in a manner which facilitates correct refitting, undo the bolts retaining the caps by one turn only to begin with. Once all have been loosened, proceed to unscrew and remove them.
7   The bearing caps can now be lifted away, together with the shells inside them. Finally, the crankshaft can be removed and the shells seated in the crankcase.
8   Remove the rear oil seal from the end of the crankshaft.

17 Gudgeon pins – removal

The pistons are retained on the connecting rods by gudgeon pins, which are an interference fit in the connecting rod small-end bore. If new pistons are to be fitted, it is strongly recommended that you take the assemblies to your GM dealer or motor engineering specialist to have this done, otherwise damage to the piston or distortion of the connecting rod may result.

18 Piston rings – removal

1   To remove the piston rings, slide them carefully over the top of the

16.4 Checking crankshaft endfloat prior to removal

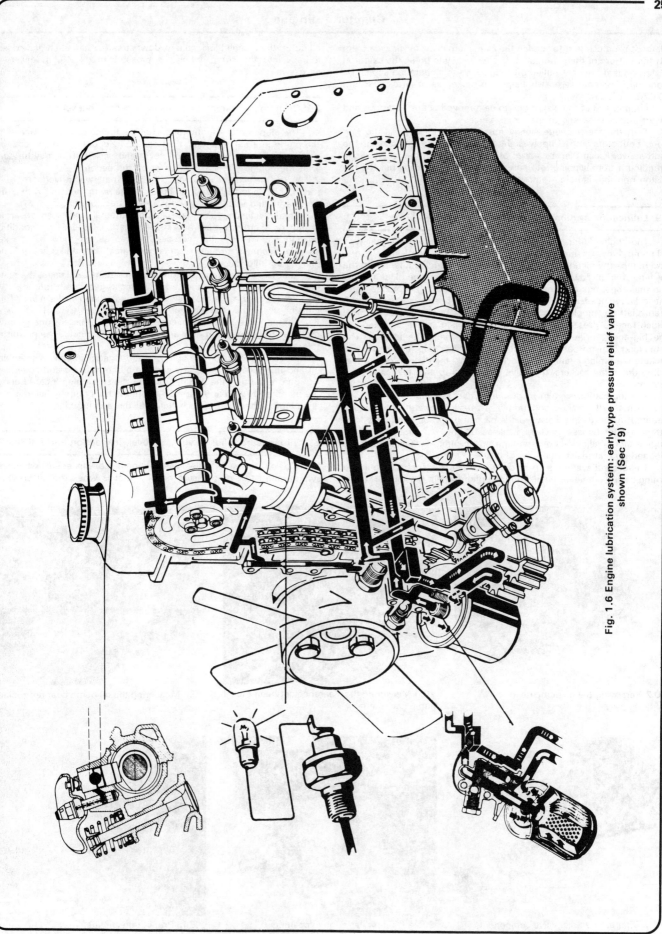

Fig. 1.6 Engine lubrication system: early type pressure relief valve shown (Sec 19)

piston, taking care not to scratch the aluminium alloy; never slide them off the bottom of the piston skirt. It is very easy to break the cast iron piston rings if they are pulled off roughly, so this operation should be done with extreme care. It is helpful to make use of an old 0.5 mm (0.020 in) feeler gauge.

2   Lift one end of the piston ring to be removed out of its groove and insert under it the end of the feeler gauge.

3   Turn the feeler gauge slowly round the piston and, as the ring comes out of its groove, apply slight upward pressure so it rests on the land above. It can then be eased off the piston with the feeler gauge stopping it from slipping into an empty groove if it is any but the top piston ring that is being removed.

19 Lubrication system – general description

The engine lubrication system is quite conventional: A gear type oil pump draws oil up from the sump, via the suction pipe and strainer, and pumps the oil under pressure into the cartridge oil filter. From the oil filter, the oil flows into galleries drilled in the engine block to feed the main bearings on the crankshaft and the moving components of the cylinder head. Oil is bled from the main bearing journals in the crankshaft to supply the big-end bearings. Therefore, the bearings which receive pressure lubrication are the main crankshaft bearings, the big-end bearings, the camshaft bearings and the tappets. The remaining moving parts receive oil by splash or drip feed and these include the timing chain and associated items, the distributor and fuel pump drive, the rockers, the valve stems and to a certain extent the pistons.

The lubrication system incorporates two safeguards. The first is common to all engines and that is a pressure operated ball valve situated in the gallery between the oil pump and oil filter. This is in effect a filter bypass valve and allows oil to pass directly into the engine block gallery – down stream of the filter – when the filter is clogged up and resists the flow of oil.

The second system is an oil pressure relief system, located in the timing casing between the oil filter and timing chain tensioner. It takes oil out of the engine block gallery, downstream of the filter, and passes it back into the sump, when the pressure of oil in that gallery is excessive.

20 Oil pump – dismantling, inspection and reassembly

1   The oil pump in an integral part of the timing cover, and access to the pump internal components is gained by undoing the six retaining screws and lifting off the pump cover and gasket. This may be done with the engine either in the car or on the bench.

2   With the cover removed, lift out the two drivegears, then thoroughly clean them and the inside of the pump housing with petrol or paraffin and wipe dry with a non-fluffy rag (photo).

3   Carefully inspect the gears, pump internal body and cover for pitting or scoring; renew any suspect parts. If the pump condition appears satisfactory, the necessary clearances may now be checked using a machined straight-edge (a good steel rule) and a set of feeler gauges as follows.

4   Refit the gears to the pump, dry at this stage, and using the feeler gauges, measure the clearance between the gear teeth (photo).

5   Now measure the protrusion of the gears above the level of the housing using the straight-edge and feeler gauges (photo).

6   Compare the measured clearances with the dimensions given in the Specifications and renew any parts that are outside the permitted tolerance.

7   When reassembling the pump, coat the gears liberally with engine oil and use a new gasket between the pump housing and cover.

8   Before starting the engine, remove the small plug located above the pump body with an Allen key and prime the pump by filling it with engine oil. When the pump is full, refit the priming plug.

21 Oil pressure relief valve – removal, inspection and refitting

1   The oil pressure relief valve should be inspected whenever symptoms of low oil pressure occur – that is when the oil pressure

20.2 Removing the oil pump gears

20.4 Measuring the clearance between the oil pump gear teeth

20.5 Measuring the oil pump gear protrusion

21.2 Oil pressure relief valve components

22.4a Oil filter cartridge in position

22.4b Priming the oil filter

warning light illuminates with the engine running at tick-over. The valve can be removed with the engine in place.

2   The relief valve is located in the oil pump cover and is retained by a large hexagon-headed plug (photo).

3   To remove the valve, undo and remove the hexagon-headed plug and lift out the spring and relief valve.

4   Clean the components with petrol or paraffin and dry with a non-fluffy rag.

5   Inspect the surface of the valve and its seat in the bore; both surfaces should be smooth and regular.

6   If there is any sign of wear or surface scoring, renew the complete valve and cover as an assembly.

7   Refit the valve in the bore, followed by the spring, then secure them with the retaining plug.

8   Prime the oil pump on completion of reassembly as described at the end of Section 20.

22 Oil filter cartridge – renewal

1   The oil filter is a complete throw-away cartridge, located at the base of the timing cover.

2   To renew the unit, simply unscrew the cartridge from the housing. It may be necessary to use a small chain strap wrench if it is tight.

3   Wipe the mating face of the housing and smear clean engine oil over the rubber seal of the new cartridge.

4   Screw the cartridge onto the housing, taking care not to cross the threads, and tighten it using your hands only (photo). The filter may be primed by removing the plug on the timing cover (photo).

5   With the cartridge in place, start the engine and check for leaks.

23 Engine components – examination for wear

When the engine has been stripped down and all parts properly cleaned, decisions have to be made as to what needs renewal. The following Sections tell the examiner what to look for. In any border-line case it is always best to decide in favour of a new part. Even if a part may still be serviceable its life will have been reduced by wear and the degree of trouble needed to renew it in the future must be taken into consideration. However, these things are relative and it depends on whether a quick 'survival' job is being done or whether the car as a whole is being regarded as having many thousands of miles of useful and economical life remaining.

24 Crankshaft – examination and renovation

1   Look at the main bearing journals and the crankpins: If there are any scratches or score marks, the shaft will need regrinding. Such conditions will nearly always be accompanied by similar deterioration in the matching bearing shells.

2   Each bearing journal should also be round and can be checked with a micrometer or caliper gauge around the periphery at several points. If there is more than 0.02 mm (0.001 in) of ovality, regrinding is necessary.

3   A main GM agent or motor engineering specialist will be able to decide to what extent regrinding is necessary and also supply the special undersize shell bearing to match whatever may need grinding off.

4   Before taking the crankshaft for regrinding, check also the cylinder bore and pistons as it may be advantageous to have the whole engine done at the same time.

5   Check the spigot bearing in the end of the crankshaft for wear, and if necessary renew it.

25 Crankshaft main and big-end bearings – examination and renovation

1   With careful servicing and regular oil and filter changes, bearings will last for a very long time. But they can still fail for unforeseen reasons. With big-end bearings, an indication is a regular rhythmic loud knocking from the crankcase. The frequency depends on engine speed and is particularly noticeable when the engine is under load

This symptom is accompanied by a fall in oil pressure although this is not normally noticeable unless an oil pressure gauge is fitted. Main bearing failure is usually indicated by serious vibration, particularly at higher engine revolutions, accompanied by a more significant drop in oil pressure and a 'rumbling' noise.

2   Big-end bearings can be removed with the engine still in the car. If the failure is sudden and the engine has a low mileage since new or overhaul, this is possibly worth doing. Bearing shells in good condition have bearing surfaces with a smooth, even matt silver/grey colour all over. Worn bearings will show patches of a different colour when the bearing metal has worn away and exposed the underlay. Damaged bearings will be pitted or scored. It is always well worthwhile fitting new shells as their cost is relatively low. If the crankshaft is in good condition, it is merely a question of obtaining another set of standard size shells. A reground crankshaft will need new bearing shells as a matter of course.

26 Cylinder bores – examination and renovation

1   A new cylinder is perfectly round and the walls parallel throughout its length. The action of the piston tends to wear the walls at right angles to the gudgeon pin due to side thrust. This wear takes place principally on that section of the cylinder swept by the piston rings.

2   It is possible to get an indication of bore wear by removing the cylinder head with the engine still in the car. With the piston down in the bore, first signs of wear can be seen and felt just below the top of the bore where the top piston ring reaches and there will be a noticeable lip. If there is no lip it is fairly reasonable to expect that bore wear is not severe and any lack of compression or excessive oil consumption is due to worn or broken piston rings or pistons.

3   If it is possible to obtain a bore measuring micrometer, measure the bore in the thrust plane below the lip and again at the bottom of the cylinder in the same plane. If the difference is more than 0.15 mm (0.006 in), a rebore is necessary. Similarly, a difference of 0.08 mm (0.003 in) or more between two measurements of the bore diameter taken at right angles to each other is a sign of ovality, calling for a rebore.

4   Any bore which is significantly scratched or scored will need reboring. This symptom usually indicates that the piston or rings are damaged also. In the event of only one cylinder being in need of reboring it will still be necessary for all four to be bored and fitted with new oversize pistons and rings. Your GM agent or local motor engineering specialist will be able to rebore and obtain the necessary matched pistons. If the crankshaft is undergoing regrinding also, it is a good idea to let the same firm renovate and reassemble the crankshaft and pistons to the block. A reputable firm normally gives a guarantee for such work.

27 Pistons and piston rings – examination and renovation

1   Worn pistons and rings can usually be diagnosed when the symptoms of excessive oil consumption and lower compression occur and are sometimes, though not always, associated with worn cylinder bores. Compression testers that fit into the spark plug hole are available and these can indicate where low compression is occurring. Wear usually accelerates the more it is left so when the symptoms occur, early action can possible save the expense of a rebore.

2   Another symptom of piston wear is piston slap – a knocking noise from the crankcase not to be confused with big-end bearing failure. It can be heard clearly at low engine speed when there is no load (idling for example) and is much less audible when the engine speed increases. Piston wear usually occurs in the skirt or lower end of the piston and is indicated by vertical streaks in the worn area which is always on the thrust side. It can also be seen where the skirt thickness is different.

3   Piston ring wear can be checked by first removing the rings from the pistons as described in Section 18. Then place the rings in the cylinder bores from the top, pushing them down about 38 mm (1.5 in) with the head of a piston (from which the rings have been removed) so that they rest square in the cylinder. Now measure the gap at the ends of the rings with a feeler gauge and compare the dimension obtained with the figures given in Specifications (photo). If the gaps are excessive the rings must be renewed.

4   The grooves in which the rings locate in the pistons can also

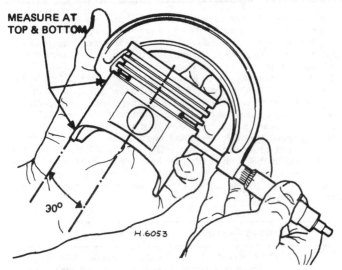

Fig. 1.7 Measuring the piston diameter (Sec 27)

27.3 Measuring piston ring gap

27.4 Measuring the piston ring clearance in the piston grooves

become enlarged in use. These clearances can be measured with the rings in position on the piston (photo) and compared with the figures given in Specifications. Excessive clearances will require renewal of the piston and rings as an assembly.

28 Connecting rods – examination and renovation

1   The connecting rods are not subject to wear but can, in the case of engine seizure, become bent or twisted. If any distortion is visible or even suspected, the rod must be renewed.
2   The rods should also be checked for hairline cracks or deep nicks and if in evidence, the rod discarded and a new one fitted.

29 Camshaft and camshaft bearings – examination and renovation

1   Carefully examine camshaft bearings for wear. If the bearings are obviously worn or pitted or the metal underlay just showing through, they must be renewed. This is an operation for your local GM agent or automobile engineering works, as it demands the use of specialised equipment. The bearings are removed using a special drift, after which the new bearings are pressed in, care being taken that the oil holes in the bearings line up with those in the block. With another special tool, the bearings are then reamed in position.
2   The camshaft itself should show no signs of wear, but, if very slight scoring marks on the cams are noticed, the score marks can be removed by a very gentle rubbing down with a very fine emery cloth or an oil stone. The greatest care should be taken to keep the cam profiles smooth.

30 Hydraulic tappets – description

1   The hydraulic tappet comprises five parts; the tappet body, spring, plunger and ball valve, rocker seat, and retaining cap.
2   The tappet operates in the following manner: Drillings in the tappet body allow the internal plunger to fill with oil. When the plunger is full, the ball valve at the base of the plunger opens, allowing oil to pass into the pressure chamber below the plunger. A spring is provided in the pressure chamber to take up rocker arm clearances.
3   When the tappet is operated by the cam lobe against the pressure of the valve spring, oil pressure in the chamber instantly increases to close the ball valve, thus locking the plunger height in the tappet body.
4   Hydraulic tappets require no periodic maintenance or adjustment apart from the initial settings described in Sections 49 and 55. Because the tappets are in direct contact with the camshaft lobes and rocker arms at all times, they are extremely quiet during normal operation, and do not exhibit the general valve train noise associated with conventional systems.
5   Should ticking or knocking noises be heard in the vicinity of the valve gear, particularly on a high mileage engine, the tappets should be dismantled and inspected for scoring, wear, or oil sludge contamination of the internal parts, as described in the following Section.

31 Hydraulic tappets – examination and renovation

1   As stated previously, hydraulic tappets are maintenance free and

Fig. 1.8 Hydraulic tappet components (Sec 30)

1   Tappet body   4   Rocker seat
2   Spring   5   Retaining cap
3   Plunger and ball valve

should only be dismantled if their operation is suspect or if they have become particularly noisy in service.

2 Each individual tappet and plunger is a matched assembly and must not be interchanged. Tappet component parts are not available separately and if found to be unserviceable, the complete tappet must be renewed. It is also likely that if one tappet is found to be internally worn, or contaminated with oil sludge or varnish deposits, the others will probably be the same.

3 To dismantle the tappets, push the plunger down against the pressure of the return spring and prise off the retaining cap using a small screwdriver. Now lift out the rocker seat, plunger and spring from the tappet body.

4 Thoroughly clean all the parts in petrol or paraffin and dry with a non-fluffy rag.

5 Carefully check the internal and external surfaces of the components for surface cracks, scoring or pitting. If wear is evident, the tappet must be renewed as an assembly.

6 Also check that all the oil feed holes are clear and the plunger moves freely in the tappet body.

7 Reassemble the tappet in the reverse order to dismantling, then immerse the tappet in clean engine oil. Move the plunger up and down in the tappet body until the tappet is primed.

32 Valve and valve seats – examination and renovation

1 With the valve removed from the cylinder head, examine the heads for signs of cracking, burning away and pitting of the edge where it seats in the port. The valve seats in the cylinder head should also be examined for the same signs. Usually, it is the valve that deteriorates first, but if a bad valve is not rectified the seat will suffer, and this is more difficult to repair.

2 Provided there are no obvious signs of serious pitting, the valve should be ground into its seat. This may be done by placing a smear of carborundum paste on the edge of the valve and, using a suction type valve holder, grinding the valve in situ. This is done with a semi-rotary action, rotating the handle of the valve holder between the hands and lifting it occasionally to redistribute the traces of paste. Use a coarse paste to start with. As soon as a matt grey unbroken line appears on both the valve and seat the valve is 'ground in'. All traces of carbon should also be cleaned from the head and neck of the valve stem. A wire brush mounted in a power drill is a quick and effective way of doing this.

3 If the valve requires renewal, it should be ground into the seat in the same way as the old valve.

4 Another form of valve wear can occur on the stem where it runs in the guide in the cylinder head. This can be detected by trying to rock the valve from side to side. If there is any movement at all it is an indication that the valve stem or guide is worn. Check the stem first with a micrometer at points along and around its length: If they are not within the specified size new valves will probably solve the problem. If the guides are worn, however, they will need reboring for oversize valves. The valve seats will also need recutting to ensure they are concentric with the stems. This work should be given to your GM dealer or local engineering works.

5 When valve seats are badly burnt or pitted, requiring renewal, inserts may be fitted – or renewed if already fitted once before – and once again this is a specialist task to be carried out by a suitable engineering firm.

6 When all valve grinding is completed, it is essential that every trace of grinding paste is removed from the valves and ports in the cylinder head. This should be done by thorough washing in petrol or paraffin and blowing out with a jet of air. If particles of carborundum should work their way into the engine, they would cause havoc with bearings or cylinder walls.

33 Cylinder head and piston crowns – decarbonising

1 When the cylinder head is removed, either in the course of an overhaul or for inspection of bores or valve condition when the engine is in the car, it is normal to remove all carbon deposits from the piston crowns and heads.

2 This is best done with a cup shaped wire brush and an electric drill, and is fairly straightforward when the engine is dismantled and the pistons removed. Sometimes hard spots of carbon are not easily

removed except by a scraper. When cleaning the pistons with a scraper, take care not to damage the surface of the piston in any way.

3 When the engine is in the car, certain precautions must be taken when decarbonising the piston crowns in order to prevent dislodged pieces of carbon falling into the interior of the engine which could cause damage to the cylinder bores, piston and rings – or if allowed into the water passages – damage to the water pump. Turn the engine so that the piston being worked on is at the top of its stroke and then mask off the adjacent cylinder bores and all surrounding water jacket orifices with paper and adhesive tape. Press grease into the gap all round the piston to keep carbon particles out and then scrape all carbon away by hand. Do not use a power drill and wire brush when the engine is in the car, as it will virtually be impossible to keep all the carbon dust clear of the engine. When completed, carefully clear out the grease around the rim of the piston with a matchstick or something similar – bringing any carbon particles with it. Repeat the process on the other piston crown. It is not recommended that a ring of carbon is left round the edge of the piston on the theory that it will aid oil consumption. This was valid in the earlier days of long stroke, low revving engines but modern engines, fuels and lubricants cause less carbon deposits anyway, and any left behind tends merely to cause hot spots.

34 Valve guides – inspection

Examine the valve guides internally for wear. If the valves are a very loose fit in the guides and there is the slightest suspicion of lateral rocking using a new valve, then the guides will have to be reamed and oversize valves fitted. This is a job best left to the local GM garage.

35 Sump – inspection

Wash out the sump in petrol and wipe dry. Inspect the exterior for signs of damage: If evident, a new sump must be obtained. To ensure an oil tight joint, scrape away all traces of the old gasket from the cylinder block mating face.

36 Timing gears, chain and cover – examination and renovation

1 Carefully inspect the teeth of the timing gears and the links of the chain for wear. Place the chain over the gears and ensure the chain is a snug fit without slackness. Renew any suspect components.

2 Examine the chain guide on the cylinder block and the chain tensioner pads in the timing cover (photo) If heavily grooved, due to the action of the chain rubbing against them, they should be renewed.

3 The crankshaft front oil seal in the timing cover should be renewed as a matter of course. The old seal may be levered out using a

36.2 Timing chain tensioner pads in the timing cover

36.3 Renewing the timing cover oil seal

Fig. 1.9 Using a cold chisel to split the flywheel ring gear (Sec 37)

Fig. 1.10 Fitting a new flywheel ring gear (Sec 37)

screwdriver, or tapped out from behind using a tube of suitable diameter. Tap a new seal squarely in position, using a medium hammer and interposed block of wood (photo).

37 Flywheel ring gear – examination and renovation

1   If the ring gear is badly worn or has teeth mising it should be renewed. The old ring can be removed from the flywheel by cutting a notch between two teeth with a hacksaw and then splitting it with a cold chisel.
2   To fit a new ring gear requires heating the ring to 230°C (446°F). This can be done by polishing four equal spaced sections of the gear, laying it on a suitable heat resistant surface (such as fire bricks) and heating it evenly with a blow lamp or torch until the polished areas turn a light yellow tinge. Do not overheat, or the hard wearing properties will be lost. The gear has a chamfered inner edge which should go against the shoulder when put on the flywheel. When hot enough, place the gear in position quickly, tapping it home if necessary and let it cool naturally without quenching in any way.

38 Engine reassembly – general

All components of the engine must be cleaned of oil, sludge and old gaskets and the working area should also be cleared and clean. In addition to the normal range of good quality socket spanners and general tools which are essential, the following must be available before reassembling begins:

> Complete set of new gaskets
> Supply of clean rags
> Clean oil can full of clean engine oil
> Torque wrench
> All new spare parts as necessary

39 Crankshaft – refitting

1   Ensure that the crankcase is thoroughly clean and all oilways are clear. A thin twist drill is useful for clearing the oilways, or if possible, they may be blown out with compressed air. Treat the crankshaft in the same fashion, then inject engine oil into the oilways.
2   Wipe the bearing shell seats in the crankcase clean, then fit the upper halves of the new main bearing shells into their seats (photo).
3   Note that there is a tab on the back of each bearing shell which engages with a groove in the seating.
4   Now fit the remaining shells into the bearing caps.
5   Four sets of bearing shells are identical and fit into the seats at positions 1 to 4. The rearmost main bearing shells incorporate the

39.2 Fitting the main bearing shell upper halves

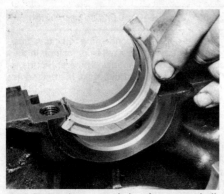

39.5 Fitting the rear main bearing upper shell half and integral thrust washer

39.6 Lubricating the bearing shells before fitting the crankshaft

39.7a Crankshaft in position in the crankcase

39.7b Applying sealer to the rear main bearing cap

39.11 Fitting the rear crankshaft oil seal

39.12 Using a torque wrench to tighten the retaining bolts

thrust washers. These shells are supplied with various thicknesses of flange in order to set correctly the crankshaft endfloat (photo).

6   Ensure the holes in the shells fitted in the crankcase seats line up and do not restrict the oil supply hole in the crankcase. Inject oil into each oilway and coat the shells liberally with engine oil (photo).

7   Carefully lower the crankshaft into position and fit each bearing cap in turn. The stepped edge of the joint face on the rear bearing cap should be lightly coated with a silicone RTV jointing compound before fitting to the crankcase (photos).

8   Screw in the bearing cap retaining bolts noting that No 2 main bearing cap bolt also carries the support bracket for the oil pick-up tube. Tighten the bolts evenly to half of the specified torque setting, then check the crankshaft for ease of rotation.

9   Should the crankshaft be stiff to turn or possess high spots, a most careful inspection should be made – preferably by a skilled mechanic – to trace the cause of the trouble. It is very seldom that trouble of this nature will be experienced when fitting the crankshaft.

10 Using a screwdriver, ease the crankshaft fully forward and measure the endfloat, with feeler gauges, between the side of the crankshaft rear journal and the thrust washers. Ensure that the clearance is within the limits given in the Specifications.

11 Lubricate the lip seal of the crankshaft rear oil seal and place it in position over the crankshaft, with the open side toward the engine. Push the seal fully into its seating in the bearing cap and crankcase (photo).

12 Now tighten the main bearing securing bolts to the torque wrench setting given in the Specifications (photo).

40 Pistons and connecting rods – reassembly

As interference type gudgeon pins are used (see Section 17) this operation must be carried out by your GM dealer or motor engineering specialists.

Fig. 1.11 Correct assembly of piston to connecting rod (Sec 40)

41 Piston rings – refitting

1   Check that the piston ring grooves and oilways are thoroughly clean and unblocked. Piston rings must always be fitted over the head of the piston and never from the bottom.

2   The easiest method to use when fitting rings is to wrap a 0.38 mm (0.015 in) feeler gauge round the top of the piston and place the rings one at a time, starting with the bottom oil control ring, over the feeler gauge.

3   The feeler gauge, complete with ring can then be slid down the

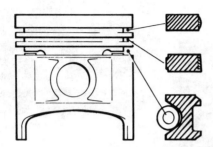

Fig. 1.12 Correct positioning of the piston rings (Sec 41)

piston over the other piston ring grooves until the correct groove is reached. The piston ring is then slid gently off the feeler gauge into the groove.

4   An alternative method is to fit the rings by holding them slightly open with the thumbs and both of the index fingers. This method requires a steady hand and great care, as it is easy to open the ring too much and break it.

5   The top compression ring and the slotted oil control ring may be fitted either way up; however the tapered second ring must be fitted with the word 'top' uppermost.

6   When all the rings are in position on the pistons, move them around to bring each ring gap approximately 120° away from the adjacent ring.

42 Pistons and connecting rod assemblies – refitting

1   Lay the piston/connecting rod assemblies out in their correct order, ready for refitting into their respective bores in the cylinder block. Remember that the connecting rods have been numbered to indicate to which cylinder they are to be fitted.

2   Clean the cylinder bores with a clean non-fluffy rag.

3   Apply some clean engine oil to the piston rings, then wrap the piston ring compressor around the first assembly to be fitted. A large diameter worm drive hose clip will serve as a ring compressor if a proper tool is not available.

4   Insert the connecting rod and piston into the top of the cylinder block and gently tap the piston through the ring compressor into the cylinder bore with a wooden or soft-headed mallet (photo). Guide the big-end of the connecting rod near to its position on the crankshaft.

5   Repeat the sequence described for the remaining three piston/connecting rod assemblies.

6   Check that all the pistons and connecting rods are the correct way around in the cylinder block. The notches in the top of the pistons should be towards the front of the engine; the oil squirt holes near the big-ends on the connecting rods should be on the manifold side of the engine. The notches in the big-end caps should all be to the rearward end of the engine.

43 Connecting rods/big-end bearings – refitting to crankshaft

1   Wipe the shell seat in the big-end of the connecting rod clean, and the underside of the new shell bearing. Fit the shell into position in the connecting rod with its locating tongue engaged with the appropriate groove in the big-end. Check that the oil squirt hole in the rod is aligned with the hole in the bearing shell.

2   Generously lubricate the crankpin journals with engine oil and turn the crankshaft so that it is in its most advantageous position for the rod to be drawn onto it.

3   Wipe the bearing shell seat in the bearing cap clean, and then the underside of the new shell. Fit the shell into the cap, engaging the shell tongue with the groove in the cap (photo).

4   Draw the big-end of the connecting rod onto the crankpin, then fit the cap into position. Make sure it is the correct way around, then insert the two retaining bolts.

5   Tighten the big-end bolts a little at first, and do not tighten fully to the specified torque until all the piston/connecting rod assemblies have been fitted and the rotational freedom of the crankshaft checked (photo).

44 Flywheel – refitting

1   Place the flywheel in position on the crankshaft and refit the retaining bolts. The bolt with the letter P stamped on its head must be refitted in its original position as was marked during disassembly (photo).

2   Tighten the retaining bolts in a diagonal and progressive sequence to the torque wrench setting given in the Specifications (photo).

3   If the needle roller bearing in the end of the crankshaft has been removed, it should now be refitted, after first smearing the rollers with medium grease (photo).

4   If desired, the clutch assembly may be refitted at this stage as described in Chapter 5.

45 Timing chain, cover and sump – reassembly

1   Begin reassembly of the timing components by placing the Woodruff keys into the slots in the forward end of the crankshaft.

2   Gently tap the timing sprocket onto the crankshaft, engaging the slot in the gear with the Woodruff key. The teeth on the gear should be next to the shoulder on the crankshaft.

3   Now slide the auxiliary drive gear onto the crankshaft with the raised face toward the timing sprocket (photo).

4   Rotate the crankshaft to bring Nos 1 and 4 pistons to TDC with the Woodruff key slot in the crankshaft pointing directly upwards.

5   If the chain guides in the timing cover and on the cylinder block were removed and have not yet been refitted, this should now be done along with the camshaft sprocket support bracket.

6   With Nos 1 and 4 pistons at TDC, and the Woodruff key slot in the crankshaft uppermost, place the timing chain in position over the crankshaft sprocket. Now fit the camshaft sprocket and position it in such a fashion that when the chain is held parallel with the guide, the dimple on the periphery of the sprocket is adjacent to the notch in the

42.4 With the piston rings compressed with a compressor tool, tap the assemblies into the cylinders

43.3 Fitting of the bearing shells to the big-end caps

43.5 Using a torque wrench to tighten the big-end retaining bolts

Are your plugs trying to tell you something?

Normal.
Grey-brown deposits, lightly coated core nose. Plugs ideally suited to engine, and engine in good condition.

Heavy Deposits.
A build up of crusty deposits, light-grey sandy colour in appearance.
Fault: Often caused by worn valve guides, excessive use of upper cylinder lubricant, or idling for long periods.

Lead Glazing.
Plug insulator firing tip appears yellow or green/yellow and shiny in appearance.
Fault: Often caused by incorrect carburation, excessive idling followed by sharp acceleration. Also check ignition timing.

Carbon fouling.
Dry, black, sooty deposits.
Fault: over-rich fuel mixture.
Check: carburettor mixture settings, float level, choke operation, air filter.

Oil fouling.
Wet, oily deposits. Fault: worn bores/piston rings or valve guides; sometimes occurs (temporarily) during running-in period.

Overheating.
Electrodes have glazed appearance, core nose very white – few deposits. Fault: plug overheating. Check: plug value, ignition timing, fuel octane rating (too low) and fuel mixture (too weak).

Electrode damage.
Electrodes burned away; core nose has burned, glazed appearance. Fault: pre-ignition. Check: for correct heat range and as for 'overheating'.

Split core nose.
(May appear initially as a crack). Fault: detonation or wrong gap-setting technique.
Check: ignition timing, cooling system, fuel mixture (too weak).

WHY DOUBLE COPPER IS BETTER FOR YOUR ENGINE.

Unique Trapezoidal Copper Cored Earth Electrode — 50% Larger Spark Area — Copper Cored Centre Electrode

Champion Double Copper plugs are the first in the world to have copper core in both centre <u>and</u> earth electrode. This innovative design means that they run cooler by up to 100°C – giving greater efficiency and longer life. These double copper cores transfer heat away from the tip of the plug faster and more efficiently. Therefore, Double Copper runs at cooler temperatures than conventional plugs giving improved acceleration response and high speed performance with no fear of pre-ignition.

Champion Double Copper plugs also feature a unique trapezoidal earth electrode giving a 50% increase in spark area. This, together with the double copper cores, offers greatly reduced electrode wear, so the spark stays stronger for longer.

 FASTER COLD STARTING

 FOR UNLEADED OR LEADED FUEL

 ELECTRODES UP TO 100°C COOLER

 BETTER ACCELERATION RESPONSE

 LOWER EMISSIONS

 50% BIGGER SPARK AREA

 THE LONGER LIFE PLUG

Plug Tips/Hot and Cold.
Spark plugs must operate within well-defined temperature limits to avoid cold fouling at one extreme and overheating at the other.
Champion and the car manufacturers work out the best plugs for an engine to give optimum performance under all conditions, from freezing cold starts to sustained high speed motorway cruising.
Plugs are often referred to as hot or cold. With Champion, the higher the number on its body, the hotter the plug, and the lower the number the cooler the plug.

Plug Cleaning
Modern plug design and materials mean that Champion no longer recommends periodic plug cleaning. Certainly don't clean your plugs with a wire brush as this can cause metal conductive paths across the nose of the insulator so impairing its performance and resulting in loss of acceleration and reduced m.p.g.
However, if plugs are removed, always carefully clean the area where the plug seats in the cylinder head as grit and dirt can sometimes cause gas leakage.
Also wipe any traces of oil or grease from plug leads as this may lead to arcing.

DOUBLE CC COPPER

1

This photographic sequence shows the steps taken to repair the dent and paintwork damage shown above. In general, the procedure for repairing a hole will be similar; where there are substantial differences, the procedure is clearly described and shown in a separate photograph.

2

First remove any trim around the dent, then hammer out the dent where access is possible. This will minimise filling. Here, after the large dent has been hammered out, the damaged area is being made slightly concave.

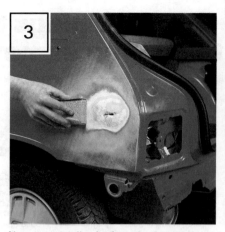

3

Next, remove all paint from the damaged area by rubbing with coarse abrasive paper or using a power drill fitted with a wire brush or abrasive pad. 'Feather' the edge of the boundary with good paintwork using a finer grade of abrasive paper.

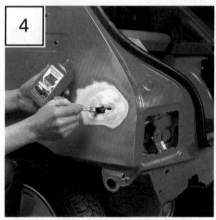

4

Where there are holes or other damage, the sheet metal should be cut away before proceeding further. The damaged area and any signs of rust should be treated with Turtle Wax Hi-Tech Rust Eater, which will also inhibit further rust formation.

5

For a large dent or hole mix Holts Body Plus Resin and Hardener according to the manufacturer's instructions and apply around the edge of the repair. Press Glass Fibre Matting over the repair area and leave for 20-30 minutes to harden. Then ...

5A

... brush more Holts Body Plus Resin and Hardener onto the matting and leave to harden. Repeat the sequence with two or three layers of matting, checking that the final layer is lower than the surrounding area. Apply Holts Body Plus Filler Paste as shown in Step 5B.

5B

For a medium dent, mix Holts Body Plus Filler Paste and Hardener according to the manufacturer's instructions and apply it with a flexible applicator. Apply thin layers of filler at 20-minute intervals, until the filler surface is slightly proud of the surrounding bodywork.

5C

For small dents and scratches use Holts No Mix Filler Paste straight from the tube. Apply it according to the instructions in thin layers, using the spatula provided. It will harden in minutes if applied outdoors and may then be used as its own knifing putty.

6

Use a plane or file for initial shaping. Then, using progressively finer grades of wet-and-dry paper, wrapped round a sanding block, and copious amounts of clean water, rub down the filler until glass smooth. 'Feather' the edges of adjoining paintwork.

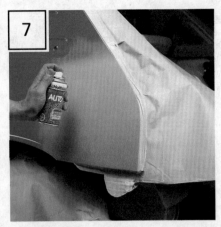

7 Protect adjoining areas before spraying the whole repair area and at least one inch of the surrounding sound paintwork with Holts Dupli-Color primer.

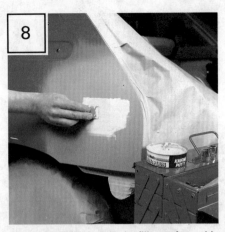

8 Fill any imperfections in the filler surface with a small amount of Holts Body Plus Knifing Putty. Using plenty of clean water, rub down the surface with a fine grade wet-and-dry paper – 400 grade is recommended – until it is really smooth.

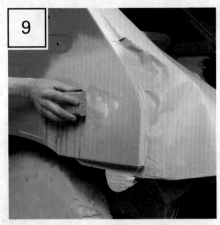

9 Carefully fill any remaining imperfections with knifing putty before applying the last coat of primer. Then rub down the surface with Holts Body Plus Rubbing Compound to ensure a really smooth surface.

10 Protect surrounding areas from overspray before applying the topcoat in several thin layers. Agitate Holts Dupli-Color aerosol thoroughly. Start at the repair centre, spraying outwards with a side-to-side motion.

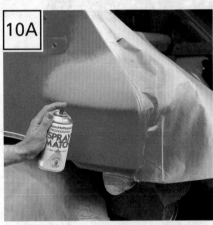

10A If the exact colour is not available off the shelf, local Holts Professional Spraymatch Centres will custom fill an aerosol to match perfectly.

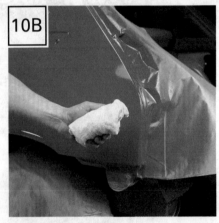

10B To identify whether a lacquer finish is required, rub a painted unrepaired part of the body with wax and a clean cloth.

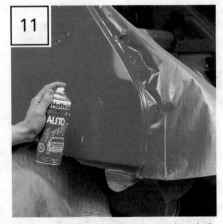

11 If *no* traces of paint appear on the cloth, spray Holts Dupli-Color clear lacquer over the repaired area to achieve the correct gloss level.

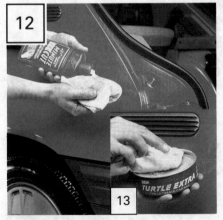

12 The paint will take about two weeks to harden fully. After this time it can be 'cut' with a mild cutting compound such as Turtle Wax Minute Cut prior to polishing with a final coating of Turtle Wax Extra.

13

14 When carrying out bodywork repairs, remember that the quality of the finished job is proportional to the time and effort expended.

44.1 Flywheel locating bolt stamped with a letter P

44.2 Tightening the flywheel retaining bolts

44.3 Crankshaft needle roller bearing in position

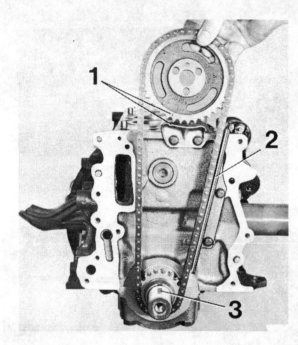

Fig. 1.13 Fitting the timing chain and sprockets (Sec 45)

Timing marks on sprocket and support plate (1) aligned with chain parallel to guide (2) and Woodruff key slot (3) facing upwards. Note that when the camshaft is fitted, No 4 piston is at TDC on its firing stroke

support bracket (photo).

7 Place a new gasket in position on the cylinder block, then refit the timing cover and the cover retaining bolts. Tighten the bolts to the specified torque (photo). Do not neglect the bolt in the water pump aperture.

8 The oil pick-up tube should now be fitted (photo). Use a new gasket at the joint face and engage the support bracket fitted to No 2 main bearing cap.

9 Coat both surfaces of the sump gasket halves with gasket sealer and place them in position on the crankcase. Now apply a silicone RTV gasket sealer to the recesses in the front timing cover and rear main bearing cap and insert the rubber end gaskets. Apply sealer liberally to the ends of the rubber gasket where they contact the cork side gaskets (photos).

10 Now place the sump carefully onto the crankcase and refit the retaining bolts. Take great care not to dislodge the gasket ends when refitting the bolts. Tighten the bolts sufficiently to compress the gasket without distortion (photos).

11 The crankshaft pulley should now be fitted and the retaining bolt tightened to the specified torque (photo).

12 With the timing cover and sump in place, turn the engine the correct way up, so that it is resting on the sump, and support it with wooden blocks.

13 Screw a new oil filter cartridge onto its location on the timing cover (see Section 22).

14 Undo and remove the small plugs located just above the oil filter and oil pump on the timing cover.

15 Inject clean engine oil into the holes until the oil pump and filter are full and the oil level reaches the priming plug holes. This will ensure that the oil pump is primed upon initial engine start-up.

46 Valve assemblies – refitting to cylinder head

1 Begin by liberally lubricating the valve stems and then inserting them into the valve guides from which they were removed (photos).

2 Fit the inlet valve stem oil seals in position over the guide protrusion (photo), then place the spring and spring cap over the valve.

45.3 Refitting the ancillary drivegear

45.6 Timing marks on sprocket and support plate

45.7 Refitting the timing cover

45.8 Refitting the oil pick-up tube

45.9a Apply silicone sealer to the front timing cover …

45.9b … and rear main bearing cap grooves …

45.9c … and fit the rubber end gasket

45.9d Apply sealer to the ends of the seals

45.10a Place the sump in position …

45.10b … and refit the retaining bolts

45.11 Refitting the crankshaft pulley

46.1a Valve assemblies laid out ready for refitting

46.1b Inserting the valve into its guide

46.2 Inlet valve stem oil seal in position

46.3 Compressing the valve spring with the compressor tool

Ensure that the inlet valve spring is fitted with the closed coils at the bottom. **Note:** *The inlet valve springs are longer than the exhaust valve springs and are not tapered.*

3   Fit the spring compressor into position and compress the spring sufficiently for the cotters to be slipped into place in the groove machined in the top of the valve stem (photo). Now release the spring compressor.

4   Assemble the exhaust valve lower seat, spring, (large diameter at the bottom), spring upper seat and cap the the valve (photos).

5   Fit the spring compressor into position and compress the spring. With the spring compressed, fit the oil seal and then the cotters to the valve stem, locating the cotters in the machined groove in the top of the valve stem (photos).

6   Now release the spring compressor and repeat this procedure until all eight valves have been assembled into the cylinder head.

7   With all the valves fitted gently tap the top of the vave stems once or twice, using a soft-faced mallet to seat the cotters and centralise the components.

47 Camshaft and hydraulic tappets – refitting

1   Wipe the lobes and journals of the camshaft clean using a non-fluffy rag, then liberally coat them in clean engine oil.

2   Clean and lubricate the camshaft bearing journals in the cylinder head in the same fashion.

3   Now carefully insert the camshaft in the cylinder head, being wary not to scratch the surfaces of the bearings as the camshaft is fitted. Support the shaft through the access aperture whilst it is being passed down into position (photo).

4   Once the camshaft is in place, the tappets may be refitted into their respective bores.

5   Place the rockers over the rocker studs, followed by the rocker ball (spherical face toward the rocker), and finally the adjusting nut (photo). Do not tighten the adjusting nuts sufficiently to open the valves, otherwise the valves may contact the pistons when the cylinder head is fitted.

46.4a Assemble the exhaust valve lower spring seat, ...

46.4b ... valve spring, ...

46.4c ... spring upper seat ...

46.4d ... and spring cap to the valve

46.5a Compress the spring and position the oil seal ...

46.5b ... and retaining cotters over the valve stem

47.3 Camshaft access aperture in cylinder head

47.5 Refitting the rocker and rocker ball to the rocker stud

6   Refit the access covers to the cylinder head, using a new gasket.
7   Now rotate the camshaft so that locating dowel for the timing chain sprocket is uppermost.

48 Cylinder head – refitting

1   As already mentioned in the previous Section, the rockers should all be slack, so that the valves remain closed. This will ensure that neither the valves nor the pistons are damaged during the fitting of the cylinder head.
2   With the engine standing on its sump, check that the crankshaft sprocket keyway is uppermost. The camshaft timing mark will not be visible, but should still be aligned with the mark on the timing plate (see Fig. 1.13).
3   Locate the circular rubber sealing ring into its locating groove in the upper face of the timing cover (photo). Using a silicone RTV jointing compound, coat the joint between the timing cover and cylinder block upper edge (photo).
4   Place a new cylinder head gasket onto the cylinder block. The gasket is marked as to which way up it should be.
5   Lower the cylinder head carefully onto the engine, taking care not to disturb the camshaft sprocket which must pass into the forward space in the cylinder head casting (photo).
6   Insert the cylinder head retaining bolts in the manifold side of the head and tighten them finger tight only at this stage.
7   Rotate the camshaft if necessary to align the dowel and bolt holes, then fit the sprocket onto the end of the camshaft (photo). Secure the sprocket in position with the three splined retaining bolts. Tighten the bolts to the specified torque (photo).
8   Now refit the timing chain tensioner to the timing cover (photo).
9   The remaining cylinder head retaining bolts can now be fitted. Rotate the engine if necessary, so that the cut-outs in the camshaft are in the correct position to allow the cylinder head bolts to be inserted.
10   Tighten the cylinder head bolts progressively and evenly in the sequence shown in Fig. 1.15 to the torque wrench settings given in Specifications (photo).

11   When the cylinder head is secure, the two additional bolts that thread into the timing cover should be tightened, observing the specified torque.
12   Now refit the plastic plug into the centre of the camshaft sprocket assembly (photo).
13   Fit the forward end camshaft cover plate, use a new gasket and tighten the bolts (threads smeared with a locking agent) to compress the gasket without deformation.
14   The camshaft endfloat can now be measured. Push the camshaft rearward as far as it will go, using a screwdriver or flat bar as a lever.
15   Using feeler gauges, measure the clearance between the plastic plug and the extended nose of the end cover. Compare the reading obtained with the correct dimensions given in the Specifications (photo).
16   The endfloat is adjusted by mechanical deformation of the end cover. Depending on the adjustment required, the extended nose of the cover will need to be tapped lightly inwards, or the cover removed and the nose tapped outward.
17   Remembering that the timing chain, camshaft and cylinder head have been fitted with No 4 piston at TDC on its firing stroke, rotate the crankshaft through 360° (thus bringing No 1 piston to TDC on its firing stroke) in preparation for refitting the distributor.

49 Hydraulic tappets – initial adjustment after overhaul

1   After engine overhaul, or at any time when the rocker arm and its adjusting nut have been removed, it will be necessary to carry out a preliminary adjustment to enable the engine to be started. Final adjustment is made with the engine running, as described in Section 55.
2   Rotate the crankshaft until one of the pistons is at TDC and both the valves for that cylinder are closed.
3   Slacken the adjusting nut on the rockers of those valves until there is a slight clearance between the rocker and the top of the valve stem.
4   Tighten the rocker adjusting nut until the clearance is eliminated and the spring inside the hydraulic tappet can be felt to be starting to compress.

48.3a Location of the rubber sealing ring in the timing cover groove

48.3b Applying silicone gasket sealer to the timing cover joint prior to cylinder head fitting

48.5 Lowering the cylinder head onto the engine

48.7a Camshaft sprocket and chain in position

48.7b Tightening the camshaft sprocket retaining bolts

48.8 Refitting the timing chain tensioner

Fig. 1.14 Location of cut-outs in camshaft (Sec 48)

Fig. 1.15 Cylinder head bolt tightening sequence (Sec 48)

5   Repeat this operation for the valves of each cylinder.

50 Engine ancillary components – refitting

The following components should be assembled onto the engine before it is refitted into the car. Refer to the relevant Chapter or Section of this manual where necessary for detailed refitting procedures.

Water pump and fan
Distributor
Inlet and exhaust manifolds and carburettor

Oil filter cartridge
Thermostat and housing
Fuel pump
Alternator and fanbelt
Rocker cover
Engine mounting brackets

51 Engine (with manual gearbox) – reconnecting

1   If the engine was removed in unit with the gearbox, it may be reattached in the following manner:
2   With the engine on the floor and suitably supported on blocks, lift up the gearbox and insert the gearbox input shaft into the centre of the clutch. Push the gearbox so that the gearbox input shaft splines pass through the internal splines of the clutch disc (photo).
3   If difficulty is experienced in engaging the splines, try turning the gearbox slightly. *On no account allow the weight of the gearbox to hang unsupported on the input shaft.*
4   With the gearbox correctly positioned on the engine, support its weight using a wooden block.
5   Secure the gearbox to the engine with the retaining bolts.
6   Refit the starter motor, the flywheel cover plate and the two lower support brackets (photos).
7   The power unit is now ready for refitting into the car.

52 Engine (with automatic transmission) – reconnecting

The procedure for reconnecting the automatic transmission to the engine is the same as described in Section 51, bearing in mind the following points:

(a) Ensure that the torque converter is in position on the transmission before reconnecting to the engine
(b) With the transmission in position, align the previously made marks between the torque converter and drive disc and refit the retaining bolts

48.10 Tightening the cylinder head bolts

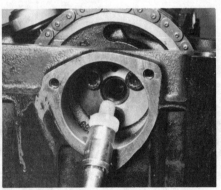

48.12 Refitting the camshaft sprocket thrust plug

48.15 Measuring the camshaft endfloat

51.2 Refitting the gearbox

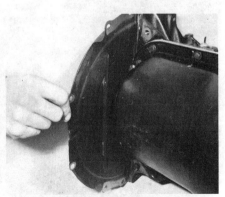

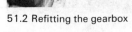

51.6a Refitting the starter motor ...

51.6b ... and flywheel cover plate

53 Engine – refitting

1   Refitting the engine is a reversal of the removal procedure. A little trouble taken in getting the engine properly slung (so it takes up a suspended angle similar to its final position) will pay off when it comes to locating it on the front engine mountings.

2   Ensure that all loose leads, cables, hoses, etc are tucked out of the way. If not, it is easy to trap one and cause additional work after the engine is refitted in the car.

3   Carefully lower the engine while an assistant guides it into position (photo). If the gearbox is still in place in the car, it may be necessary to turn the crankshaft slightly to engage the splines of the gearbox input shaft.

4   The engine is likely to be stiff to turn over initially if new bearings or pistons and rings have been fitted, and it will save a lot of frustration if the battery is well charged. After a rebore the stiffness may initially be more than the battery can cope with, so be prepared to connect another battery in parallel with jump leads.

5   The following check list should ensure the engine starts safely and with the minimum of delay:

(a)   Fuel lines connected and tightened
(b)   Water hoses connected and secured with clips
(c)   Coolant drain plug fitted and tightened
(d)   Cooling system replenished
(e)   Sump drain plug fitted and tight
(f)   Oil in engine
(g)   LT wiring connected to distributor and coil
(h)   Choke, temperature gauge, and oil pressure warning light wires connected
(j)   Spark plugs tight
(k)   Rotor arm fitted in distributor
(l)   Distributor cap and HT leads correctly fitted
(m)   Throttle linkage connected
(n)   Earth strap connected
(p)   Starter motor leads connected
(q)   Alternator leads connected
(r)   Battery fully charged and leads connected
(s)   Oil or fluid in gearbox or transmission

54 Engine – initial start-up after overhaul or major repair

1   Make sure the battery is fully charged and all lubricants, coolant and fuel are replenished.

2   If the fuel system has been dismantled, it will require several revolutions of the engine on the starter motor to pump the petrol up to the carburettor, so be prepared for this.

3   As soon as the engine fires and runs, keep it going at a fast idle only and bring it up to normal working temperature.

4   When the engine is initially started, there will be a lot of noise from the hydraulic tappets until they fill with oil. This may take two or three minutes and the engine may appear to be running unevenly during this time. This is quite normal and is nothing to be alarmed about, providing no other noises are heard from other parts of the engine at the same time.

5   As the engine warms up, there will be odd smells and some smoke from parts getting hot and burning off oil deposits. The signs to look for are leaks of water, petrol or oil, which will be obvious, if serious. Check also the exhaust pipe and manifold connections, as these do not always find their exact gastight position until the heat and vibration have acted upon them, and it is almost certain they will require further tightening. This should be done, of course, with the engine stopped.

6   When normal running temperature has been reached, adjust the engine idling speed as described in Chapter 3.

7   Stop the engine and wait a few minutes to see if any lubricant or coolant is dripping out when the engine is stationary.

8   After the engine has reached normal operating temperature, carry out Stage 3 of the cylinder head bolt tightening sequence (see Specifications).
Also, check the manifold bolts and sump bolts.

9   The hydraulic tappet final adjustment should now be carried out,

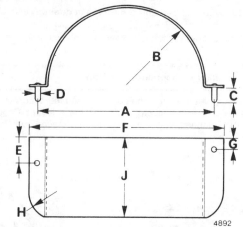

Fig. 1.16 Temporary chain guard and oil baffle dimensions (Sec 55)

A	168 mm (6.614 in)		F	180 mm (7.087 in)
B	75 mm (2.953 in)		G	10 mm (0.394 in)
C	12 mm (0.472 in)		H	25 mm (0.984 in)
D	4.8 mm (0.189 in)		J	70 mm (2.756 in)
E	23 mm (0.905 in)			

53.3 Refitting the engine (note the angle)

55.2 Temporary chain guard in position on the engine

as described in Section 55.

10 Road test the car to check that the timing is correct and the engine is delivering the necessary smoothness and power. Do not race the engine – if new bearings and/or pistons have been fitted, it should be treated as a new engine and run in at a reduced speed for the first 1000 miles (1610 km).

55 Hydraulic tappets – final adjustment after overhaul

1 Make up a temporary chain guard and oil baffle from 18 or 20 swg mild steel sheet (see Fig. 1.16).
2 Run the engine until it achieves normal operating temperature, then switch it off, remove the rocker cover and fit the chain guard (photo).

3 Start the engine, and when it is again at normal operating temperature (and running at idling speed), slacken one of the rocker adjusting nuts until the rocker arm starts rattling.
4 Tighten the rocker adjusting nut slowly until the rocker arm just stops rattling. Now tighten the nut by a quarter of a turn and wait ten seconds until the engine runs smoothly again. Tighten the nut by three further quarter turns, waiting ten seconds between each quarter turn until the nut has been tightened one full turn from the position where the rocker stopped rattling.
5 It is important that this procedure is followed exactly, as this method of adjustment preloads the plunger slowly and allows the tappet to adjust itself to the changed preload. By so doing, the risk of plunger damage – or of the engine running unevenly through compression loss – is eliminated.
6 The adjusting sequence must be carried out on each rocker arm in turn.

56 Fault diagnosis – engine

Symptom	Reason(s)
Engine turns over but will not start	Ignition damp or wet
	Ignition leads to spark plugs loose
	Shorted or disconnected low tension leads
	Dirty, incorrectly set or pitted contact breaker points
	Faulty condenser
	Defective ignition switch
	Ignition LT leads connected wrong way round
	Faulty coil
	Contact breaker point spring earthed or broken
	No petrol in petrol tank
	Vapour lock in fuel line (in hot conditions or at high altitude)
	Blocked float chamber needle valve
	Fuel pump filter blocked
	Choked or blocked carburettor jets
	Faulty fuel pump
	Too much choke allowing too rich a mixture to wet plugs
	Float damaged or leaking or needle not seating
	Float lever incorrectly adjusted
Engine stalls and will not start	Ignition failure – sudden
	Ignition failure – misfiring precludes total stoppage
	Ignition failure – in severe rain or after traversing water splash
	No petrol in petrol tank
	Petrol tank breather choked
	Sudden obstruction in carburettor
	Water in fuel system
Engine misfires or idles unevenly	Ignition leads loose
	Battery earth strap loose on body attachment point
	Engine earth lead loose
	Low tension leads to terminals on coil loose
	Low tension lead from coil to distributor loose
	Dirty or incorrectly gapped spark plugs
	Dirty, incorrectly set or pitted contact breaker points
	Tracking across distributor cap
	Ignition too retarded
	Faulty coil
	Mixture too weak
	Air leak in carburettor
	Air leak at inlet manifold to cylinder head, or inlet manifold to carburettor
	Burnt out exhaust valves
	Sticking or leaking valves
	Weak or broken valve springs
	Worn valve guides or stems
	Worn pistons and piston rings

Symptom	Reason(s)
Lack of power and poor compression	Burnt out exhaust valves
	Sticking or leaking valves
	Worn valve guides and stems
	Weak or broken valve springs
	Blown cylinder head gasket (accompanied by increase in noise)
	Worn pistons and piston rings
	Worn or scored cylinder bores
	Ignition timing wrongly set. Too advanced or retarded
	Contact breaker points incorrectly gapped
	Valve timing incorrect
	Incorrectly set spark plugs
	Carburettor too rich or too weak
	Dirty contact breaker points
	Fuel filters blocked causing top end fuel starvation
	Distributor automatic balance weights or vacuum advance and retard mechanisms not functioning correctly
	Faulty fuel pump giving top end fuel starvation
Excessive oil consumption	Badly worn, perished or missing valve stem oil seals
	Excessively worn valve stems and valve guides
	Worn piston rings
	Worn pistons and cylinder bores
	Excessive piston ring gap allowing blow-by
	Piston oil return holes choked
Oil being lost due to leaks	Leaking oil filter gasket
	Leaking rocker cover gasket
	Leaking timing cover gasket
	Leaking sump gasket
	Loose sump plug
Unusual noises from engine	Worn valve gear (noisy tapping from rocker covers)
	Worn big-end bearing (regular heavy knocking)
	Worn main bearings (rumbling and vibration)
	Worn crankshaft (knocking, rumbling and vibration)

Chapter 2 Cooling system

For modifications, and information applicable to later models, see Supplement at end of manual

Contents

Specifications

System type .... Pressurised, pump assisted thermo-syphon

Thermostat
Type ....

Starts to open ....

Fully open ....

Wax

87°C (189°F)

102°C (216°F)

Radiator
Type ....

Pressure cap opens ....

Corrugated fin

102 to 115 kPa (14.5 to 16.3 lbf/in²)

Fan
Manual transmission ....

Automatic transmission ....

5-blade, rigid drive

5-blade, viscous clutch drive

Cooling system capacity (including heater)
Manual transmission ....

Automatic transmission ....

6.1 litres (10.7 Imp pints)

6.0 litres (10.5 Imp pints)

Torque wrench settings

	Nm	lbf ft
Water pump	15	11
Thermostat cover	16	12
Temperature sender	11	8

1 General description

The engine cooling water is circulated by a water pump assisted, thermo-syphon system. The system is pressurised to prevent loss of cooling water down the overflow pipe with the radiator cap in position and to prevent premature boiling in adverse conditions. Cooling system pressure is maintained by a spring-loaded radiator cap. This has the effect of increasing the boiling point of the coolant. If the water temperature rises above the increased boiling point, the extra pressure in the system forces the internal part of the cap off its seat thus exposing the overflow pipe, down which the steam from the boiling water escapes, thereby relieving the pressure. It is therefore important to check that the radiator cap is in good condition and that the spring behind the sealing washer has not weakened.

The cooling system comprises the radiator, downflow or crossflow type dependent on model, top and bottom water hoses, heater hoses, the impeller water pump (mounted on the front of the engine, it carries the fan blades and is driven by the fanbelt), the thermostat and the drain tap in the engine block. On vehicles equipped with automatic transmission, a viscous drive cooling fan is used. This type of fan rotates at pulley speed at low engine rpm, and at a speed slower than that of the pulley at high engine rpm. This has the effect of reducing

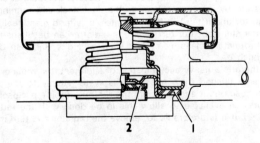

Fig. 2.1 Radiator pressure cap (Sec 1)

1 Pressure valve   *2 Vacuum valve*

the power consuming drag of the fan blades at high speed when sufficient cooling air is provided by the forward motion of the vehicle. These vehicles also have a transmission oil cooler located in the lower portion of the radiator. The system functions in the following fashion: Cold water in the bottom of the radiator circulates up the lower radiator hose to the water pump, where it is pushed round the water passages in the cylinder block, helping to keep the cylinder bores and pistons cool.

The water then travels down the radiator where it is rapidly cooled by the in-rush of cold air through the radiator core, which is created by both the fan and the motion of the car. The water, now much cooler, reaches the bottom of the radiator when the cycle is repeated.

When the engine is cold the thermostat (which is a valve that opens and closes according to the temperature of the water) maintains the circulation of the same water in the engine.

Only when the correct minimum operating temperature has been reached, as shown in the Specifications, does the thermostat begin to open, allowing water to return to the radiator.

2 Routine maintenance

1   Check the level of coolant weekly, or more frequently if the engine has a tendency to overheat. Under normal conditions, coolant loss is negligible and any need for frequent topping-up should be investigated.
2   Always top-up with a mixture of one part of approved antifreeze, to three parts water using soft water, if available. This ratio of antifreeze to water should be maintained all year round to act as a corrosion inhibitor and its strength increased if necessary during winter months according to climatic conditions (refer to Section 13).
3   Keep the radiator core free from debris, such as dead insects and leaves.
4   Check the fanbelt tension regularly and also examine all the hoses for signs of deterioration and leakage.
5   To ensure reliable operation, renew all the hoses every 30 000 miles (50 000 km).

3 Cooling system – draining

1   If possible, ensure the engine is cold before draining the coolant to avoid the risk of scalding.
2   Remove the radiator filler cap. If the engine is hot, this must be done very cautiously, because a sudden release of pressure can result in the coolant boiling and blowing out. On a hot engine, place a cloth over the cap and turn it very gently to release the pressure slowly.
3   Place a suitable container beneath the radiator, disconnect the bottom hose and allow the coolant to drain (photo).
4   The cylinder block may be drained completely, by removing the drain plug located at the rear right-hand side of the engine.

4 Cooling system – flushing

1   In time, the cooling system will lose its efficiency because of a build-up of rust and sediment in the radiator and engine water passages. To clean the system out, remove the radiator filler cap and block drain plug. Disconnect the bottom hose at the radiator and flush the system by inserting a hose in the filler neck and running water through for about ten to fifteen minutes. If, after a reasonable period the water still does not run clear, the radiator can be flushed with a good proprietary cleaning system such as Holts Radflush or Holts Speedflush.
2   If there is a heavy accumulation of sediment, the radiator should be reverse flushed by connecting the water supply to the radiator bottom hose outlet and allowing it to run out of the tap. Special hose adaptors are available to allow this to be done with the radiator in position, but it is preferable to remove the radiator and turn it upside down.

5 Cooling system – filling

1   Ensure the cylinder block drain plug is screwed in firmly and all cooling system hoses are in position and secured with hose clips.
2   Unscrew the small bleed plug on the top of the thermostat housing to allow air trapped in the cylinder block to escape as the system is filled (photo).
3   Using a mixture of one part antifreeze to three parts water, (in winter months a greater proportion of antifreeze may be required, according to regional climatic conditions), fill the cooling system

slowly to minimise air-locks. Ensure the heater control is in the 'HOT' position otherwise an air-lock may form in the heater.
4   Do not fill the system higher than 40 mm (1.5 in) from the top of the filler neck, because the coolant expands when heated and overfilling will result in coolant overflowing.
5   When the system is full, refit the bleed plug and radiator filler cap, then run the engine until normal temperature has been reached. Allow the engine to cool, then check and top-up the coolant level, if necessary.

6 Radiator – removal and refitting

1   Drain the cooling system as described in Section 3.
2   On automatic transmission models, place a tray beneath the oil cooler unions at the base of the radiator, wipe the unions clean and undo them. Quickly plug the pipe ends and the oil cooler unions, to prevent the loss of fluid and the ingress of dirt.
3   Remove the radiator top hose and the bottom hose also (if not already removed) as part of the radiator draining operation.
4   If a radiator cowl is fitted, remove the securing screws and lift the cowl rearwards over the fan.
5   Using a pair of pliers, compress the two retaining clips, one on each side of the radiator, and lift them out of their mounting brackets (photo).
6   Lift out the radiator, taking care not to damage the radiator core or the fan blades (photo).
7   With the radiator removed from the car, inspect the core and top and bottom tanks for damage or signs of leaks. If the radiator requires repair, it is better to fit an exchange radiator or have the repair done by a specialist. In an emergency, minor leaks can be cured with a radiator sealant such as Holts Radweld.
8   Inspect the radiator hoses for cracks or damage resulting from overtightening the clips and fit new hoses if the old ones have deteriorated. Renew the hose clips if the old ones are damaged or corroded.
9   Refitting the radiator is the reverse sequence to removal (photo). If any new hoses have been fitted, it will be found easier to position them onto the radiator outlets if their bores are first smeared with soap or rubber grease.
10 After refitting the radiator and hoses, tighten the hose clips and refill the cooling system.
11 On automatic transmission models, reconnect the oil cooler pipes and top-up the transmission with the recommended grade of fluid. If necessary, refer to Chapter 6.

7 Thermostat – removal and refitting

1   Drain the cooling system as described in Section 3.
2   Slacken the clips securing the top hose to the thermostat cover and remove the hose (photo).
3   Undo and remove the two bolts securing the thermostat cover to the housing, noting that the right-hand bolt also carries a heater hose support bracket.
4   Tap the thermostat cover with a soft-faced mallet if necessary to unstick it and lift the cover away (photo).
5   Carefully ease the thermostat out of its housing (photo).
6   Before refitting the thermostat, thoroughly clean the recess into which the thermostat fits, and clean all traces of old gasket from the joint faces of the housing and thermostat cover.
7   To refit the thermostat, place it in position in the housing, locating it squarely in the recess, and with the spring on the thermostat pointing downward.
8   Locate a new gasket, lightly coated with gasket cement, on the housing and refit the cover, hose bracket and retaining bolts, tightened to the specified torque.
9   Refit the hoses, tighten the clips and refill the cooling system.

8 Thermostat – testing

1   Remove the thermostat as described in the previous Section.
2   Place the thermostat the right way up in a pan of water, with a thermometer to measure the water temperature.
3   Heat the water and note the temperature at which the thermostat begins to open and is fully open. If these are not within the

3.3 Radiator bottom hose connections

5.2 Cooling system bleed plug located in the thermostat cover

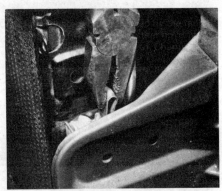

6.5 Removing the radiator retaining clips

6.6 Radiator removal

6.9 Location of radiator lower mounting

7.2 Removing the radiator top hose

7.4 Lifting off the thermostat cover

7.5 Withdrawing the thermostat

9.5 Undoing the fan retaining bolts using an Allen key

Specifications, fit a new thermostat. A defective thermostat will either fail to open, or will not open fully.

4   Allow the water to cool and note the temperatures at which the thermostat begins to close and is fully closed. If the valve does not seat properly in the closed position, fit a new thermostat.

9   Water pump – removal and refitting

1   Drain the cooling system as described in Section 3.
2   Remove the radiator and plastic cowl, if fitted, as described in Section 6.
3   If the vehicle is fitted with power steering, remove the pump drivebelt as described in Chapter 11.
4   Loosen the alternator mounting bolt and adjusting arm bolt, and push the alternator in toward the engine. Lift the fanbelt off the three pulleys and remove it.
5   Using a suitable Allen key, undo and remove the retaining bolts,

then withdraw the fan and pulley from the water pump flange (photo).
6   Slacken the hose clips and withdraw the heater hose and the radiator bottom hose from their respective positions on the water pump.
7   Undo and remove the six retaining bolts, then lift the pump from its location on the timing case.
8   Before refitting the pump, remove all traces of old gasket and jointing compound from the joint face of the timing case and water pump.
9   Apply jointing compound to both faces of a new gasket and position it accurately on the pump.
10   Position the water pump on the timing case and refit the retaining bolts finger tight first, then progressively tighten them in a diagonal sequence to the specified torque.
11   Refit the pulley and fan to the water pump followed by the fanbelt, adjusted as described in Section 11. The power steering drivebelt should now be refitted, where applicable, refering to Chapter 11 if necessary
12   Reconnect the water pump bottom hose and heater hose and fully

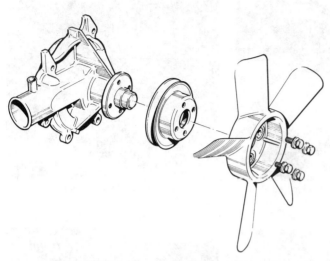

Fig. 2.2 Water pump and fan assembly (Sec 9)

tighten the clips.
13 Refit the radiator as described in Section 6 and refill the cooling
system as detailed in Section 5.

10 Water pump – overhaul

1   Water pump failure is indicated by leaks, noisy operation, and/or
slackness in the pump spindle bearing.
2   It is not possible to renew individual components on these water
pumps, therefore in the event of pump failure a new or exchange unit
must be fitted.

Fig. 2.3 Alternator mounting and adjusting bolts (Sec 11)

1   *Lower mounting bolt*   3   *Upper mounting bolt (where*
2   *Adjusting arm bolt*   *fitted)*

11 Fanbelt – removal, refitting and tensioning

1   If the vehicle is fitted with power steering, it will be necessary to
remove the power steering drivebelt before removing or refitting the
fanbelt.
2   Loosen the alternator adjusting and mounting bolts, then move the
alternator toward the engine as far as possible.
3   Slip the belt over the edge of the alternator pulley, the remove it
from the fan and crankshaft pulleys.
4   Before refitting, examine the belt for cracks or deterioration; if at
all suspicious, renew the belt.
5   Pass the new belt around the crankshaft and fan pulley, then ease
it over the edge of the alternator pulley.
6   Carefully lever the alternator away from the engine until the belt
can be deflected by finger pressure approximately 13 mm (0.5 in) at
a point midway between the alternator and water pump pulleys
(photo).
7   With the alternator held in this position, tighten the mounting and
adjusting bolts, then recheck the tension.
8   It is important to maintain correct belt tension. The belt being too
slack will result in its slipping and reducing the efficiency of the
alternator and cooling system. A belt too tight will cause excessive
wear to the water pump and alternator bearings.
9   With the fanbelt refitted and correctly tensioned, the power
steering drivebelt, where applicable, should be refitted and tensioned
as described in Chapter 11.
10 Always recheck the tension of a new belt after approximately 250
miles (400 km) as slight stretching will probably have taken place and
further adjustment may be required.

12 Temperature gauge and sender unit – removal, refitting and testing

1   If the temperature gauge fails to work, either the gauge, the
sender unit or the wiring and connections are at fault.
2   It is not possible to repair either the gauge or the sender unit, as
they are both sealed assemblies and must be replaced by new units it
at fault.
3   A quick check can be made when attempting to isolate a possible
fault, by removing the electrical lead from the sender unit and earthing
it on a suitable, non-painted, engine bolt or component. With the
ignition switched on, the temperature gauge should read maximum. If
this is the case, the sender unit is at fault. If no reading is shown on
the gauge, the gauge or wiring are faulty.
4   Removal and refitting of the temperature gauge is described in
Chapter 10.
5   To remove the sender unit, first drain the cooling system as
described in Section 3.
6   Detach the electrical lead from the sender unit and unscrew it

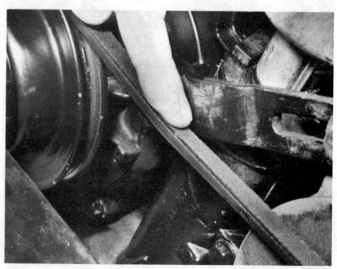

11.6 Checking the fanbelt tension

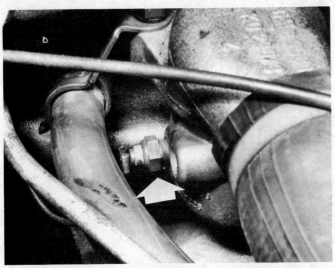

12.6 Location of the temperature gauge sender unit in the timing cover

from its location in the thermostat housing (photo).

7 Apply a trace of jointing compound to the threads of the sender and refit the unit to the thermostat housing.

8 Refit the electrical lead, and refill the cooling system.

13 Antifreeze

1 Owing to its corrosion inhibiting properties, a mixture of three parts water to one part antifreeze should be maintained in the cooling system all year round. In winter months, this ratio should be increased as necessary to suit the climatic condition in your area.

2 Preferably use an ethylene glycol based antifreeze, conforming to BS3151, BS3152, or BS6580 (Duckhams Universal Antifreeze and Summer Coolant). It is not recommended that an alcohol-based antifreeze is used due to its high evaporation rate.

3 The table below shows the proportion of antifreeze and the degree of protection:

Antifreeze %	Commences to freeze °C (°F)	Frozen °C (°F)
25	−12 (+10)	− 26 (−15)
33⅓	−20 (− 4)	−35 (−31)
40	−24 (−11)	−41 (−42)
50	−36 (−33)	−48 (−53)

Note: *Never use antifreeze in the windscreen washer reservoir as it will cause damage to the paintwork*

14 Fault diagnosis – cooling system

Symptom	Reason(s)
Overheating	Insufficient water in cooling system Fanbelt slipping (accompanied by a shrieking noise on rapid engine acceleration) Radiator core blocked or radiator grille restricted Bottom water hose collapsed, impeding flow Ignition advance and retard incorrectly set (accompanied by loss of power, and perhaps, misfiring) Carburettor incorrectly adjusted (mixture too weak) Exhaust system partially blocked Oil level in sump too low Blown cylinder head gasket (water/steam being forced down the radiator overflow pipe under pressure) Engine not yet run in Brakes binding
Underheating	Thermostat jammed open Incorrect thermostat fitted allowing premature opening of valve Thermostat missing
Loss of cooling water	Loose clips on water hoses Top, bottom or bypass water hoses perished and leaking Radiator core leaking Thermostat gasket leaking Radiator pressure cap spring worn or seal ineffective Blown cylinder head gasket (pressure in system) forcing water/steam down overflow pipe) Cylinder wall or head cracked

Chapter 3 Fuel and exhaust systems

For modifications, and information applicable to later models, see Supplement at end of manual

Contents

Specifications

Fuel pump

Type	Mechanical, driven by eccentric on distributor shaft
Delivery pressure	19.6 to 25.5 kPa (2.8 to 3.7 lbf/in²) at 2000 rpm

Fuel tank capacity

Saloon	65 litres (14.3 gallons)
Estate	70 litres (15.4 gallons)

Fuel filter

Type	Nylon mesh
Location	Fuel pump cover and carburettor inlet union

Fuel type

98 RON (4 star)

Air cleaner

Type	Thermostatically controlled
Element:	
2.0 litre carburettor engine (up to 1983)	Champion W130
2.0 litre carburettor engine (1984 on)	Champion U512
2.0 litre fuel injection engine	Champion U502

Carburettor

Type	GM Varajet II twin barrel downdraught
Throttle flap diameter:	
Primary	35 mm (1.38 in)
Secondary	46 mm (1.81 in)
Venturi diameter:	
Primary	26 mm (1.03 in)
Secondary	32 mm (1.26 in)
Idling speed	800 to 850 rpm
Fast idle speed	2000 to 2100
Mixture % CO	1.5 to 2.5%
Choke flap gap	3.5 mm (0.14 in)
Baffle plate lever to pull rod clearance	0.1 to 0.3 mm (0.004 to 0.012 in)
Automatic choke setting	Pointer 1 division towards R from centre
Pump piston setting	10.4 to 10.8 mm (0.41 to 0.42 in)
Float height	7.5 to 8.5 mm (0.29 to 0.33 in) below bowl top face
Throttle damper plunger travel	3.5 mm (0.14 in)

Torque wrench settings

	Nm	lbf ft
Fuel pump-to-timing cover	15	11
Carburettor-to-manifold	18	13
Exhaust pipe-to-manifold	35	26
Exhaust pipe U-bolts	15	11

1 General description

The fuel system comprises a fuel tank, a mechanically operated fuel pump, and a GM Varajet II carburettor. The fuel tank is positioned below the luggage compartment and is held in position by two retaining straps. An integral part of the fuel tank is the filler neck, which passes through the right-hand rear quarter panel and also contains the tank ventilation hoses. The fuel tank also houses the combined fuel outlet pipe and fuel gauge sender unit, located on the front face of the tank.

The mechanical fuel pump is located on the left-hand side of the engine and is operated by a plunger driven off an eccentric on the distributor driveshaft. Located in the fuel pump is a nylon filter, and access is gained by removing the pump top cover.

Petrol is drawn from the tank by the pump and delivered to the carburettor. The petrol level in the carburettor is controlled by a float operated needle valve. Petrol flows past the needle valve until the float rises to a predetermined level and closes the needle valve. As the fuel level in the float chamber drops, the needle valve opens again and a further supply of petrol is delivered to the carburettor by the pump.

Carburettor enrichment for cold starting is provided by an electrically operated automatic choke and intake air temperature is thermostatically regulated by the air cleaner which houses a disposable paper element.

2 Air cleaner – description and operation

A thermostatically controlled air cleaner is used to regulate the temperature of the air entering the carburettor according to ambient temperatures and engine load. The air cleaner has two sources of supply, through the normal intake (cool air), or from a heat shroud mounted on the exhaust manifold.

The air flow through the cleaner is controlled by a flap valve in the air cleaner spout, which covers or exposes the hot or cool air ports, according to engine temperature and manifold vacuum.

The vacuum motor operates the flap valve and holds it fully open when the temperature in the air cleaner is below 35°C (95°F). This allows only hot air to enter the air cleaner, irrespective of engine load.

When the air intake temperature reaches approximately 35°C (95°F), the vacuum motor opens or closes the flap valve, dependent entirely on manifold vacuum. Thus during light or constant throttle applications, the flap valve will remain open, supplying the carburettor with hot air, and will close under heavy throttle application so that only cool air enters the carburettor.

When the temperature in the air cleaner rises above approximately 45°C (113°F) the vacuum motor closes the flap valve, therefore allowing only cool air to enter the carburettor under all operating conditions.

The vacuum motor is operated by vacuum created in the inlet manifold and is controlled by a temperature sensing unit located inside the air cleaner.

3 Air cleaner – operating check

1 With the engine stationary, check that the flap valve is fully closed. The flap valve can be observed through the intake spout using a mirror.
2 With the engine cold, below 35°C (95°F), start it and check the operation of the flap valve. At idle, the flap valve should be fully open, allowing only warm air from the exhaust manifold to enter the air cleaner.
3 If the flap valve operates as described above, the air cleaner is functioning correctly.
4 If the flap valve remains closed when the engine is started, check the vacuum lines for leaks and renew if necessary.
5 If the vacuum lines are in order and the flap valve remains closed when the engine is started, the vacuum motor and/or heat sensor must be at fault. Testing of these units requires a vacuum pump and gauge, and should therefore be entrusted to your local main GM dealer.

4 Air cleaner – removal, servicing and refitting

Removal and refitting

1 The renewable paper element type air cleaner is fitted onto the top of the carburettor installation and is retained in position by a single central securing nut. To remove the air cleaner assembly, proceed as follows:
2 Undo and remove the retaining nut and washer from the centre of the air cleaner (photo).
3 If the filter only is to be removed, detach the wire clips around the circumference of the air cleaner and lift off the top cover. The paper element may now be lifted out (photo).
4 To remove the air cleaner body, carefully lift it off the carburettor and detach the pre-heating hose, engine breather hose, and vacuum supply line (photos).
5 Refitting the air cleaner is the reverse sequence to removal.

Servicing

6 Carefully inspect the element for signs of splitting, cracking or permanent distortion, and if evident, a new element should be fitted. A new element must be fitted every 24 000 miles (40 000 km) or earlier, if the car is being operated in dirty or dusty conditions.
7 With the air cleaner removed, a close inspection should be made of the vacuum motor and flap valve, the temperature sensing unit

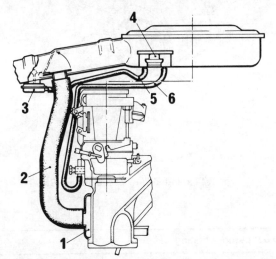

Fig. 3.1 Thermostatically controlled air cleaner components (Sec 2)

1 Manifold shroud	4 Temperature sensor
2 Pre-heating hose	5 Vacuum operating hose
3 Vacuum motor	6 Vacuum supply hose

4.2 Removing the air cleaner retaining nut

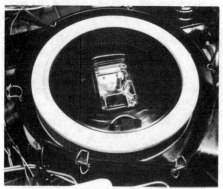

4.3 Removing the air cleaner filter element

4.4a Detach the breather hose ...

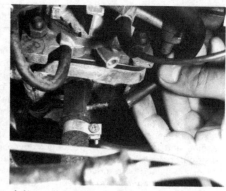

4.4b ... and vacuum supply line as the air cleaner is lifted off

4.7 Air cleaner temperature sensing unit

4.8 Removing the vacuum motor and flap valve from the air cleaner

4.9 Correct fitting of vacuum motor retaining wire clip

(photo) and the vacuum supply lines. Inspect the components for damage: Ensure that they are securely attached to the air cleaner and that the supply lines are in order and secure.

8   If required, the vacuum motor and flap valve may br removed from the air cleaner spout, by detaching the wire retaining clip and lifting off the motor and flap valve (photo).

9   When the vacuum motor is refitted, ensure that the retaining clip is positioned correctly (photo).

5   Fuel pump – description

The mechanical fuel pump is mounted on the lower left-hand side of the engine below the alternator, and is driven by an eccentric on the distributor driveshaft.

It is not possible to dismantle this type of pump for repairs, other than for cleaning the filter and sediment cap. Should a fault appear in the pump, it may be tested, and if confirmed, the pump must be discarded and a new one obtained.

6   Fuel pump – routine servicing

1   At intervals of 12 000 miles (20 000 km), the fuel pump filter, sediment cap and pumping chamber should be cleaned as follows:

2   Jack up the front of the car and support it on firmly based axle stands.

3   Undo the retaining clip and pull off the fuel inlet pipe from the pump sediment cap. Plug the pipe with a bolt or metal rod of suitable diameter immediately, to prevent loss of fuel.

4   With the fuel pipe removed, undo the retaining screw and lift off the sediment cap, filter and gasket from the pump body.

5   Using a stiff paintbrush and clean petrol, thoroughly clean the sediment cap, filter and pumping chamber to remove any sediment.

6   Reassembly is the reverse sequence to dismantling. Do not over-tighten the centre screw, as it could distort the sediment cap.

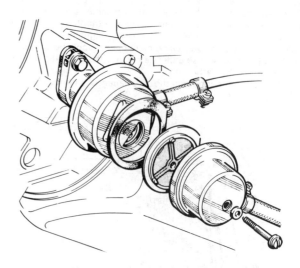

Fig. 3.2 Exploded view of fuel pump (Sec 6)

7   Fuel pump – testing

Assuming that the fuel lines and unions are in good condition and that there are no leaks anywhere, check the performance of the fuel pump in the following manner: Disconnect the fuel pipe at the carburettor inlet union, and the HT lead to the coil and, with a suitable container or large rag in position to catch the ejected fuel, turn the engine over. A good spurt of petrol should emerge from the end of the pipe every second revolution.

8 Fuel pump – removal and refitting

1 Jack up the front of the car and support it on firmly based axle stands.
2 Undo the two fuel pipe retaining clips and remove the pipes from the pump (photo). Plug the pipes immediately using a bolt or metal rod of suitable diameter to prevent loss of fuel and dirt ingress.
3 Undo and remove the two fuel pump retaining bolts and carefully withdraw the pump from the engine (photo).
4 Refitting is the reverse sequence to removal. Apply a trace of gasket sealer to the gasket faces before refitting, and tighten the retaining bolts to the specified torque wrench setting when the pump is fitted.

9 Fuel tank – removal and refitting

1 Petrol is a highly volatile and dangerous liquid, and certain precautions must be observed when working with it or near it (as will be the case during removal of the fuel tank)

  (a) *Always work in an open or well ventilated area, never over a pit. Petrol vapour is heavier than air and will gather in a pit or confined space creating a highly explosive environment*
  (b) *Ensure that the tank is less than quarter full before removal. This will reduce the risk of spillage and make the tank more manoeuverable. If necessary, syphon off a quantity of petrol into suitably marked sealed metal containers before removing the tank*
  (c) *When the fuel tank is removed seal off the filler neck to prevent evaporation (an old non-locking petrol cap is ideal)*

2 Having positioned the car in such a manner as to observe the above precautions, jack it up at the rear and place firmly based axle stands under the rear axle.
3 Remove the filler cap and the sealing grommet located between the filler neck and the rear quarter panel (photo).

4 From underneath the car, disconnect the electrical connections to the fuel gauge sender unit.
5 Slacken the clip securing the flexible petrol hose to the underbody mounted petrol pipe. Pull the hose off the pipe and plug the end with a bolt or metal rod of suitable diameter.
6 Support the tank on a jack or blocks, then undo and remove the bolts securing the tank retaining straps to the underbody (photos).
7 With the aid of an assistant, take the weight of the tank and withdraw it from under the car.
8 Refitting is the reverse procedure to removal.

10 Fuel tank – cleaning

1 With time it is likely that sediment will collect in the bottom of the fuel tank. Condensation, resulting in rust and other impurities, will usually be found in the fuel tank of any car more than three or four years old.
2 When the tank is removed it should be vigorously flushed out and turned upside down. If facilities are available at the local garage the tank may be steam cleaned and the exterior repainted with a lead based paint.
3 Never weld or bring a naked light close to an empty fuel tank until it has been steam cleaned out for at least two hours or washed internally with boiling water and detergent and allowed to stand for at least three hours.

11 Fuel gauge sender unit – removal and refitting

1 The fuel gauge sender unit can be removed with the fuel tank in position.
2 Jack up the rear of the car and place stands under the axle.
3 Ensure the level of fuel in the tank is below that of the sender unit, and if necessary, syphon off a quantity of fuel before proceeding. Observe the precautions listed in Section 9 before handling fuel.
4 The two electrical connections may now be removed from the unit

8.2 Removing the fuel pipe retaining clips

8.3 Withdrawing the fuel pump

9.3 Fuel tank filler cap and sealing grommet

9.6a Fuel tank front ...

9.6b ... and rear retaining straps

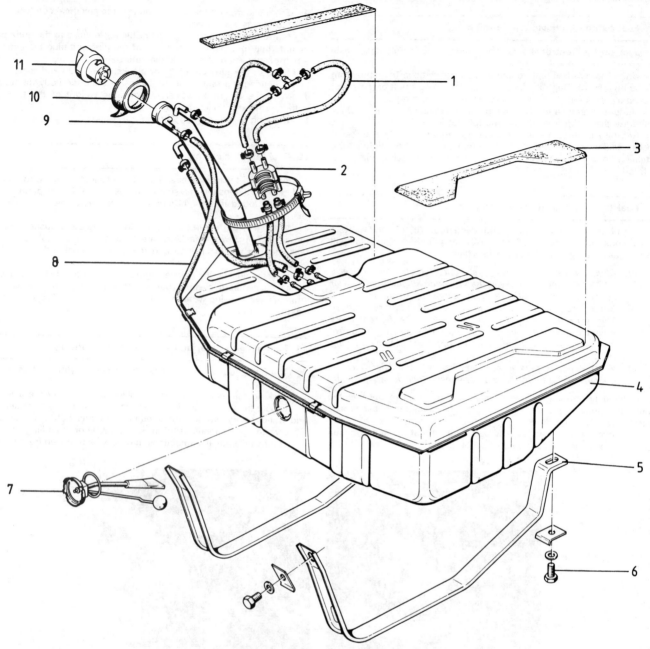

Fig. 3.3 Fuel tank and venting system (Sec 9)

1	Vent hose	4	Fuel tank	7	Sender unit	10	Grommet
2	Vent container	5	Retaining strap	8	Vent hose	11	Filler cap
3	Mounting pad	6	Retaining bolt	9	Filler neck		

and the petrol hose withdrawn after first slackening the retaining clip
(photo). Plug the end of the hose upon removal.
5   Using a soft metal drift, carefully tap the sender unit retaining ring
anti-clockwise and withdraw the complete unit from the tank.
6   Refitting is the reverse sequence to removal, but always use a new
gasket smeared with jointing compound and ensure the sender unit is
fitted with the float hanging downwards.

12 Accelerator linkage – adjustment

Manual transmission models
1   Remove the air cleaner, referring to Section 4 if necessary.
2   Measure the length of the accelerator linkage adjustable control
rod and adjust if necessary, until the distance between the two

balljoints is 76 mm (3 in).
3   Adjust the idling speed as described in Section 18.
4   Loosen the two locknuts on the linkage support bracket, then
working inside the car, adjust the pedal stop screw until the distance
between the throttle pedal rod and the floor is 50 mm (2 in) (photo).
5   With the throttle pedal and the throttle lever fully released, adjust
the two locknuts on the linkage support to provide a small amount of
slack in the inner cable.
6   Tighten both locknuts and refit the air cleaner.

Automatic transmission models
7   Adjustment of the accelerator linkage on models equipped with
automatic transmission is the same as that described for those with
manual transmission, except that paragraph 2 does not apply. However, after making an adjustment it is advisable to check the

11.4 Fuel gauge sender unit electrical connections and petrol hose

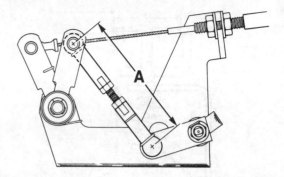

Fig. 3.4 Accelerator linkage control rod adjustment (Sec 12)
Dimension A = 76 mm (3 in)

adjustment of the kickdown cable as described in Chapter 6, Section 12.

8 Automatic transmission models also have a throttle damper fitted to the carburettor linkage. It should not normally be necessary to alter the original factory setting. If adjustment should, however, be necessary, proceed as follows:

9 Run the engine until normal operating temperatures have been attained, then check, and if necessary adjust, the idling speed to the figures given in Specifications (see also Section 18).

10 Stop the engine and open the throttle slightly, until the operating lever is just touching the damper plunger. Now measure the distance between the lever and the damper body (see Fig. 3.6). Release the throttle and allow it to close. Take a second measurement of the lever and damper body. The difference between these two measurements represents plunger travel, and should be 3.5 mm (0.14 in).

11 To adjust the damper, slacken the locknut and rotate the damper body until the correct plunger travel dimension is attained.

12 Tighten the locknut and refit the air cleaner.

13 Accelerator cable – removal and refitting

1 Withdraw the five plastic retaining buttons and lift out the kick panel from under the right-hand side of the dashboard.

2 Disconnect the inner accelerator cable, complete with tension spring, from the top of the accelerator pedal.

3 Working in the engine compartment, release the small spring retaining clip and lift off the cable ball socket from the lever of the throttle linkage.

4 Undo and remove the adjusting locknut, and remove the outer cable from the support bracket.

5 Pull the cable and grommet through the opening in the bulkhead and withdraw the complete cable from the engine compartment.

6 Refitting the accelerator cable is the reverse sequence to removal. With the cable in position, carry out the adjustment procedure described in Section 12.

14 Accelerator pedal – removal and refitting

1 The accelerator pedal is removed by disconnecting the accelerator cable (and kickdown cable for vehicles with automatic transmission) from the top of the pedal. The circlip retaining the accelerator pedal pivot can then be removed and the pivot and pedal lifted out.

2 Refitting is the reverse sequence to removal.

15 Carburettor – general description

The GM Varajet II carburettor is of the twin barrel downdraught

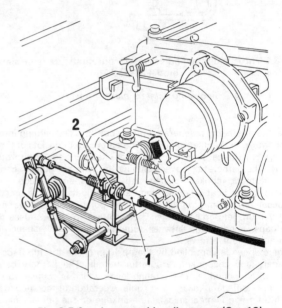

Fig. 3.5 Accelerator cable adjustment (Sec 12)

1 *Accelerator cable* 2 *Adjusting locknuts*

12.4 Accelerator pedal adjusting stop screw (arrowed)

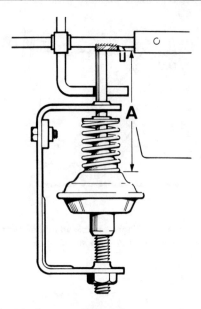

Fig. 3.6 Throttle damper adjustment – automatic transmission models (Sec 12)

A = measuring point for plunger travel

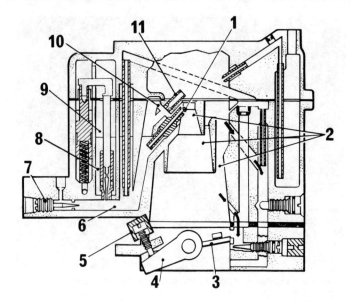

Fig. 3.7 Cutaway view of Varajet II carburettor (Sec 16)

1	Mixture outlet tube	7	Partial load needle valve
2	Auxiliary venturi (triple		(sealed)
	concentric)	8	Main jet
3	Throttle flap (primary barrel)	9	Partial load needle valve
4	Throttle flap lever	10	Air passage
5	Throttle stop screw	11	Air baffle
6	Main fuel passage		

type, each barrel being a separate system but both discharging into a common intake in the inlet manifold. The carburettor consists of three main castings: The carburettor cover, float chamber body and throttle flap body. The carburettor cover contains the twin air intakes, choke plates, automatic choke housing and the immersion tubes. Incorporated in the float chamber body are the floats and fuel needle valve, accelerator pump, partial load valve, pump suction valve, and integral venturi, jets and drillings. The throttle flap body houses the throttle flaps, spindles and linkages, together with the idle speed and mixture adjustment screws.

Engine speed is controlled by the position of the throttle flaps in the primary and secondary carburettor barrels. The primary barrel throttle flap is opened by an operating lever, which is coupled to the accelerator pedal via a linkage and cable. Operation of the secondary barrel throttle flap is mechanical, via a linkage on the primary flap.

Fuel enrichment for cold starting is provided by an electrically activated automatic choke.

16 Carburettor – operating principles

When starting the engine from cold, the bi-metallic strip tensions the choke flap spindle, thus allowing the choke flap to restrict the main air supply into the carburettor. Electric heating elements increase the temperature around the spring when the ignition is on, thus causing its tension to decrease. This decreasing tension of the bi-metal spring opens the choke flap progressively over a predetermined period of between two and three minutes. When the choke is closed, a high vacuum condition is created below the choke flap which drains the original over-rich mixture necessary for cold starting out of the discharge port in the auxiliary venturi. A linkage on the choke flap is connected to the throttle spindle, via a stepped cam, to give the required increase in engine speed necessary when the engine is cold. A vacuum controlled override unit is also incorporated, one of its functions being to prevent the mixture from becoming too rich during fast idle warm-up conditions.

Two idling mixture systems are used to control engine idling speed and idling mixture strength. Fuel from the idle system immersion tube is mixed with air drawn in through the idle air port, and this mixture is then passed down a vertical drilling to be further diluted with air entering a bypass drilling in the float chamber body. The resulting vapour is regulated by the mixture control screw, and passes out through a small hole below the throttle flap. An additional mixture system is used in conjunction with the idling mixture system, to provide sensitive adjustment of the idling speed and mixture settings.

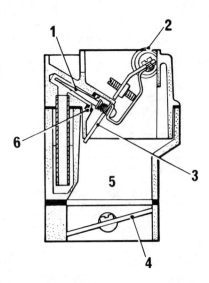

Fig. 3.8 Cutaway view of carburettor secondary barrel (Sec 16)

1	Full load needle valve	4	Throttle flap
2	Baffle flap spring	5	Venturi
3	Baffle flap	6	Jet baffle

This second system is regulated by the additional mixture control screw.

Fuel is supplied to the engine between idling and full load by the primary barrel main jet system. At wide throttle openings, the depression created around the mixture outlet (due to air speed in the venturi) is sufficient to maintain a flow of fuel from the mixture outlet tube. At reduced throttle openings, the flow of fuel is limited by the partial load valve.

The secondary barrel main jet system comes into operation when the primary barrel throttle flap is approximately two thirds open. This system provides additional enrichment of the mixture during hard acceleration and at high engine speeds.

As the secondary barrel throttle flap begins to open, a partial vacuum is created below the secondary barrel baffle flap. This flap is spring-loaded and is connected to the full load needle valve. As the vacuum increases with wider throttle openings, the tension of the baffle flap spring is overcome and the flap opens. The needle valve, being connected to the flap, is drawn off its seat and fuel is allowed to enter the air stream, providing the necessary high speed enrichment.

The vacuum controlled override system described previously is also used to hold the baffle flap shut initially, during hard acceleration, and thus prevent over-weakening of the mixture due to the increased air entering the venturi.

A full load enrichment valve, an accelerator pump and a further series of jets and drillings are incorporated in the two systems to provide smooth transition between primary and secondary throttle flap opening and to eliminate flat spots under all engine load conditions.

17 Carburettor adjustments – general

1 The GM Varajet II carburettor is provided with three idling adjustment screws. These are the primary barrel throttle flap stop screw, the mixture control screw and the additional idling mixture screw. The additional idling mixture screw controls the engine idling speed within set parameters, and may be adjusted without the use of special equipment as it does not appreciably alter the idling speed air/fuel mixture.

2 Due to the construction of this type of carburettor, and the very low level of carbon monoxide (CO) emission for which it was designed, the mixture control screw should not be adjusted without the use of a proper CO meter, (exhaust gas analyser).

3 The setting of the primary barrel throttle flap stop screw is established in production relative to the vacuum valve obtained at the carburettor vacuum advance connection. The screw is then sealed with a plastic cap. Incorrect adjustment of this screw will adversely affect the ignition vacuum advance operation, and the functioning of the carburettor progression system.

4 Adjustment of the primary barrel throttle flap stop screw will only be necessary if the required idling speed and exhaust gas condition cannot be achieved using the other two adjusting screws. If this is the case, adjustment should be entrusted to your GM main dealer, as a manometer is required to measure the vacuum valve controlled by the primary barrel throttle flap.

18 Carburettor – adjustments

Idle speed adjustment

1 Start the engine and allow it to warm up to its normal operating temperature.

2 Connect a tachometer (if not already fitted) following the manufacturer's instructions.

3 When the engine has reached normal operating temperature, blip the throttle to ensure the automatic choke fast idle cam is in the idling position. On cars equipped with automatic transmission, place the selector lever in the P position.

4 Using a small screwdriver, adjust the additional idling mixture screw (Fig. 3.9) until the specified idling speed (as given in the Specifications) is obtained.

Idle mixture adjustment

5 Connect a CO meter to the car, following the manufacturer's instructions.

6 With the engine at normal operating temperature, check that the CO reading falls within the limits given in the Specifications.

7 If the CO reading is incorrect, adjust the mixture control screw (Fig. 3.9) until the correct CO level is achieved. Now check, and if necessary readjust, the idling speed.

8 Switch off the engine and disconnect the CO meter. **Note:** *If the required idling speed and exhaust gas condition are not obtainable using the procedure described, it is likely that the primary barrel throttle flap is incorrectly adjusted (see Section 17)*

Fast idle adjustment

9 Before carrying out the fast idle adjustment, make sure that the normal engine idling performance is satisfactory, and that the engine

Fig. 3.9 Carburettor idling adjustment screws (Sec 18)
1 Ignition vacuum advance
*   connection*
2 Additional idling mixture
*   screw*
3 Mixture control screw

Fig. 3.10 Primary barrel throttle flap adjusting screw (Sec 18)

Fig. 3.11 Fast idle regulating screw (Sec 18)

is at its normal operating temperature.

10 Remove the air cleaner and blank off the air cleaner vacuum supply outlet.

11 Open the throttle flap slightly, and position the stepped fast idle cam so the regulating screw is resting on the centre step of the cam when the throttle flap is released.

12 Without depressing the accelerator pedal, start the engine.

13 Refer to the Specifications at the beginning of this Chapter, and adjust the regulating screw if necessary, until the specified fast idling speed is obtained.

14 Switch off the engine, disconnect the tachometer and refit the air cleaner.

19.3 Carburettor fuel pipe union nut

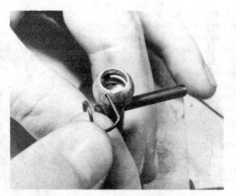

19.9a Refitting the wire retaining clip to the throttle linkage

19.9b Correct positioning of linkage

19 Carburettor – removal and refitting

1   Disconnect the battery earth terminal.

2   Remove the air cleaner, referring to Section 4 if necessary.

3   Undo and remove the fuel pipe from the carburettor union, then tape over the end to prevent dirt ingress (photo).

4   Disconnect the ignition vacuum advance hose from the carburettor.

5   Using a small screwdriver, prise up and remove the small wire clip that retains the ball of the throttle linkage to the carburettor throttle flap spindle.

6   Undo and remove the two retaining bolts, and lift the throttle linkage support plate complete with linkage off the inlet manifold.

7   Remove the electrical lead from the choke housing.

8   Undo and remove the four retaining nuts, then carefully lift the carburettor and gasket off the manifold.

9   Refitting the carburettor is the reverse sequence to removal, bearing in mind the following points:

(a) Ensure the mating surfaces are clean and always use a new gasket

(b) When fitting the throttle linkage, make sure the pin on the linkage is engaged with the fork of the carburettor throttle flap spindle (photo) and the wire retaining clip is correctly positioned (photo)

(c) Check the engine idle speed, and adjust if necessary, as described in Section 18

20 Carburettor dismantling and reassembly – general

1   With time, the component parts of the carburettor will wear and petrol consumption increase. The diameter of drillings and jets may alter, and air and fuel leaks may develop around spindles and other moving parts. Because of the high degree of precision involved it is best to purchase an exchange carburettor. This is one of the few instances where it is better to take the latter course rather than to rebuild the component oneself.

2   It may be necessary to partially dismantle the carburettor to clear a blocked jet. The accelerator pump itself may need attention and gaskets may need renewal. Providing care is taken, there is no reason why the carburettor may not be completely reconditioned at home, but ensure a full repair kit can be obtained before you strip the carburettor down. *Never* clean out jets with wire or similar but blow them out with compressed air or air from a car tyre pump.

21 Carburettor – dismantling, cleaning and inspection

1   Prepare a clean, uncluttered working area on the bench and have at the ready an assortment of trays or containers to store the various parts as they are dismantled. The carburettor contains a number of small precision assemblies, as well as numerous small jets and springs, which must be handled with extreme care to avoid damage. Providing you take your time, and follow the procedure below, the carburettor can be dismantled and reassembled quite easily, however.

2   Begin by removing the carburettor from the engine as described in Section 19, and thoroughly clean the exterior.

3   Undo and remove the fuel union nut on the side of the float chamber, then withdraw the fuel filter.

4   Undo and remove the three securing screws then lift off the automatic choke retaining ring and choke body, followed by the vacuum unit.

5   The accelerator pump actuating lever is removed next, after undoing the pivot screw and lifting off the operating rod. On some versions, a circlip is used to retain the rod to the lever, and this must also be removed if fitted.

6   Using a small screwdriver, prise off the circlips securing the choke flap operating link and the fast idle cam assembly, then slide the complete assembly off its pivot post.

7   Next, undo and remove the seven screws securing the carburettor cover to the float chamber body. Very carefully lift off the cover, making sure the gasket stays behind on the float chamber body. With the cover removed, it will be seen that the four immersion tubes protrude from the bottom of the cover. These tubes are permanently fixed in the cover, and if damaged, a new cover will have to be obtained; take care when handling this assembly.

8   Carefully lift out the accelerator pump piston and return spring from their locations in the float chamber body (Fig. 3.14).

9   The gasket can now be removed from the float chamber body. Lift it carefully over the partial load needle valve which protrudes through a slot cut in the centre of the gasket.

10   Next, lift off the float chamber filler, followed by the float assembly and needle valve.

11   A threaded collar retains the partial load needle valve in position. Using a pair of pointed-nosed pliers or similar tool, unscrew the collar and remove the valve. Take care not to mislay the piston return spring, which is located in the chamber beneath the valve collar (Fig. 3.15).

Fig. 3.12 Carburettor cover retaining screws (Sec 21)

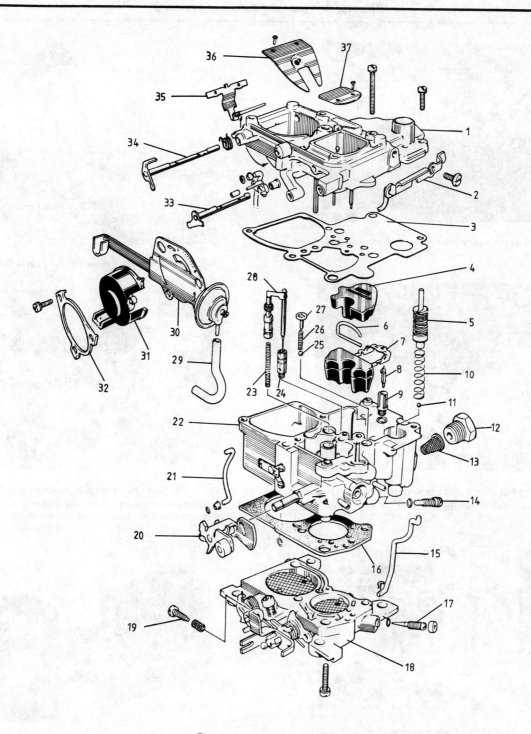

Fig. 3.13 Exploded view of carburettor (Sec 21)

1 Carburettor cover
2 Accelerator pump actuating lever
3 Gasket
4 Float filler
5 Accelerator pump piston
6 Float pivot clip
7 Float assembly
8 Needle valve
9 Needle valve seat
10 Accelerator pump return spring

11 Check ball
12 Union nut
13 Filter
14 Additional idling mixture screw
15 Accelerator pump operating rod
16 Gasket
17 Mixture control screw
18 Throttle flap body
19 Fast idle regulating screw

20 Fast idle cam assembly
21 Choke flap operating link
22 Float chamber body
23 Piston return spring (partial load valve)
24 Main jet
25 Pump suction valve check ball
26 Pump suction valve spring
27 Pump suction valve spring retainer

28 Partial load valve
29 Vacuum hose
30 Vacuum unit
31 Automatic choke housing
32 Retaining ring
33 Choke flap spindle
34 Baffle flap spindle
35 Full load needle valve mounting plate
36 Baffle flap
37 Choke flap

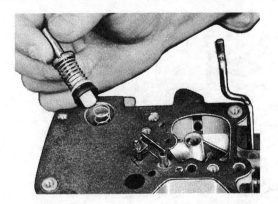

Fig. 3.14 Lifting out the accelerator pump piston and return spring (Sec 21)

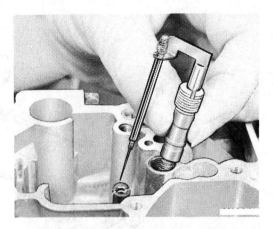

Fig. 3.15 Removing the partial load valve (Sec 21)

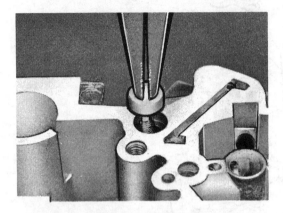

Fig. 3.16 Using flat-nosed pliers to withdraw the pump suction valve spring retainer (Sec 21)

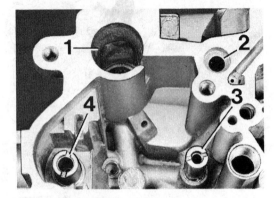

Fig. 3.17 Float chamber body jet locations (Sec 21)

1 Accelerator pump bore	3 Main jet
2 Pump suction valve bore	4 Float needle valve seat

Fig. 3.18 Throttle flap body securing screws (Sec 21)

Fig. 3.19 Lifting off the throttle flap body (Sec 21)

12 Using flat-nosed pliers, withdraw the pump suction valve spring retainer and spring. The retainer is a push fit in the float chamber body and is removed by pulling upwards.

13 Turn the float chamber upside down over a tray and retrieve the two steel balls that will now drop out. The smaller ball is the accelerator pump check ball and the larger is the pump suction valve check ball.

14 The main jet and float needle valve seat may now be removed using a screwdriver.

15 The float chamber body may now be separated from the throttle flap body, by undoing the four screws and lifting apart the two components. Take care not to damage the gasket on separation.

16 If the mixture control screw and additional idling mixture screw are to be removed, first screw them fully in whilst counting the number of turns taken. Record this figure and then remove the screws. It will now be possible to refit the adjusting screws in approximately the same position when the carburettor is reassembled.

17 With the carburettor now completely dismantled, thoroughly clean out the float chamber, top cover and throttle flap body. Clean all the jets and passageways using clean dry compressed air, if possible. Check the float assembly for signs of damage or leaking. Inspect the rubber seal of the accelerator pump piston for swelling or deterioration, and the small valve springs for damage. Examine the mixture screws and needle valve for signs of wear, and the throttle plates and choke flap for ease of operation. Renew defective parts as necessary. Apply suction to the hose on the vacuum unit and observe the

movement of the pullrod. If the pullrod fails to move, and no resistance to suction is felt, it is likely that the diaphragm is punctured necessitating renewal of the vacuum unit.

22 Carburettor – reassembly

1   Begin reassembly by refitting the mixture control screw and additional idling mixture screw to their respective locations in the throttle flap body and float chamber body. Screw them both fully in, then unscrew them an equal number of turns as was noted during removal.

2   Place the gasket in position on the float chamber body and refit the throttle flap body. Refit and fully tighten the four securing screws. With the assembly secure, check that the primary barrel throttle flap return spring is engaged on the arm on the linkage connecting link (Fig. 3.20).

3   The main jet and the float needle valve seat may now be secured into place in the float chamber body.

4   The two small steel balls are next refitted, the larger ball into the suction valve bore and the smaller ball into the accelerator pump bore. Ensure that the accelerator pump ball locates in the recess at the bottom of the pump bore.

5   Place the pump suction valve spring in position over the ball, then refit the spring retainer by pushing it down firmly to the shoulder in the bore.

6   Refit the partial load needle valve return spring to the float chamber body, followed by the valve assembly. Carefully guide the needle valve into the jet, then tighten the retaining collar.

7   Place the float needle valve into its valve seat, after first hooking the valve spring onto the float platform. Now guide the float pivot clip into position in the two vertical slots in the float chamber body.

8   To check the float level, hold the needle valve closed using moderate finger pressure on the float bracket and pivot clip. Measure the distance between the top of the float and the upper edge of the chamber body. Compare the recorded dimension with the figure given in the Specifications, and if necessary, alter the float level by bending the float bracket slightly.

9   When the float level has been set correctly place the float filler in position with the slot located over the float pivot clip.

10 Place the gasket in position, locating it carefully over the partial load valve.

11 Refit the accelerator pump spring, followed by the accelerator pump piston, then place the carburettor cover in position over the float chamber body. Refit the securing screws, and as they are progressively tightened, check that the accelerator pump piston moves freely in its bore.

12 Refit the fast idle cam assembly and the choke flap operating link, and secure with the two circlips.

13 Engage the accelerator pump actuating lever with the operating rod, then secure the lever with the retaining screw.

14 With the throttle plate closed, measure the distance between the top face of the carburettor cover and the upper edge of the accelerator pump piston (Fig. 3.24). This is the accelerator pump piston setting, and must correspond to the figure given in the Specifications. If the setting is incorrect, bend the actuating lever at the groove in the lower edge as necessary to give the required dimension.

15 Refit the automatic choke vacuum unit, choke cover and retaining ring, and secure with the three screws. As the cover is fitted, engage the choke flap tang with the formed end of the bi-metal spring coil; as the retaining ring is tightened, position the pointer on the cover adjacent to the mark immediately to the right of the centre mark (Figs. 3.25 and 3.26).

16 Finally, refit the fuel line filter and union nut.

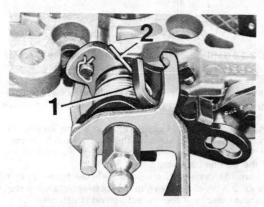

Fig. 3.20 Throttle flap return spring (2) correctly located on connecting link arm (1) (Sec 22)

Fig. 3.21 Float needle valve spring positioned on float platform (Sec 22)

Fig. 3.22 Measuring the float level (Sec 22)

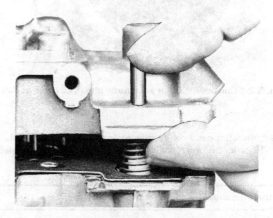

Fig. 3.23 Checking free movement of accelerator pump piston (Sec 22)

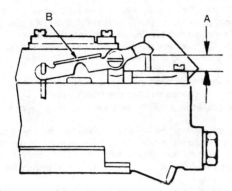

Fig. 3.24 Accelerator pump piston setting (Sec 22)

Dimension A = 10.4 to 10.8 mm (0.41 to 0.42 in), B is the adjustment point

Fig. 3.25 Automatic choke cover refitted with loop on spring coil (1) engaged with choke flap tang (2) (Sec 22)

Fig. 3.26 Correct fitting of automatic choke cover (Sec 22)

17 The carburettor can now be refitted to the engine as described in Section 19, and the idling adjustments carried out as detailed in Section 18.

23 Automatic choke – adjustment

1 Start the engine and warm it up to normal operating temperature. Ensure the engine idling performance (as described in Section 18) is satisfactory, then switch off the engine and remove the air cleaner.

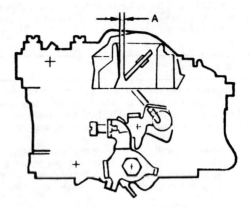

Fig. 3.27 Automatic choke flap gap (Sec 23)

Dimension A = 3.5 mm (0.14 in)

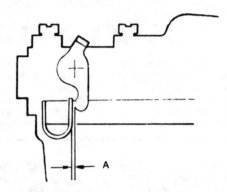

Fig. 3.28 Baffle plate lever to pullrod clearance (Sec 23)

Dimension A = 0.1 to 0.3 mm (0.004 to 0.012 in)

2 Slightly open the throttle flap and position the fast idle cam so the adjusting screw locates on the centre stop of the cam when the throttle flap is released.

3 Without depressing the accelerator, start the engine. With the engine running at a fast idle, rotate the choke flap fully in the closing direction, then measure the clearance between the edge of the choke flap and the throttle barrel bore (Fig. 3.27).

4 Compare the dimension obtained with the figure quoted in the Specifications. If the choke flap gap is excessive, rotate the stop screw on the vacuum unit until the correct setting is achieved.

5 If the gap is smaller than the stated dimension, the linkage should be bent back slightly to provide a clearance between the stop and baffle plate lever before rotating the adjusting screw.

6 With the choke flap gap correctly adjusted, measure the clearance between the baffle plate lever and the pullrod. Refer to Specifications for the correct dimension, and if necessary, bend the pullrod end slightly to achieve the required setting.

7 The choke flap gap should also be checked with the engine stationary as follows:

8 Position the choke linkage so that the choke flap is closed and the fast idle adjusting screw is located on the centre step of the cam.

9 Disconnect the vacuum unit supply hose from the carburettor outlet.

10 Apply sufficient suction to the hose to enable the pullrod to move the baffle plate lever into contact with the stop. Now measure the clearance between the edge of the choke flap and the throttle barrel bore. If adjustment is required, follow the procedure described in paragraphs 4 and 5 of this Section.

11 When adjustment is complete, refit the air cleaner and refit the vacuum hose.

24 Exhaust system – general description

The exhaust system comprises a cast iron exhaust manifold, a twin

25.3 Exhaust tailpipe rear mounting

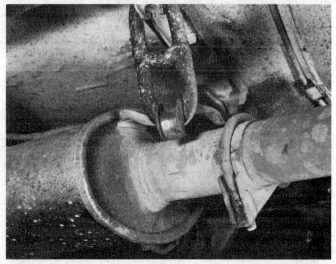

25.4 Intermediate pipe mounting rings

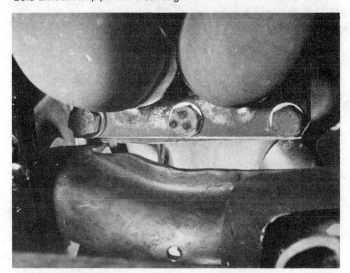

25.5a The three exhaust manifold flange retaining bolts accessible from beneath the car

25.5b Separating the exhaust pipe to manifold flange joint

branch front pipe, an intermediate pipe and silencer and a tailpipe and resonator. The three sections of the system are joined together by two U-bolt type clamps.

The system is flexibly attached to the floor pan by two circular rubber mountings at the front of the intermediate pipe, and a rubber damping block at the tailpipe.

At regular intervals, the system should be checked for corrosion, joint leakage, the condition and security of the flexible mountings and the tightness of the joints.

25 Exhaust system – renewal

1 If possible, raise the car on a ramp or place it over an inspection pit. Alternatively, jack up the car and support it on axle stands to obtain the maximum amount of working height underneath.
2 Slacken the nuts securing the two U-bolt clamps and slide the clamps off the joints.
3 Apply penetrating fluid to the two joints, then disconnect the tailpipe from the rear rubber mounting block (photo). Now twist the tailpipe back and forth to free the joint and then remove the pipe.
4 In the same manner, twist the intermediate pipe back and forth to free the joint, after first removing the two rubber mounting rings (photo). When the joint has separated, withdraw the intermediate pipe over the rear axle and out from under the car.
5 The six bolts securing the front pipe to the manifold can now be undone. These bolts are extremely inaccessible, and a socket and long

extension is useful, as well as a small spanner (photo). A steady bracket is also fitted, and if this is loosened at its attachment point on the engine, it can be moved rearward sufficiently to allow the front pipe to be lowered and withdrawn from under the car. Take care to avoid damaging the gasket as the pipe is removed (photo).
6 To refit the system, clean the joint faces on the pipe ends with emery cloth. Renew the rubber mountings if they show signs of deterioration.
7 Place the gasket in position and refit the front pipe, securing bolts and steady bracket.
8 Apply exhaust sealing compound such as Holts Firegum to the end of the front pipe, position the intermediate pipe over the axle and connect the two pipes. Refit the rubber mountings and U-bolt clamp, but do not tighten the clamp at this stage.
9 Apply sealing compound to the tailpipe joint and couple it to the intermediate pipe. Reconnect the rubber mounting block and loosely fit the U-clamp.
10 Twist the two sections as necessary, until sufficient clearance exists between the exhaust system and the underbody or underbody attachments. Ensure that the system is not under tension in any way, then tighten the U-bolt clamps.
11 Recheck that all joints and mountings are secure, then run the engine and check for leaks.
12 Holts Flexiwrap or Holts Gun Gum exhaust repair systems can be used for effective repairs to exhaust pipes and silencer boxes, including ends and bends. Holts Flexiwrap is an MOT approved permanent exhaust repair.

26 Fault diagnosis – fuel and exhaust systems

Symptom	Reason(s)
Engine difficult to start when cold	Automatic choke incorrectly adjusted Automatic choke not functioning (choke plate not closing) Insufficient fuel in float chamber *See also 'Fault diagnosis – ignition system'*
Engine difficult to start when hot	Automatic choke incorrectly adjusted Automatic choke electrical lead broken or disconnected Air cleaner dirty or choked Insufficient fuel in float chamber *See also 'Fault diagnosis – ignition system'*
Engine will not idle or idles erratically	Air cleaner dirty or choked Carburettor idle speed and/or mixture settings incorrectly set Blocked carburettor jets or internal passages Air leaks at carburettor or manifold joint faces Automatic choke or fast idle adjustments incorrect Generally worn carburettor
Engine performance poor, accompanied by hesitation, missing and/or cutting out	Blocked carburettor jets or internal passages Float level incorrect Fuel filter blocked Fuel pump faulty or delivery pressure low Fuel tank vent blocked Fuel lines restricted Air leaks at carburettor or manifold joint faces Engine internal components worn, broken or out of adjustment *See also 'Fault diagnosis – engine' and 'Fault diagnosis – ignition system'*
Fuel consumption excessive	Air cleaner dirty or choked Fuel leaking from carburettor, fuel pump or fuel line Float chamber flooding Generally worn carburettor Tyres under-inflated Brakes binding
Excessive noise from exhaust system	Leaking exhaust on manifold joints Leaking, corroded, or damaged silencer, pipe, or resonator

Chapter 4 Ignition system

For modifications, and information applicable to later models, see Supplement at end of manual

Contents

Specifications

Spark plugs

Type	Champion RL82YCC or RL82YC
Electrode gap:	
RL82YCC spark plugs	0.8 mm (0.032 in)
RL82YC spark plugs	0.7 mm (0.028 in)

Ignition coil

Type	Bosch or Delco Remy
Primary coil resistance	1.2 to 1.8 ohms
Starting voltage	12 volts (approx)
Running voltage	4.5 to 6 volts

Distributor

Type	Bosch
Automatic advance	Mechanical and vacuum
Drive	Skew gear from crankshaft
Contact breaker gap	0.40 mm (0.016 in)
Dwell angle	47° to 53°
Ignition timing	5° BTDC (pointer in flywheel housing aligned with steel ball in flywheel)
Firing order	1–3–4–2

Torque wrench settings

	Nm	lbf ft
Spark plugs	40	30

1 General description

In order that the engine can run correctly, it is necessary for an electrical spark to ignite the fuel/air mixture in the combustion chamber at exactly the right moment in relation to engine speed and load.

The ignition system is divided into two circuits, low tension and high tension. The low tension (LT), or primary circuit, consists of the battery ignition switch, low tension or primary coil windings, and the contact breaker points and condenser, both located at the distributor. The high tension (HT), or secondary circuit, consists of the high tension or secondary coil winding, the heavy ignition lead from the centre of the coil to the distributor cap, and the rotor arm and the spark plug leads. The ignition system is based on feeding low tension voltage from the battery to the coil where it is converted to high tension voltage. The high tension voltage is powerful enough to jump the spark plug gap in the cylinders many times a second under high compression pressures, providing the system is in good condition and all adjustments are correct.

The wiring harness includes a high resistance wire in the ignition coil feed circuit and it is very important that only a 'ballast resistor' type ignition coil is used. During starting this 'ballast resistor' wire is bypassed, allowing the full available battery voltage to be fed to the coil. This ensures that during cold starting, when the starter motor current draw would be high, sufficient voltage is still available at the coil to produce a powerful spark. It is therefore essential that only the correct type of coil is used. Under normal running the 12 volt supply is directed through the ballast resistor before reaching the coil.

The ignition advance is controlled both mechanically and by vacuum, to ensure that the spark occurs at just the right instant for the particular engine load and speed. The mechanical governor comprises two lead weights, which move out from the distributor shafts as the engine speed rises, due to centrifugal force. The vacuum control consists of a diaphragm, one side of which is connected via a small bore tube to the carburettor, and the other side to the contact breaker plate. Depression in the inlet manifold and carburettor, which varies with engine speed and throttle opening, causes the diaphragm to move, so moving the contact breaker plate, and advancing or retarding the spark.

2 Contact breaker points – adjustment

1 Slide back the distributor cap protective cover and release the two distributor cap retaining clips. Lift off the cap, together with the HT leads and cover, from the distributor.
2 Clean the inside and outside of the cap with a clean, dry cloth. Scrape away any small deposits from the four terminal studs inside the cap and examine it thoroughly for cracks or surface deterioration.

Fig. 4.1 Lifting off the distributor cap protective cover; arrows indicate retaining buttons (Sec 2)

2.6a Slacken the retaining screw ...

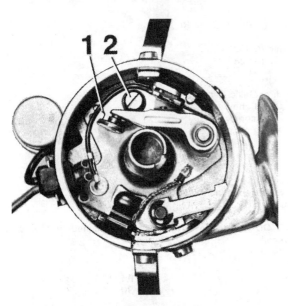

Fig. 4.2 Contact breaker points adjustment (Sec 2)

1   Slot for screwdriver   2   Retaining screw

2.6b ... then move the contacts until the correct gap is achieved

Inspect the carbon brush contact in the centre of the cap to ensure it is not broken and stands proud of the plastic surface. Renew the cap if it is cracked or if the carbon brush or terminal studs are excessively corroded or worn away.

3   Lift off the rotor arm followed by the protective plastic cover located over the contact breaker assembly.

4   Gently prise the contact breaker points open and examine the condition of their faces. If they are rough, pitted, or dirty, it will be necessary to renew them before proceeding with the adjustment.

5   Assuming the points are satisfactory or have been renewed, measure the gap between the points by turning the engine over until the contact breaker arm is on the peak of one of the four cam lobes and the points are fully open. A 0.4 mm (0.016 in) feeler gauge should now fit between the points.

6   If the points are too close or too far apart, slacken the contact plate securing screw and move the contact plate in the desired direction until the correct setting has been obtained. Tighten the retaining screw then recheck the gap (photos).

7   Refit the plastic cover and rotor arm, followed by the distributor cap and protective cover.

8   On modern engines, setting the contact breaker gap in the distributor using feeler gauges must be regarded as a basic adjustment only. For optimum engine performance, the dwell angle must be checked. The dwell angle is the number of degrees through which the distributor cam turns during the period between the instance of closure and opening of the contact breaker points. Checking the dwell angle not only gives a more accurate setting of the contact breaker gap but also evens out any variations in the gap which could be caused by wear in the distributor shaft or its bushes, or difference in height of any of the cam peaks.

9   The angle should be checked with a dwell meter connected in accordance with the maker's instructions. Refer to the Specifications for the correct dwell angle. If the dwell angle is too large, increase the points gap, if too small, reduce the points gap.

10 The dwell angle should always be adjusted before checking and adjusting the ignition timing.

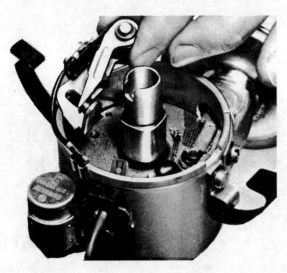

Fig. 4.3 Removing the contact breaker points (Sec 3)

5.1 Removing the distributor cap

3 Contact breaker points – removal and refitting

1   If the contact breaker points are burned, pitted or badly worn, they must be renewed; any attempt to file or grind them down will destroy the special facing.
2   Having removed the distributor cap, rotor arm and contact breaker cover as described in the previous Section, undo and remove the screw securing the contact breaker points to the baseplate.
3   Remove the LT lead spade connector and lift out the contact breaker assembly.
4   Refitting the points is the reverse sequence to removal. Smear a trace of grease onto the cam to lubricate the moving heel of the contact breaker arm, before refitting the points.
5   With the points in position, adjust the contact breaker gap as described in Section 2.

4 Condenser – removal, testing and refitting

1   The purpose of the condenser (sometimes known as a capacitor) is to ensure that when the contact breaker points open, there is no sparking across them, which would cause rapid wear of their faces and prevent the rapid collapse of the magnetic field in the coil. This would cause a reduction in coil HT voltage and ultimately lead to engine misfire.
2   If the engine becomes very difficult to start, or begins to miss after several miles of running, and the contact breaker points show signs of excessive burning, the condition of the condenser must be suspect. A further test can be made by separating the points by hand with the ignition switched on. If this is accompanied by a strong bright flash, it is indicative that the condenser has failed.
3   Without special test equipment, the only sure way to diagnose condenser trouble is to substitute a suspect unit with a new one and note if there is any improvement.
4   To remove the condenser from the distributor, take off the distributor cap, rotor arm and plastic cover.
5   Withdraw the contact breaker points LT lead from the spade terminal, located inside the distributor casing.
6   Separate the LT lead connecting the coil to the distributor at the cable joining connector.
7   Undo and remove the screws securing the condenser and LT lead assembly to the distributor casing and lift off the complete assembly. Note that the condenser is supplied complete with LT lead and LT spade tag and mounting grommet.
8   Refitting the condenser is the reverse procedure to removal.

5 Distributor – removal and refitting

1   Slide back the distributor cap protective cover and release the two

Fig. 4.4 Correct position of rotor arm in relation to distributor body, prior to removal (Sec 5)

distributor cap retaining clips. Lift off the cap, together with the HT leads and cover, from the distributor and place it to one side (photo). Disconnect the LT lead at the cable connector.
2   Pull the rotor arm off the distributor shaft and lift out the protective plastic cover, located over the contact breaker assembly. Now refit the rotor arm onto the distributor shaft.
3   Turn the engine by means of the fan, in the correct direction of rotation until the rotor arm is pointing toward the notch on the side of the distributor body (see Fig. 4.4).
4   Scribe a line, using a small file, between the flange at the base of the distributor and the upper edge of the timing cover (photo). This will ensure that when the distributor is refitted, the ignition timing setting will not be lost.
5   Referring to Chapter 3 if necessary, undo and remove the two bolts securing the petrol pump to the base of the timing cover and lift out the pump. The petrol pump is operated by a cam on the distributor driveshaft. It is therefore necessary to remove the pump to allow the distributor and driveshaft to be withdrawn.
6   Undo and remove the distributor clamp plate and bolt, then carefully lift the distributor off the timing cover. Recover the gasket at

5.4 Scribe a line between the distributor and timing cover flanges prior to removal

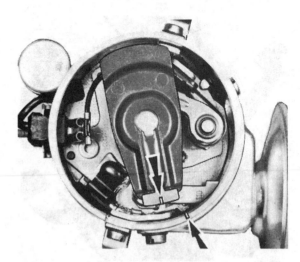

Fig. 4.5 Correct position of rotor arm in relation to distributor body prior to fitting (Sec 5)

the base of the distributor flange, if still intact.

7   Before refitting the distributor, ensure that the engine has not been inadvertently turned and No 1 piston is on the compression stroke. This can be checked by removing the valve rocker cover and No 1 spark plug. As the piston is moved back and forth off the TDC position, (observed through the spark plug hole), both valve rocker arms of No 4 cylinder should move slightly. This indicates No 1 cylinder on the compression stroke.

8   As the distributor is lowered into position in the timing cover, the distributor shaft will rotate slightly as the drivegear on the distributor shaft engages with the drivegear on the crankshaft. To compensate for this, position the rotor arm as shown in Fig. 4.5, prior to fitting the distributor. It will also be necessary to insert a long screwdriver down the opening in the timing cover and rotate the oil pump drivegear by a corresponding amount in the same direction.

9   Place a new gasket in position on the timing cover, and while holding the distributor and shaft in the correct position, insert the assembly into the timing cover aperture.

10   When the distributor shaft has seated fully into the oil pump gear slot, check that the distributor driveshaft has rotated to the correct position.

11   Align the previously made marks on the distributor flange and timing cover, then refit the clamp plate and bolt. Reconnect the LT connection at the cable connector.

12   Refit the fuel pump, followed by No 1 spark plug and the valve rocker cover if previously removed, then recheck the ignition timing as described in Section 11.

Fig. 4.6 Correct setting of oil pump drivegear prior to fitting the distributor (Sec 5)

6   Distributor – dismantling

1   With the distributor on the bench, remove the rotor arm from the distributor shaft.

2   Remove the contact breaker points as described in Section 3.

3   Undo and remove the condenser securing screw and lift away the condenser and connector.

4   Next, carefully remove the U-shaped clip from the pullrod of the vacuum unit.

5   Undo and remove the two vacuum unit securing screws and withdraw the unit from the side of the distributor body.

6   The distributor cap spring clip retainer may be removed by undoing and removing the screws and lifting away the clips and retainers. **Note**: *This is the limit of dismantling which may be undertaken, since none of the parts beneath the breaker plate (including the drivegear) can be renewed separately.*

Fig. 4.7 Removing the vacuum unit pullrod retaining clip (Sec 6)

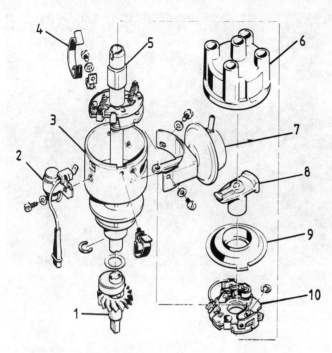

Fig. 4.8 Exploded view of distributor (Sec 6)

1 Distributor shaft	6 Distributor cap
2 Condenser assembly	7 Vacuum unit
3 Distributor body	8 Rotor arm
4 Retaining clip	9 Cover
5 Cam and advance weights	10 Contact assembly

9.3 Lubricating the distributor

7 Distributor – inspection and repair

1   Check the contact breaker points for wear, burning or pitting; renew if necessary.

2   Examine the rotor arm for cracks and ensure that it is a snug fit on the distributor shaft. Any slight burning apparent on the end of the metal portion of the arm may be removed with a fine file. If the rotor arm is badly burned, cracked or a loose fit on the shaft, it should be renewed.

3   Hold the gear at the base of the distributor with one hand and turn the upper distributor shaft with the other. Firm spring resistance should be felt, with no slackness or binding apparent. Also, check there

is no side play of the shaft relative to the distributor body. Any faults noticed during this inspection will necessitate renewal of the complete distributor, as component parts are not available separately.

4   The vacuum unit may be checked for correct operation, by sucking the vacuum pipe connection while observing the action of the pullrod. If no movement of the pullrod is apparent when suction is applied to the vacuum pipe, it is likely that the diaphragm in the vacuum unit is punctured, necessitating renewal of the unit.

8 Distributor – reassembly

1   Place the distributor cap retaining spring clip and retainers on the outside of the distributor body and secure the retainers with the two screws.

2   Position the contact breaker point assembly in the breaker plate in such a manner that the entire lower surface of the assembly contacts the plate. Refit the contact breaker points assembly securing screw but do not fully tighten yet.

3   Hook the diaphragm assembly pullrod into contact with the pivot pin.

4   Secure the diaphragm to the distributor body with the two screws. Also refit the condenser to the terminal side of the diaphragm bracket securing screw. The condenser must firmly contact its lower stop on the housing.

5   Smear a trace of grease to the cam to lubricate the moving heel of the contact breaker arm.

6   Reset the contact breaker points as described in Section 2, then refit the rotor arm. The distributor may now be refitted to the engine as described in Section 5.

9 Distributor – lubrication

1   It is important that the distributor cam is lubricated with petroleum jelly or grease at 6000 miles (10 000 km) or 6 monthly intervals. Also the automatic timing control weights and cam spindle are lubricated with engine oil.

2   Great care should be taken not to use too much lubricant; any excess that finds its way onto the contact breaker points could cause burning and misfiring.

3   To gain access to the cam spindle, lift away the distributor cap and rotor arm. Apply no more than two drops of engine oil onto the felt pad. This will run down the spindle when the engine is hot and lubricate the bearings (photo).

4   To lubricate the automatic timing control, allow a few drops of oil to pass through the holes in the contact breaker baseplate through which the four-sided cam emerges. Apply not more than one drop of oil to the pivot post of the moving contact breaker point. Wipe away excess oil and refit the rotor arm and distributor cap.

10 Spark plugs and HT leads

1   The correct functioning of the spark plugs is vital for the correct running and efficiency of the engine. It is essential that the plugs fitted are appropriate for the engine, and the suitable type is specified at the beginning of this chapter. If this type is used and the engine is in good condition, the spark plugs should not need attention between scheduled replacement intervals. Spark plug cleaning is rarely necessary and should not be attempted unless specialised equipment is available as damage can easily be caused to the firing ends.

2   Examination of the spark plugs will give a good indication of the overall condition of the engine.

3   If the insulator nose of the spark plug is clean and white, with no deposits, this is indicative of a weak mixture, or too hot a plug (a hot plug transfers heat away from the electrode slowly – a cold plug transfers it away quickly).

4   The plugs fitted as standard are as listed in the Specifications at the beginning of this Chapter. If the tip and insulator noses are covered with hard black-looking deposits, then this is indicative that the mixture is too rich. Should the plug be black and oily, it is likely that the engine is fairly worn, as well as the mixture being too rich.

5   If the insulator nose is covered with light tan to greyish brown deposits, the mixture is correct, and it is likely that the engine is in good condition.

6   The spark plug gap is of considerable importance, as, if it is too large or too small, the size of the spark and its efficiency will be seriously impaired. The spark plug gap should be set to the figure given in the Specifications at the beginning of this Chapter.

7   To set it, measure the gap with a feeler gauge, and then bend open, or close, the outer plug electrode until the correct gap is achieved. The centre electrode should never be bent as this may crack the insulation and cause plug failure if nothing worse.

8   When refitting the plugs, remember to use new washers, and refit the leads from the distributor in the correct firing order, which is given in the Specifications.

9   The plug leads require no routine attention other than being kept clean and wiped over regularly.

10 At intervals of 6000 miles (10 000 km) or 6 months, pull the leads off the plugs and distributor one at a time and make sure no water has found its way onto the connections. Remove any corrosion from the brass ends, wipe the collars on top of the distributor, and refit the leads.

11.4 Ignition timing adjusted with steel ball in flywheel in line with pointer

11 Ignition timing – adjustment

1   For prolonged engine life, efficient running performance and economy, it is essential for the fuel/air mixture in the combustion chambers to be ignited by the spark plugs at precisely the right moment in relation to engine speed and load. For this to occur, the ignition timing must be set accurately, and should be checked at regular intervals, or whenever the position of the distributor has been altered. Before checking or adjusting the ignition timing, ensure that the contact breaker points are correctly adjusted as described in Section 2.

2   To check the timing, turn the engine by hand in the normal direction of rotation until No 1 piston is approaching TDC on the compression stroke. This can be checked by removing the No 1 spark plug and feeling the pressure being developed in the cylinder, or by removing the rocker cover and observing when the valves of No 4 cylinder are rocking, ie the inlet valve is just opening and the exhaust valve is just closing. If this check is not made, it is all too easy to set the timing 180° out, as both No 1 and No 4 pistons approach TDC at the same time but only one will be on the compression stroke.

3   Remove the distributor cap and check that the rotor arm is pointing toward the No 1 cylinder HT lead segment in the cap. If this is not the case, ensure that the distributor is fitted correctly as described in Section 5, then repeat the procedure given in paragraph 2 of this Section.

4   Continue turning the engine in the normal direction of rotation until the steel ball in the flywheel is directly in line with the pointer on the flywheel housing (photo). This indicates 5° BTDC, and with the engine in this position, the points should be just opening.

5   If adjustment is necessary, slacken the clamp bolt at the base of the distributor. Rotate the distributor body clockwise slightly, until the points are fully closed. Then turn it anti-clockwise slowly, until the points just begin to open. Now tighten the clamp bolt and refit the distributor cap.

6   Difficulty is sometimes experienced in determining exactly when the contact breaker points open. This can easily be ascertained by connecting a 12 volt bulb in parallel with the contact breaker points (one lead to earth and the other to the coil/distributor low tension terminal). Switch on the ignition and rotate the distributor body until the bulb lights, indicating that the points have just opened.

7   Set in this way, the timing should be approximately correct, but a more accurate method is by using a stroboscopic timing light. This allows the timing to be adjusted with the engine running and therefore compensation for any backlash or wear in the distributor drivegear or shaft, or the distributor itself.

8   To adjust the timing using a stroboscopic timing light, first disconnect the vacuum advance pipe at the distributor and plug the pipe. Run the engine to normal operating temperature, check and if necessary adjust the idling speed, then switch off.

9   Connect the timing light between No 1 spark plug and No 1 spark plug HT lead, following the manufacturer's instructions.

10 Start the engine and point the timing light at the pointer in the flywheel housing. The steel ball in the flywheel will appear stationary,

and if the timing is correct, the ball will be directly in line with the pointer.

11 If they are not directly opposite each other, slacken the distributor clamp bolt and turn the distributor slightly one way or the other until the marks line up. Tighten the clamp bolt and recheck the timing.

12 If the engine speed is now increased, the steel ball in the flywheel will appear to move away from the pointer, indicating that the centrifugal advance is operating. If the vacuum pipe is reconnected, the operation of the vacuum unit can be checked by revving the engine and observing the timing marks. **Note**: *To check the amount of ignition advance the timing light must include an advance meter.*

13 When the checks are complete, switch off the engine, remove the timing light and reconnect the HT lead to the spark plug.

14 Since the ignition timing setting enables the firing point to be correctly related to the grade of fuel used, the fullest advantage of a change of grade from that recommended for the engine, will only be attained by readjustment of the ignition setting.

12 Ignition system – fault finding

1   By far the majority of breakdown and running troubles are caused by faults in the ignition system, either in the low tension or high tension circuits.

2   There are two main symptoms indicating ignition system faults. Either the engine will not start or fire, or the engine is difficult to start and misfires. If it is a regular misfire, ie the engine is running on only two or three cylinders, the fault is likely to be in the secondary or high tension circuit. If the misfiring is intermittent, the fault could be in either the high or low tension circuits. If the car stops suddenly or will not start at all, it is likely the fault is in the low tension circuit. Loss of power and overheating (apart from faulty carburation settings) are normally due to faults in the distributor or to incorrect ignition timing.

3   The following fault finding guide should be used in conjunction with the fault diagnosis section at the end of this Chapter.

Engine fails to start

4   If the engine fails to start and the car was running normally when it was last used, first check that there is fuel in the petrol tank. If the engine turns over normally on the starter motor and the battery is evidently well charged, the fault may be in either the high or low tension circuits. First check the HT circuit. If the battery is known to be fully charged, the ignition light comes on and the starter motor fails to turn the engine *check the tightness of the leads on the battery terminals* and also the secureness of the earth lead to its connection to the body. It is quite common for the leads to have worked loose, even if they look and feel secure. If one of the battery terminal post gets very hot when trying to work the starter motor, this is a sure

indication of a faulty connection to that terminal.

5 One of the most common reasons for bad starting is wet or damp spark plug leads and distributor. Remove the distributor cap. If condensation is visible internally dry the cap with a rag and also wipe over the leads. Refit the cap. A moisture dispersant, such as Holts Wet Start, can be very effective in these situations. To prevent the problem recurring Holts Damp Start can be used to provide a sealing coat, so excluding any further moisture from the ignition system. In extreme difficulty, Holts Cold Start will help to start a car when only a very poor spark occurs.

6 If the engine still fails to start, check that the current is reaching the plugs, by disconnecting each plug lead in turn at the spark plug end, and holding the end of the cable about 5 mm ($\frac{3}{16}$) away from the cylinder block. Spin the engine on the starter motor.

7 Sparking between the end of the cable and the block should be fairly strong with a strong regular blue spark. (Hold the lead with rubber to avoid electric shocks). If current is reaching the plugs, remove them and clean and regap them. The engine should now start.

8 If there is no spark at the plug leads, take off the HT lead from the centre of the distributor cap and hold it to the block as before. Spin the engine on the starter once more. A rapid succession of blue sparks between the end of the lead and the block indicate that the coil is in order and that the distributor cap is cracked, the rotor arm faulty, or the carbon brush in the top of the distributor cap is not making good contact with the rotor arm. Possibly, the points are in bad condition. Renew them as described in this Chapter, Sections 2 and 3.

9 If there are no sparks from the end of the lead from the coil, check the connections at the coil end of the lead. If it is in order, start checking the low tension circuit.

10 Use a 12v voltmeter or a 12v bulb and two lengths of wire. With the ignition switched on and the points open, test between the low tension wire to the coil (it is marked SW or +) and earth. No reading indicates a break in the supply from the ignition switch. Check the connections at the switch to see if any are loose. Refit them and the engine should run. A reading shows a faulty coil or condenser, or broken lead between the coil and the distributor.

11 Detach the condenser from the distributor body, and with the points open, test between the moving point and earth. If there is now a reading then the fault is in the condenser. Fit a new one as described in this Chapter, Section 4.

12 With no reading from the moving point to earth, take a reading between earth and the CB or negative (–) terminal of the coil. A reading here shows a broken wire which will need to be renewed between the coil and distributor. No reading confirms that the coil has failed and must be renewed, after which the engine will run once more. Remember to refit the condenser wire to the points assembly. For these tests it is sufficient to separate the points with a piece of dry paper while testing with the points open.

Engine misfires

13 If the engine misfires regularly, run it at a fast idling speed. Pull off each of the plug caps in turn and listen to the note of the engine. Hold the plug cap in a dry cloth or with a rubber glove as additional protection against a shock from the HT supply.

14 No difference in engine running will be noticed when the lead from the defective circuit is removed. Removing the lead from one of the good cylinders will accentuate the misfire.

15 Remove the plug leads from the end of the defective plug and hold it abut 5 mm ($\frac{3}{16}$ in) away from the block. Re-start the engine. If the sparking is fairly strong and regular, the fault must lie in the spark plug.

16 The plug may be loose, the insulation may be cracked, or the points may have burnt away giving too wide a gap for the spark to jump. Worse still, one of the points may have broken off. Either renew the plug, or clean it; reset the gap, and then test it.

17 If there is no spark at the end of the plug lead, or if it is weak and intermittent, check the ignition lead from the distributor to the plug. If the insulation is cracked or perished, renew the lead. Check the connections at the distributor cap.

18 If there is still no spark, examine the distributor cap carefully for tracking. This can be recognised by a very thin black line running between two or more electrodes, or between an electrode and some other part of the distributor. These lines are paths which now conduct electricity across the cap thus letting it run to earth. The only answer is a new distributor cap.

19 Apart from the ignition timing being incorrect other causes of misfiring have already been dealt with under the section dealing with the failure of the engine to start. To recap – these are that:

(a) The coil may be faulty giving an intermittent misfire
(b) There may be a damaged wire or loose connection in the low tension circuit
(c) The condenser may be short circuiting
(d) There may be a mechanical fault in the distributor (broken driving spindle or contact breaker spring)

20 If the ignition timing is too far retarded, it should be noted that the engine will tend to overheat, and there will be a quite noticeable drop in power. If the engine is overheating and the power is down, and the ignition timing is correct, the carburettor should be checked, as it is likely that this is where the fault lies.

---

13 Fault diagnosis – ignition system

Symptom	Reason(s)
Engine turns over normally but fails to start	Dampness or condensation on cap, or HT leads
	No current reaching spark plugs
	Spark plugs wet, dirty or incorrectly adjusted
	Faulty HT leads or loose connections
	Distributor cap cracked or tracking between segments
	Rotor arm cracked or making poor contact with centre electrode
	Faulty or incorrectly adjusted contact breaker points
	Faulty coil or condenser
	Broken or loose wiring connections in ignition circuit
	See also 'Fault diagnosis – fuel system'
Engine misfires	Worn, dirty, or incorrectly adjusted spark plugs
	Faulty HT leads or loose connections
	Distributor cap cracked or tracking between segments
	Faulty coil or condenser
	Broken or loose wiring connections in ignition circuit
	Worn or damaged engine internal components
	See also 'Fault diagnosis – engine' and 'Fault diagnosis – fuel system'

Chapter 5 Clutch

For modifications, and information applicable to later models, see Supplement at end of manual

Contents

Specifications

Type.. Single dry plate, diaphragm spring, cable operated

Lining diameter
Inner.. 131 mm (5.16 in)
Outer.. 204 mm (8.03 in)

Lining thickness... 9.50 ± 0.25 mm (0.3740 ± 0.0098 in)

Number of torsion springs...................................... 4

Torque wrench settings	Nm	lbf ft
Bellhousing-to-engine	45	33
Pressure plate-to-flywheel	22	16

1 General description

All manual transmission models are equipped with a single plate diaphragm spring clutch. The unit comprises a steel cover which is dowelled and bolted to the rear face of the flywheel, and contains the pressure plate and diaphragm spring.

The clutch disc is free to slide along the splined gearbox motion shaft, and is held in position between the flywheel and the pressure plate by the pressure of the diaphragm spring. Friction lining material is riveted to the clutch disc, which has a spring cushioned hub to absorb transmission shocks and help ensure a smooth take-up of the drive.

The clutch is actuated by a cable controlled by the clutch pedal. The clutch mechanism consists of a release fork and bearing which are in permanent contact with the release fingers on the pressure plate assembly. Wear of the friction material in the clutch is adjusted out by means of an adjuster located on the bellhousing.

Depressing the clutch pedal actuates the clutch release arm by means of the cable. The release arm pushes the release bearing forward to bear against the diaphragm fingers, so moving the centre of the diaphragm spring inwards. As the centre of the spring is pushed in, the outside of the spring pivots out, so moving the pressure plate backwards and disengaging the pressure plate from the clutch disc. When the clutch pedal is released, the diaphragm spring forces the pressure plate into contact with the friction linings on the clutch disc. The disc is now firmly sandwiched between the pressure plate and the flywheel, thus transmitting engine power to the gearbox.

All models are fitted with a 'clutch worn' warning light on the instrument panel. This light is activated by a switch on the clutch pedal bracket. As wear takes place on the clutch friction linings, the pedal 'at rest' position alters, thus bringing the pedal into contact with the switch. The warning light is then illuminated, thus informing the driver that clutch adjustment is necessary.

2 Clutch free play – adjustment

1 The correct positioning of the clutch release fork is critical for smooth and efficient operation of the clutch assembly. Adjustment is carried out by first altering the position of the release fork pivot bolt to obtain a set dimension and then altering the position of the clutch pedal if necessary, by adjusting the length of the operating cable. These adjustments should be checked periodically, or immediately should the 'clutch worn' warning light on the instrument panel illuminate.

2 To adjust the clutch, first chock the rear wheels, jack up the front

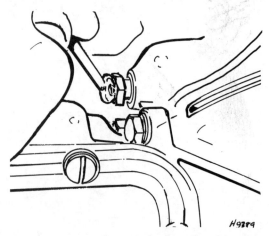

Fig. 5.1 Clutch release fork adjusting bolt and locknut (Sec 2)

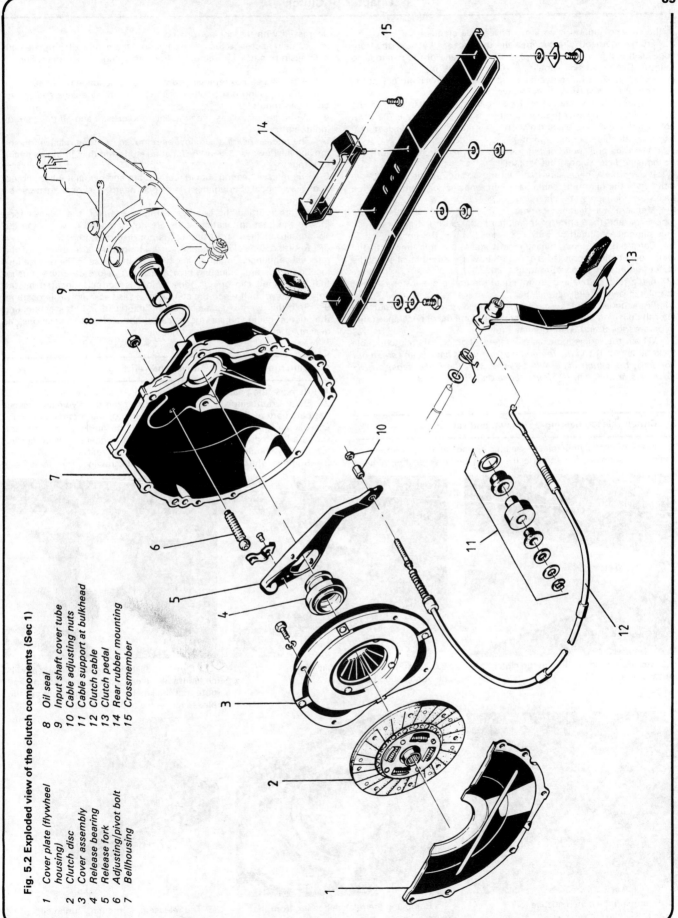

Fig. 5.2 Exploded view of the clutch components (Sec 1)

1 Cover plate (flywheel
   housing)
2 Clutch disc
3 Cover assembly
4 Release bearing
5 Release fork
6 Adjusting/pivot bolt
7 Bellhousing

8 Oil seal
9 Input shaft cover tube
10 Cable adjusting nuts
11 Cable support at bulkhead
12 Clutch cable
13 Clutch pedal
14 Rear rubber mounting
15 Crossmember

of the car and support it on firmly based axle stands.

3   From underneath the car, measure the distance between the front edge of the clutch release fork and the front face of the bellhousing (photo). This dimension should be 109 mm (4.29 in)

4   If the measured distance does not fall within this limit, adjust the position of the release fork as follows.

5   Slacken off the pivot bolt locknut located on the side of the bellhousing, then screw the pivot bolt in or out, as required. The pivot bolt is rather inaccessible and a short open-ended spanner is useful for carrying out this operation (photo).

6   When the prescribed distance exists between the release fork and bellhousing face, tighten the locknut.

7   It is normally necessary to adjust the position of the clutch pedal only when the operating cable has been renewed, or if difficulties are being experienced when changing gear.

8   Measure the distance between the outer edge of the steering wheel rim and the centre of the clutch pedal, with the pedal at rest. This dimension should be 596 $\pm$ 20 mm (23.5 $\pm$ 0.8 in).

9   Carry out the above measurement again, but this time with the clutch pedal fully depressed. The length now measured must equal the above dimension *plus* 155 mm (6.1 in).

10 If the recorded values do not equal the above dimensions, adjust the clutch pedal height as follows.

11 From underneath the car, slacken the clutch cable locknut and alter the position of the cable adjusting nut until the dimensions stated in paragraphs 8 and 9 are obtained (photo).

12 When the adjustment is complete, tighten the clutch cable locknut. **Note:** *When the foregoing adjustments have been carried out correctly, the clutch pedal will be level with the brake pedal on RH drive cars or 20.0 mm (0.79 in) above on LH drive cars.*

3   Clutch release bearing – removal and refitting

1   Wear of the clutch release bearing is indicated by a squealing noise or roughness, felt through the clutch pedal when the pedal is depressed with the engine running.

2   To gain access to the release bearing, the gearbox (complete with bellhousing) must be removed from the engine, as described in Chapter 6.

3   With the gearbox removed from the car, disengage the release fork from the adjusting pivot bolt by sliding the fork sideways and off the bolt head (photo).

4   Withdraw the release bearing and fork forward and off the gearbox input shaft.

5   The release bearing can now be removed from the release fork, by moving it sideways to clear the locating studs and then lifting away the fork (photo).

6   The release bearing should feel smooth and be quiet when turned. If any evidence of roughness is felt or heard, the bearing must be renewed.

7   Before refitting the bearing, carefully examine the release fork. Ensure the bearing locating studs are not damaged or worn and the spring clip on the rear of the fork is not distorted (photo).

8   Refitting the release bearing is a straightforward reversal of the removal sequence. Smear a trace of medium grease to the release fork locating studs and adjusting pivot bolt head before assembly. Ensure that the spring clip on the release fork is correctly located on the adjusting pivot bolt when the complete release assembly is in position.

9   Refit the gearbox as described in Chapter 6, and after connecting the clutch cable, adjust the release fork and pedal positions, as described in Section 2 of this Chapter.

4   Clutch assembly – removal and refitting

1   Remove the gearbox and bellhousing, as described in Chapter 6.

2   Before removing the clutch assembly from the flywheel, inspect the periphery of the clutch cover in the area of the retaining bolts for any aligning marks that may be visible. If no markings are present, scribe a line between the clutch cover and flywheel to ensure correct reassembly should the original components be refitted.

3   Remove the clutch assembly by unscrewing the four bolts

2.3 Measuring the position of the clutch release fork

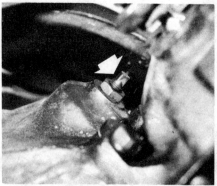

2.5 Location of clutch release fork pivot/adjusting bolt

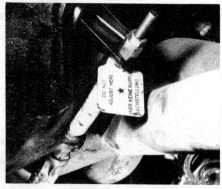

2.11 Clutch pedal height is adjusted by altering the length of the cable at the adjusting nuts (note that the label refers to adjustment of the release fork – see text)

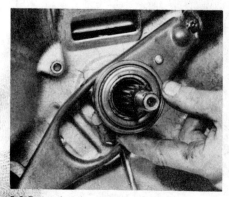

3.3 Removing the clutch release fork

3.5 Removing the release bearing from the release fork

3.7 The release fork retaining spring clip

securing the clutch cover to the rear face of the flywheel. Unscrew the diagonally opposite bolts half a turn at a time, to prevent distortion of the cover flange.

4   With the bolts removed, lift the clutch assembly off the flywheel locating dowels. The clutch disc will fall out at this stage – it is not attached to the clutch cover assembly, or flywheel.

5   It is important that no oil or grease is allowed to come into contact with the clutch disc friction linings, or the pressure plate and flywheel faces. It is advisable to handle the parts with clean hands and to wipe off the pressure plate and flywheel faces with a clean, dry rag before inspection or refitting commences.

6   To refit the clutch, place the clutch disc against the flywheel with the words 'SCHWUNGRAD' or 'FLYWHEEL SIDE' toward the flywheel. On no account should the clutch disc be refitted the wrong way round; it is impossible to operate the clutch with the friction disc incorrectly fitted.

7   Place the clutch cover assembly on the flywheel with the alignment marks in line. Refit the four bolts and tighten them finger tight, so that the clutch disc is gripped, but can still be moved.

8   The clutch disc must now be centralised so that when the engine and gearbox are mated, the gearbox input shaft splines will pass through the splines in the centre of the hub.

9   Centralisation can be carried out quite easily by inserting a round bar or long screwdriver through the hole in the centre of the clutch, so that the end of the bar rests in the small hole in the end of the crankshaft containing the input shaft spigot bearing. Moving the bar sideways, or up and down, will move the clutch disc in whichever direction is necessary to achieve centralisation.

10 Centralisation is easily judged by removing the bar and viewing the clutch disc hub in relation to the crankshaft spigot bearing and the hole in the centre of the diaphragm spring. When the hub appears exactly in the centre, all is correct. Alternatively, if an old input shaft, or a universal clutch aligning tool (photo), can be obtained, this will eliminate all the guesswork, obviating the need for visual alignment.

11 Tighten the cover retaining bolts fully in a diagonal sequence to ensure the cover plate is pulled down evenly without distortion of the flange. Tighten the bolts to the torque setting given in the Specifications.

12 Refit the gearbox to the engine as described in Chapter 6 and, after connecting the clutch cable, adjust the release fork, and if necessary, the pedal positions as described in Section 2 of this Chapter.

5   Clutch assembly – inspection

1   With the clutch disc and pressure plate removed from the flywheel, clean off all traces of asbestos dust using a dry cloth. This is best done outside or in a well ventilated area; *asbestos dust is harmful and must not be inhaled.*

2   Examine the clutch disc friction linings for wear and loose rivets, and the disc for rim distortion, cracks, broken hub springs and worn splines (photo). The surface of the friction linings may be highly glazed, but as long as the clutch material pattern can be clearly seen, this is satisfactory. If the friction material is less than 1.58 mm (0.0625 in) above the rivet heads, or if the linings are black in appearance (indicating oil contamination), the disc must be renewed. If oil contamination is evident, usually from a leaking crankshaft rear oil seal or gearbox input shaft seal, the leak must be rectified before refitting the clutch assembly.

3   Check the machined faces of the flywheel and pressure plate. If either is grooved or heavily scored, it should be machined until smooth, or preferably, renewed.

4   If the pressure plate is cracked or split, or if the diaphragm spring is damaged or its pressure suspect, a new unit must be fitted.

5   Also, check the release bearing for smoothness of operation. There should be no harshness or slackness in it. It should spin reasonably freely, bearing in mind it has been pre-packed with grease.

6   When considering renewing clutch components individually, bear in mind that new parts (or parts from different manufacturers) do not always bed into old ones satisfactorily. A clutch pressure plate or disc renewed separately may sometimes cause judder or snatch. Although expensive, the clutch pressure plate, disc and release bearing should be renewed together, as a complete assembly, wherever possible.

6   Clutch cable – removal and refitting

1   Chock the rear wheels, jack up the front of the car and support it on firmly based axle stands.

2   From underneath the car, measure and record the length of exposed threads before removing the old cable, so that a preliminary adjustment may be made when the new cable is fitted.

3   Undo and remove the capped adjusting nut from the end of the clutch cable, then withdraw the cable from the clutch release fork and bellhousing flange (photo).

4   From inside the car, prise out the five retaining buttons and lift out the trim panel from under the dash.

5   Disconnect the clutch pedal return spring and withdraw the hooked end of the cable from the slot on the clutch pedal.

6   Withdraw the upper end of the cable into the engine compartment, and remove the complete cable from the car.

7   Insert the upper end of the new cable into the entry hole in the bulkhead and assemble the hooked end to the clutch pedal.

8   Reconnect the clutch pedal return spring and refit the trim pad under the dash.

9   Locate the lower end of the cable through the bellhousing and into the clutch release fork.

10 Screw on the capped adjusting nut until approximately the same length of threads exist as were previously recorded.

4.10 Using a universal clutch aligning tool to centralise the clutch disc

5.2 Clutch components laid out for inspection

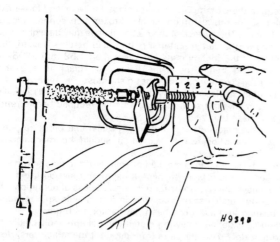

Fig. 5.3 Measuring the length of exposed cable threads (Sec 6)

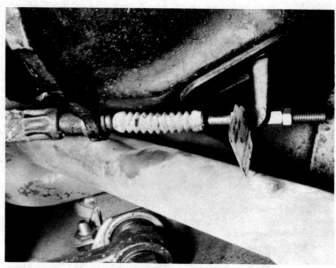

6.3 Location of clutch cable in bellhousing flange and clutch release fork

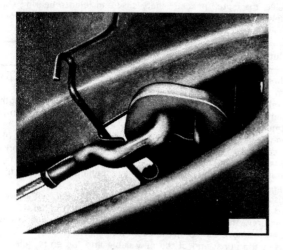

Fig. 5.4 Clutch cable hooked end fitted to pedal (Sec 6)

11 Depress the clutch pedal once or twice to settle the cable, then adjust the clutch release fork and pedal positions as described in Section 2.

7 Clutch pedal and bushes – removal and refitting

1 The clutch pedal pivots on the same axis as the brake pedal. Removal and refitting procedures for both pedals and pedal bushes may be found in Chapter 9.

8 Fault diagnosis – clutch

Symptom	Reason(s)
Difficulty changing or engaging gears	Clutch adjustment incorrect Clutch disc sticking to flywheel or pressure plate due to possible oil contamination* Clutch disc seized on gearbox input shaft splines Gearbox input shaft seized in crankshaft spigot bearing Excessive crankshaft endfloat
Squeal, harshness or roughness when clutch pedal is depressed	Worn clutch release bearing Worn or broken pressure plate fingers
Engine revs increase with no appreciable increase in vehicle road speed	Clutch adjustment incorrect Clutch disc or pressure plate excessively worn Oil present on clutch disc friction linings
Excessive judder when moving off from rest	Oil or grease contamination of clutch disc friction linings. Loose or worn engine or gearbox mountings Broken or incorrectly assembled clutch pressure plate or diaphragm spring Excess run-out of flywheel

*This condition may also be due to the clutch disc being rusted to the flywheel or pressure plate. It is possible to free it by applying the handbrake, depressing the clutch pedal, engaging top gear and operating the starter motor. If really badly corroded, then the engine will not turn over, but in the majority of cases the clutch disc will free. Once the engine starts, rev it up and slip the clutch several times to clear the rust deposits.

Chapter 6
Manual gearbox and automatic transmission

For modifications, and information applicable to later models, see Supplement at end of manual

Contents

Specifications

Manual gearbox

Number of gears	4 forward, 1 reverse
Type of gears	Helical, constant mesh
Synchromesh	All forward gears
Gear ratios:	
First	3.640:1
Second	2.120:1
Third	1.336:1
Fourth	1.000:1
Reverse	3.522:1
Reverse gear relay lever endfloat	0.1 to 0.3 mm (0.004 to 0.012 in)
Lubricant type/specification	Hypoid gear oil, viscosity SAE 80EP (Duckhams Hypoid 80)
Lubricant capacity	1.1 litres (1.9 Imp pints)

Automatic transmission

Type	GM
Selector lever positions	P, R, N, D, 2, 1
Gear ratios:	
First	2.40:1
Second	1.48:1
Third	1.00:1
Reverse	1.92:1
Lubricant type/specification	Dexron II type ATF (Duckhams D-Matic)
Fluid capacity	4.7 litres (8.3 Imp pints) – dry
	2.1 litres (3.7 Imp pints) – top-up after draining

Torque wrench settings

	Nm	lbf ft
Manual gearbox		
Bellhousing-to-engine	45	33
Gearbox-to-bellhousing	30	22
Bellhousing splash shield	22	16
Extension housing-to-gearbox	30	22
Rear mounting-to-gearbox	22	16
Rear mounting-to-crossmember	20	15
Crossmember-to-body	40	30
Reversing light switch	25	18
Automatic transmission		
Bellhousing-to-engine	40	30
Converter-to-drive disc	55	41
Drive disc-to-crankshaft	60	44
Bellhousing splash shield	22	16
Rear mounting-to-transmission	45	33
Rear mounting-to-crossmember	20	15
Crossmember-to-body	40	30
Fluid lines at oil cooler	22	16

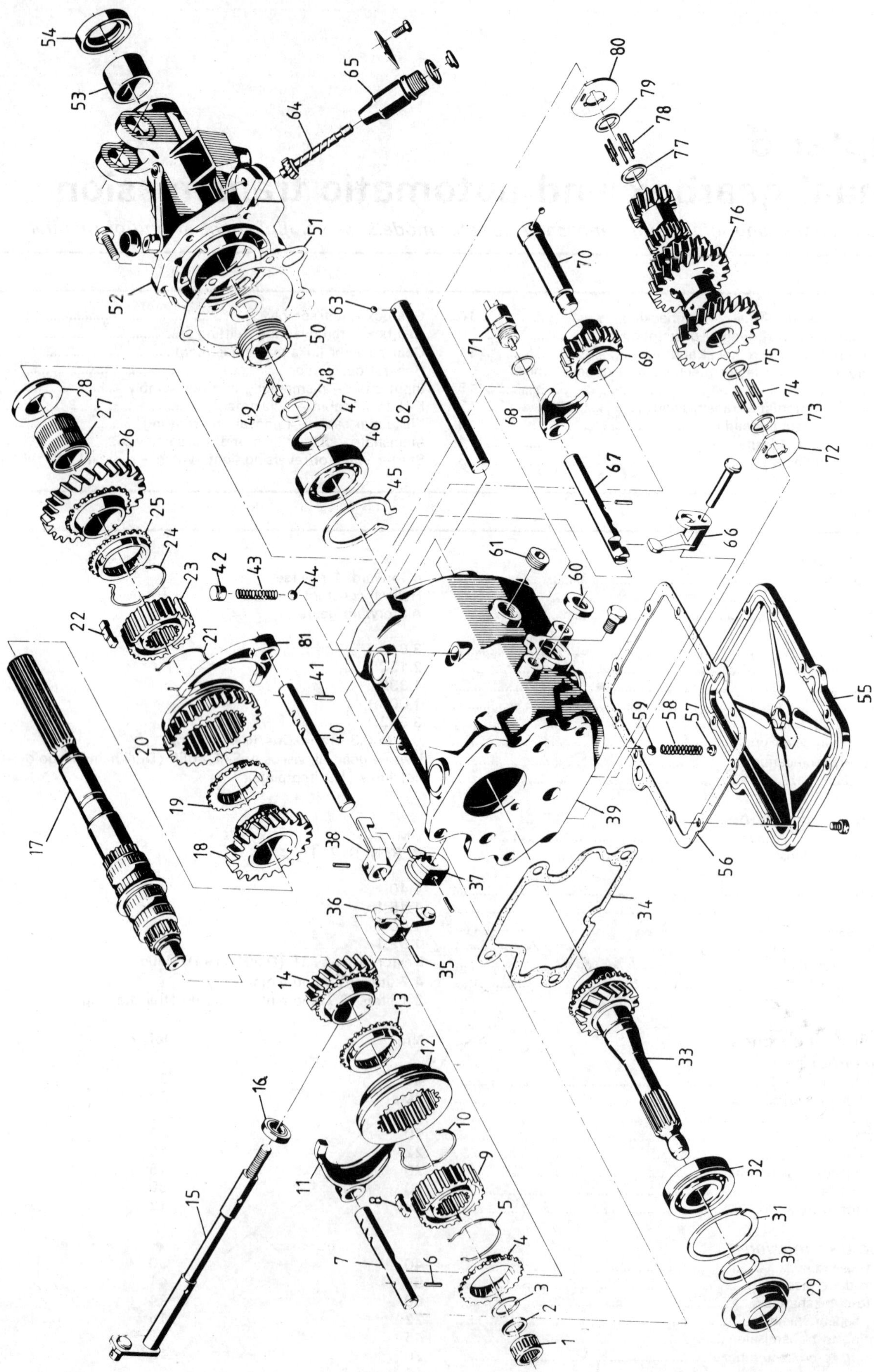
1
2
3
4
5
6
7
8
9
10
11
12
13
14
15
16
17
18
19
20
21
22
23
24
25
26
27
28
29
30
31
32
33
34
35
36
37
38
39
40
41
42
43
44
45
46
47
48
49
50
51
52
53
54
55
56
57
58
59
60
61
62
63
64
65
66
67
68
69
70
71
72
73
74
75
76
77
78
79
80
81

Fig. 6.1 Exploded view of manual gearbox (Sec 1)

1 Input shaft needle roller bearing
2 Bearing spacer
3 Circlip
4 4th gear synchroniser cone
5 Sliding key front retaining spring
6 Roll pin
7 3rd/4th selector rod
8 Sliding key
9 3rd/4th synchromesh hub
10 Sliding key rear retaining spring
11 3rd/4th synchromesh ring
12 3rd/4th synchroniser cone
13 3rd gear synchroniser cone
14 3rd gear
15 Transverse selector shaft
16 Oil seal
17 Mainshaft
18 2nd gear
19 2nd gear synchroniser cone
20 1st/2nd synchromesh ring
21 Sliding key front retaining spring
22 Sliding key
23 1st/2nd synchromesh hub
24 Sliding key rear retaining spring
25 1st gear synchroniser cone
26 1st gear
27 Needle roller bearing
28 Bearing spacer
29 Input shaft oil seal
30 Input shaft bearing retainer circlip
31 Outer locating circlip
32 Input shaft bearing
33 Input shaft
34 Gasket
35 Rollpin
36 3rd/4th relay lever
37 1st/2nd and reverse relay lever
38 1st/2nd shift dog
39 Gearbox casing
40 1st/2nd selector rod
41 Roll pin
42 Retaining plug
43 Detent spring
44 Detent ball
45 Mainshaft bearing retaining circlip
46 Mainshaft bearing
47 Dished washer
48 Circlip
49 Speedometer drivegear retaining spring clip
50 Speedometer drivegear
51 Gasket
52 Rear extension housing
53 Propeller shaft support bearing
54 Rear oil seal
55 Gearbox cover
56 Gasket
57 Retaining cap
58 Detent spring
59 Detent ball
60 Oil seal
61 Filler plug
62 Layshaft
63 Layshaft locating ball
64 Speedometer driven gear
65 Speedometer driven gear housing
66 Reverse gear relay lever
67 Reverse selector rod
68 Reverse selector fork
69 Reverse idler gear
70 Reverse idler gear shaft
71 Reversing light switch
72 Thrust washer
73 Spacer shim
74 Needle roller bearings
75 Layshaft gear cluster
76 Layshaft gear cluster
77 Spacer shim
78 Needle roller bearings
79 Spacer shim
80 Thrust washer
81 1st/2nd selector fork

1 General description

The manual transmission fitted to all models covered by this manual comprises four forward and one reverse gear. All forward gears are engaged through synchromesh units to obtain smooth, silent gear changes.

The transmission comprises four main assemblies, a detachable bellhousing, main gearbox assembly, rear extension housing and remote control gear change. Access to the gearbox internal components is provided by a detachable cover bolted to the bottom of the gearbox.

Housed within the gearbox assembly are the input shaft, the layshaft, the mainshaft, gear clusters and synchro hubs, and the selector fork rods and shafts. The input shaft and all forward gears on the mainshaft are in constant mesh with their corresponding gears on the layshaft gear cluster, and are helically cut to achieve quiet running.

Movement of the gear lever is transmitted to the selector forks via the remote control linkage and a series of relay rods and shafts. The forks act on the synchronising rings on a hub splined to the mainshaft. The rings are moved forward or rearward against the gear to be engaged. A female cone is carried with the synchronising ring to bear against a male cone on the gear to be engaged. The friction between the two cones as they come together serves to bring the gear train speed to that of the synchronising ring on the mainshaft. Once the speeds are synchronised, the ring can pass further to fully engage the gear. Keys, sprung in the synchroniser hub, act to keep the ring in place once it has positively engaged the gear selected.

When reverse gear is selected, an idler gear is moved into mesh by the reverse selector fork, with the toothed first/second synchronising ring and the layshaft gear cluster. The reverse idler gear, the toothed first/second synchronising ring and the corresponding gear on the layshaft gear cluster all have straight cut spur teeth; synchromesh action is not provided.

In addition to the manual gearbox, a GM three-speed automatic transmission is available as a factory option. Further information regarding this unit will be found in Section 8 of this Chapter.

2 Gearbox – removal and refitting

1 The gearbox (complete with bellhousing) can be separated from the rear of the engine and lowered from under the car, or the gearbox only can be removed, leaving the bellhousing still in position. Either method may be adopted, depending on whether the gearbox is being removed for renewal or overhaul, or whether the complete assembly is being withdrawn to provide access to the clutch or flywheel. It is also possible to lift out the complete engine and transmission as a unit through the engine compartment, as described in Chapter 1.
2 Having decided on the method of removal, proceed as follows: if a hoist or inspection pit is not available, run the back of the car up a pair of ramps, or jack it up and fit axle stands. Next, jack up the front of the car and support it on stands.
3 For safety reasons, disconnect the battery earth terminal.
4 From inside the car, remove the centre console as described in Chapter 12.
5 With the centre console removed, slide the upper rubber boot up the gear lever, then detach the lower inner rubber boot from the rubber seal. Slide the inner rubber boot up the lever also, to expose the gear lever linkage.
6 Disconnect the tension spring from the end of the gear lever, then prise off the small circlip from the front of the gear lever pivot pin (photos).
7 Withdraw the pivot pin rearwards and lift out the gear lever (photos).
8 Unhook the remaining rubber seal downwards and off the lip on the transmission tunnel.
9 Working beneath the car, remove the propeller shaft as described in Chapter 7. With the propeller shaft removed, wrap some polythene around the end of the gearbox, and secure with string or elastic bands to stop any oil running out.
10 Undo and remove the knurled nut securing the speedometer cable to the gearbox, and withdraw the cable (photo).
11 From the rear of the gearbox, detach the two reversing light switch wires (photo).
12 If the gearbox only is being removed (leaving the bellhousing in

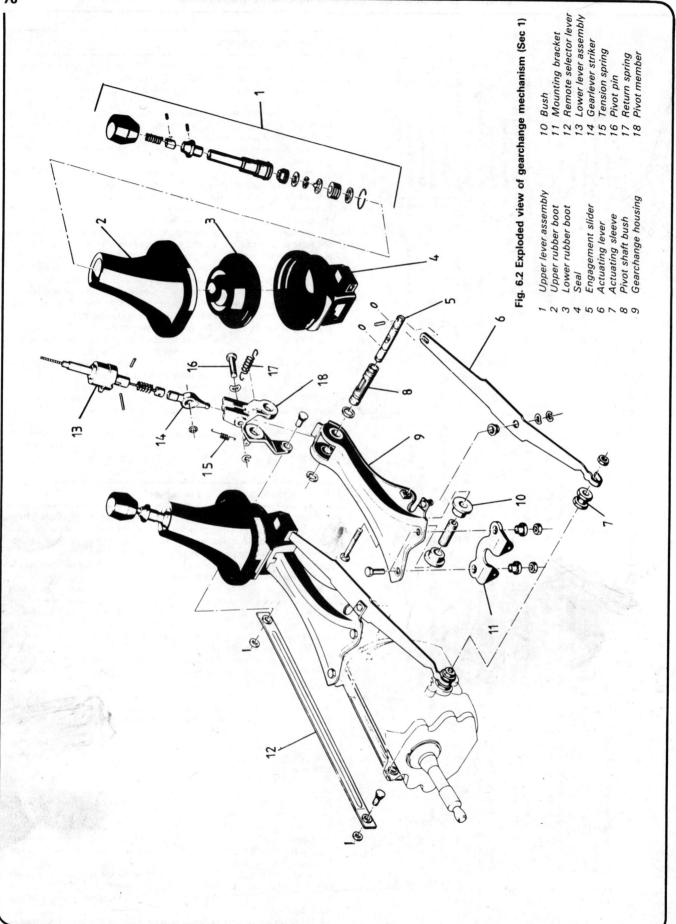

Fig. 6.2 Exploded view of gearchange mechanism (Sec 1)

1 Upper lever assembly
2 Upper rubber boot
3 Lower rubber boot
4 Seal
5 Engagement slider
6 Actuating lever
7 Actuating sleeve
8 Pivot shaft bush
9 Gearchange housing
10 Bush
11 Mounting bracket
12 Remote selector lever
13 Lower lever assembly
14 Gearlever striker
15 Tension spring
16 Pivot pin
17 Return spring
18 Pivot member

2.6a Disconnect the gear lever tension spring ...

2.6b ... and then remove the circlip from the pivot pin

2.7a Slide out the pivot pin ...

2.7b ... and lift off the gear lever

2.10 Removing the speedometer cable knurled nut

2.11 Reversing light switch electrical connections

2.13a Remove the crossmember mounting bolts and lift off the crossmember

2.13b Gearbox mounting with crossmember removed

position on the engine), suitably support the weight of the gearbox, using a jack or axle stand. Support the engine sump in the same manner, using a block of wood between the sump and jack or stand, so that the engine does not drop when the gearbox is removed.

13 Undo and remove the two nuts securing the gearbox mountings to the crossmember, and the two bolts and locktabs that secure the crossmember to the chassis (photo). Lift away the crossmember (photo).

14 Undo and remove the four bolts retaining the gearbox to the bellhousing.

15 The assistance may now be required of a second person, who should be ready to help in taking the weight of the gearbox if necessary.

16 Carefully separate the gearbox from the bellhousing by sliding it rearwards. Do not allow the weight of the gearbox to hang on the input shaft, as it is easily damaged. When the input shaft has been fully withdrawn from the bellhousing, lower the gearbox and slide it out from under the car. Remove the gasket from the bellhousing.

17 If the gearbox is to be removed complete with bellhousing, proceed in the following manner.

18 Before disconnecting the clutch cable, measure and record the length of exposed threads visible from the adjusting nuts to the end of the cable. This measurement is necessary so that an initial cable setting may be obtained when the cable is refitted.

19 Now undo and remove the adjusting nut and locknut, then withdraw the cable from the clutch release fork and bellhousing flange.

20 Working in the engine compartment, make a note of the electrical connections on the starter motor solenoid, then disconnect them.

21 Undo and remove the two bolts securing the starter motor to the cylinder block flange and the single bolt retaining the motor rear steady bracket to the cylinder block. Now lift off the starter motor.

22 Support the weight of the gearbox, using a jack or axle stand. Support the engine sump in the same manner, using a block of wood between the sump and jack or stand, so the engine does not drop when the gearbox is removed.

23 Undo and remove the bolts securing the bellhousing to the

cylinder block, and the bolts retaining the two support brackets and flywheel cover plate to the bellhousing.

24 Undo and remove the two nuts securing the gearbox mountings to the crossmember, then bend back the locktabs and remove the two crossmember retaining bolts. Now lift away the crossmember.

25 The assistance of a second person is now required, who should be ready to help in taking the weight of the gearbox.

26 Separate the gearbox and bellhousing from the engine by sliding it rearwards until the input shaft is fully disengaged from the clutch assembly. *Do not allow the weight of the gearbox to hang on the input shaft; it is easily damaged.* With the gearbox and bellhousing clear of the clutch assembly, lower it to the ground and withdraw the unit from under the car.

27 Refitting the gearbox is the reverse sequence to removal bearing in mind the following points:

(a) *If the gearbox has been separated from the bellhousing, use a new gasket between the mating faces lightly coated with gasket sealer*

(b) *Check that the input shaft cover/tube is correctly positioned with the two tabs pointing downward and located in the recess (photo)*

(c) *Position the oil seal over the input shaft, with the hollow side toward the bearing, before refitting the gearbox to the bellhousing*

(d) *If the clutch cable has been disconnected, adjust the locknuts to expose the same length of cable noted upon removal, then refer to Chapter 5 for the correct adjustment procedure*

(e) *Check and if necessary top-up the gearbox oil level on completion of refitting (photo)*

---

3 Gearbox – dismantling

1 Thoroughly clean the exterior of the gearbox with paraffin or a water soluble degreasing agent, then dry it with compressed air or a non-fluffy rag.

2 Place the complete unit on a firm bench or table, and ensure you have the following tools available, in addition to the normal range of spanners, etc:

(a) *Good quality circlip pliers; two pairs – one expanding and one contracting*

(b) *Soft-faced mallet*

(c) *Drifts, steel and brass; approximately 10 mm (0.39 in)*

(d) *Small pin punch*

(e) *Engineer's vice mounted on firm bench*

(f) *Small containers or trays for needle rollers etc*

(g) *Selection of metal tubing and angle iron*

Having gathered together the above mentioned tools, read through

this complete Section before starting work, to familiarise yourself with the dismantling sequence.

3 It is advisable to drain the oil from the gearbox at this stage. The gearbox is not provided with a drain plug, and removal of the bottom cover is necessary to allow the oil to drain. This is best done by inverting the gearbox so the cover is uppermost. Undo the ten screws and lift off the cover. Retrieve the selector shaft detent spring from its location in the gearbox casing. There is a steel ball located under the spring, that may fall out when the oil is drained. Be prepared for this to happen. Now carefully tip the gearbox onto its side, draining the oil into a suitable container.

4 When all the oil has drained, temporarily refit the cover with two screws fitted finger tight.

5 The remote control gear linkage is next removed. Extract the split pin securing the remote selector lever to the gearbox transverse selector shaft. Recover the washer.

6 Undo and remove the two bolts and nuts securing the remote control unit to the bracket on the gearbox, and the single bolt retaining the remote control unit to the gearbox extension housing. The unit can now be lifted off.

7 If the gearbox was removed complete with bellhousing, undo and remove the four retaining bolts and separate the two units. The clutch release fork and release bearing may be removed from the bellhousing by referring to Chapter 5.

8 The speedometer driven gear can now be withdrawn from the extension housing after undoing the bolt and lifting off the retaining plate.

9 Undo and remove the reversing light switch from the rear of the gearbox casing.

10 Undo and remove the two bottom cover securing screws that were temporarily refitted after draining the oil. Lift off the cover and, if the steel selector shaft detent ball did not drop out when the oil was drained, turn the gearbox over and tap the side of the case until the ball emerges.

11 Undo and remove the five bolts securing the rear extension housing to the gearbox. Now rotate the extension housing until the layshaft is exposed.

12 Using a drift of suitable diameter, tap out the layshaft from front to rear. As the layshaft starts to emerge from the rear of the gearbox, recover the small steel locating ball from the dimple in the end of the shaft (Fig. 6.3).

13 With the layshaft removed, carefully lift out the layshaft gear cluster complete with the two thrust washers. Take care not to lose the needle roller bearings located in each end of the gear cluster.

14 The reverse gear relay lever and pivot are next removed. Use a soft metal drift to drive the pivot towards the centre of the gearbox, then lift out the pivot and relay lever (Fig. 6.4).

15 Position the transverse selector shaft so that the roll pins securing the 1st/2nd and 3rd/4th gear relay levers are as near to the vertical position as possible (Fig. 6.5).

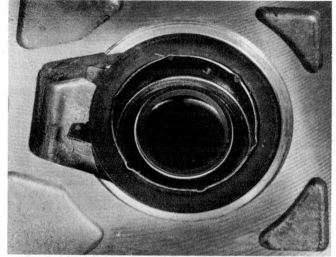

2.27a Input shaft cover tube correctly located in the bellhousing with the tabs in the recess

2.27b Topping up the gearbox oil

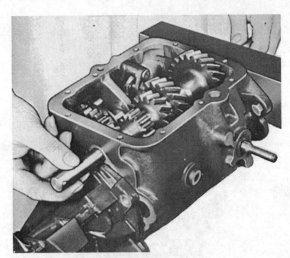

Fig. 6.3 Withdrawing the layshaft from the rear of the gearbox casing (Sec 3)

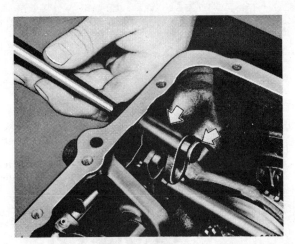

Fig. 6.4 Removing the reverse gear relay lever and pivot pin (Sec 3)

Fig. 6.5 Location of the two transverse selector shaft rollpins (Sec 3)

Fig. 6.6 Selector shaft detent ball and spring retaining plug (Sec 3)

Fig. 6.7 Location of the four selector fork and shift fork rollpins (Sec 3)

17 Now undo and remove the locknut and actuating sleeve from the end of the transverse selector shaft, protruding from the right-hand side of the gearbox casing. The transverse selector shaft can now be withdrawn from the left, and the two relay levers recovered.

18 Turn the gearbox the correct way up and withdraw the two plugs which retain another pair of selector shaft detent balls and springs. These plugs can be stubborn, and the best method of removal is to engage a thin strip of metal in the groove and prise upwards. Once the plugs have been removed, lift out the springs, turn the gearbox over again, and tap the side of the casing until the two balls drop out.

19 Engage first gear, then using the thin punch, tap out the four remaining roll pins securing the three selector forks and the shift fork to the selector rods. Tap the pin down sufficiently to clear the selector rods only. Do not tap the pins completely out, or they will foul the gearbox casing.

20 With the roll pins clear of the selector rods, rotate the extension housing to provide access and tap out the rods from rear to front.

21 When the selector rods have been removed, lift out the three selector forks and the shift dog.

22 Pull the extension housing rearwards and withdraw the housing and complete mainshaft assembly from the gearbox casing. Now remove the input shaft and bearing, by pulling the shaft and bearing forward and out of the casing.

23 The reverse idler gear and shaft may be removed if necessary, by tapping the shaft rearwards with a soft metal drift. Take care not to lose the small locating ball situated in a dimple on the shaft.

16 Using a thin punch, drive out the roll pin from the 3rd/4th gear relay lever first, followed by the 1st/2nd gear relay lever roll pin.

4   Gearbox components – inspection

1   Thoroughly clean the inside of the gearbox casing and check for any dropped needle rollers or roll pins.
2   Carefully clean and then examine all the component parts for general wear, distortion, slackness of fit, and damage to machined faces.
3   Examine the gears for excessive wear and chipping of the teeth. Renew them as necessary.
4   Examine the layshaft for signs of wear, where the needle rollers bear. If a small ridge can be felt at either end of the shaft, or if any scoring is evident, it will be necessary to renew the shaft and the needle rollers. If worn, the thrust washers at each end must also be renewed.
5   The four synchroniser cones are likely to be badly worn, and it is false economy not to renew them. New cones will improve the smoothness and speed of the gearchange considerably.
6   The needle roller bearing and cage, located between the nose of the mainshaft and the annulus in the rear of the input shaft, is also liable to wear, and should be renewed as a matter of course.
7   Examine the condition of the two ball bearing assemblies, one on the input shaft and one on the mainshaft. Check them for looseness between the inner and outer races and for general wear or noisy operation. Normally they should be renewed on a gearbox that is being overhauled.
8   If either of the synchroniser assemblies is worn, which will be the case if the vehicle has been jumping out of gear, it will be necessary to obtain complete assemblies; the parts are not sold individually.
9   Examine the ends of the selector forks, where they rub against the channels in the periphery of the synchroniser rings. If possible, compare the selector forks with new units to help determine the wear that has occurred. Renew them if worn.
10 The input shaft oil seal, extension housing oil seal, the two tranverse shaft oil seals, and all gearbox gaskets should be renewed as a matter of course. The transverse shaft oil seals and the extension housing oil seal can be removed by prising out with a screwdriver or flat strip of metal. New seals are then tapped into place, using a tube or block of wood to spread the load.

5   Input shaft – dismantling and reassembly

1   Place the input shaft bearing in a soft-jawed vice, with the splined end of the shaft uppermost.
2   Using circlip pliers remove the circlip which retains the bearing in position, then drive the input shaft downwards and out of the bearing, using a soft-faced mallet.
3   Remove the large circlip from the groove in the bearing outer track and transfer it to the new bearing.
4   Slide the new bearing onto the input shaft with the large circlip on the bearing outer track offset toward the front.
5   Position the bearing on top of the vice jaws, with the splined end of the input shaft pointing downwards between the jaws. Using a drift located in the spigot bearing hole in the rear of the input shaft, drift the shaft into the bearing. Alternatively, place the input shaft on the bench and tap on the bearing, using a long tube of suitable diameter.
6   With the bearing in place, refit the small retaining circlip (photo).

6   Mainshaft – dismantling and reassembly

1   With the mainshaft assembly on the bench, extract the circlip and withdraw the extension housing from the rear of the mainshaft.
2   Remove the needle roller bearing, (if still in place), the bearing spacer, the 3rd/4th synchromesh ring and the three sliding keys and front key retaining spring from the front of the mainshaft.
3   The speedometer drivegear is next removed from the rear of the mainshaft, after depressing the spring steel retaining clip.
4   After removing the speedometer drivegear, extract the circlip and dished washer retaining the rear bearing in position.
5   To remove the mainshaft rear bearing, position two strips of angle iron or similar material under the edge of the bearing and clamp this assembly in a vice, using a block of wood as a spacer (photo). With the bearing thus supported, drive the mainshaft out of the bearing, using a soft-faced mallet.

5.6 Input shaft, bearing and circlip correctly assembled

Fig. 6.8 Using circlip pliers to extract the mainshaft bearing retaining circlip (Sec 6)

Fig. 6.9 3rd/4th gear synchro components removed from the front of the mainshaft (Sec 6)

6.5 Removing the mainshaft rear bearing

6.13a Slide the third speed gear onto the mainshaft ...

Fig. 6.10 1st gear and 1st/2nd synchro components removed from the rear of the mainshaft (Sec 6)

6.13b ... then place the synchromesh cone on the gear

Fig. 6.11 Removing the circlip from the front of the mainshaft (Sec 6)

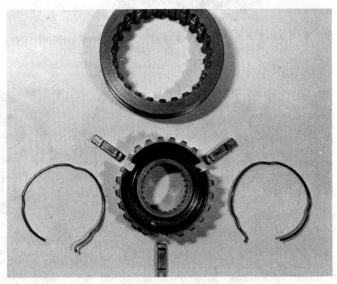

6.14a The 3rd/4th speed synchro components

6   Now withdraw the bearing spacer, large circlip and first speed gear from the end of the mainshaft.

7   Slide the 1st/2nd synchromesh ring off the hub and recover the three sliding keys and rear key retaining spring, the synchromesh cones and needle roller bearing.

8   The two gears and two synchro hubs that still remain on the mainshaft can now be removed.

9   Position the two strips of angle iron or similar material, as used for the rear bearing removal, under the second speed gear. Drive the mainshaft downwards until the synchro hub is free, then lift off the hub and second speed gear. **Note:** *There is a shoulder preventing the hub and gear from being removed toward the front end of the mainshaft.*

10 From the front of the mainshaft, extract the 3rd/4th synchro hub retaining circlip.

11 Using the two strips of angle iron positioned behind third speed gear, and with the splined end of the mainshaft pointing downward, clamp the assembly in the vice. Drive the mainshaft downward with a soft-faced mallet, then withdraw the 3rd/4th synchro hub and third speed gear.

12 The mainshaft reassembly procedure can now begin, using new parts as necessary.

13 Slide the third speed gear onto the front end of the mainshaft, then position the synchromesh cone on the third speed gear (photos).

14 Locate the synchromesh key retaining spring onto the rear face of the 3rd/4th speed synchro hub (photo), then place the hub on the front end of the mainshaft with the raised centre of the hub facing away from the third speed gear (photo). Support the mainshaft in the vice and, using a socket or tube of suitable diameter, tap the hub fully onto the shaft (photo).

15 Slide the second speed gear over the rear of the mainshaft (photo), then place the synchromesh cone in position on the gear.

16 The 1st/2nd speed synchro hub can now be assembled. Slide the synchromesh ring over the hub, then position the three keys into the slots in the hub. **Note:** *The sliding keys for the 1st/2nd synchro hub*

are longer than those of the 3rd/4th hub and do not have arrows on their faces. With the keys in place, locate a retaining spring over the keys, ensuring that the turned up end engages one of the keys. Now turn the hub over and place the second retaining spring in position. Locate the turned up end in the same key, and check the other ends of the springs point in opposite directions.

17 Fit the assembled hub onto the mainshaft (photo), with the selector fork groove toward the rear of the shaft.

18 Place the assembly in the vice so that the 1st/2nd synchro hub is resting on the protected vice jaws. Using a tube of suitable diameter placed over the front of the mainshaft, tap the shaft into the 1st/2nd synchro hub. Ensure that the sliding keys engage with the slots in the synchromesh cone as the hub is tapped into position (photo).

19 Next to be fitted is the inner sleeve, in which the first speed gear needle roller bearing runs. This sleeve is an interference fit on the mainshaft when cold, but if it is heated in front of an electric fire for a few minutes, or in an oven at approximately 150°C (300°F), it can be slid over the mainshaft quite easily.

20 With the inner sleeve in position, slide the needle roller bearing over the end of the mainshaft and onto the sleeve (photo).

21 Place the remaining 1st/2nd synchromesh cone onto the first speed gear, then fit the gear to the needle roller bearing (photo).

22 Position the bearing spacer on the mainshaft next, with the chamfered side toward the rear of the shaft (photo), followed by the large circlip.

23 Now refit the rear mainshaft bearing. Support the assembly in the vice so the bearing is resting on the vice jaws, and drift the mainshaft into the bearing using a soft-faced mallet.

24 Slide the dished washer over the rear of the mainshaft, followed by the circlip. Tap the circlip down with a tube of suitable diameter, to compress the dished washer and allow the circlip to engage its groove (photos).

25 Place the speedometer drivegear spring clip in position, then slide the drivegear up the mainshaft and engage the clip (photos).

Fig. 6.12 3rd/4th synchro sliding keys assembled with arrows facing front of mainshaft (Sec 6)

Fig. 6.13 Correct fitting of sliding key retaining springs (Sec 6)

6.14a The 3rd/4th speed synchro components

6.14c ... then fit the hub to the mainshaft with the raised centre away from the third speed gear

6.14d Tapping the hub into position on the mainshaft

6.15 Refitting the 2nd speed gear to the mainshaft

6.17 Refitting the 1st/2nd synchro hub with the selector fork groove to the rear

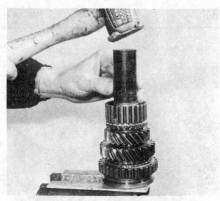

6.18 Tapping the 1st/2nd selector hub into position on the mainshaft

6.20 1st speed gear needle roller bearing in position on the sleeve

6.21 Fitting the 1st speed gear

6.22 The bearing spacer is fitted with the chamfered side to the rear

6.24a Place the dished washer onto the mainshaft …

6.24b … followed by the circlip

6.25a Position the speedometer drivegear and retaining clip on the mainshaft …

6.25b … and engage the clip and gear

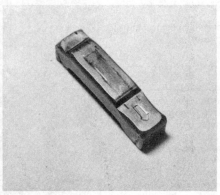

6.26a Arrows on 3rd/4th sliding keys must face forward

6.26b Assembling the 3rd/4th synchro

6.27a Fit the outer sliding key retaining ring, ...

6.27b ... the retaining circlip ...

6.27c ... and bearing spacer

6.28 Refitting the mainshaft to the extension housing

26 The 3rd/4th synchro unit at the front of the mainshaft can now be assembled. The procedure is the same as previously described for the 1st/2nd synchro hub, except that the arrows on the sliding keys must face the front of the mainshaft, and the selector fork groove on the synchromesh ring also faces forward (photos).
27 With the hub assembled, fit the retaining circlip (photo) followed by the bearing spacer (photos).
28 Insert the assembled mainshaft into the extension housing, and retain the two assemblies with the large circlip (photo).

7   Gearbox – reassembly

1   Commence reassembly by refitting the reverse idler gear and shaft. Fit the gear with the selector fork groove toward the front of the gearbox and tap the shaft into position, using a suitable drift. Take care not to lose the locating ball, which fits in a dimple on the shaft (photo).
2   Coat a new gasket on both sides with medium grease and place it in position on the extension housing assembly into the gearbox casing (photo).
3   Position the reverse idler gear selector fork on the gear, with the chamfered side facing forward. Slide the selector rod into the casing and align the roll pin hole with the slot on the fork (photo). Tap in the roll pin, leaving 2 mm (0.079 in) exposed (photo).

7.1 Reverse idler gear in position in the casing

7.2 Refitting the mainshaft and extension housing to the gearbox casing

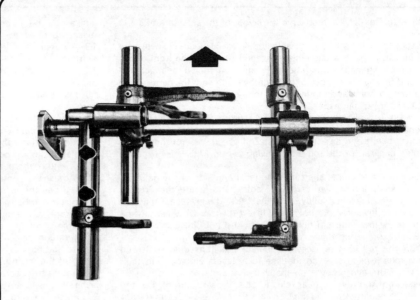

Fig. 6.14 Layout of the gear selector linkage (Sec 7)

7.3a Refitting the reverse idler selector shaft and fork

7.3b Tapping the reverse idler selector fork rollpin into position

7.5a Refitting the 3rd/4th selector rod to the fork ...

7.5b ... then the roll pin ...

7.5c ... leaving 2 mm (0.079 in) exposed

7.6 1st/2nd selector rod, selector fork and shift dog refitted

7.7a Insert the transverse shaft ...

4   Refer to Fig. 6.14 and observe the layout of the selector forks and rods.

5   Place the 3rd/4th speed selector fork in position over the synchromesh ring. Now slide in the selector rod from the front of the gearbox and engage the fork (photo). Position the rod so the machined half round face is uppermost, and the groove is toward the centre. Line up the roll pin holes and tap in the pin (photo). Leave approximately 2 mm (0.079 in) of pin exposed (photo).

6   The 1st/2nd selector rod can now be refitted. Slide the rod in from the front of the gearbox, with the machined flat uppermost. Engage the selector rod shift dog and then the 1st/2nd speed selector fork. Align the holes and tap in the roll pins, leaving 2 mm (0.079 in) exposed (photo).

7   Insert the transverse shaft into the left-hand side of the gearbox. Slide the shaft through, toward the centre, and locate the 3rd/4th selector shaft relay lever, followed by the 1st/2nd relay lever. Align the 1st/2nd relay lever roll pin holes and insert the pin. Now line up the 3rd/4th relay lever roll pin holes and refit the roll pin. Leave 2 mm (0.079 in) exposed on these pins also (photos).

8   With the roll pins refitted, manipulate the transverse shaft and selector rods if necessary, so that the relay levers engage with their respective slots and grooves on the shift fork and selector rods.

9   Next, refit the reverse gear relay lever and pivot (photo). Tap the pivot into the gearbox casing until a clearance of 0.1 to 0.3 mm (0.004 to 0.012 in) exists between the head of the pivot and the relay lever. Measure this clearance with feeler gauges (photo).

10 Lubricate the input shaft needle roller bearing, using the correct grade of gear oil, and place the bearing on the front of the mainshaft (photo). Place the synchromesh cone on the 3rd/4th synchro unit.

11 Now refit the input shaft to the front of the gearbox (photo), pushing it fully home until the large circlip is in contact with the gearbox face.

12 Before proceeding further, check the operation of the gear selectors by operating the transverse shaft. This is only a rough guide, as the detent balls and springs have not yet been refitted, and the input shaft and mainshaft are not secure. It will, however, give an indication as to whether the assembly is correct up to this point. If anything is amiss, go back and recheck *now* before carrying on with the reassembly.

13 Assuming everything is satisfactory so far, the layshaft can now be refitted.

14 Smear both ends of the layshaft gear cluster bore with medium grease.

15 Insert one of the spacer shims fully into the end of the gear cluster bore.

16 Now fit the needle roller bearings, followed by the second spacer shim, then smear some more grease over the needle rollers to retain them in position (photos).

17 Repeat this procedure for the second set of needle rollers at the cother end of the gear cluster.

18 If possible, obtain a tube or metal rod the same length and diameter as the layshaft, and insert it into the gear cluster. This will retain the needle rollers in position and reduce the possibility of their falling out as the layshaft is refitted.

19 Smear some grease on the rear face of the gear cluster thrust washers and place them in position on the gearbox casing (photos). Ensure that the tab on the rear face of the thrust washers locates in the notch of the casing.

20 Rotate the gearbox extension housing to provide clearance for the layshaft to be inserted from the rear.

21 Place the steel locating ball into the dimple on the layshaft, and retain it in position with a trace of grease (photo).

22 Now carefully lower the layshaft gear cluster into the gearbox, taking care not to dislodge the thrust washers.

23 Line up the gear cluster and very carefully insert the layshaft from the rear of the gearbox (photo).

24 Push the layshaft fully into the gearbox until the locating ball enters its seat (photos).

25 After coating their threads with a jointing compound, the bolts securing the extension housing can be refitted and tightened to the specified torque. The upper two bolts also retain the remote control gear change mounting bracket (photo).

26 Place the detent ball and spring in position, then refit the gearbox cover, using a new gasket (photos).

7.7b ... and slide on the 3rd/4th and 1st/2nd relay levers

7.7c Transverse shaft and relay levers fitted

7.9a Fit the reverse gear relay lever and pivot ...

7.9b ... then measure the relay lever endfloat

7.10 Refit the input shaft needle bearing ...

7.11 ... followed by the input shaft

7.16a Refit the layshaft gear cluster needle roller bearings and retain with grease ...

7.16b ... then place the spacer shim over the needles

7.19a The layshaft gear cluster front thrust washer ...

7.19b ... and rear thrust washer in position

7.21 Layshaft locating steel ball in position

7.23 Insert the layshaft through the rear of the casing

7.24a Push the shaft through the gear cluster

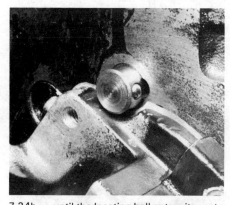

7.24b ... until the locating ball enters its seat

7.25 Refitting the extension housing retaining bolts and gearchange support bracket

7.26a Refit the detent ball and spring ...

7.26b ... and then the gearbox cover

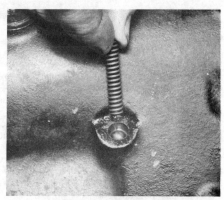

7.27 Refitting the two remaining detent balls, springs and plugs

7.28a Refitting the reversing light switch ...

7.28b ... the speedometer driven gear ...

7.28c ... and retaining plate and bolt

7.31a The remote gearchange housing is secured with two upper ...

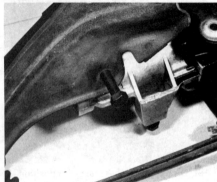

7.31b ... and one lower retaining bolts

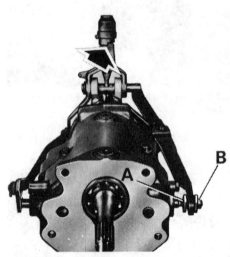

Fig. 6.15 Adjustment of the gearchange remote control linkage (Sec 7)

Actuating sleeve – A
Locknut – B
Gearlever stop – arrowed

7.31c Finally refit the remote selector lever

7.33 Adjusting the transverse shaft actuating sleeve

27 Turn the gearbox over and refit the remaining two detent balls and springs, retaining them in position with the two plugs (photo).

28 Now refit the reversing light switch (photo) and the speedometer driven gear, retaining plate and bolt (photos).

29 The gearchange remote control linkage can now be refitted and adjusted.

30 First, refit the actuating sleeve and locknut to the gearbox transverse shaft, but do not tighten the locknut at this stage.

31 Place the remote control gearchange in position and secure it with the three bolts (photo). Refit the remote selector lever to the transverse shaft and secure it with a new split pin (photos).

32 To adjust the linkage, temporarily refit the gear lever, but do not assemble the tension spring.

33 Engage second gear and adjust the actuating sleeve on the transverse shaft (photo) to bring the stop at the base of the gearlever into contact with the raised portion of the intermediate shift lever bracket. Now turn the actuating sleeve back a quarter of a turn and tighten the locknut.

34 With the adjustment complete, check that it is possible to engage all the gears. If this adjustment is incorrect, it will be difficult to engage second gear. If this is found to be the case during road test, further adjustment will be necessary. The actuating sleeve can be adjusted with the gearbox fitted, from underneath the car.

35 Position a new gasket on the front face of the gearbox, then slide the new oil seal over the input shaft.

36 If the gearbox was removed complete with bellhousing, this should now be refitted, tightening the bolts to the specified torque.

37 The gearbox can now be refitted to the car, as described in Section 2. Remember to refill the gearbox with the correct grade of oil when refitted.

8 Fault diagnosis – Manual gearbox

Symptom	Reason(s)
Weak or ineffective synchromesh	Synchroniser cones worn or damaged
Gearbox jumps out of gear	Worn synchroniser hubs and rings Selector forks badly worn Detent balls and springs worn Excessive endfloat on mainshaft
Excessive noise	Incorrect grade of oil in gearbox or level too low Worn gearbox bearings Chipped or broken gear teeth Worn layshaft or needle roller bearings
Difficulty in engaging gears	Incorrect clutch adjustment Clutch disc sticking to flywheel or pressure plate Gearbox input shaft binding in crankshaft spigot bearing

9 Automatic transmission – general description

A three-speed automatic transmission of GM manufacture is available as an option, in place of the manual transmission fitted as standard.

The transmission comprises two basic systems: the torque converter, which takes the place of the conventional clutch, and a torque/speed responsive hydraulically operated epicyclic gearbox. A transmission oil cooler, incorporated in the radiator, is also fitted to maintain the transmission fluid at the correct operating temperature.

Due to the complexity of the automatic transmission unit, any adjustments (made necessary by sub-standard performance) or overhaul work should be left to the local main agents, who will have the special equipment for fault diagnosis and rectification. The contents of the following Sections are therefore confined to supplying general information and any service information and instruction that can be used by the owner.

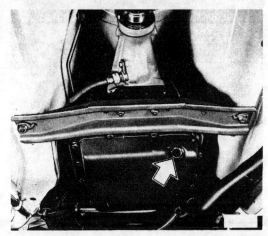

Fig. 6.16 Automatic transmission fluid drain plug (Sec 11)

10 Automatic transmission – fluid level checking

1 Every 6000 miles (10 000 km), the automatic transmission fluid level should be checked with the engine and transmission at normal operating temperatures. A road journey of 15 miles (20 km) minimum will achieve this.
2 With the vehicle standing on level ground, leave the engine running and place the selector lever in P or N.
3 Withdraw the transmission dipstick, wipe it clean, re-insert it, withdraw it a second time and read off the level.
4 If necessary, top-up with the specified fluid to the 'F' mark. The distance between 'ADD' and 'F' on the dipstick is 0.56 litre (1 Imp pint)
5 If the dipstick is marked '+ 20°C' on one side and '+90°C' on the other the fluid level may be checked with the engine and transmission hot or cold. In this case, top-up with the specified fluid to the 'MAX' mark. Never overfill the transmission.
6 Always keep the area around the dipstick/filler tube clean; dirt particles entering the transmission could cause severe malfunctions.

11 Automatic transmission – removal and refitting

1 Any suspected faults must be referred to the main agent before unit removal, as with this type of transmission the fault must be confirmed, using specialist equipment, before the transmission is removed from the car.
2 If a ramp or inspection pit is not available, jack up the rear of the car and place axle stands under the rear axle. Now jack up the front of the car and support it on ramps or stands.
3 Disconnect the battery earth terminal.
4 Place a container of approximately 3.5 litres (6.3 Imp pints) capacity beneath the transmission, remove the drain plug, and drain the transmission fluid.

5 Remove the propeller shaft, as described in Chapter 7.
6 When the transmission fluid has drained, undo the clamp screws and disconnect the two rubber fluid hoses from the fluid pipes. Plug their ends to prevent dirt ingress and further fluid loss.
7 Undo and remove the knurled nut securing the speedometer cable to the transmission, and withdraw the cable.
8 Disconnect the transmission selector rod from the transmission selector lever.
9 Undo and remove the six bolts and the support bracket securing the exhaust pipe to the manifold flange. These bolts are inaccessible without a socket and long extension as well as a small spanner.
0 Next, undo and remove the bolts securing the engine/bellhousing brackets on either side of the sump and lift off the brackets.
11 Working inside the engine compartment, detach the three wire clips securing the kickdown cable to the transmission fluid filler pipe.
12 Position the fan in such a fashion that when the engine is tipped back, the radiator top hose will pass between the blades.
13 Place a jack beneath the transmission, bend back the locktabs and undo and remove the bolts securing the transmission crossmember to the body.
14 Lower the jack approximately 150 mm (6 in).
15 Disconnect the modulator pipe support clip, then remove the modulator pipe from the diaphragm connection at the rear of the transmission.
16 Undo and remove the kickdown cable angle bracket retaining bolt from the right-hand side of the transmission. Now pull the cable end out of the transmission and disconnect the cable end from the kickdown valve.
17 Undo and remove the bolts securing the torque converter splash shield to the front face of the bellhousing, and lift off the shield.
18 The three bolts securing the torque converter to the drive disc can

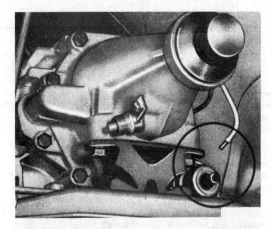

Fig. 6.17 Modulator diaphragm and pipe location (Sec 11)

Fig. 6.18 Kickdown cable retaining bracket (Sec 11)

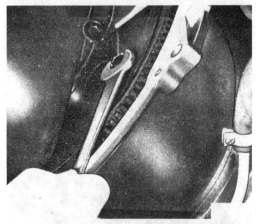

Fig. 6.19 Unbolting the torque converter from the drive disc (Sec 11)

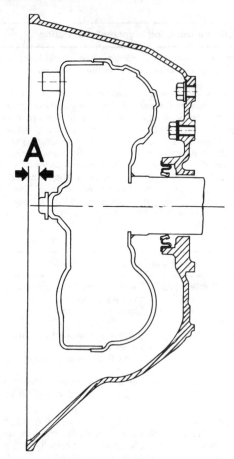

Fig. 6.20 Correct fitting of torque converter (Sec 11)

Dimension A = 5 to 7 mm (0.20 to 0.28 in)

now be removed. To do so rotate the engine using a spanner on the crankshaft pulley nut, and undo each bolt in turn, as it becomes accessible through the opening previously covered by the splash shield. If an alignment mark is not apparent between the torque converter and the drive disc (adjacent to one of the retaining bolts), suitably mark the two components, using a dab of white paint.

19 Next, undo and remove all the bolts securing the transmission bellhousing to the engine.

20 Place a second jack beneath the engine sump to support the engine when the transmission is removed.

21 Remove the rubber grommet from the bottom of the bellhousing, then make a final check that all pipes, cables and wires have been disconnected from the transmission.

22 With the help of an assistant to take the weight of the transmission, lower the jack and withdraw the transmission from the engine. The torque converter must remain in position on the transmission during removal. If necessary, prise it off the drive disc, using a screwdriver inserted through the opening in the bottom of the bellhousing.

23 Lower the transmission to the ground and remove it from under the car. Keep the front of the transmission raised slightly, to prevent the torque converter sliding off, and when convenient arrange to support the converter on the transmission with an improvised prop.

24 Refitting the transmission unit is the reverse of the removal procedure, bearing in mind the following points:

(a) *Before refitting, check that the torque converter is properly seated on the transmission driving gear. Refer to Fig. 6.20 and check that the clearance between the bellhousing flange and torque converter centring pin is 5 to 7 mm (0.20 to 0.28 in)*

(b) *When refitting the torque converter to drive disc retaining bolts, line up the previously made alignment marks, then fit all three bolts finger tight, then progressively tighten to the*

specified torque

(c) *Fill the transmission with the correct grade of fluid upon completion of the refitting*

(d) *Check and if necessary adjust the gear selector lever and kickdown cable as described in Sections 12 and 13 respectively*

---

12 Gear selector linkage – adjustment

---

1 Jack up the front of the car and support it on firmly based axle stands.

2   Position the gear selector lever in the P position.
3   From underneath the car, disconnect the selector rod from the transmission selector lever.
4   Now move the transmission selector lever rearwards as far as possible, if not already in this position.
5   Apply slight rearward pressure to the selector rod, and adjust the clevis until the bore in the clevis aligns with the bore of the selector lever. Now screw in the clevis by one further turn, ie shorten the rod.
6   Reconnect the selector lever to the selector rod and lower the car to the ground.

13 Kickdown cable – adjustment

1   Before carrying out adjustments to the kickdown cable, ensure that the accelerator cable adjustment is correct as described in Chapter 3.
2   Place a block of wood 10 mm (0.4 in) thick between the accelerator pedal and the floor (see Fig. 6.21).
3   Fully depress the accelerator pedal and wedge it in this position with a length of wood placed between the pedal and the front seat.
4   Loosen the clamp around the kickdown cable at the point where the cable emerges through the bulkhead and into the engine compartment.
5   Pull the sleeve of the cable through the clamp until resistance can be felt. This will happen when the ball on the end of the cable comes into firm contact with the grommet on the end of the accelerator pedal.
6   Hold the cable sleeve in this position and tighten the clamp.

14 Kickdown cable – removal and refitting

1   Jack up the rear of the car and place firmly based axle stands under the rear axle. Now jack up the front of the car and support it on stands or ramps.
2   Disconnect the battery earth terminal.
3   From inside the car, prise out the retaining buttons and lift off the lower trim panel under the dash.
4   Disconnect the kickdown cable from its attachment at the top of the accelerator pedal.
5   Remove the clamp from the kickdown cable at the point where it emerges through the bulkhead and into the engine compartment. Now pull the cable through and into the engine compartment.
6   Disconnect the clips securing the kickdown cable to the transmission fluid filler tube.
7   Using a socket and long extension, and small spanner as necessary, undo and remove the six bolts and support bracket securing the exhaust pipe to the manifold flange.
8   Place a jack beneath the transmission, then bend back the locktabs and undo and remove the bolts securing the transmission crossmember to the body.
9   Lower the transmission until there is sufficient clearance to provide access to the kickdown cable where it enters the right-hand side of the transmission. If necessary, turn the fan so the blades do not foul the radiator hose.
10   Undo and remove the kickdown cable retaining bolt and angle bracket.
11   Pull the cable out of the transmission and disconnect the cable end from the kickdown valve. Now withdraw the cable from under the car.
12   Refitting the new cable is the reverse sequence to removal. with the refitting completed, adjust the kickdown cable as described in Section 13, then check, and if necessary top-up, the transmission fluid level.

15 Automatic transmission selector mechanism – removal and refitting

1   Jack up the front of the car and support it on firmly based axle stands.
2   Disconnect the battery earth terminal.
3   From inside the car, remove the securing screws and lift the selector lever cover off the centre console.
4   Now remove the centre console as described in Chapter 12.
5   Pull the illuminating lamp off the selector lever.
6   Undo and remove the starter inhibitor/reversing light switch securing screws; lift off the switch.
7   From underneath the car, undo and remove the nut securing the selector lever to the intermediate shaft.
8   Move the selector lever sideways and withdraw it from the car.
9   Refitting is the reverse sequence to removal.

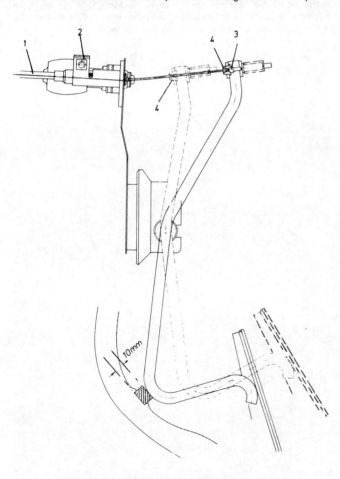

Fig. 6.21 Kickdown cable adjustment (Sec 13)

1   *Kickdown cable*   3   *Cable ball*
2   *Retaining clamp*   4   *Accelerator pedal grommet*

Fig. 6.22 Kickdown cable clamp at bulkhead (Sec 15)

Fig. 6.23 Removing the illuminating lamp from the selector lever
(Sec 15)

Fig. 6.24 Withdrawing the starter inhibitor/reversing light switch
(Sec 15)

16 Starter inhibitor/reversing light switch – removal and refitting

1   This switch is screwed to the transmission tunnel at the base of the gear selector lever and is actuated by a pin on the selector lever
2   The switch is non-adjustable and is a sealed unit. If found to be faulty, it must be renewed.
3   Access to the switch is gained by removing the selector lever

cover and centre console, as described in the previous Section.

17 Fault diagnosis – automatic transmission

Faults in these units are nearly always the result of incorrect adjustment of the selector linkage or downshift cable, or low fluid level. Internal faults should be diagnosed by your main GM dealer, who has the necessary equipment to carry out the work.

Chapter 7 Propeller shaft

Contents

Specifications

Type .... Two-piece tubular with front rubber drive coupling, centre support bearing and constant velocity joint and rear universal joint

	Nm	lbf ft
Torque wrench settings		
Rubber drive coupling retaining bolts	75	55
Centre bearing-to-floor assembly..	20	15
Universal joint U-bolts	12	9

1 General description

Drive is transmitted from the gearbox to the rear axle by means of a finely balanced tubular propeller shaft, split into two halves and supported at the centre by a rubber mounted bearing.

The propeller shaft is fitted with a rubber coupling at the front, a constant velocity (CV) joint at the centre and a universal joint at the rear. These units cater for vertical movement of the rear axle and slight movement of the complete power unit on its rubber mountings.

Fore and aft movement of the rear axle is absorbed by a sliding spline, located at the gearbox end. At the opposite end of the shaft, the universal joint bearing caps are secured to the rear axle flange by two U-bolts, nuts and lockwashers.

With the exception of the rubber coupling, none of the units on the propeller shaft are renewable separately, and in the event of wear being detected in the joints or centre bearing, it will be necessary to renew the propeller shaft as a complete assembly.

2 Propeller shaft – inspection

1 At periodic intervals, the propeller shaft front rubber drive coupling, centre support bearing, constant velocity joint and rear universal joint should be carefully inspected for wear, damage or excessive free play as follows.

2 Examine the front rubber coupling for swelling or deterioration of the rubber due to oil contamination, or cracking of the rubber around the mounting bolts. If wear has reached an advanced stage, the joint should be renewed. If oil contamination is apparent, this will probably be due to a leaking gearbox rear oil seal, and should be rectified as soon as possible. The mounting bolts should also be checked for tightness, referring to the torque wrench settings at the beginning of this Chapter.

3 Next, inspect the centre support bearing for cracks in the rubber or slackness of the mounting bolts. It is not possible to renew the centre bearing separately, and if excessive wear is apparent, it will be necessary to renew the complete propeller shaft.

4 Wear in the universal joint needle roller bearings and constant velocity joint balls is characterised by vibration in the transmission, clonks on taking up the drive and, in extreme cases of universal joint wear, metallic squeaking and ultimately grating and shrieking sounds as the bearings break up.

5 The universal joint and constant velocity joint can be checked for wear with the propeller shaft in position, by trying to turn the shaft back and forth with one hand while holding the rear axle flange or constant velocity joint housing with the other hand. Any movement felt between the propeller shaft and rear axle flange or constant velocity joint housing is indicative of considerable wear. As in the case of the centre support bearing, any wear in the above mentioned components will necessitate renewal of the complete propeller shaft assembly.

3 Propeller shaft – removal and refitting

1 Chock the front wheels, jack up the rear of the car and support it on firmly based axle stands.

2 The propeller shaft is carefully balanced to fine limits, and it is important that it is refitted in exactly the same position it was in prior to its removal. Scribe a mark on the rear universal joint bearing cap and rear axle flange to ensure refitment in its original position.

3 Bend back the locktabs, then undo and remove the four U-bolt retaining nuts securing the universal joint to the rear axle flange. Lever out the U-bolts, using a screwdriver, but do not disengage the joint from the axle flange at this stage (photos).

4 Moving to the centre of the car, detach the handbrake cable steady spring from the centre bearing mounting bracket.

5 Supporting the weight of the shaft, undo and remove the two outer retaining bolts securing the centre bearing mounting bracket to the underbody (photo).

6 Slide the propeller shaft forward slightly and separate the rear universal joint from the rear axle flange, then move it rearwards to disengage it from the gearbox mainshaft splines (photo). Do not allow the two halves of the propeller shaft to adopt an angle greater than 15° to each other as this will place excessive strain on the constant velocity joint.

7 With both ends of the propeller shaft detached from their respective locations, move the assembly forward, over the handbrake cable and out from under the car.

8 Refitting the propeller shaft is the reverse of the removal sequence. Ensure that the marks made previously on the universal joint and axle flange are in line, tighten the U-bolt retaining nuts to the specified torque and secure with new locktabs.

3.3a Bend back the locktabs ...

3.3b ... and remove the universal joint retaining nuts and U-bolts

3.5 Centre support bracket, mounting bracket and retaining bolts

3.6 Disengaging the front of the propeller shaft from the mainshaft splines

4   Propeller shaft rubber drive coupling – removal and refitting

1   Remove the propeller shaft from the car as described in the previous Section.
2   Mark the relationship of the propeller shaft sliding forward section with the tubular centre section. This is necessary to ensure correct orientation of these two units when the new coupling is fitted, and maintain the balance of the propeller shaft.

3   Undo and remove the nuts and bolts securing the rubber coupling to the front and centre propeller shaft sections. Separate the sections and lift out the coupling.
4   Refitting the rubber coupling is the reverse procedure to removal. Ensure that the previously made marks are in line and tighten the retaining bolts to the specified torque.
5   Refit the propeller shaft to the car, as described in the previous Section.

5 Fault diagnosis – propeller shaft

Symptom	Reason(s)
Vibration	Worn rear universal joint or constant velocity joint
	Worn centre support bearing
	Worn front rubber drive coupling
	Propeller shaft out of balance
	Propeller shaft distorted
Knock or clunk when taking up drive	Worn rear universal joint bearings
	Worn rear axle drive pinion splines
	Loose universal joint U-bolts
	Worn rear axle halfshaft splines
	Excessive backlash in rear axle gears
	Worn propeller shaft constant velocity joint

Chapter 8 Rear axle

For modifications, and information applicable to later models, see Supplement at end of manual

Contents

Specifications

Type .... Semi-floating, hypoid

Axle ratio 3.67:1

Number of gearteeth
Crownwheel 33
Pinion 9

Oil type/specification .... Hypoid gear oil, viscosity SAE 90EP (Duckhams Hypoid 90S)

Oil capacity .... 1.2 litres (2.1 Imp pints)

Torque wrench settings

	Nm	lbf ft
Propeller shaft U-bolts	12	9
Rear axle cover plate	35	26
Upper suspension arm at chassis	65	48
Upper suspension arm at axle	65	48
Lower suspension arm at chassis	105	77
Lower suspension arm at axle	105	77
Anti-roll bar-to-upper arm	15	11
Panhard rod-to-chassis	105	77
Panhard rod-to-axle	60	44
Shock absorber lower mountings (not estate car)	45	33
Shock absorber lower mountings (estate car only)	23	17
Halfshaft bearing retaining plate	60	44
Wheel nuts	90	66

1 General description

The semi-floating rear axle assembly comprises a hypoid gear differential housed in a banjo type solid axle casing. A limited slip differential is available as an option. The differential is integral with the axle casing and the rear axle must be removed from the car to carry out any repairs to the differential.

The axleshafts (halfshafts), are splined at their inner ends into the differential gears, while their outer ends are supported by ball bearings. Oil seals are fitted to each end of the axle casing.

Coil spring suspension is used, in conjunction with upper and lower trailing arms which control fore and aft movement of the axle. Lateral movement is prevented by a Panhard rod, and an anti-roll bar is fitted to minimise body roll.

The axle casing is not fitted with a drain plug. It is therefore necessary to remove the differential cover plate to drain the axle oil.

The overhaul and repair of a differential assembly is a highly skilled task requiring special tools and equipment, and it is not recommended that the DIY mechanic should attempt this job. The best policy, in the event of differential failure or excessive noise, is to obtain a factory exchange reconditioned unit.

2 Rear axle – removal and refitting

1 Chock the front wheels, jack up the rear of the car and support it on firmly based axle stands, placed along the chassis side-members.
2 Mark the relationship of the wheel to the wheel studs and remove both rear roadwheels.
3 Refer to Chapter 9, and remove the rear brake drums.
4 Detach the handbrake cable from the brake shoes, by moving the operating lever on the rear shoes toward the wheel hub and withdrawing the cable from the hooked end (Fig. 8.2).
5 Prise off the retaining spring clip securing the cable to the inside of each brake backplate, and withdraw the cable from the rear of the backplates.
6 Undo and remove the rigid brake pipe union from the flexible brake hose, then plug the end of the pipe to prevent fluid loss and dirt ingress (Fig. 8.3).
7 Withdraw the retaining clip from the flexible hose, and lift off the hose from its mounting bracket. Plug, or tape over, the end of the hose to prevent dirt ingress.
8 Undo and remove the nuts and U-bolts securing the propeller shaft to the rear axle flange after marking each part for relocation. Tie up the propeller shaft from a convenient place on the vehicle underbody. Do not allow the shaft to hang down; this will place undue strain on the centre support bearing (Fig. 8.4).
9 Place a sturdy jack beneath the differential casing and raise the axle slightly.
10 Undo and remove the nuts and bolts securing the Panhard rod and the shock absorbers to the axle casing. On estate cars, bend up the protective cover flap to gain access to the Panhard rod mounting bolt.
11 Lower the jack until there is no tension on the coil springs.

Fig. 8.1 Exploded view of rear axle (Sec 1)

1	Pinion oil seal	12	Pinion
2	Front pinion bearing	13	Axle casing
3	Collapsible spacer	14	Brake drum
4	Rear pinion bearing	15	Brake assembly
5	Bearing cap	16	Halfshaft
6	Cover gasket	17	Bearing retaining plate
7	Differential cover	18	Water deflector
8	Differential pinion	19	Halfshaft bearing
9	Differential cage	20	O-ring seal
10	Differential bearing	21	Retaining ring
11	Crownwheel		

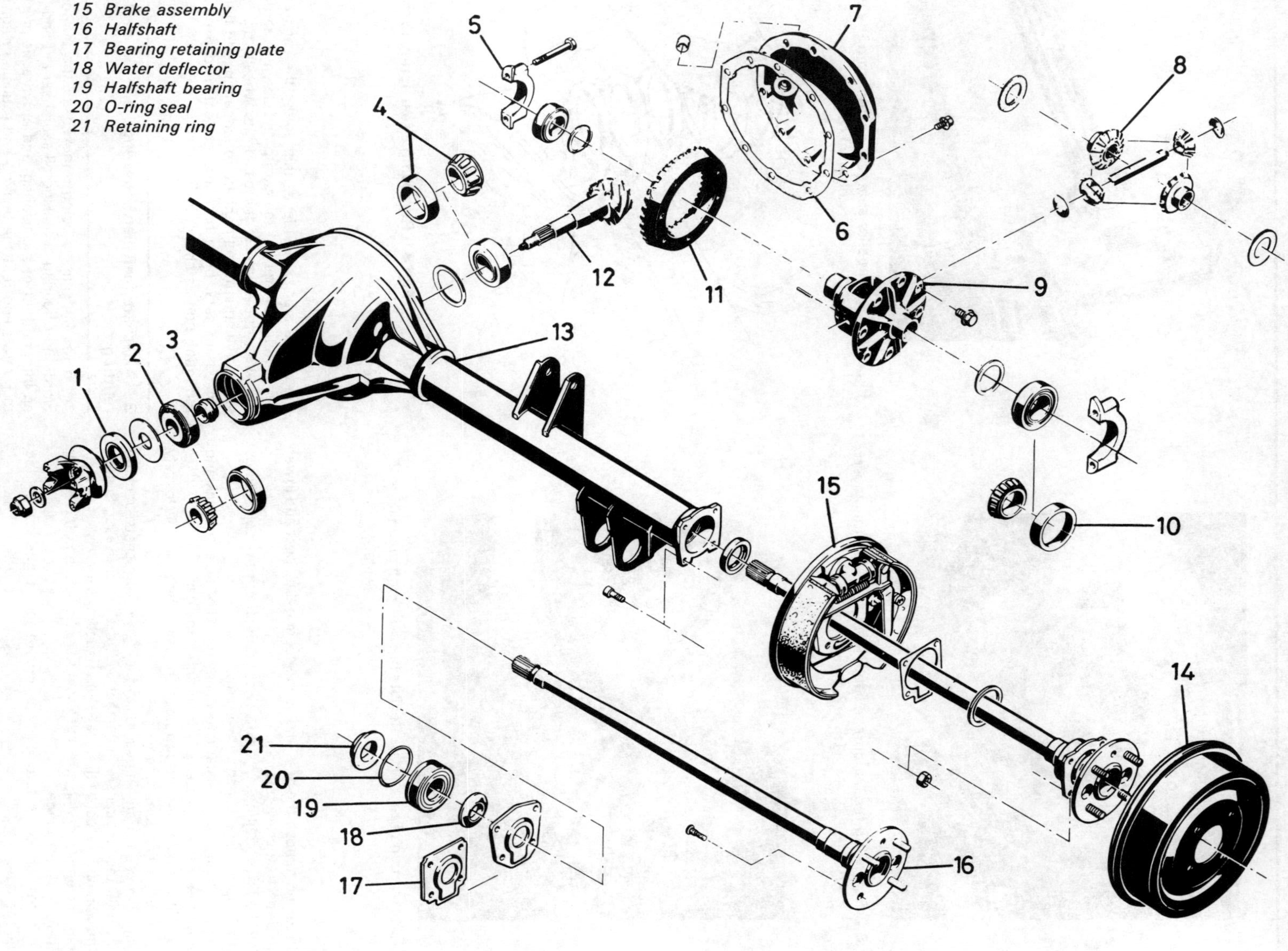

Fig. 8.2 Removing the handbrake cable from the operating lever (Sec 2)

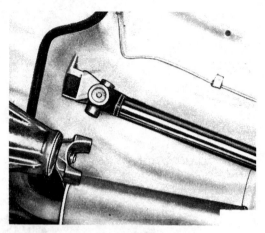

Fig. 8.4 The propeller shaft supported from the underbody after removal (Sec 2)

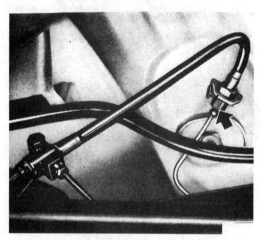

Fig. 8.3 Location of rear brake flexible hose-to-pipe union (Sec 2)

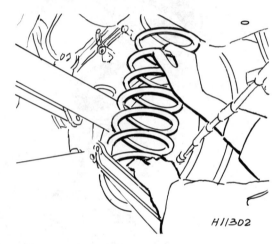

Fig. 8.5 Removing a rear spring (Sec 2)

12 Undo and remove the nuts and bolts securing the upper and lower trailing arms to the axle casing.

13 Pull the lower trailing arms downward and lift out the coil springs from their spring seats in the lower arms.

14 With the help of an assistant, to steady the axle, lower the jack and withdraw the rear axle assembly from under the car.

15 To refit the axle, raise it into position, using the jack, and loosely fit the lower trailing arm mountings.

16 Place the coil springs in position in their lower arm seats. Jack up the axle until the springs are in contact with their upper seats. Ensure that the springs are correctly located and seating squarely.

17 Refit the upper trailing arm and Panhard rod mountings, but do not tighten fully at this stage.

18 Refit the shock absorber lower mountings, tightened to the specified torque.

19 Position the propeller shaft universal coupling on the axle flange and secure it with the U-bolts, new locktabs and nuts tightened to the specified torque.

20 Insert the brake hose into its bracket and retain it with the spring clip. Remove the protective tape or plugs from the hose and brake pipe and reconnect the unions.

21 Insert the handbrake cable through the openings in the brake backplates, and lock them in position with the retaining clips.

22 Reconnect the handbrake cable to the brake shoes and refit the brake drum.

23 Bleed the rear brakes, and adjust the brake shoes if necessary, as described in Chapter 9.

24 Refit the wheels in their original positions, check, and if necessary,

top-up the rear axle oil level, then lower the car to the ground.

25 Bounce the rear of the car up and down to settle the suspension.

26 With the weight of the car on its wheels, tighten the upper and lower trailing arm and Panhard rod mountings to the specified torque. On estate cars, bend back the protective cap on the Panhard rod mounting bolt as shown in Fig. 8.6.

3 Axleshaft (halfshaft), bearings and oil seal – removal and refitting

1 If the halfshaft is being removed for the purpose of renewing a worn outer bearing or leaking oil seal, bear in mind that the oil seal is an integral part of the bearing, and a hydraulic press will be required to remove and refit the bearing and retaining ring. Your local garage should be able to do this for you, but ensure these facilities are available before commencing this operation.

2 To remove the halfshaft, begin by jacking up the rear of the car and supporting it on firmly based axle stands. Mark the relationship of the wheel to the wheel stud and remove the appropriate roadwheel.

3 Remove the brake drum, referring to Chapter 9 if necessary, then, using a socket and extension bar inserted through the aperture in the halfshaft flange, remove the four nuts and bolts securing the brake backplate and bearing retainer to the axle casing.

4 The halfshaft may now be withdrawn from the axle by gently tapping the circumference of the flange with a soft-faced mallet. If the shaft is a tight fit, a small slide hammer can be made quite easily from two lengths of tubing, two suitable bolts and a washer (photos).

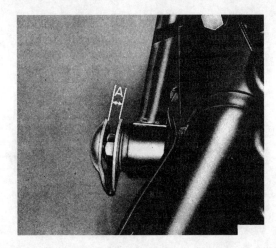

Fig. 8.6 Correct position of Panhard rod mounting bolt protective cap (Sec 2)

Dimension A = 19 mm (0.75 in)

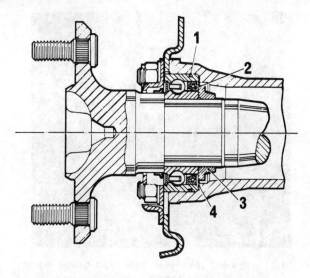

Fig. 8.7 Sectional view of halfshaft bearing (Sec 3)

1　Outer sealing ring　　　3　Bearing retaining ring
2　Inner seal　　　　　　　4　Shims

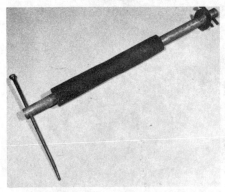

3.4a A simple slide hammer to remove the halfshafts can be made from tubing and suitable bolts

3.4b Using the slide hammer to withdraw the halfshaft

3.4c Removing the halfshaft

5　With the halfshaft removed, recover the shim from the bearing recess in the axle casing.
6　Support the halfshaft firmly in a vice and, using a cold chisel and medium hammer, split the bearing retaining ring, then slide the ring off the halfshaft.
7　With the retaining ring removed, the bearing can now be withdrawn from the halfshaft, using a hydraulic press, as previously described.
8　Before refitting a new bearing, examine the water deflector located behind the bearing retainer plate. If the deflector is damaged, it should be renewed. Ensure that when fitted, the deflector is positioned below the shoulder of the bearing land and with the flange on the deflector toward the bearing.
9　Press a new bearing onto the halfshaft, with the O-ring oil seal groove toward the splined end of the shaft, followed by a new retaining ring, flanged side toward the bearing (photo).
10　Before refitting the halfshaft, the depth of the bearing seat in the axle casing must be determined using a depth gauge, and shims then added or subtracted as necessary, to provide a slight preload on the bearing. This is only necessary if a new bearing has been fitted. If the original components are being reused, the existing shims need not be altered.
11　Before taking a depth measurement, refit the brake backplate to the axle casing, with new gaskets both sides, and lightly secure it in place with the nuts.
12　Measure the depth of the bearing recess from the brake backplate to the shoulder in the axle casing.

Fig. 8.8 Removing the shim from the recess in the axle casing (Sec 3)

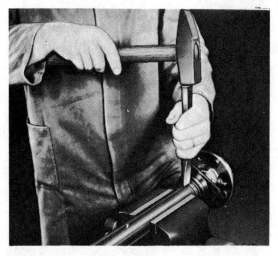

Fig. 8.9 Using a cold chisel to split the bearing retaining ring
(Sec 3)

Fig. 8.10 Correct positioning of water deflector with flange toward
bearing (Sec 3)

Fig. 8.11 Ensure bearing O-ring oil seal is toward splined end
of halfshaft (Sec 3)

3.9 Halfshaft bearing correctly fitted

Fig. 8.12 Measuring the depth of the bearing recess (Sec 3)

13 Now measure the width of the bearing. The difference in these two measurements is the thickness of shims required. The allowable tolerance is 0.05 mm (0.0020 in) of axial play to 0.15 mm (0.0059 in) of interference.

14 Having calculated the number of shims required and placed them in position on the axle casing, the halfshaft may be carefully inserted into the axle. Twist the shaft slightly, if necessary, to align the splines and top it fully home with a soft-faced mallet.

15 Refit the nuts and bolts to the bearing retaining plate and tighten them evenly to the specified torque.

16 Refit the brake drum and roadwheel, and lower the car to the ground.

4 Differential pinion oil seal – removal and refitting

1   Chock the front wheels and jack up the rear of the car, supporting it on firmly based axle stands.

2   Bend back the locktabs, then undo and remove the nuts and U-bolts securing the propeller shaft universal joint to the pinion flange after marking each part for relocation. Tie up the propeller shaft from a suitable place on the underbody. Do not allow the shaft to hang down; this will place excessive strain on the centre bearing.

3   Using a punch, or small file, accurately mark the relationship of the pinion flange and the locknut to the pinion shaft. This is necessary to

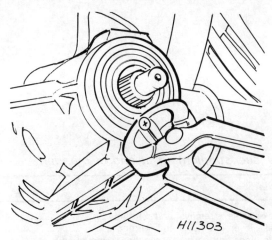

Fig. 8.13 Removal of pinion oil seal (Sec 4)

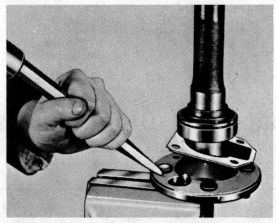

Fig. 8.14 Wheel stud removal using cold chisel (Sec 5)

ensure that the correct preload is maintained on the pinion bearings through the collapsible spacer when the assembly is refitted.

4   Temporarily refit one of the U-bolts to the pinion flange. Using a bar, or stout screwdriver, inserted through the U-bolt to prevent the flange turning, undo and remove the centre locknut.

5   Place a tray, or suitable container, beneath the pinion flange, and, using a small puller or a soft-faced mallet, withdraw the pinion flange from the shaft. As it is not possible to drain the axle casing, a quantity of oil will be released as the flange is withdrawn.

6   The oil seal can now be removed, by drilling a small hole in the flat face of the seal, inserting a self-tapping screw and pulling out the seal with pliers or pincers.

7   Lubricate the lips of a new oil seal with gear oil and place it in position on the axle casing. Using a tube of suitable diameter, tap in the seal until it is flush with the edge of the casing.

8   Refit the pinion flange in its original position, followed by the locknut tightened until the previously made marks are in line. Now tighten the locknut by a further eighth of a turn.

9   Place the propeller shaft in position and secure it with the U-bolts

and nuts. Use new locktabs and tighten the nuts to the specified torque.

10 Refill the axle with the correct grade of oil and lower the car to the ground.

5   Wheel stud – removal and refitting

1   Remove the rear axle halfshaft as described in Section 3.

2   Support the halfshaft in a vice and drill a 13 mm (0.5 in) shallow hole in the head of the stud.

3   Chisel off the head of the stud, then tap out the stud, using a drift of suitable diameter.

4   Tap or press in a new stud, ensuring that the splines on the stud and halfshaft flange are aligned.

5   Working on the outer face of the flange, peen over the base of the stud at three places around its circumference, using a centre punch.

6   Refit the halfshaft to the rear axle, as described in Section 3.

6   Fault diagnosis – rear axle

Symptom	Reason(s)
Vibration	Out of balance propeller shaft Worn halfshaft bearings Loose pinion flange U-bolts Out of balance rear wheels
High pitched whine on drive or overrun	Insufficient lubricant Incorrect crownwheel and pinion mesh Worn gear and differential components generally
'Clunk' on acceleration and deceleration	Incorrect crownwheel and pinion mesh Worn halfshaft or differential splines Loose pinion flange U-bolts Worn drive pinion flange splines Worn propeller shaft universal joint, centre bearing or rubber coupling
Oil leakage	Leaking pinion or halfshaft oil seal or differential cover gasket

Chapter 9 Braking system

For modifications, and information applicable to later models, see Supplement at end of manual

Contents

Specifications

Type .... Disc front, drum rear, dual hydraulic circuit – servo assisted

Brake pedal free travel .... 6 to 9 mm (0.24 to 0.35 in)

Brake fluid type/specification .... Hydraulic fluid to SAE J1703/DOT 3 (Duckhams Universal Brake and
Clutch Fluid)

Master cylinder
Type .... Tandem
Manufacture .... Delco or ATE

Disc brakes
Disc diameter .... 246 mm (9.685 in)
Disc thickness .... 12.7 mm (0.5 in)
Disc run-out .... 0.20 mm (0.0079 in) maximum
Minimum pad thickness (total including backing) .... 7 mm (0.275 in)

Drum brakes
Drum diameter .... 230 mm (9.055 in)
Drum run-out .... 0.1 mm (0.0039 in) maximum

Servo unit
Type .... 203.2 mm (8 in) single diaphragm
Manufacture .... Delco or ATE

Handbrake
Type .... Mechanically operated – acting on rear brake only

Torque wrench settings

	Nm	lbf ft
Caliper retaining bolts	95	70
Disc-to-wheel hub bolts	50	36
Splash shield bolts	4	3
Rear backplate-to-axle bolts	60	44
Master cylinder-to-servo	18	13
Servo-to-mounting bracket	20	15
Servo bracket-to-bulkhead	20	15
Wheel cylinder-to-backplate	8	6
Handbrake lever-to-body	20	15
Bleed screw-to-caliper	4	3
Bleed screw-to-wheel cylinder	9	7

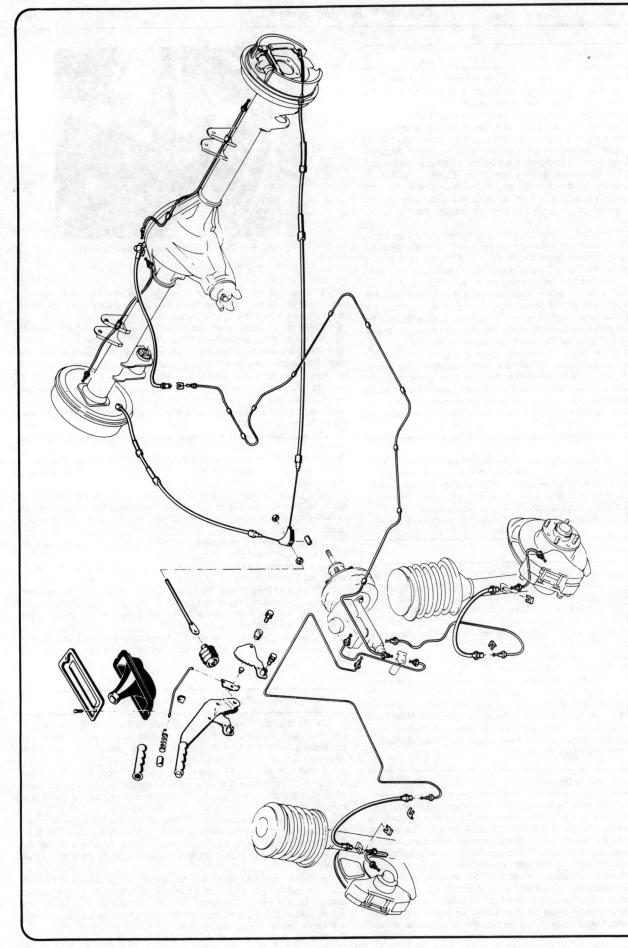

Fig. 9.1 Layout of the braking system hydraulic and mechanical components (Sec 1)

1   General description

Disc brakes are fitted to the front wheels and drum brakes are fitted to the rear. All are operated under servo assistance from the brake pedal, this being connected to the master cylinder and servo assembly, mounted on the engine compartment bulkhead.

The hydraulic system is of the dual line principle, whereby the front disc brake calipers have a separate hydraulic system to that of the rear drum brake wheel cylinders, so that if failure of the hydraulic pipes to the front or rear brakes occurs, half the braking system is still operative. Servo assistance in this condition is still available. A regulating (pressure proportioning) valve is incorporated in the rear brake circuit to restrict hydraulic fluid pressure to the rear brakes. This prevents rear wheel lock-up, due to forward weight transfer under heavy braking.

The front brake disc is secured to the hub flange and the caliper is mounted on the suspension strut, so the disc is able to rotate between the two halves of the caliper. Inside each half of the caliper is a hydraulic cylinder, this being interconnected by a drilling which allows hydraulic fluid pressure to be transmitted to both halves. A piston operates in each cylinder and is in contact with the outer face of the brake pad. By depressing the brake pedal, hydraulic fluid pressure is transmitted to the caliper by a system of metal and flexible hoses. The pistons are thus moved outwards so pushing the pads onto the face of the disc and slowing down the rotational speed of the disc.

The rear drum brakes have one twin piston wheel cylinder operating two brake shoes. When the brake pedal is depressed, hydraulic fluid pressure is transmitted to the rear brake wheel cylinder, via the regulator, by a system of metal and flexible pipes. The pressure moves the pistons outwards, so pushing the shoe linings into contact with the inside circumference of the brake drum, and slowing down its rotational speed.

The handbrake provides an independent mechanical means of rear brake shoe application.

Adjustment of the braking system is provided by an eccentric cam adjuster, operating on each rear brake shoe, periodic adjustment being necessary to compensate for wear on the brake shoe friction linings. The front disc brakes require no adjustment, as the pistons in the brake calipers automatically compensate for brake pad wear. An independent means of handbrake adjustment is provided on the cable.

2   Braking system – adjustment

1   As wear takes place on the friction material of the front disc brake pads and rear drum brake shoes, adjustment will be necessary to reduce the extra brake pedal travel that will result.
2   The front disc brake pads adjust themselves automatically, by moving closer to the disc as wear takes place on the pad linings.
3   The rear brake shoes are individually adjusted, by two eccentric cam adjusters located in each brake backplate. The cam adjusters are operated by turning a hexagon-headed bolt attached to each adjuster, accessible from the rear of the backplate.
4   To adjust the rear brakes, chock the front wheels, jack up the rear of the car and support it on stands. Release the handbrake.
5   Using a suitable spanner, turn the adjuster in the direction of the arrow stamped on the backplate until the wheel is locked. Now back off the adjuster until the wheel is just free to turn without binding.
6   Carry out this operation on the second adjuster, then repeat the procedure for the other rear wheel.

3   Hydraulic system – bleeding

1   Whenever the brake hydraulic system has been dismantled to renew a pipe or hose (or if any other major part has been disconnected in any way), air will be introduced into the pipe system. The system will therefore require 'bleeding' in order to remove this air and restore the effectiveness of the system. The design of the braking system is such that the front and rear hydraulic circuits are entirely separate. Therefore, if a front or rear pipe only has been disconnected, it will only be necessary to bleed that circuit and not the entire system.
2   During the bleeding operation, the level of hydraulic fluid in the master cylinder reservoir must be maintained at least half full, to prevent any further air from entering the system via the reservoir and master cylinder.

Fig. 9.2 Adjusting the rear brakes (Sec 2)

A   Adjuster arrow (visible on most vehicles)

3   Gather together a clean jar, tubing of approximately 300 mm (12 in) in length and of suitable diameter to fit tightly over the bleed screws, and a new tin of the correct hydraulic fluid.
4   Clean all the brake pipes and hoses, and check that all connections are tight and the bleed screws closed.
5   To bleed the front hydraulic circuit, clean the area around the bleed valves on the brake caliper and start on the caliper which is furthest away from the master cylinder.
6   Remove the rubber dust cap from the end of the bleed screw and connect one end of the tubing to the screw. Insert the other end of the tube in the jar containing approximately 25 mm (1 inch) of clean hydraulic fluid.
7   Use a suitable ring spanner and unscrew the bleed screw about half a turn.
8   An assistant should now slowly depress the brake pedal, stopping at the end of its stroke and holding it there while the bleed screw is tightened.
9   The pedal should then be released, the bleed screw opened again and the process repeated until clean hydraulic fluid, free from air bubbles, emerges. *Keep a check of the fluid level in the reservoir during this operation.*
10   When bleeding is complete for the first caliper, fully tighten the bleed screw, and refit the dust cap.
11   The procedure described in paragraphs 6 to 10 should now be repeated for the second front wheel.
12   The rear brakes should be bled in the same manner as the front. It may be necessary to jack up the rear of the car to gain access to the rear bleed screws. If so, be sure it is well supported on stands, with chocks at the front wheels.
13   When bleeding is complete, top-up the level of hydraulic fluid in the master cylinder, using fresh fluid. *Never re-use the old hydraulic fluid.*

4   Front brake pads – removal and refitting

1   Chock the rear wheels, apply the handbrake, jack up the front of the car and support it on firmly based axle stands. Mark the relationship of the wheel to the wheel studs and remove the front wheel.
2   Either Girling or ATE brake calipers are fitted. Both types are similar in construction, the main differences being the type of brake pad retaining pins used to secure the pads in position in the brake caliper.
3   On models fitted with ATE calipers, the retaining pins are removed by tapping them inwards, towards the car, using a thin punch (Fig. 9.4). To remove the retaining pins on Girling calipers, withdraw the spring clips and tap the pins outwards, away from the car, using a thin punch (photos).
4   With the retaining pins removed, lift off the spreader spring plate and then withdraw the brake pads one at a time from the caliper (photo). If they are initially tight, use a screwdriver inserted in the slot on the brake pad and lever against the edge of the caliper. Lift out the anti-rattle shims, if not already removed with the pads.
5   Inspect the thickness of the brake pad friction material. If the total

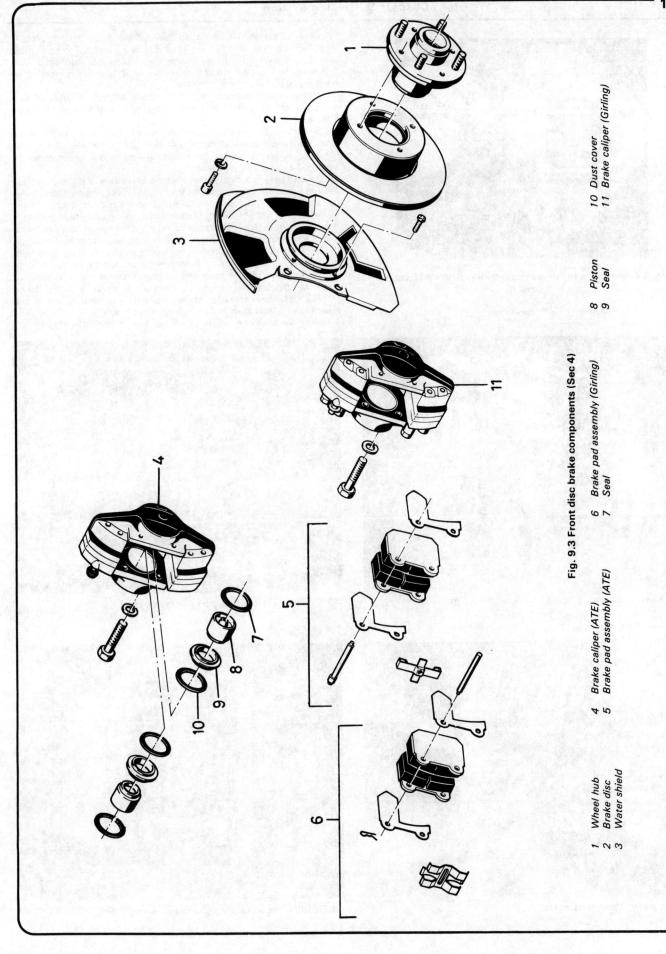

Fig. 9.3 Front disc brake components (Sec 4)

1 Wheel hub
2 Brake disc
3 Water shield

4 Brake caliper (ATE)
5 Brake pad assembly (ATE)

6 Brake pad assembly (Girling)
7 Seal

8 Piston
9 Seal

10 Dust cover
11 Brake caliper (Girling)

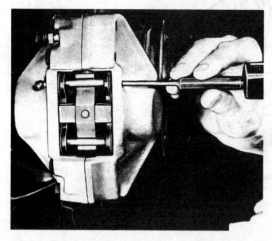

Fig. 9.4 Removing the brake pad retaining pins – ATE caliper (Sec 4)

thickness of the brake pad friction material and metal backing plate is less than 7 mm (0.27 in), the pads must be renewed. The pads must also be renewed if there is any sign of oil or hydraulic fluid contamination of the friction material, or if any heavy scoring or cracking is visible on the pad face.

6   When renewing brake pads, they should always be renewed as a complete set (4 pads); uneven braking or pulling to one side may otherwise occur.

7   With the pads removed, carefully inspect the surface of the brake disc. Concentric scores up to 0.4 mm (0.015 in) are acceptable; however, if deeper scores are found, the brake disc must either be skimmed or preferably renewed.

8   To refit the pads, first ensure that the brake caliper pistons and pad seating areas are clean and free from dust and corrosion. Using a flat bar as a lever, gently push the caliper pistons back into their cylinders as far as they will go. This operation will cause a quantity of hydraulic fluid to be returned to the master cylinder via the hydraulic pipes. Place absorbent rags around the master cylinder reservoir to collect any fluid that may overflow, or preferably, drain off a small quantity of fluid from the master cylinder reservoir before retracting the caliper pistons.

9   Fit the new friction pads and anti-rattle shims with the notch or arrow on the shims pointing downwards, ie away from the bleed nipple. Place the spreader spring plate in position and refit the retaining pins and spring clips, where fitted (photo).

10 With the brake pads correctly fitted, fully depress the brake pedal

4.3a Remove the spring clips from the retaining pins ...

4.3b ... then withdraw the pins (Girling calipers)

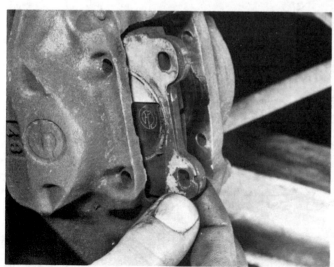

4.4 Removing the brake pads

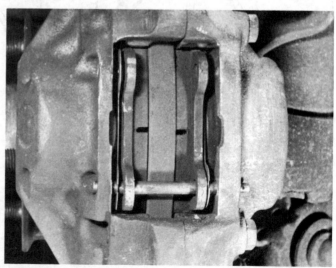

4.9 Refitting the brake pads, shims and retaining pins

several times to bring the caliper pistons into contact with the friction pads.

11 Check the hydraulic fluid level in the brake master cylinder reservoir, and top-up if necessary.

12 Refit the roadwheel in the original position and lower the car to the ground.

13 New brake pads should be bedded in slowly, over a period of 120 miles (200 km). During this time, avoid unnecessary panic stops or prolonged heavy brake applications.

5 Front disc brake caliper – removal and refitting

1 Chock the rear wheels, apply the handbrake, jack up the front of the car and support it on firmly based axle stands. Mark the relationship of the wheel to the wheel studs and remove the front wheel.

2 Remove the front brake pads, as described in Section 4, and store them in a safe place, face up, to avoid contamination of the friction material.

3 Wipe clean the area around the brake pipe-to-flexible hose union on the suspension strut. Using two spanners, undo and remove the brake pipe union nut from the hose and carefully withdraw the pipe. To prevent hydraulic fluid loss, clamp the flexible hose using a proprietary brake hose clamp. If a clamp is not available, a tapered wooden plug inserted in the end of the hose is satisfactory.

4 Undo and remove the two bolts securing the caliper to the suspension strut, then lift off the caliper over the brake disc.

5 To refit the caliper, place it in position over the disc and line up the two bolt holes. Refit the securing bolts and tighten them to the torque setting given in the Specifications.

6 Reconnect the brake pipe union nut to the flexible hose, taking care not to cross-thread the nut during the initial turns.

7 Refit the front brake pads, as described in Section 4.

8 Bleed the front brakes, as described in Section 3. Providing precautions were taken to avoid hydraulic fluid loss, it should only be necessary to bleed the brake caliper that was removed.

9 Refit the roadwheel in its original position and lower the car to the ground.

6 Front brake disc – removal and refitting

1 Chock the rear wheels, apply the handbrake, jack up the front of the car and support it on firmly based axle stands. Mark the relationship of the wheel to the wheel studs and remove the front wheel.

2 Using a pair of pliers, withdraw the lower retainer plate that secures the flexible hose and pipe to the bracket on the suspension strut (photo).

3 Undo and remove the two brake caliper-to-suspension-strut securing bolts, and carefully lift off the brake caliper (complete with pads) over the brake disc. At the same time, slide the flexible hose out of its mounting bracket on the suspension strut and tie the complete caliper assembly out of the way, using a length of wire attached to a spring coil and caliper bolt hole. By removing the brake caliper in this way, the hydraulic system is kept closed. It will not therefore be necessary to bleed the system when the caliper is refitted.

4 By judicious tapping and levering, remove the grease cap from the centre of the hub.

5 Withdraw the split pin, then undo and remove the hub and nut and thrust washer.

6 The front hub and brake disc can now be withdrawn, taking care to hold the outer wheel bearing inner race in position as the hub assembly is lifted off the stub axle.

7 To separate the brake disc from the wheel hub, special tool No KM-322 (M10, twelve-splined wrench) will be required, to remove the hub-to-disc securing bolts. With the bolts removed, the brake disc can be withdrawn from the rear of the wheel hub.

8 Carefully inspect the surface of the disc. Concentric scores up to 0.4 mm (0.015 in) are acceptable. Also, minute surface cracks due to localised surface heating are to be expected. However, if the disc is severely grooved (or if larger cracks are evident), the disc must be renewed. **Note**: *In order to maintain uniform braking, both front discs must exhibit the same surface characteristics with respect to depth of grooving and surface finish. For this reason, front disc brakes should*

6.2 Removing the brake hose retaining plate

Fig. 9.5 Location of the two caliper retaining bolts and brake hose securing clip (Sec 6)

always be renewed in pairs.

9 Refitting the brake disc is the reverse sequence to removal, bearing in mind the following points:

(a) *When refitting the brake disc to the hub, ensure that the mating faces are perfectly clean and free from corrosion. Tighten the securing bolts to the torque setting given in the Specifications*

(b) *Adjust the front wheel bearings to give the correct hub endfloat, as described in Chapter 11*

(c) *With the front wheel bearings correctly adjusted, check the brake disc run-out using a dial indicator, or feeler gauges inserted between the edge of the caliper and the disc surface, while slowly rotating the disc. Compare the figures obtained with those given in the Specifications. Excess run-out can lead to brake and steering judder, and is caused by wear or distortion of the disc, hub, or disc-to-hub mating face*

7 Front disc brake caliper – overhaul

1 Remove the brake caliper, as described in Section 5.

2 Withdraw the circlip and protective rubber dust cover fitted over the ends of the pistons and edges of the caliper.

3 Place a thin, flat block of wood over one piston and hold the block

and piston in place, using a small G-clamp.

4   The unclamped piston may now be forced out of the caliper, using a compressed air jet or the nozzle of a car foot pump held firmly against the metal hydraulic pipe attached to the caliper.

5   With the first piston removed, use the block of wood and the G-clamp to seal off the cylinder opening on the caliper, and repeat the above procedure to remove the remaining piston.

6   Thoroughly clean the caliper and pistons, using clean hydraulic fluid or methylated spirit. *Under no circumstances should the two halves of the caliper be separated.*

7   With all components thoroughly cleaned, the two caliper seals can be removed using a thin blunt instrument such as a plastic knitting needle.

8   Inspect the dismantled components carefully for corrosion, scratches or wear. New seals are available in the form of a brake caliper repair kit, and should be renewed as a matter of course. If severe corrosion, scoring, or wear is apparent on the pistons or caliper cylinders, the complete caliper will have to be renewed, as these parts are not available separately.

9   Immerse the caliper cylinder seals in clean hydraulic fluid and carefully fit them to the annular groove in the cylinder, using the fingers only.

10   Liberally coat the pistons with clean hydraulic fluid, and place them in position in the cylinder bore with the machined flat toward the bleed nipple. Ensure the pistons are inserted squarely without binding, and the seal does not become dislodged. Do not push the pistons fully into their cylinders at this stage.

11   Fit the protective rubber dust covers to the pistons, ensuring that they are correctly seated in the piston and caliper grooves.

12   Place one of the brake pad anti-rattle shims in position over the piston, with the notch on the edge of the shim away from the bleed nipple. The shim should locate squarely over the machined recess in the piston (photo). If necessary, rotate the piston slightly. Check both pistons in this way.

13   Push the pistons fully into their bores and refit the rubber dust cover retaining circlips.

14   The caliper may now be refitted to the car, as described in Section 5.

8   Rear brake drums and shoes – removal, inspection and refitting

1   Chock the front wheels, jack up the rear of the car and support it on firmly based axle stands. Mark the relationship of the wheel to the wheel studs and remove the rear wheel.

2   Mark the relationship of the brake drum to the axle flange, and remove the drum securing clip (where fitted) from the wheel stud.

3   Back off the two brake shoe adjusters from the rear of the backplate, until the shoes offer no resistance to the drum. The brake drum can now be withdrawn (photo). If it is initially tight, tap its circumference, using a soft-faced mallet.

4   Before dismantling the brake shoes, observe the components in their assembled condition. Make a note of the location of the pull-off springs and handbrake linkage, noting also which way round the various parts are fitted. Check for any hydraulic fluid leaks from the wheel cylinder or oil leaks from the halfshaft oil seal. Have an assistant

7.12 Anti-rattle shim locating recess in caliper piston

slowly depress the brake pedal, and observe the action of the wheel cylinder pistons. See that they are both free to operate and that they return under the action of the brake shoe pull-off springs when the pedal is released. The condition of the brake shoe friction linings and drum can also be inspected at this time. If the friction linings are less than 1.5 mm (0.06 in) above the rivet heads, or if there is any sign of oil or grease contamination, they must be renewed. Always renew brake shoes in complete axle sets (four shoes), even if only one shoe is worn; uneven braking and imbalance may otherwise occur.

5   To remove the brake shoes, begin by removing the shoe retaining springs in the centre of each brake shoe. Use a pair of pliers to release the spring retainers, rotating them through 90°. Lift away the springs, retainers, and washers from each brake shoe web (photo).

6   The handbrake cable can now be detached by moving the operating lever, secured to the rear brake shoe, towards the wheel hub and disconnecting the end of the cable from the hooked end of the lever (photo).

7   Using a small screwdriver, ease the coil of the lower brake shoe return spring out from under the lip of the bottom brake shoe pivot post (photo).

8   Using a sturdy screwdriver, or flat bar if necessary, lift the bottom of each brake shoe off the lower pivot post. This will relieve the tension on the lower return spring and allow it to be removed from the two brake shoes (photo).

9   Carefully manipulate the top of each brake shoe from its location in the wheel cylinder piston (photo). Lift off the two shoes, complete with the top pull-off spring and the forked handbrake relay lever (photo).

10   With the shoes removed from the backplate extract the top pull-off spring and relay lever (photo).

11   Thoroughly clean all traces of dust from the brake shoes, backplate

8.3 Removing the rear brake drum

8.5 Removing the brake shoe retaining springs

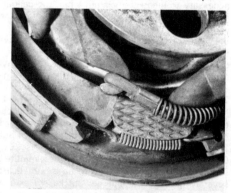

8.6 Detaching the handbrake cable from the rear brake shoe operating lever

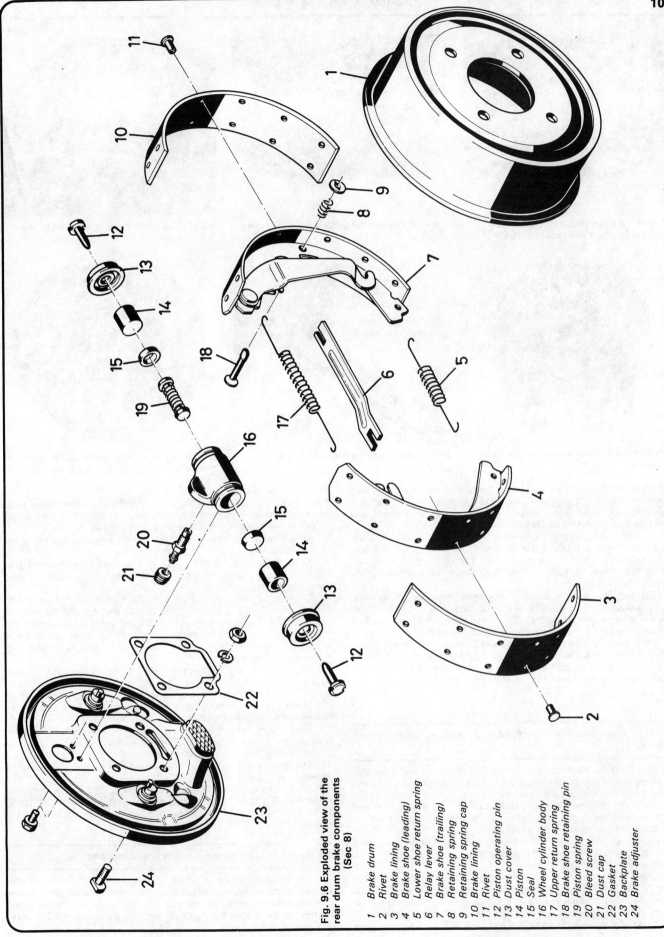

Fig. 9.6 Exploded view of the rear drum brake components (Sec 8)

1   Brake drum
2   Rivet
3   Brake lining
4   Brake shoe (leading)
5   Lower shoe return spring
6   Relay lever
7   Brake shoe (trailing)
8   Retaining spring
9   Retaining spring cap
10 Brake lining
11 Rivet
12 Piston operating pin
13 Dust cover
14 Piston
15 Seal
16 Wheel cylinder body
17 Upper return spring
18 Brake shoe retaining pin
19 Piston spring
20 Bleed screw
21 Dust cap
22 Gasket
23 Backplate
24 Brake adjuster

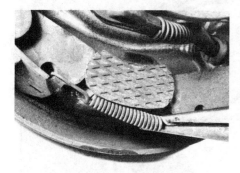

8.7 Ease the lower return spring out from under the lip of the pivot post ...

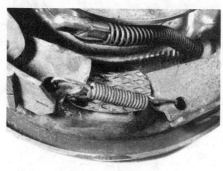

8.8 ... then lever the brake shoe off the pivot post

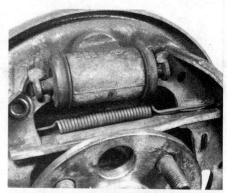

8.9a Manipulate the top of each brake shoe from the wheel cylinder piston pins

8.9b Removing the brake shoes from the backplate

8.10 Removing the top pull-off spring and relay lever

8.13 Smear high melting point brake grease to these areas before refitting the brake shoes

and drum, using a cloth and stiff brush. Ensure the working area is well ventilated during this operation; asbestos dust is harmful and should not be inhaled. Brake dust is the prime cause of judder and squeal, and therefore it is important to clean away all traces.

12 Check that the brake backplate, wheel cylinder and pivot post are secure and that the two brake adjusters are free to turn. If any hydraulic fluid or oil leaks are apparent (or if any defects were noticed during the initial inspection), they should now be rectified before refitting the brake shoes.

13 Refitting the brake shoes is the reverse sequence to removal. Smear a trace of brake grease to the brake shoe pivot posts and wheel cylinder piston locations before fitting the shoes (photo). *Do not allow grease to come into contact with the friction material.*

14 With the back shoes reassembled and the drum in position, pump the brake pedal once or twice to centralise the shoes, then adjust the rear brakes, as described in Section 2. Refit the roadwheel in its original position and lower the car to the ground.

9 Rear drum brake wheel cylinders – removal, overhaul and refitting

1 Chock the front wheels, jack up the rear of the car and support it on firmly based axle stands. Mark the relationship of the wheel to the wheel studs and remove the rear wheel.

2 Mark the relationship of the brake drum to the axle flange, and remove the brake drum securing spring clip from the wheel stud.

3 Back off the two brake shoe adjusters from the rear of the backplate until the shoes offer no resistance to the drum. The brake drum can now be withdrawn. If it is initially tight, tap its circumference using a soft-faced mallet.

4 Using a proprietary brake hose clamp, clamp the flexible brake hose just in front of the rear axle. This will prevent hydraulic fluid loss when the brake pipe union on the wheel cylinder is undone. If a hose clamp is not available, plug the end of the pipe when it is removed.

5 Undo and remove the union nut and carefully withdraw the brake

pipe from the rear of the wheel cylinder.

6 Turn the two brake shoe adjusters until the shoes are moved as far as possible away from the wheel cylinder. This will allow the cylinder to be removed without disturbing the brake shoes.

7 Undo and remove the two wheel cylinder retaining bolts from the rear of the backplate, and lift off the cylinder.

8 With the cylinder removed and laid out on a clean uncluttered working area, proceed by removing the rubber dust covers, pistons, piston seals and spring.

9 Thoroughly clean all the parts in clean hydraulic fluid or methylated spirit. Carefully examine the pistons and cylinder for wear or scoring, and if evident, renew the complete wheel cylinder. If the components are in a satisfactory condition, a new set of seals, available in the form of a wheel cylinder repair kit, must be obtained. *Never re-use old seals.*

10 Begin reassembly by thoroughly lubricating all the parts in clean hydraulic fluid. Place the spring in position in the centre of the cylinder bore, then insert the two cup seals (one on each side of the spring), with their larger diameter or lip toward the spring. Make sure the lip enters the bore cleanly and does not tuck over.

11 Next, insert the two pistons (one either side) with their flat sides toward the spring. Finally, place the two dust covers in position, ensuring they contact the collar on the outside of the cylinder body.

12 The wheel cylinder may now be refitted to the backplate, using the reverse sequence to removal.

13 When reassembly is complete, bleed the rear brakes, as described in Section 3, and adjust the brake shoes, as described in Section 2. Refit the roadwheel in its original position and lower the car to the ground.

10 Rear brake backplate – removal and refitting

1 The brake backplate retaining bolts also retain the axle halfshaft and halfshaft bearing in position. Both these components must first be removed before the backplate can be withdrawn. The removal and refitting procedure for the halfshaft and bearing is described in detail in Chapter 8, Section 3.

2   With the halfshaft removed, the brake shoes and hydraulic wheel cylinder can now be removed from the backplate by referring to Sections 8 and 9 respectively of this Chapter.

3   Before lifting the backplate off the axle casing, extract the handbrake cable locking clip securing the cable to the front face of the backplate and withdraw the cable toward the centre of the car.

4   The backplate can now be removed from the axle casing.

5   Refitting the backplate is the reverse sequence to removal, bearing in mind the following points:

(a) *Use a new gasket between the backplate and axle casing, lightly coated with gasket cement*

(b) *When reassembly is complete, bleed the rear brakes as described in Section 3, then adjust the brake shoes as described in Section 2*

11 Handbrake cable – adjustment

1   Chock the front wheels, jack up the rear of the car and support it on firmly based axle stands. Release the handbrake.

2   Before carrying out any adjustment of the handbrake cable, ensure the brake shoes are correctly adjusted, as described in Section 2, and the handbrake cable is firmly supported in the guides on the rear suspension arms and underbody. Check also that the handbrake linkage operates correctly, by pulling down on the cable just behind the compensating yoke while an assistant turns the rear wheels. Each wheel should lock when the cable is pulled down, and be free to turn when it is released. If this is not the case, investigate the cause of any problems noticed, before proceeding with the cable adjustment.

3   With the cable and linkage correctly adjusted, the rear brakes should just begin to take effect with the handbrake lever pulled up to the third notch on the ratchet.

4   To adjust the cable, set the handbrake lever to the third notch, and working beneath the car, slacken the two locknuts securing the threaded relay rod to the compensation yoke (photo). By adjusting the position of the locknuts, the yoke is moved forward or backward along the relay rod, thus increasing or decreasing the tension in the cable. Adjust the yoke so the brake shoes are just dragging on the drums, then tighten the locknuts.

5   Operate the handbrake lever and check that the wheels lock on full application, and do not bind when the handbrake is released.

12 Handbrake cable – removal and refitting

1   Chock the front wheels, jack up the rear of the car and support it on firmly based axle stands. Mark the relationship of the rear wheels to the wheel studs and remove both rear wheels.

2   Remove both rear brake drums, as described in Section 8.

3   Detach the handbrake cable from the brake shoes, by moving the operating lever on the rear shoes toward the wheel hub and withdrawing the cable from the hooked end.

4   Prise off the retaining spring clip securing the cable to each brake backplate, and withdraw the cable from the rear of the backplates.

5   Undo and remove the locknut securing the compensating yoke to the threaded relay rod, then slide the yoke off the rod.

6   Detach the outer cable from its mounting points on the rear suspension lower arms and underbody, then remove the cable from beneath the car.

7   Refitting the cable is the reverse sequence to removal.

8   With the cable in position and the brake drums and roadwheels refitted, adjust the cable as described in Section 11.

13 Handbrake lever – removal and refitting

1   Chock the front wheels, jack up the rear of the car and support it on firmly based axle stands.

2   From underneath the car, undo and remove the two locknuts securing the handbrake cable compensating yoke to the relay rod. Slide off the compensating yoke and the rubber boot from the relay rod.

3   Refer to Chapter 12 and remove the left-hand front seat and the centre console, if a full length console is fitted.

4   Undo and remove the screws securing the left-hand door sill trim

11.4 Handbrake cable adjusting nuts and compensating yoke

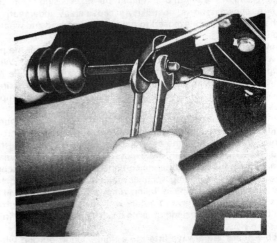

Fig. 9.7 Adjusting the handbrake cable (Sec 11)

Fig. 9.8 Disconnecting the handbrake cable from the brake shoe operating lever (Sec 12)

strip, and lift off the trim.

5   Undo and remove the two securing screws and lift off the handbrake lever trim plate, if fitted.

6   Fold back the carpet sufficiently to gain access to the two handbrake lever retaining bolts on the left-hand side of the transmission tunnel. Remove the bolts.

7   Withdrw the handbrake lever out of its mounting slightly, and remove the single bolt retaining the handbrake warning light switch to the lever. Lift off the switch and withdraw the handbrake completely from its location in the transmission tunnel.

8   Refitting the handbrake lever is the reverse sequence to removal. With the lever fitted, adjust the handbrake cable as described in Section 11.

14 Hydraulic pipes and hoses – inspection, removal and refitting

1   The rigid metal brake pipes and the three flexible brake hoses, their connections, unions and mountings should periodically be carefully examined.

2   Examine first all the unions for signs of leaks. Then look at the flexible hoses for signs of fraying and chafing (as well as for leaks). This is only a preliminary inspection of the flexible hoses, as exterior condition does not necessarily indicate interior condition which will be considered later.

3   The steel pipes must be examined equally carefully. They must be thoroughly cleaned and examined for signs of dents or other percussive damage, rust and corrosion. Rust and corrosion should be scraped off, and, if the depth of pitting in the pipes is significant, they will require renewal. This is most likely in those areas underneath the body where the pipes are exposed to the full force of road and weather conditions (photos).

4   If any section of pipe is to be removed, plug or tape over the pipe unions when they are undone, to minimise hydraulic fluid loss. When removing a pipe which is 'downstream' from a flexible hose (ie rear axle or front caliper brake pipes) the hose may be compressed using a brake hose clamp. This will eliminate hydraulic fluid loss and simplify bleeding when the pipe is refitted.

5   Rigid pipe removal is usually quite straightforward. The unions at each end are undone and the pipe drawn out of the connection. The clips which may hold it to the car body are bent back and it is then removed. Underneath the car, the exposed union can be particularly stubborn, defying the efforts of an open-ended spanner. As few people will have the special split ring spanner required, a self-grip wrench is the only answer. If the pipe is being renewed, new unions will be provided. If not, one will have to put up with the possibility of burring over the flats on the unions and of using a self-grip wrench for refitting also.

6   Flexible hoses are always fitted to a rigid support bracket where they join a rigid pipe. The rigid pipe unions must first be removed from the flexible union, which is then detached from its support bracket, by withdrawing the locking plate with a pair of pliers.

7   Once the flexible hose is removed, examine the internal bore. If clear of fluid, it should be possible to see through it. Any specks of rubber which come out, or signs of restriction in the bore, mean that the inner lining is breaking up and the hose must be renewed.

8   Rigid pipes which need renewing can usually be purchased from your local dealer where they have the pipe, unions and special tools to make them up. All they need to know is the pipe length required and the type of flare used at the ends of the pipe. These may be different at each end of the same pipe. If possible, it is a good idea to take the old pipe along as a pattern.

9   Refitting of pipes is a straightforward reversal of the removal procedure. It is best to get all the sets (bends) made prior to refitting. Also, any acute bends should be put in by the garage on a bending machine otherwise there is the possibility of kinking them, and restricting the bore area, and thus, fluid flow.

10   With the pipes refitted, the braking system must be bled as described in Section 3.

15 Master cylinder – removal and refitting

1   Either a Delco or ATE master cylinder may be fitted to models covered by this manual. Both are of the twin system, 'tandem type' and are similar in construction and external appearance. The easiest way to identify the type of cylinder is by the location of the fluid

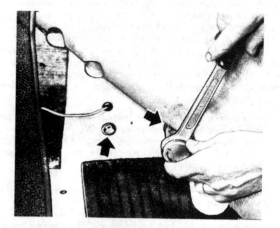

Fig. 9.9 Location of handbrake lever retaining bolts (Sec 13)

14.3a Hydraulic pipe to hose rear connector

14.3b Hydraulic pipe rear three-way union on axle

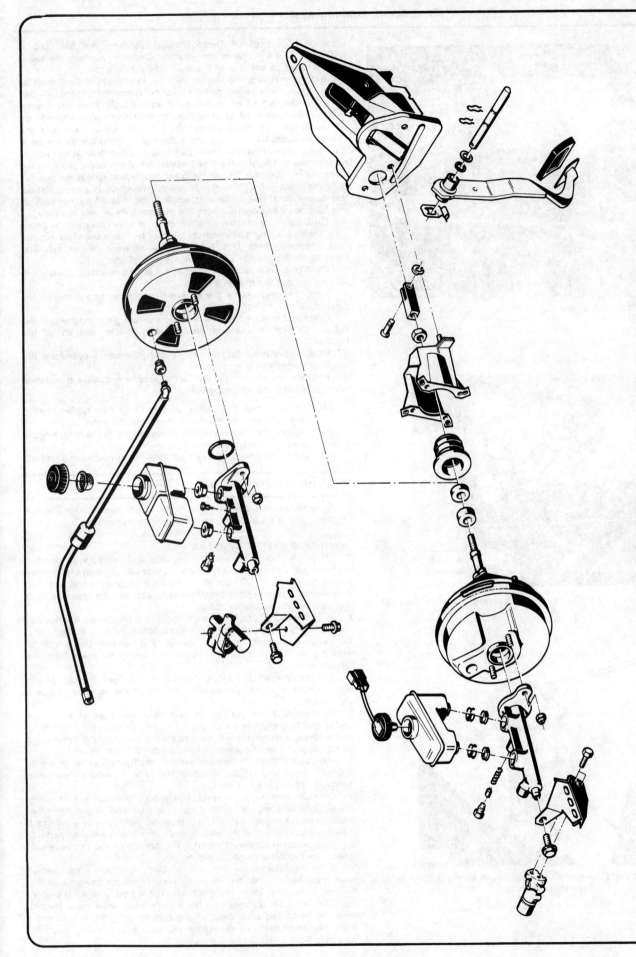

Fig. 9.10 The master cylinder, vacuum servo unit and pedal components (Sec 15)

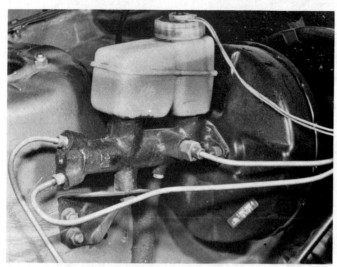

15.1 ATE master cylinder and fluid reservoir

Fig. 9.11 Removing the Delco master cylinder reservoir (Sec 15)

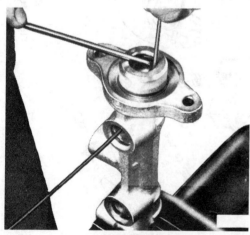

Fig. 9.12 Removing the rear piston lockring from the Delco master cylinder (Sec 16)

reservoir filler cap: on Delco master cylinders, the filler cap is positioned in the centre of the reservoir. On ATE cylinders, the cap is located towards the rear of the fluid reservoir (photo).

2   Before removing the master cylinder, the hydraulic fluid must be drained from the reservoir and the reservoir removed from the cylinder.

3   With the aid of an assistant, drain the fluid from the master cylinder reservoir and master cylinder, by attaching a plastic bleed tube to one of the front brake caliper bleed nipples. Undo the nipple one turn, then pump the fluid out into a clean glass container by means of the brake pedal. Hold the brake pedal against the floor at the end of each stroke and tighten the bleed nipple. When the pedal has returned to its normal position, loosen the bleed nipple and repeat the process until the front half of the master cylinder reservoir is empty. Repeat this operation at one of the rear wheel cylinder bleed nipples until all the fluid has been drained from the master cylinder and reservoir.

4   On Delco type master cylinders, press the two reservoir retaining clips inwards, using a screwdriver inserted between the reservoir and master cylinder body (Fig. 9.11); tip the reservoir to one side and carefully lift it upwards and off the master cylinder.

5   On ATE type master cylinders, firmly lift the reservoir upwards to remove it from the master cylinder.

6   Undo and remove the three brake pipe unions, then withdraw the pipes from the master cylinder.

7   Undo and remove the nuts and bolts securing the master cylinder support bracket to the body and master cylinder, and lift off the bracket.

8   Undo and remove the two nuts securing the master cylinder to the servo and withdraw the cylinder.

9   Refitting the master cylinder is the reverse sequence to removal bearing in mind the following points:

  (a) *On ATE master cylinders, always use a new rubber sealing ring between the master cylinder and the servo unit*
  (b) *Tighten the master cylinder securing nuts to the torque figure given in the Specifications*
  (c) *Bleed the complete braking system, as described in Section 3*

16 Master cylinder – overhaul

1   Remove the master cylinder from the car, as described in Section 15, and place it on a clean, uncluttered working surface.

Delco type master cylinders

2   Mount the cylinder in a soft-jawed vice, and using a well rounded bar or tube of suitable diameter, push the rear piston down the cylinder bore approximately 100 mm (4 in). Retain the piston in this position, by inserting a blunt-ended length of stiff wire into the reservoir inlet port nearest the mounting flange.

3   With the rear piston held down, use two screwdrivers to prise out the locking ring from the internal groove in the cylinder body.

4   Release the tension on the piston and remove the length of retaining wire. Lift out the rear piston and spring assembly from the cylinder bore.

5   Tap the cylinder on a block of wood, and retrieve the front piston as it emerges from the cylinder bore. Recover the seals, spring support and spring.

6   To dismantle the rear piston assembly, use a small socket or similar tool to compress the spring sufficiently to expose the retaining circlip. Using a small screwdriver, extract the circlip and withdraw the spring support sleeve, spring and seals from the rear piston.

7   Thoroughly clean all components in methylated spirit or clean hydraulic fluid, and lay them out in the order in which they were removed, ready for inspection.

8   Carefully examine the internal cylinder bore and pistons for scoring or wear, and all components for damage or distortion. In order that the seals may adequately maintain hydraulic fluid pressure without leakage, the condition of the pistons and cylinder bore must be perfect. If in any doubt whatsoever about the condition of the components, renew the complete master cylinder.

9   If the master cylinder is in a satisfactory condition, a new set of seals must be obtained before reassembly. These are available in the form of a master cylinder repair kit, obtainable from your local dealer.

10   To reassemble the master cylinder, note which way round the old seals are fitted and slide them off the pistons using the fingers only. Refit the new seals in the same manner, after coating them in hydraulic fluid.

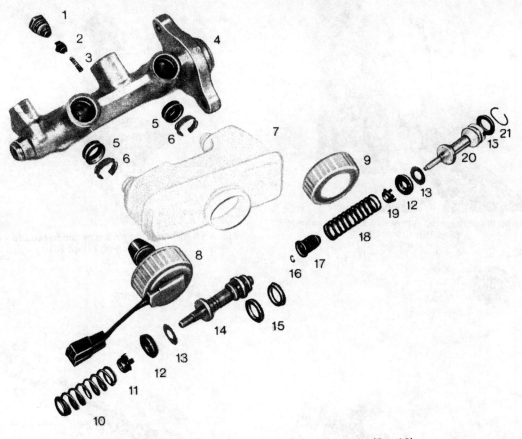

Fig. 9.13 Exploded view of the Delco master cylinder (Sec 16)

1 Pre-pressure valve housing	7 Brake fluid reservoir	12 Primary cup	17 Spring support sleeve
2 Pre-pressure valve	8 Cap with monitor unit	13 Fill disk	18 Rear piston spring
3 Spring	9 Cap without monitor unit	14 Front piston	19 Support ring
4 Master cylinder housing	10 Front piston spring	15 Secondary cups	20 Rear piston
5 Reservoir seals	11 Spring support	16 Lockring	21 Lockring
6 Retaining clips			

11 Compress the spring on the rear piston, using a small socket, then secure the spring and support sleeve in position, using a new retaining circlip.

12 Thoroughly lubricate the two piston assemblies and the master cylinder bore in clean hydraulic fluid. Slide the front piston spring and spring support into the cylinder bore, followed by the front piston assembly.

13 Insert the rear piston assembly into the cylinder bore. Push the piston down the bore and temporarily retain it in place, using the rounded bar and stiff wire, as described in the dismantling sequence.

14 Fit a new piston retaining circlip into the groove in the cylinder bore, ensuring that it is squarely seated.

15 Release the tension on the piston and remove the length of retaining wire.

16 The master cylinder may now be refitted to the car.

ATE type master cylinders

17 Mount the cylinder in a soft-jawed vice and, using a pair of circlip pliers, remove the piston retaining circlip from the groove in the cylinder bore. Apply gentle downward pressure to the exposed piston pushrod to relieve spring tension on the circlip during removal.

18 Withdraw the rear piston assembly from the cylinder, ensuring that the piston stop rings do not catch in the circlip groove as the piston assembly is lifted out.

19 Using a well rounded bar or tube of suitable diameter, apply downward pressure to the front piston. At the same time, undo and remove the piston stop screw from the cylinder bore.

20 Tap the master cylinder on a block of wood until the front piston emerges from the cylinder bore. Withdraw the piston completely and

recover the spring, spring support and seals.

21 Unscrew the small retaining screw securing the spring to the rear piston, supporting the spring at the same time to prevent it flying off as the screw is undone. Withdraw the spring, spring retainer and support ring.

22 Thoroughly clean all components in methylated spirit or clean

Fig. 9.14 Removing the rear piston pushrod from the ATE master cylinder (Sec 16)

Fig. 9.15 Removing the piston stop screw – ATE master cylinder
(Sec 16)

Fig. 9.16 Removing the front piston assembly – ATE master
cylinder (Sec 16)

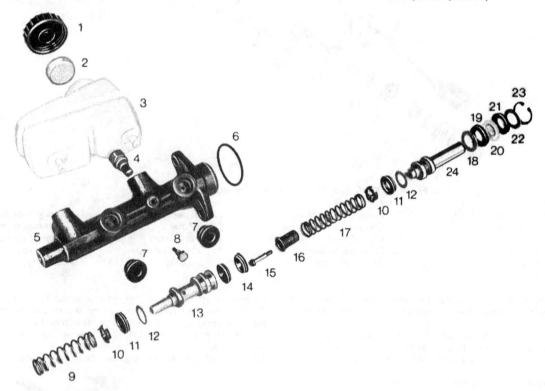

Fig. 9.17 Exploded view of the ATE master cylinder (Sec 16)

1	Cap for reservoir	7	Reservoir plugs	13	Intermediate piston	19	Secondary cup
2	Screen	8	Stop screw	14	Separator cup	20	Intermediate ring
3	Fluid reservoir	9	Pressure spring	15	Restraint screw	21	Vacuum cup
4	Pre-pressure valve	10	Support ring	16	Spring sleeve	22	Stop ring
5	Master cylinder housing	11	Primary cup	17	Pressure spring	23	Lockring
6	O-ring	12	Fill disk	18	Bearing ring	24	Pushrod

hydraulic fluid, and lay them out in the order in which they were
removed, ready for inspection.

23 Carefully, examine the internal cylinder bore and pistons for
scoring or wear, and all components for damage or distortion. In order
that the seals may adequately maintain hydraulic fluid pressure
without leakage, the condition of the pistons and cylinder bore must be
perfect. If in any doubt whatsoever about the condition of the
components, renew the complete master cylinder.

24 If the master cylinder is in a satisfactory condition, a new set of
seals must be obtained before reassembly. These are available in the

form of a master cylinder repair kit, obtainable from your local dealer.

25 To reassemble the master cylinder, note which way round the old
seals and spacers are fitted, then slide them off the pistons, using the
fingers only. Thoroughly lubricate the new seals in clean hydraulic fluid
and refit them in the same manner.

26 Compress the spring on the rear piston and secure the spring and
spring sleeve with the small retaining screw.

27 Coat the piston assemblies and cylinder bore with clean hydraulic
fluid. Insert the front spring and spring support into the cylinder,
followed by the front piston assembly.

28 Apply downward pressure to the front piston, using a drift of suitable diameter, and refit the piston stop screw to the cylinder body.
29 Refit the rear piston assembly, spring end first, into the cylinder bore. Apply downward pressure to the piston pushrod and insert the retaining circlip into its groove in the cylinder. Ensure that the circlip is squarely seated in the groove.
30 The master cylinder may now be refitted to the car.

17 Brake servo unit – general description, maintenance and adjustment

A vacuum servo unit is fitted into the brake hydraulic circuit in series with the master cylinder, to provide power assistance to the driver when the brake pedal is depressed. The unit operates by vacuum obtained from the induction manifold and comprises, basically, a booster diaphragm and a non-return valve.

The servo unit and hydraulic master cylinder are connected together so that the servo unit piston rod acts as the master cylinder pushrod. The driver's braking effort is transmitted through another pushrod to the servo unit piston and its built-in control system. The servo unit piston does not fit tightly into the cylinder, but has a strong diaphragm to keep its edges in constant contact with the cylinder wall so ensuring an air tight seal between the two parts. The forward chamber is held under vacuum conditions created in the inlet manifold of the engine and, during periods when the brake pedal is not in use, the controls open a passage to the rear chamber, so placing it under vacuum. When the brake pedal is depressed, the vacuum passage to the rear chamber is cut off and the chamber opened to atmospheric pressure. The consequent rush of air pushes the servo piston forward in the vacuum chamber and operates the main pushrod to the master cylinder. The controls are designed so that assistance is given under all conditions and, when the brakes are not required, vacuum in the rear chamber is established when the brake pedal is released. Air from the atmosphere entering the rear chamber is passed through a small air filter.

Maintenance and adjustments

1 The brake servo unit operation can be checked easily without any special tools. Proceed as follows:
2 Stop the engine and clear the servo of any vacuum by depressing the brake pedal several times.
3 Once the servo is cleared, keep the brake pedal depressed and start the engine. If the servo unit is in proper working order, the brake pedal should move further downwards, under even foot pressure, due to the effect of the inlet manifold vacuum on the servo diaphragms.
4 If the brake pedal does not move further downwards, the servo system is not operating properly, and the vacuum hoses from the inlet manifold to the servo should be inspected. The vacuum control valve should also be checked. This valve is in the vacuum hose to prevent air flowing into the vacuum side of the servo from the inlet manifold when the engine stops. It is in effect a one way valve.
5 If the brake servo operates properly in the test, but still gives less

effective service on the road, the air filter through which air flows into the servo should be inspected. A dirty filter will limit the formation of a difference in pressure across the servo diaphragm.
6 The servo unit itself cannot be repaired and therefore a complete replacement is necessary if the measures described are not effective.
7 *Air filter refitment:* From inside the car, detach the brake pedal from the servo pushrod, then remove the rubber boot over the pushrod housing and air filter.
8 Once the boot has been removed, extract the filter, silencer and retainer from the servo housing bore.
9 Refitting follows the reversal of the removal procedure. The retainer can be driven into position with a light soft-faced hammer. The slots in the filter and silencer should be spaced by 180 degrees.
10 *Vacuum control valve:* The valve is located in the vacuum hose to prevent air flowing into the servo when the engine stops. It is not repairable and therefore when defective must be renewed.
11 The valve should be located near to the inlet manifold union and the arrows on the valve casing should point towards the inlet manifold. Make sure all the hose clips are properly located and tightened: the system must be airtight.

18 Brake servo unit – removal and refitting

1 Remove the master cylinder, as described in Section 15.
2 Disconnect the vacuum hose from the servo unit.
3 Detach the five plastic buttons securing the kick-panel under the dash and lift out the panel.
4 Detach the servo unit pushrod from the brake pedal.
5 Disconnect the brake pedal return spring from the mounting stud retainer. Then remove the retainer and the stud.
6 Undo and remove the nuts securing the servo unit mounting bracket to the bulkhead and lift out the servo unit (complete with bracket) from the engine compartment.
7 Now undo and remove the four nuts, and separate the servo unit from its mounting bracket.
8 Refitting the servo follows the reverse sequence to removal, but adjust the pedal free play, as described in Section 19.

19 Brake and clutch pedals – removal and refitting

1 Withdraw the five retaining buttons and lift out the kick-panel from the lower right-hand side of the dash.
2 Lift out the heater/demister duct from above the pedal bracket.
3 Refer to Chapter 12 and remove the dashboard lower sections to provide access to the pedal bracket.
4 Remove the stop light switch from the pedal bracket.
5 Disconnect the clutch pedal return spring and then detach the clutch cable from the forked end of the clutch pedal.
6 Remove the pedal retaining spring clip, the pedal return spring and the brake servo pushrod clevis pin from the brake pedal.
7 Withdraw the pedal pivot rod retaining clip and then slide the rod

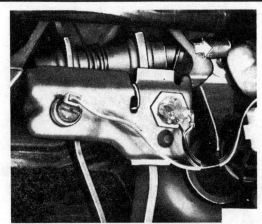

Fig. 9.18 Withdrawing the brake and clutch pedal pivot rod – pre-1979 models (Sec 19)

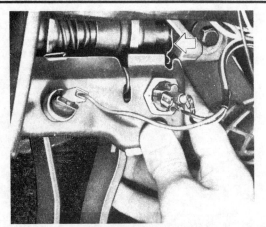

Fig. 9.19 Refitting the pedal pivot retaining clips – pre-1979 models (Sec 19)

to the right and out of the two pedals and mounting bracket. Note that on 1979 models, each pedal is mounted on a separate shaft incorporating two spring clips.

8   The brake and clutch pedals can now be withdrawn from under the dash.

9   Examine the brake pedal bushes for wear, and renew if necessary. It is unlikely that the pivot rod will be worn, but if so, it should also be renewed.

10   Refitting the brake pedals is the reverse of the removal sequence, but lubricate the moving surfaces with a little grease and adjust the brake pedal free play as follows: depress the brake pedal several times to release any vacuum from the servo unit. Slacken the locknut at the fork of the piston rod and turn the rod until the specified free play is obtained at the pedal pad. Tighten the locknut after making adjustment.

20   Brake pressure control valve – removal and refitting

1   A brake pressure sensing valve, incorporating a pressure differential warning actuator on certain models, is located in the engine compartment, bolted to the left-hand side of the inner panel (photo).

2   The valve is connected into the hydraulic pipeline to the rear brakes, and is basically a reducing valve. Under heavy braking conditions, the fluid pressure to the front brakes is maintained at the normal rate, while the valve reduces the pressure to the rear brakes, thus minimising the possibilities of the rear wheels locking.

3   The pressure differential warning actuator, incorporated in the pressure control valve on certain models, is a pressure-conscious switch. Should a failure of the front or rear hydraulic circuit occur, the switch will be activated and a warning light on the instrument panel will be illuminated, thus informing the driver immediately of front or rear hydraulic circuit failure. Should this occur, the switch must be reset after repairing the fault and bleeding the brakes, by depressing

20.1 Location of brake pressure control valve on left-hand side inner panel

the rubber plunger located between the two electrical connections on the switch.

4   The valve and actuator can be removed by undoing and removing the hydraulic lines and the bracket bolts, and lifting off. The valve and actuator cannot be dismantled and if faulty, should be replaced with new units.

5   After refitting, it will be necessary to bleed the brakes, as described in Section 3.

21 Fault diagnosis – braking system

Before diagnosing faults from the following chart, check that any braking irregularities are not caused by:

    (a) Uneven and incorrect tyre pressures
    (b) Incorrect 'mix' of radial and crossply tyres
    (c) Wear in the steering mechanism
    (d) Defects in the suspension and dampers
    (e) Misalignment of the bodyframe

Symptom	Reason(s)
Pedal travels a long way before the brakes operate	Brake shoes set too far from the drums
Stopping ability poor, even though pedal pressure is firm	Linings, discs or drums badly worn or scored One or more wheel hydraulic cylinders seized, resulting in some brake shoes not pressing against the drums (or pads against discs) Brake linings contaminated with oil Wrong type of linings fitted (too hard) Brake shoes wrongly assembled Servo unit not functioning
Car veers to one side when the brakes are applied	Brake pads or linings on one side are contaminated with oil Hydraulic wheel cylinder(s) on one side partially or fully seized A mixture of lining materials fitted between sides Brake discs not matched Unequal wear between sides caused by partially seized wheel cylinders
Pedal feels spongy when the brakes are applied	Air is present in the hydraulic system
Pedal feels springy when the brakes are applied	Brake linings not bedded into the drums (after fitting new ones) Master cylinder or brake backplate mounting bolts loose Severe wear in brake drums causing distortion when brakes are applied Discs out of true
Pedal travels right down with little or no resistance and brakes are virtually non-operative	Leak in hydraulic system resulting in lack of pressure for operating wheel cylinders If no signs of leakage are apparent the master cylinder internal seals are failing to sustain pressure
Binding, juddering, overheating	One or a combination of reasons given above

Chapter 10 Electrical system

For modifications, and information applicable to later models, see Supplement at end of manual

Contents

Specifications

Battery .... 12 volt, 44 amp hour at 20 hour rate

Windscreen wiper blades .... Champion C45-01

Alternator

Bosch type

Voltage	14 volt
Output	45 or 55 amp
Brush length	5 mm (0.2 in) minimum
Slip rings:	
Permissible eccentricity	0.03 mm (0.001 in) maximum
Minimum diameter	31.5 mm (1.24 in)
Regulator voltage	13.7 to 14.5 volts

Delco Remy type

Voltage	14 volt
Output	45 or 55 amp
Brush length	10 mm (0.39 in) minimum
Slip rings:	
Permissible eccentricity	0.08 mm (0.003 in) maximum
Minimum diameter	21 mm (0.83 in)
Regulator voltage	14.5 to 15 volts

Starter motor
Bosch type
Brush length	13 mm (0.51 in) minimum
Commutator:	
Permissible eccentricity	0.03 mm (0.001 in) maximum
Minimum diameter	33.5 mm (1.31 in)
Solenoid pull-in voltage	7.5 volts minimum

Delco Remy type
Brush length	7.0 mm (0.27 in) minimum
Commutator:	
Permissible eccentricity	0.05 mm (0.002 in) maximum
Minimum diameter	37.0 mm (1.46 in)
Solenoid pull-in voltage	8 volts minimum

Bulb data
Type	Wattage	Description
Head	60/55	Quartz Halogen
Side	4	Miniature centre contact
Stop/tail	21/5	Small centre cap
Turn signal	21	Small centre contact
Side repeater	4	Small bayonet cap
Number plate:		
Saloon	5	Festoon
Estate	10	Small centre contact
Reverse	21	Small centre contact
Fog:		
Front	55	Quartz Halogen
Rear	21	Small centre contact
Courtesy lights	10	Festoon
Instruments, panel lights and warning lights	1.2	Miniature wedge-base capless
Alternator warning	3	Wedge-base capless
Glove compartment	5	Festoon

Torque wrench settings
	Nm	lbf in
Alternator through-bolts:		
Bosch	5.5	48
Delco Remy	7	62
Alternator pulley nut:		lbf ft
Bosch	41	30
Delco Remy	68	50
Starter mounting bolts	70	52

1 General description

The electrical system is of the 12 volt negative earth type and the major components comprise a 12 volt battery of which the negative terminal is earthed, an alternator which is driven from the crankshaft pulley, and a starter motor.

The battery supplies a steady amount of current for the ignition, lighting and other electrical circuits and provides a reserve of electricity when the current consumed by the electrical equipment exceeds that being produced by the alternator.

The alternator has its own regulator which ensures a high output if the battery is in a low state of charge or the demand from the electrical equipment is high, and a low output if the battery is fully charged and there is little demand for the electrical equipment.

When fitting electrical accessories to cars with a negative earth system it is important, if they contain silicone diodes or transistors, that they are connected correctly, otherwise serious damage may result to the components concerned. Items such as radios, tape players, electronic ignition systems, electronic tachometer, automatic dipping etc, should all be checked for correct polarity.

It is important that the battery is disconnected before removing the alternator output lead as this is live at all times. Also, if body repairs are to be carried out using electric arc welding equipment the alternator must be disconnected otherwise serious damage can be caused to the more delicate instruments. Whenever the battery has to be disconnected it must always be reconnected with the negative terminal earthed. Do *not* disconnect the battery with the engine running. If 'jumper cables' are used to start the car, they *must* be connected correctly – positive to positive and negative to negative.

2 Battery – removal and refitting

1   The battery is located on a tray fitted to the left-hand wing valance of the engine compartment. It should be removed once every three months for cleaning and testing.
2   Slacken the negative terminal clamp bolt and lift off the terminal. Now slacken the bolt and lift off the positive terminal (photo).
3   Undo and remove the bolt securing the battery mounting clamp plate to the tray and lift away the clamp plate (photo). Carefully lift the battery out of the tray and hold it vertically to ensure none of the electrolyte is spilled.
4   Refitting is a direct reversal of this procedure. **Note:** *Refit the positive lead before the negative lead and smear the terminals with petroleum jelly to prevent corrosion. Never use an ordinary grease.*

3 Battery – maintenance and inspection

1   Check the battery electrolyte level weekly, by lifting off the cover or removing the individual cell plugs. The tops of the plates should be just covered by the electrolyte. If not, add distilled water so that they are. *Do not add extra water with the idea of reducing the intervals of topping-up.* This will merely dilute the electrolyte and reduce charging and current retention efficiency. On batteries fitted with patent covers, troughs, glass balls and so on, follow the instructions marked on the cover of the battery to ensure correct addition of water.
2   Keep the battery clean and dry all over by wiping it with a dry cloth. A damp top surface could cause tracking between the two terminal posts with consequent draining of power.

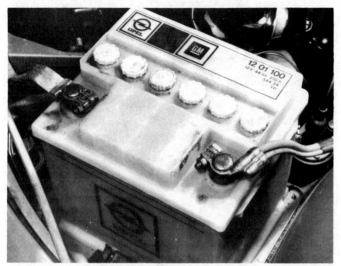

2.2 Battery positive and negative terminal connections

2.3 Battery retaining clamp and bolt

3   Every three months, remove the battery and check the support tray clamp and battery terminal connections for signs of corrosion — usually indicated by a whitish green crystalline deposit. Wash this off with clean water to which a little ammonia or washing soda has been added. Then treat the terminals with petroleum jelly and the battery mounting with suitable protective paint to prevent the metal being eaten away.

4   If the electrolyte level needs an excessive amount of replenishment but no leaks are apparent, it could be due to over-charging as a result of the battery having been run down and then left to recharge from the vehicle rather than an outside source. If the battery has been heavily discharged for one reason or another, it is best to have it continuously charged at a low amperage for a period of many hours. If it is charged from the car's system under such conditions, the charging will be intermittent and greatly varied in intensity. This does not do the battery any good at all. If the battery needs topping-up frequently, even when it is known to be in good condition and not too old, then the voltage regulator should be checked to ensure that the charging output is being correctly controlled. An elderly battery, however, may need topping-up more than a new one, because it needs to take in more charging current. Do not worry about this, provided it gives satisfactory service.

5   When checking a battery's condition, a hydrometer should be used. On some batteries, where the terminals of each of the six cells are exposed, a discharge tester can be used to check the condition of any one cell also. On modern batteries, the use of a discharge tester is no longer regarded as useful, as the renewal or repair of cells is not an economic proposition. The tables in the following Section give the hydrometer readings for various states of charge. A further check can be made when the battery is undergoing a charge. If, towards the end of the charge, when the cells are meant to be 'gassing' (bubbling), one cell appears not to be, this indicates the cell or cells in question are probably breaking down and the life of the battery is limited.

4   Battery – charging and electrolyte replenishment

1   It is possible that in winter (when the load on the battery cannot be recuperated during normal driving time) external charging is desirable. This is best done overnight at a 'trickle' rate of 1 to 1.5 amps. Alternatively, a 3 to 4 amp rate can be used over a period of four hours or so. Check the specific gravity in the latter case and stop the charge when the reading is correct. Most modern charging sets reduce the rate automatically when the fully charged state is neared. Rapid boost charges of 30 to 60 amps or more may get you out of trouble or can be used on a battery that has seen better days anyhow. They are not advised for a good battery that may have run flat for some reason.

2   Electrolyte replenishment should not normally be necessary unless an accident or some other cause, such as contamination, arises. If it is

necessary, then it is best first to discharge the battery completely and then tip out all the remaining liquid from all cells. Acquire a quantity of mixed electrolyte from a battery shop or garage according to the specifications in the table given next. The quantity required will depend on the type of battery but 3 or 4 pints should be more than enough for most. When the electrolyte has been put into the battery, a slow charge – not exceeding one amp – should be given for as long as is necessary to fully charge the battery. This could be up to 36 hours. Specific gravities for hydrometer readings (check each cell) – 12 volt batteries are as follows:

	Climate below 80°F (26.7°C)	Climate above 80°F (26.7°C)
Fully charged	1.270 to 1.290	1.210 to 1.230
Half-charged	1.190 to 1.210	1.120 to 1.150
Discharged completely	1.110 to 1.130	1.050 to 1.070

Note: If the electrolyte temperature is significantly different from 60°F (15.6°C), then the specific gravity will be affected. For every 5°F (2.8°C) it will increase or decrease with the temperature by 0.002. When the vehicle is being used in cold climates, it is essential to maintain the battery fully charged because the charge affects the freezing point of the electrolyte. The densities below have been corrected to suit measurement at 80°F (26.7°C)

Specific gravity	1.200	freezes	–35°F
Specific gravity	1.160	freezes	0°F

5   Alternator – general description, removal and refitting

1   Either a Bosch or Delco Remy alternator may be fitted. Both types are similar in construction, comprising basically an aluminium casing housing a three-phase star-connected stator. A rotor carrying the field windings rotates within the stator and is belt-driven from the crankshaft pulley.

2   The alternator is fitted with an integral voltage regulator located within the end casing.

3   The main advantage of the alternator over its predecessor, the dynamo, lies in its ability to provide a high charge at low revolutions. Driving slowly in heavy traffic with a dynamo invariably means no charge is reaching the battery. In similar conditions even with the wiper, heater, lights and perhaps radio switched on the alternator will ensure a charge reaches the battery.

4   To remove the alternator, first disconnect the negative (earth) battery terminal.

5   Unplug and unscrew all the wiring connectors from the rear of the alternator (photo).

6   Undo and remove the fanbelt tension adjustment bolt from the alternator and retrieve the lockwasher, plain washer and nut (photo).

7   Next loosen the pivot bolt beneath the alternator and push the unit

5.5 Position of alternator wiring connections (Delco Remy)

5.6 Fanbelt tension adjusting bolt at top of alternator

5.7 Alternator lower mounting pivot bolt

towards the engine to permit the fanbelt to be removed from the alternator pulley (photo).

8   Now swing the alternator down to expose the pivot bolt which can then be removed to release the unit from the engine. **Note:** *An earthing wire may be connected from the alternator through-bolts to the rear mounting bracket retaining bolt, in which case the bolt will have to be removed and the wire disconnected.*

9   Refit the alternator, using the reverse procedure to removal. Adjust the fanbelt tension so that there is approximately 13 mm (0.5 in) deflection, using light finger pressure, at a point midway between the alternator and crankshaft pulleys.

6 Alternator – fault finding and repair

Due to the specialist knowledge and equipment required to test or service an alternator, it is recommended that if the performance is

suspect, the car be taken to an automobile electrician who will have the facilities for such work. Because of this recommendation, information is limited to the inspection and renewal of the brushes. Should the alternator not charge or the system be suspect, the following points may be checked before seeking further assistance:

(a)   Check the fanbelt tension, as described in Section 5
(b)   Check the battery, as described in Section 3
(c)   Check all electrical cable connections for cleanliness and security

7 Alternator brushes (Delco Remy) – inspection, removal and refitting

1   Remove the alternator from the engine, as described in Section 5.
2   Scribe a line across the stator casing and front end cover to ensure

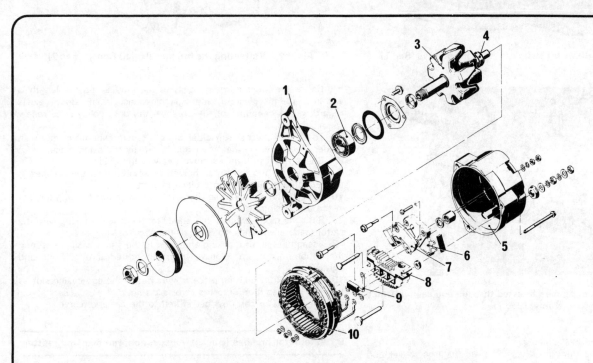

Fig. 10.1 Exploded view of Delco Remy alternator (Sec 7)

1 Drive end bracket	4 Slip rings	7 Brush holder	9 Auxiliary diodes
2 Drive end bearing	5 Slip ring end bracket	8 Rectifier	10 Stator
3 Rotor	6 Regulator		

Fig. 10.2 Delco Remy alternator through-bolts (Sec 7)

Fig. 10.3 Stator (1) and diode (2) terminal nuts (Delco Remy)
(Sec 7)

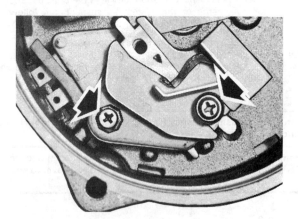

Fig. 10.4 Delco Remy brush holder retaining screws (Sec 7)

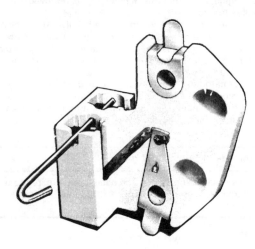

Fig. 10.5 Retracting the brushes (Delco Remy) (Sec 7)

Fig. 10.6 Brush retracting wire inserted through end casing (Delco
Remy) (Sec 7)

6   Check the brushes move freely in the guides and the length is
within the limit given in the Specifications. If any doubt exists
regarding the condition of the brushes, the best policy is to renew
them.
7   To fit new brushes, unsolder the old brush leads from the brush
holder and solder on the new leads in exactly the same place.
8   Check the new brushes move freely in the guides.
9   Before refitting the brush holder assembly retain the brushes in
the retracted position using a piece of wire.
10 Refit the brush holder so that the wire protrudes through the slot
in the end casing.
11 Refit the diode bracket and stator to the casing, making sure the
stator leads are in their correct positions.
12 Assemble the front casing and rotor to the stator casing, ensuring
the scribe marks are aligned. Insert the three through-bolts and
tighten.
13 Now carefully pull the piece of wire out of the end casing slot so
that the brushes drop onto the rotor slip ring.
14 The alternator can now be refitted to the car and tested.

---

8   Alternator brushes (Bosch) – inspection, removal and refitting

---

1   Undo and remove the two screws, spring and plain washers that
secure the brush box to the rear of the brush end housing. Lift away
the brush box (Fig. 10.8).
2   Check the carbon brushes are able to slide smoothly in their
guides without any sign of binding.
3   Measure the length of brushes; if they have worn below the
specified limit, they must be renewed.

correct location when reassembling.
3   Remove the three through-bolts, and prise the front cover and
rotor away from the rear end casing and stator.
4   Remove the three nuts and washers securing the stator leads to
the rectifier and lift away the stator assembly, then remove the
terminal screw and lift out the diode bracket.
5   Undo the two screws retaining the brush holder and voltage
regulator to the end casing and remove the brush holder assembly.
Note that the inner screw is insulated.

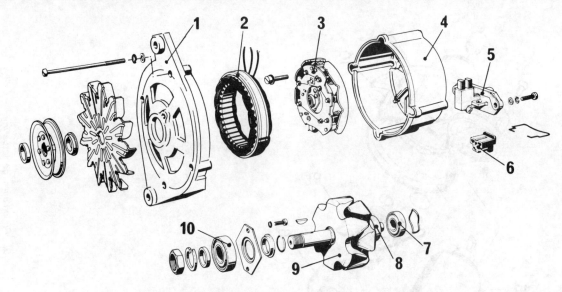

Fig. 10.7 Exploded view of the Bosch alternator (Sec 8)

1	Drive end bracket	4	Slip ring end bracket	7	Slip ring end bearing	9	Rotor
2	Stator	5	Brush holder	8	Slip rings	10	Drive end bearing
3	Heat sink plate	6	Connector plug				

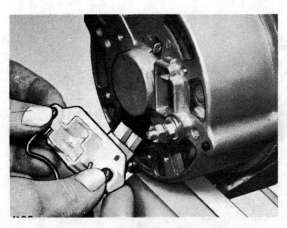

Fig. 10.8 Removing the brush holder (Bosch) (Sec 8)

4   Hold the brush wire with a pair of engineer's pliers and unsolder it from the brush box. Lift away the two brushes.

5   Insert the new brushes and check they are free to move in their guides. If they bind, lightly polish with a very fine file.

6   Solder the brush wire ends to the brush box, taking care that solder is not allowed to pass to the stranded wire.

7   Whenever new brushes are fitted new springs should also be fitted.

8   Refitting the brush box is the reverse sequence to removal.

9   Starter motor – general description

GM have fitted Delco Remy and Bosch starters during the production of this range of cars. They are both of the pre-engaging type and comprise a dc series wound motor, switched by a solenoid mounted on the top of the motor. The solenoid also serves to move the motor pinion into engagement with the ring gear on the flywheel periphery, before the switch contacts are closed to supply electrical power to the starter motor. The motor pinion is mounted on a carriage which engages a spiral spline on the motor shaft. The carriage incorporates an overspeed clutch which allows the pinion gear to be driven at a speed greater than starter motor speed when the engine starts. Once the engine has started and the starter switch is released,

the solenoid cuts off the power from the motor and moves the pinion and carriage back from engagement with the flywheel ring gear.

The construction of the two makes of starter motor is quite similar and the removal, refitting, dismantling, inspection and reassembly procedures detailed here will serve for both motors. Significant differences will be noted.

10   Starter motor – testing on engine

1   If the starter motor fails to turn the engine when the switch is operated there are four possible reasons why:

(a)   The battery is faulty
(b)   The electrical connections between the switch, solenoid, battery and starter motor are somewhere failing to pass the necessary current from the battery through the starter to earth
(c)   The solenoid switch is faulty
(d)   The starter motor is either jammed or electrically defective

2   To check the battery, switch on the headlights. If they dim after a few seconds, the battery is in a discharged state. If the lights glow brightly, operate the starter switch and see what happens to the lights. If they dim, power is reaching the starter motor but failing to turn it. Therefore check it is not jammed by placing the car in gear (manual transmission only) and rocking it to and fro. Should the motor not be jammed, it will have to be removed for proper inspection. If the starter turns slowly when switched on, proceed to the next check.

3   If, when the starter switch is operated, the lights stay bright, insufficient power is reaching the motor. Remove the battery connections, starter/solenoid power connections and the engine earth strap and thoroughly clean and refit them. Smear petroleum jelly around the battery connections to prevent corrosion. Corroded connections are the most frequent cause of electric system malfunctions.

4   When the above checks and cleaning tasks have been carried out, but without success, you will have possibly heard a clicking noise each time the starter switch is operated. This is the solenoid switch operating, but it does not necessarily follow that the main contacts are closing properly (if no clicking has been heard from the solenoid, it is certainly defective). The solenoid contact can be checked by putting a voltmeter or bulb across the main cable connection of the starter side of the solenoid and earth. When the switch is operated, there should be a reading or lighted bulb. If there is no reading or lighted bulb, the solenoid unit is faulty and should be renewed.

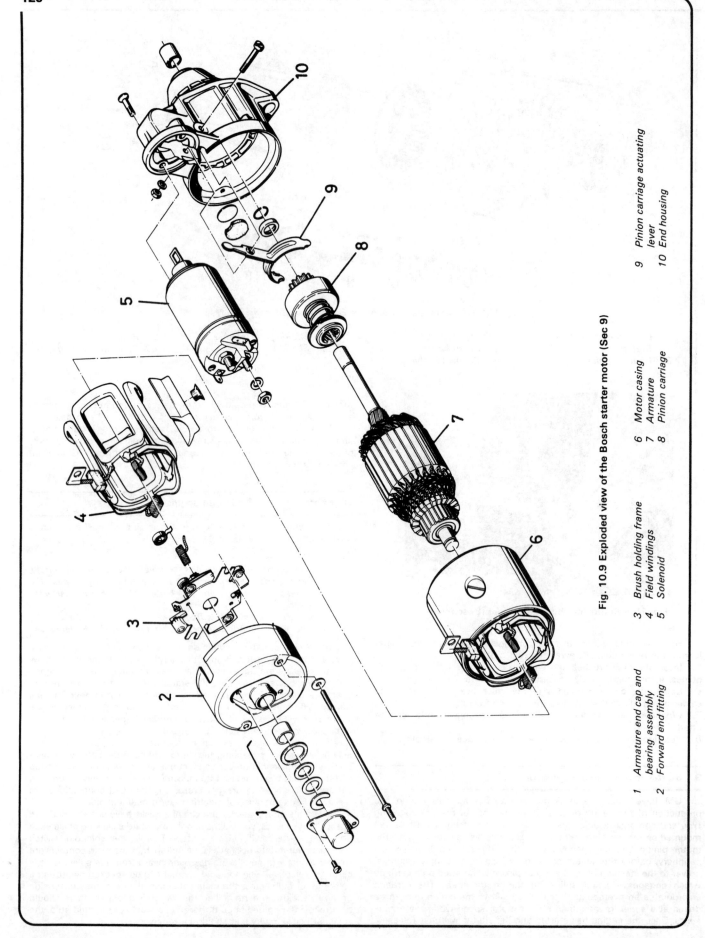

Fig. 10.9 Exploded view of the Bosch starter motor (Sec 9)

1 Armature end cap and
   bearing assembly
2 Forward end fitting
3 Brush holding frame
4 Field windings
5 Solenoid
6 Motor casing
7 Armature
8 Pinion carriage
9 Pinion carriage actuating
   lever
10 End housing

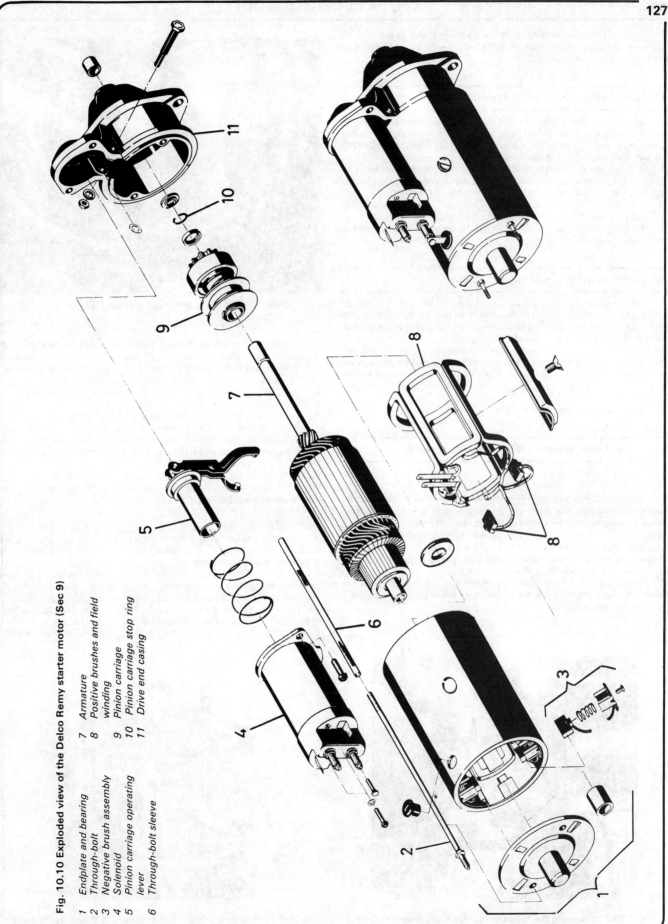

Fig. 10.10 Exploded view of the Delco Remy starter motor (Sec 9)

1 Endplate and bearing
2 Through-bolt
3 Negative brush assembly
4 Solenoid
5 Pinion carriage operating
  lever
6 Through-bolt sleeve
7 Armature
8 Positive brushes and field
  winding
9 Pinion carriage
10 Pinion carriage stop ring
11 Drive end casing

5   Finally, if it is established that the solenoid is not faulty and 12 volts are getting to the starter, then the motor is faulty and should be removed for inspection.

11 Starter motor – removal and refitting

1   With the engine in the car, the starter is quite accessible at the lower right-hand side of the engine. It is secured to the clutch bellhousing and engine cylinder block by two bolts and a terminal stud on the front end of the starter motor.
2   Remove the earth (negative) lead from the battery, then proceed to disconnect the solenoid and motor electrical connections. Identify the leads as necessary to ensure correct refitment (photo).
3   Remove the bolts and studs which secure the solenoid/motor assembly to the engine. The motor can be lifted clear.
4   Refitting the starter motor assembly is the exact reversal of the removal procedure.

12 Starter solenoid – removal and refitting

1   The solenoid is retained by two bolts to the pinion carriage operating mechanism casing. Remove the two bolts, retrieve the lockwashers and remove the electrical power connection to the motor. Extract the solenoid from the end casing.
2   Note that the Bosch starter/solenoid assembly differs from the Delco Remy described above – the solenoid is retained by two screws to the end casing and is extracted after unhooking the solenoid switch shaft from the pinion carriage actuating arm mounted in the end casing.
3   Refitting of the solenoid follows the reversal of removal.

13 Starter motor brushes – inspection and renewal

Bosch
1   With the starter removed from the engine and on a clean bench, begin by removing the armature end cap which is secured by two small screws on the front end of the motor. Remove the armature retaining clip, washers and the rubber sealing ring which were exposed. Undo and remove the two long bolts which hold the motor assembly together. The front end cover can now be removed to reveal the brushes and mounting plate.
2   Take the brushes from under the holder and slip the holder off the armature shaft. Retrieve the spacer washers between the brush plate and the armature block.

11.2 Correct location of starter motor solenoid electrical connections

3   Inspect the brushes; if they are worn down to less than the minimum length given in the Specifications, they should be renewed. When soldering new brushes in place hold the connecting wire in a pair of pliers to prevent molten solder running into the wire strands and destroying its flexibility. A 12 to 15 watt 'pencil' soldering iron is quite sufficient for this task.
4   Wipe the starter motor armature and commutator clean with a non-fluffy rag, wetted with carbon tetrachloride.
5   Reassemble the brushes into the holder and refit the holder over the armature shaft remembering to fit the two washers between the holder and armature.
6   Refit the motor end cover and secure with two long bolts.
7   Refit the armature shaft end cap after fitting the rubber sealing ring, washer and shaft clip.

Delco Remy
8   With the motor removed from the engine and ready on a clean bench, begin by undoing and removing the two long bolts which hold the motor assembly together.
9   The front end plate can then be removed from the motor to reveal the brushes, holders and armature of the motor.
10   The brush holders are secured to the motor casing by rivets.
11   The 'positive' brushes are connected to the static field windings; the negative brushes are connected to the motor casing.
12   If the brushes are worn to less than the minimum length given in

Fig. 10.11 Removing the brush holder from the Bosch starter motor – note the spacers (arrowed) (Sec 13)

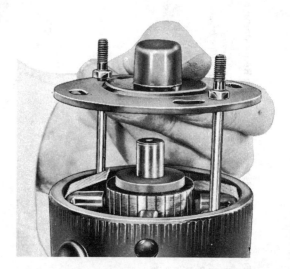

Fig. 10.12 Removing the endplate from the Delco Remy starter motor (Sec 13)

the Specifications, they should be renewed; always renew all four.

13 When soldering new positive brushes, hold the connecting wires in a pair of pliers to prevent the solder from running into the wire strands and reducing its flexibility. Use a 12 to 15 watt pencil soldering iron.

14 The negative brushes are renewed complete with the holder. Drill out the rivet holding the worn brush and mounting in place, remove and discard the worn brush unit. Offer up the new brush and mounting, insert the rivet from the inside of the casing and with a light hammer and punch close the rivet to secure the new brush mounting.

15 Clean the motor armature and commutator with a non-fluffy rag, wet with carbon tetrachloride.

16 Refit the armature into the motor and slip the brushes into position on the commutator.

17 Refit the motor endplate and screw in the long bolts which hold the motor assembly together. Check that the motor shaft turns freely, without any hint of an obstruction.

14 Starter motor – pinion carriage mechanism

1 With the starter motor removed from the engine and placed on a clean bench, remove the solenoid unit as detailed in Section 12 of this Chapter.

2 Remove the motor casing endplate as directed in Section 14 in order to gain access to the brushes.

3 *Bosch:* Remove the brushes from the brush holder, and slip holder off the armature shaft, retrieving the two spacing washers.

4 Pull the motor casing (complete with static field windings) off the armature, which is held in the motor assembly rear end casing.

5 Undo the nut and remove the bolt which is the pivot for the pinion carriage actuating lever, mounted in the rear end casing.

6 The end casing can now be separated from the armature and pin assembly.

7 Lift the forked lever from the pinion carriage.

8 Next, remove the compensating washer from the rear end of the armature shaft and tap the snap-ring retaining ring back toward the pinion carriage to reveal the snap-ring.

9 With a small screwdriver, prise the snap-ring open and slip it off the motor shaft. Clean burrs off the edge of the ring groove.

10 Slide the pinion carriage off the motor shaft. The pinion carriage cannot be dismantled and if deemed faulty should be renewed. The spiral spline on which the pinion runs should be thoroughly cleaned, then lightly lubricated with grease.

11 Reassembly follows the exact reversal of the dismantling procedure.

12 Make sure, during reassembly of Delco Remy motors, that the long bolts which hold the assembly together pass through the insulating sleeves which protect the static field windings.

15 Starter motor – checking armature and static field windings

1 Follow the instructions given in Section 14 of this Chapter and dismantle the motor to gain access to the armature and the motor casing with the static field windings attached.

2 The armature windings may be checked for a short onto the motor shaft/armature core, and for an open circuit in the windings.

3 Using a test circuit comprising two probes, a bulb and 12v battery, touch the commutator bars with one probe, whilst holding the other against the armature metal. The test bulb should not light up.

4 To check the armature windings for open circuit, replace the bulb with an ammeter (0 to 10 amp). Touch commutator bars (90° spaced) with the probes and note the ammeter reading. The readings should all be the same; considerable deviation (25%) indicates open circuits or windings insulation breakdown.

5 The battery and bulb circuit is used to check the static field windings. Touch one probe onto each winding termination and hold the other against the metal of the motor casing. The test bulb must not light up. Remember to touch the positive brushes to check for short circuits properly.

6 Faulty armatures or field windings should be renewed, though individual new spares may be difficult to obtain, and it will possibly be necessary to purchase an exchange motor unit.

16 Windscreen wiper mechanism – fault diagnosis and rectification

1 Should the windscreen wipers fail, or work very slowly, check the terminals and connections in the multi-plug socket for loose connections or broken wires. Make sure that the insulation on all the wiring is sound. If this is in order, check the current the motor is taking, by connecting an ammeter in the circuit and turning on the wiper switch. Consumption should be between 2.3 and 3.1 amps.

2 If no current is passing through the motor, check the switch is operating correctly and the fuse has not blown.

17 Windscreen wiper components – removal and refitting

Wiper blades

1 To remove the wiper blades, depress the retaining catch on the wiper arm and slide the blade off the pivot pin (photos).

2 Refit the blades using the reverse procedure to removal.

Wiper arms

3 Lift up the protective cap at the base of the wiper arm.

4 Undo and remove the wiper arm retaining nut, then prise the arm off the spindle, using a wide bladed screwdriver (photo).

5 With the wiper spindles in the 'parked' position, refit the blades using the reverse sequence to removal.

Windscreen wiper motor and linkage

6 Open the bonnet and disconnect the battery earth terminal.

7 Remove both windscreen wiper arms, then undo and remove the two wiper spindle retaining nuts, washers and rubber spacers.

8 Remove the bonnet sealing strip, then lift out the plastic wiper motor cover grille.

9 Disconnect the multi-plug wiring connector and the earth lead from the wiper motor (photo).

10 Slide the motor mounting plate out of the mounting grommet, then carefully withdraw the complete wiper motor and spindle linkage assembly from the upper cowl panel.

11 To remove the wiper motor from the mounting bracket, undo and remove the nut securing the wiper cranking arm to the motor, then unscrew the three retaining screws. The motor can now be lifted off the mounting bracket.

12 Refitting the assembly is the reverse sequence to removal. Ensure the washer pipe is routed under the motor.

18 Windscreen wiper motor – renovation

1 Release the two spring clips and pull the casing off the armature and gear housing.

2 Remove the four screws and lift off the gear housing cover. The main gear and driveshaft can now be withdrawn from the housing. Do not lose the thrust washer on the driveshaft.

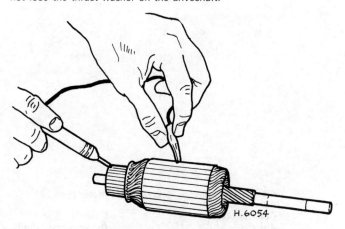

Fig. 10.13 Testing the starter armature with a test probe (Sec 15)

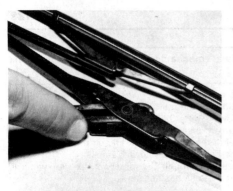
17.1a Depress the catch on the side of the wiper arm ...

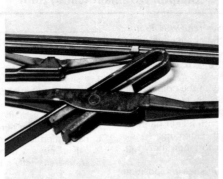
17.1b ... and slide off the wiper blade

17.4 Wiper arm retaining nut and washer

Fig. 10.14 Location of the bonnet sealing strip and wiper motor grille (Sec 17)

17.9 Wiper motor multi-plug connector and earth lead

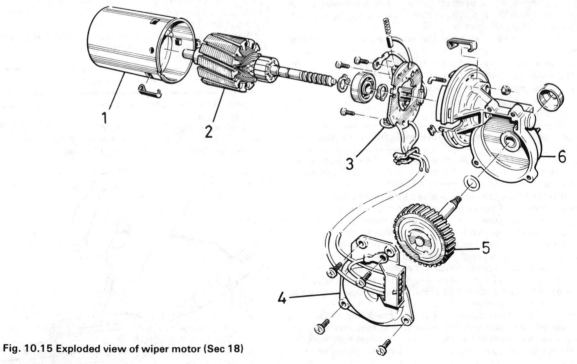
Fig. 10.15 Exploded view of wiper motor (Sec 18)

1	Outer casing	4	Contact cover
2	Armature	5	Drivegear and shaft
3	Brush holder plate	6	Gear housing

3   Slacken the bearing retaining nut and withdraw the armature and bearing assembly, taking care not to contaminate the brushes with grease.
4   The brush assembly can be removed from the gear housing by undoing the three retaining screws.
5   Check the bushes and bearing for wear and renew if necessary. The brushes should be renewed as a matter of course.
6   Clean the contacts on the gear housing cover, using very fine emery paper.
7   Clean the commutator with a piece of clean cloth soaked in solvent and check that the insulation between the segments is free from metallic dust.
8   If nothing obviously wrong with the motor can be found, take the armature to an electrical specialist and have it checked for insulation failure.
9   Wash out the gear housing in petrol and repack with grease.
10   To refit the armature and bearing, retract the brushes out of the way, and carefully insert the armature shaft and bearing into the gear housing.
11   Before tightening the bearing retaining nut, make sure the L-shaped retainer is hooked over the outer race of the bearing.
12   Continue to reassemble the motor, using the reverse procedure to dismantling.
13   Finally, refit the motor to the car, as described in Section 11.

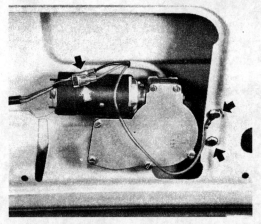

Fig. 10.16 Tailgate wiper motor wiring connector and mountings (Sec 19)

19   Tailgate wiper components (estate car) – removal and refitting

1   Disconnect the battery earth terminal.
2   Open the tailgate and remove the inner trim panel.
3   Disconnect the electrical cable block connector at the motor, then undo and remove the bolt and washer securing the earth connection to the tailgate.
4   Lift up the wiper arm protective cap, then undo and remove the nut securing the wiper arm to the spindle. Now carefully prise the arm off the spindle.
5   With the wiper arm removed, the nut securing the wiper spindle to the tailgate can be removed and the complete motor and gearbox withdrawn from inside the car.
6   Renovation of the wiper motor follows the same procedure described in Section 18 for the windscreen wiper motor.
7   Refitting is the reverse sequence to removal. With the assembly fitted and in the park position, refit the wiper arm so that a clearance of 22 mm (0.87 in) exists between the edge of the blade and the rubber window seal.

20   Windscreen washer pump – removal and refitting

1   Disconnect the battery earth terminal.
2   Disconnect the electrical connection at the washer pump and pull off the water outlet hose.
3   Lift the washer reservoir upwards and out of its bracket.
4   The pump can now be removed by pulling upwards and out of its rubber gasket (photo).
5   Refitting the pump is the reverse sequence to removal.

21   Tailgate washer pump (estate car) – removal and refitting

1   The tailgate washer pump and water reservoir are located alongside the spare wheel under the luggage compartment floor.
2   Removal and refitting of the pump follows the same procedure described for the windscreen washer pump.

22   Horn – testing, removal and refitting

1   The single horn is located behind the radiator grille.
2   If the horn fails to operate, remove the radiator grille, referring to Chapter 13 if necessary, and disconnect the two wires from the horn.
3   Connect a test lamp across the two horn wires, then have an assistant press the horn button. If the test lamp illuminates, the horn is at fault and should be renewed.
4   If the lamp fails to illuminate, the fuse may have blown or the horn switch may be at fault.

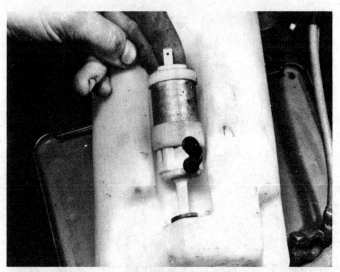

20.4 Removing the windscreen washer pump

5   To remove the horn, disconnect the two wires, undo and remove the retaining bolt and lift away the horn (photo).
6   Refitting follows the reverse sequence to removal.

23   Horn button switch – removal, inspection and refitting

1   The switch consists of a button, located in the centre of the steering wheel, and a spring-loaded finger which contacts a slip ring at the top of the steering column. Sports steering wheels are equipped with two additional switch buttons on either side of the central spoke.
2   To remove the switches, disconnect the battery earth terminal first.
3   Now carefully prise out the horn button from the centre of the steering wheel and disconnect the cables (photos). The additional buttons on sports wheels are removed in the same manner (photo). The switches cannot be dismantled, and if faulty must be renewed.
4   To gain access to the contact finger and slip ring, remove the steering wheel as described in Chapter 11.
5   With the wheel removed, the contact finger and slip ring may be inspected and the contacts cleaned. Further dismantling is not possible, and if the components are faulty, renewal is the only course of action.
6   Refitting is the reverse sequence to removal.

22.5 Horn location behind grille panel, and wiring connector positions

23.3a The horn button is removed by prising upwards

23.3b Location of the horn button wiring connectors

23.3c Removing the additional finger switches on sports steering wheels

24 Flasher unit – removal and refitting

The direction indicator lights and hazard warning lights are operated by the same flasher unit. The unit is plugged into the fusebox located on the right-hand side of the steering column below the instrument panel. To unplug the unit, simply pull it out in a downward direction. When refitting a new unit, align the terminals with those in the fusebox and push it home.

25 Steering column combination switch – removal and refitting

1   Open the bonnet and disconnect the battery earth terminal.
2   Remove the steering wheel as described in Chapter 11.
3   Undo and remove the three retaining screws, then lift off the steering column upper and lower shrouds (photo).
4   Disconnect the three multi-plug wiring connectors.
5   Undo and remove the three mounting screws and lift the switch assembly off the steering column (photo).
6   Refitting is the reverse sequence to removal.

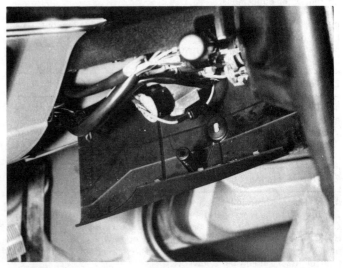

25.3 Lifting off the steering column shrouds

25.5 Withdrawing the combination switch off the steering column

28.1 The headlight assembly plastic cover is removed by turning anti-clockwise

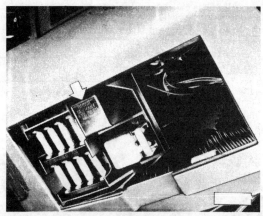

Fig. 10.17 Location of the flasher unit in the fuse box (Sec 24)

Fig. 10.18 Removing the ignition switch lock barrel (Sec 26)

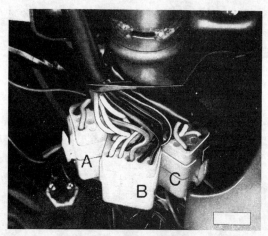

Fig. 10.19 Steering column multi-plug connection (Sec 26)

A Ignition switch cable
   connector
B Turn signal and headlight

   Dimmer cable connector
C Windscreen wiper switch
   cable connector

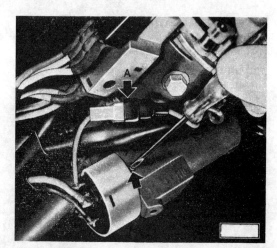

Fig. 10.20 Ignition switch contact assembly securing screw (arrowed) and additional connector (A) (Sec 26)

26 Ignition switch contact assembly and lock barrel – removal and refitting

1   Open the bonnet and disconnect the battery earth terminal.
2   Undo and remove the three retaining screws, then lift off the steering column lower shroud.
3   To remove the lock barrel, turn the ignition key to the 'I' position, depress the small detent spring with an electrician's screwdriver and lift out the lock barrel.
4   Refit the barrel, following the reverse of the above procedure.
5   To remove the switch contact assembly, disconnect the multi-plug (see Fig. 10.19) and the additional wiring connector, adjacent to the switch.
6   Unscrew the two retaining grubscrews and lift off the contact assembly. **Note:** *To avoid damage to the steering lock, the lock barrel and switch contact assembly should not be removed at the same time.*
7   Refitting is the reverse of the removal sequence.

27 Headlights – alignment and adjustment

1   Alignment is achieved by adjustment with two nylon special bolts, to be found on the headlight retaining frame. They are accessible from the inside of the engine compartment.
2   To avoid dazzling oncoming traffic due to incorrect setting, and contravening the lighting laws, it is strongly recommended that the headlights are aligned by a garage equipped with the proper optical type beam setter.
3   Holts Amber Lamp is useful for temporarily changing the headlight colour to conform with the normal usage on Continental Europe.

28 Headlight and sidelight bulbs – removal and refitting

1   Open the bonnet and remove the large plastic cap from the rear of the headlight assembly by rotating it anti-clockwise (photo).
2   Pull off the electrical plug connector (photo).
3   Remove the bulb retaining plate by pushing it inwards and turning it anti-clockwise (photo). The sidelight bulb can now be removed if required.
4   Lift the headlight bulb out of the reflector assembly (photo). Avoid touching the glass of the bulb with your fingers; this could cause premature failure of the bulb.
5   Refit the bulb, following the reverse procedure to removal. Note that the metal rim of the bulb has a projection which must engage in the slot on the reflector.

29 Headlight lens unit – removal and refitting

1   Open the bonnet and remove the bulb retaining plate and headlight bulb, as described in the previous Section.
2   Disconnect the wires from the bulb retaining plate, prise out the grommet and pull the wiring harness out of the headlight shell (photo).
3   Turn the indicator bulb holder anti-clockwise and lift it out the lens unit (photo).
4   Remove the radiator grille, then undo and remove the mounting screws and withdraw the lens unit (photo).
5   To separate the indicator housing, compress the two spring clips and withdraw the indicator housing from the headlight unit (photos).
6   Refitting follows the reverse sequence to removal. It is advisable to have the headlight alignment checked after refitting the lens unit.

30 Front turn indicator bulbs – removal and refitting

1   Open the bonnet and turn the indicator bulb holder anti-clockwise to release it from the lens unit.
2   The bulb is removed by depressing slightly and turning anti-clockwise, then lifting out.

28.2 Electrical connector at rear of headlight bulb

28.3 Remove the bulb retaining plate by depressing and turning anti-clockwise

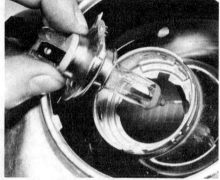

28.4 Lifting out the headlight bulb

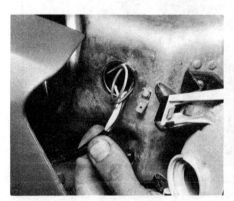

29.2 Removing the wiring harness through the grommet aperture in the headlight shell

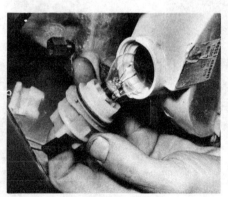

29.3 Removing the turn indicator bulb holder and bulb

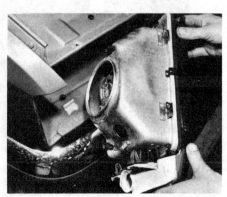

29.4 Withdrawing the lens unit from the car

29.5a The turn indicator housing is separated by compressing the two spring clips ...

29.5b ... and lifting the housing off the headlight shell

31.2 Lifting off the rear light cluster protective cover

31.3a Withdrawing the turn and sidelight bulb holders ...

31.3b ... and the stop and reversing light holders

32.1a Prise the number plate bulb holder upwards ...

32.1b ... and lift off

32.2 Spread the tag and lift the lens housing off the bulb holder

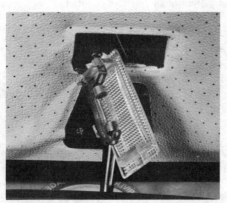

33.2 Removing the interior courtesy light bulb holder

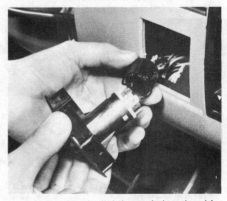

34.1 Removing the lighting switch and multi-plug connector

31 Rear light bulbs – removal and refitting

Saloon car
1   Access to the rear light cluster bulbs is gained from inside the luggage compartment.
2   Lift off the protective plastic covers (photo).
3   Spread the bulb holder retainers slightly and lift out the bulb holders (photos).
4   The bulbs can now be removed by depressing and turning the bulb slightly, then lifting them out.

Estate car
5   Undo and remove the two rear lens retaining screws and withdraw the lens.
6   The bulbs can now be removed by depressing and turning slightly, then lifting them out.

32 Rear number plate light – removal and refitting

1   Insert a screwdriver through the slot on the right-hand side of the plastic housing and prise the unit out of the bumper (photos).
2   Spread the plastic tag at the base of the bulb holder and lift the lens housing off the bulb holder (photo).
3   The bulb can now be renewed and the unit reassembled.

33 Courtesy lights – removal and refitting

1   The interior light, boot illuminating light, glove box light and engine compartment light are all removed as follows:
2   Prise the lens and bulb holder from its location using a thin screwdriver (photo).
3   Spread the contacts and lift out the festoon type bulbs.
4   Place a new bulb in position and refit the lens.

34 Light switch and instrument panel switches – removal and refitting

1   These switches are all a push fit into their respective locations, and are removed by prising out with a screwdriver (photo).
2   With the switch removed from its location, pull off the wiring plug and illuminating bulb holder, then lift away the switch.
3   Refitting is the reverse sequence to removal.

35 Reversing light switch – removal and refitting

1   The reversing light switch on cars with manual transmission is located at the rear of the gearbox and is activated by the selector shaft when reverse gear is selected. On vehicles equipped with automatic transmission, the switch is fitted to the gear selector lever.
2   To remove the switch on vehicles fitted with manual transmission,

Fig. 10.21 Instrument panel switch removal (Sec 34)

jack up the front of the car and support it on axle stands.
3   Disconnect the two wires and unscrew the switch from the gearbox (photo).
4   Refitting is the reverse sequence to removal.
5   To remove the reversing light switch on vehicles equipped with automatic transmission, refer to Chapter 6, Section 15.

36 Door pillar switches – removal and refitting

1   These switches are removed by simply unscrewing the retaining screw, lifting out the switch and disconnecting the electrical connection (photo).
2   Refitting is the reverse of the above sequence.

37 Brake light and clutch warning light switches – removal and refitting

1   Prise out the five retaining buttons securing the trim panel to the lower dash.
2   Disconnect the wires to the switches and unscrew them from the pedal bracket (photo).
3   Refitting is the reverse sequence to removal.

38 Handbrake warning light switch – removal and refitting

1   Remove the handbrake lever as described in Chapter 9.
2   Disconnect the electrical lead, then undo and remove the switch retaining bolt.
3   The switch can now be lifted off the handbrake lever.
4   Refitting is the reverse sequence to removal.

35.3 The reversing light switch is located at the rear of the gearbox

36.1 Front door pillar switch

37.2 Location of brake light switch on pedal bracket

39 Instrument panel – removal and refitting

1 Disconnect the battery earth terminal.
2 Unscrew and remove the upper retaining screw, press the instrument cowl together at the top and bottom centres, and carefully lift out (photos).
3 Remove the two lower and one upper instrument panel retaining screws (photo).
4 From inside the engine compartment, push the speedometer cable through the grommet in the bulkhead as far as it will go.
5 Now tip the instrument cluster upwards at the bottom and withdraw it far enough to allow the speedometer cable to be removed from the rear. This is done by depressing the spring clip and pulling off the cable.
6 The instrument panel can now be withdrawn, the two wires and socket connector removed and the panel lifted away.
7 Refitting is the reverse sequence to removal.

40 Instruments, warning lights, printed circuit and voltage stabilizer – removal and refitting

1 Remove the instrument panel, as described in the previous Section.
2 The exact details concerning the number and type of securing screws retaining the instruments in position will vary according to the instrument fitted and model type, but this will be obvious upon inspection.
3 The warning lights are removed by twisting the bulb holders and lifting them out. The bulbs are a push fit in the holders (photos).
4 To remove the voltage stabilizer, press the heat conductor plate together and lift out the unit.
5 The printed circuit is removed by sliding it sideways and lifting it out after first removing all the instruments.
6 Refitting of all the components on the instrument panel follows the reverse sequence to removal.

41 Speedometer cable – removal and refitting

1 Jack up the front of the car and support it on firmly based axle stands.
2 Disconnect the battery earth terminal.
3 Referring to Section 39, paragraphs 2 to 5, withdraw the instrument panel and disconnect the speedometer cable from the speedometer.
4 With the cable disconnected, prise out the bulkhead grommet and pull the cable through into the engine compartment.
5 Working underneath the car, unscrew the knurled nut securing the lower end of the cable to the gearbox, then lift off the cable.
6 Remove the cable from the guide clips on the underbody and withdraw the cable from under the car.
7 Refitting is the reverse sequence to removal.

42 Cigarette lighter – removal and refitting

1 The cigarette lighter is retained in the lower instrument panel by means of a slotted plate.
2 To remove the lighter, first disconnect the battery earth terminal.
3 Pull out the lighter element, then insert a pair of round-nosed pliers into the element socket.
4 Spread the pliers and rotate the socket to the left.
5 Now withdraw the socket from the instrument panel and disconnect the electrical connections.
6 Refitting is the reverse sequence to removal.

43 Fuses and relays

1 The fuses and relays are located behind a removable panel, below the instrument panel on the right of the steering column (photo).
2 The layout of the fuse block and the fuse and relay locations are shown in Fig. 10.24. The fuse box has provisions for fourteen fuses and four relays; however some locations will be vacant, depending on options fitted and model type. On certain models, additional line fuses (located between the steering column and fuse box) are used to protect optional equipment circuits.
3 Fuse failure may be diagnosed by the simultaneous failure of several electrical systems.
4 If a fuse blows, it must be replaced with a fuse of the same rating. If the new fuse blows immediately the particular electrical service is operated, there is a fault in the system and the circuit must be carefully inspected to find the cause of the trouble.
5 To renew a fuse, simply pull it downwards and out of its holder. Relays are renewed in the same fashion.
6 The fuses and their respective circuits are as follows:

Fuse	Rating	Function
1	5 amp	Right side and tail lights
2	5 amp	Left side and tail lights
3	5 amp	Number plate light, engine compartment light, instrument lights
4	5 amp	Courtesy light, luggage compartment light, hazard warning system, electric clock
5	16 amp	Windscreen wipers, heater blower
6	8 amp	Reversing lights, cigarette lighter
7	5 amp	Stop lights, direction indicators
8	8 amp	Horn, choke preheater
9	16 amp	Long range headlights (optional)
10	16 amp	Fog lights (optional)
13		Vacant
14	16 amp	Electrically operated sunroof

7 The four relays and their functions are as follows:

Location	Function
A	Flasher unit
B	Rear window heater
C	Fog lights (optional)
D	Driving lights (optional)

39.2a Removing the instrument cowl retaining screw …

39.2b … and lifting out the cowl by pressing the centres together

39.3 Removing the instrument panel retaining screws

40.3a Removing the instrument panel warning light ...

40.3b ... and illuminating light bulb holder

Fig. 10.22 Removing the voltage stabilizer from the instrument panel (Sec 40)

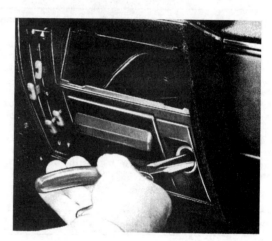

Fig. 10.23 Using pliers to withdraw the cigarette lighter (Sec 42)

43.1 The fuses and relays are located behind a removable panel on the right-hand side of the dash

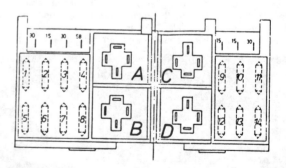

Fig. 10.24 Fuse and relay locations in the fuse box (Sec 43)

A   Flasher
B   Rear window heater relay
C   Foglight relay
D   Driving light relay

44 Radios and tape players – fitting (general

A radio or tape player is an expensive item to buy and will only give its best performance if fitted properly. It is useless to expect concert hall performance from a unit that is suspended from the dash panel on string with its speaker resting on the back seat or parcel shelf! If you do not wish to do the fitting yourself there are many in-car entertainment specialists who can do the fitting for you.

Make sure the unit purchased is of the same polarity as the car, and ensure that units with adjustable polarity are correctly set before commencing fitting.

It is difficult to give specific information with regard to fitting, as final positioning of the radio/tape player, speakers and aerial is entirely a matter of personal preference. However, the following paragraphs give guidelines to follow, which are relevant to all installations.

Radios

Most radios are a standardised size on 7 in wide, by 2 in deep – this ensures that they will fit into the radio aperture provided in most cars. If your car does not have such an aperture, then the radio must be fitted in a suitable position either in, or beneath, the dash panel. Alternatively, a special console can be purchased which will fit between the dash panel and the floor, or on the transmission tunnel. These consoles can also be used for additional switches and instrumentation if required. Where no radio aperture is provided, the following points should be borne in mind before deciding exactly where to fit the unit:

(a) the unit must be within easy reach of the driver wearing a seat belt

(b) The unit must not be mounted in close proximity to an electronic tachometer, the ignition switch and its wiring, or the flasher unit and associated wiring

(c) the unit must be mounted within reach of the aerial lead, and in such a place that the aerial lead will not have to be routed near the components detailed in the preceding paragraph (b)

(d) The unit should not be positioned in a place where it might cause injury to the car occupants in an accident; for instance, under the dash panel above the driver's or passenger's legs

(e) The unit must be fitted really securely

Some radios will have mounting brackets provided together with instructions: others will need to be fitted using drilled and slotted metal strips, bent to form mounting brackets – these strips are available from most accessory shops. The unit must be properly earthed, by fitting a separate earthing lead between the casing of the radio and the vehicle frame.

Use the radio manufacturers' instructions when wiring the radio into the vehicle's electrical system. If no instructions are available, refer to the relevant wiring diagram to find the location of the radio 'feed' connection in the vehicle's wiring circuit. A 1 to 2 amp 'in-line' fuse must be fitted in the radio's feed wire – a choke may also be necessary (see next Section).

The type of aerial used, and its fitted position is a matter of personal preference. In general the taller the aerial, the better the reception. It is best to fit a fully retractable aerial – especially if a mechanical car-wash is used or if you live in an area where cars tend to be vandalised. In this respect electric aerials which are raised and lowered automatically when switching the radio on or off are convenient,c but are more likely to give trouble than the manual type.[

When choosing a site for the aerial the following points should be considered:

(a) The aerial lead should be as short as possible – this means that the aerial should be mounted at the front of the car

(b) The aerial must be mounted as far away from the distributor and HT leads as possible

(c) The part of the aerial which protrudes beneath the mounting point must not foul the roadwheels, or anything else

(d) If possible the aerial should be positioned so that the coxial lead does not have to be routed through the engine compartment

(e) The plane of the panel on which the aerial is mounted should not be so steeply angled that the aerial cannot be mounted vertically (in relation to the 'end-on' aspect of the car). Most aerials have a small amount of adjustment available

Having decided on a mounting position, a relatively large hole will have to be made in the panel. The exact size of the hole will depend upon the specific aerial being fitted, although, generally, the hole required is of 19 mm (0.75 in) diameter. On metal bodied cars, a 'tank-cutter' of the relevant diameter is the best tool to use for making the hole. This tool needs a small diameter pilot hole drilled through the panel, through which, the tool clamping bolt is inserted. When the hole has been made the raw edges should be de-burred with a file and then painted, to prevent corrosion.

Fit the aerial according to the manufacturer's instructions. If the aerial is very tall, or if it protrudes beneath the mounting panel for a considerable distance, it is a good idea to fit a stay between the aerial and the vehicle's frame. This stay can be manufactured from the slotted and drilled metal strips previously mentioned. The stay should be securely screwed or bolted in place. For best reception, it is advisable to fit an earth lead between the aerial and the vehicle frame.

It will probably be necessary to drill one or two holes through bodywork panels in order to feed the aerial lead into the interior of the car. Where this is the case, ensure that the holes are fitted with rubber grommets to protect the cable, and to stop possible entry of water.

Positioning and fitting of the speaker depends mainly on its type. Generally, the speaker is designed to fit directly into the aperture already provided in the car (usually in the shelf behind the rear seats, or in the top of the dash panel). Where this is the case, fitting the speaker is just a matter of removing the protective grille from the aperture and screwing or bolting the speaker in place. Take great care not to damage the speaker diaphragm whilst doing this. It is a good idea to fit a 'gasket' between the speaker frame and the mounting panel, in order to prevent vibration – some speakers will already have such a gasket fitted.

If a 'pod' type speaker was supplied with the radio, the best acoustic results will normally be obtained by mounting it on the shelf behind the rear seat. The pod can be secured to the mounting panel with self-tapping screws.

When connecting a rear mounted speaker to the radio, the wires should be routed through the vehicle beneath the carpets or floor mats – preferably the middle, or along the side of the floorpan, where they will not be trodden on by passengers. Make the relevant connections as directed by the radio manufacturer.

By now you will have several yards of additional wiring in the car; use PVC tape to secure this wiring out of harm's way. Do not leave electrical leads dangling. Ensure that all new electrical connections are properly made (wires twisted together will not do) and completely secure.

The radio should now be working, but before you pack away your tools it will be necessary to 'trim' the radio to the aerial. If specific instructions are not provided by the radio manufacturer, proceed as follows. Find a station with a low signal strength on the medium wave band, slowly turn the trim screw of the radio in, or out, until the loudest reception of the selected station is obtained – the set is then trimmed to the aerial.

Tape players

Fitting instructions for both cartridges and cassette stereo type players are the same, and in general the same rules apply as when fitting a radio. Tape players are not usually prone to electrical inference like radios – although it can occur – so positioning is not so critical. If possible, the player should be mounted on an 'even-keel'. Also, it must be possible for a driver wearing a seat belt to reach the unit in order to change or turn over tapes.

For the best results from speakers designed to be recessed into a panel, mount them so that the back of the speaker protrudes into an enclosed chamber within the car (eg door interiors or the boot cavity).

To fit recessed type speakers in the front doors, first check that there is sufficient room to mount the speakers in each door without it fouling the latch or window winding mechanism. Hold the speaker against the skin of the door, and draw a line around the periphery of the speaker. With the speaker removed draw a second 'cutting' line, within the first, to allow enough room for the entry of the speaker back, but, at the same time, providing a broad seat for the speaker flange. When you are sure that the 'cutting-line' is correct, drill a series of holes around its periphery. Pass a hacksaw blade through one of the holes and then cut through the metal between the holes until the centre section of the panel falls out.

De-burr the edges of the hole, then paint the raw metal to prevent corrosion. Cut a corresponding hole in the door trim panel – ensuring that it will be completely covered by the speaker grille. Now drill a hole in the door edge and a corresponding hole in the door surround. These holes are to feed the speaker leads through – so fit grommets. Pass the speaker leads through the door trim, door skin and out through the holes in the side of the door and door surround. Refit the door trim panel, then secure the speaker to the door using self-tapping screws. Note that if the speaker is fitted with a shield to prevent water dripping on it, ensure that this shield is at the top.

Pod type speakers can be fastened to the shelf behind the rear seat, or anywhere else offering a corresponding mounting point on each side of the car. If the pod speakers are mounted on each side of the shelf behind the rear seat, it is a good idea to drill several large diameter holes through to the boot cavity beneath each speaker – this will improve the sound reproduction. Pod speakers sometimes offer a better reproduction quality if they face the rear window – which then acts as a reflector – so it is worthwhile to do a little experimenting before finally fixing the speaker.

45 Radios and tape players – suppression of interference (general)

To eliminate buzzes and other unwanted noises costs very little and is not as difficult as sometimes thought. With a modicum of common sense and patience, and following the instructions in the following paragraphs, interferences can be virtually eliminated.

The first cause for concern is the generator. The noise this makes over the radio is like an electric mixer and the noise speeds up when you rev up (if you wish to prove the point, you can remove the drivebelt and try it). The remedy for this is simple; connect a $1.0 \mu F$ to $3.0 \mu F$ capacitor between earth, probably the bolt that holds down the generator base, and the *large* terminal on the dynamo or alternator.

This is most important: *If you connect it to the small terminal, you will probably damage the generator permanently (see Fig. 10.25).*

A second common cause of electrical interference is the ignition system. Here a $1.0 \mu F$ capacitor must be connected between earth and the 'SW' or '+' terminal on the coil (see Fig. 10.26). This may stop the 'tick-tick-tick' sound that comes over the speaker. Next comes the spark itself.

There are several ways of curing interferences from the ignition HT system. One is to use carbon film HT leads but these have a tendency to 'snap' inside, and you don't know, then, why you are firing on only half your cylinders. So the second, and more successful method is to use resistive spark plug caps (see Fig. 10.27) of about 10 000 ohm to 15 000 ohm resistance. If, due to lack of room, these cannot be used, an alternative is to use 'in-line' suppressors (Fig. 10.27) – if the interference is not too bad, you may get away with only one suppressor in the coil to distributor line. If the interference does continue (a 'clacking' noise), doctor all HT leads.

At this stage, it is advisable to check that the radio is well earthed, also the aerial, and to see that the aerial plug is pushed well into the set and that the radio is properly trimmed (see preceding Section). In addition, check that the wire which supplies the power to the set is as short as possible and does not wander all over the car. At this stage, it is a good idea to check that the fuse is of the correct rating. For most sets this will be about 1 to 2 amps.

At this point, the more usual causes of interference have been suppressed. If the problem still exists, a look at the cause of interference may help to pinpoint the component generating the stray electrical discharges.

The radio picks up electromagnetic waves in the air; now some are made by radio stations and other broadcasters and some, not wanted, are made by the car. The home made signals are produced by stray electrical discharges floating around the car. Common producers of

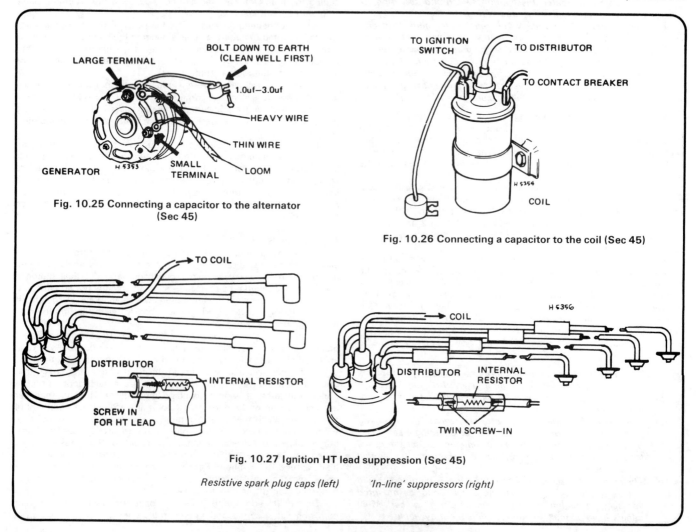

Fig. 10.25 Connecting a capacitor to the alternator (Sec 45)

Fig. 10.26 Connecting a capacitor to the coil (Sec 45)

Fig. 10.27 Ignition HT lead suppression (Sec 45)

Resistive spark plug caps (left)   *'In-line' suppressors (right)* these signals are electric motors; ie, the windscreen wipers, electric screen washers, electric window winders, heater fan or an electric aerial if fitted. Other sources of interference are electric fuel pumps, flashing turn signals, and instruments. The remedy for these cases is shown in Fig. 10.28 for an electric motor whose interference is not too bad and Fig. 10.29 for instrument suppression. Turn signals are not normally suppressed. In recent years, radio manufacturers have included in the line (live) of the radio, in addition to the fuse, an 'in-line' choke. If your installation lacks one of these, put one in as shown in Fig. 10.30. All the foregoing components are available from radio shops or accessory shops. For a transistor radio, a 2A choke should be adequate. If you have an electric clock fitted, this should be suppressed by connecting a 0.5 μF capacitor directly across it as shown for a motor in Fig. 10.28.

If, after all this, you are still experiencing radio interference, first assess how bad it is, for the human ear can filter out unobstrusive unwanted noises quite easily. But if you are still adamant about eradicating the noise, then continue.

As a first step, a few 'experts' seem to favour a screen between the radio and the engine. This is OK as far as it goes, literally! – for the whole set is screened and if interference can get past that, then a small piece of aluminium is not going to stop it.

A more sensible way of screening is to discover if interference is coming down the wires. First, take the live lead; interference can get between the set and the choke (hence the reason for keeping the wires short). One remedy here is to screen the wire and this is done by buying screened wire and fitting that. The loudspeaker lead could be screened also to prevent 'pick-up' getting back to the radio – although this is unlikely.

Without doubt, the worst source of radio interference comes from the ignition HT leads, even if they have been suppressed. The ideal way of suppressing these is to slide screening tubes over the leads themselves. As this is impractical, we can place an aluminium shield over the majority of the lead areas. In a V- or twin-cam engine, this is relatively easy but for a straight engine the results are not particularly good.

Now for the really impossible cases, here are a few tips to try out. Where metal comes into contact with metal, an electrical disturbance is caused which is why good clean connections are essential. To remove interference due to overlapping or butting panels, you must bridge the join with a wide braided earth strap (like that from the frame to the engine/transmission). The most common moving parts that

could create noise and should be strapped are, in order of importance:

(a) Silencer to frame
(b) Exhaust pipe to engine block and frame
(c) Air cleaner to frame
(d) Front and rear bumpers to frame
(e) Steering column to frame
(f) Bonnet and boot lids to frame
(g) Soft top frame to frame on soft tops

These faults are most pronounced when the engine is either idling or labouring under loads. Although the moving parts are already connected with nuts, bolts, etc, these do tend to rust and corrode, thus creating a high resistance interference source.

If you have a 'ragged' sounding pulse when mobile, this could be wheel or tyre static. This can be cured by buying some anti-static powder and sprinkling it liberally inside the tyres.

If the interference takes the shape of a high pitched screeching noise that changes its note when the car is in motion and only comes now and then, this could be related to the aerial, especially if it is of the telescopic or whip type. This source can be cured quite simply by pushing a small rubber ball on top of the aerial (yes, really!) as this breaks the electric field before it can form; but it would be much better to buy yourself a new aerial of a reputable brand. If, on the other hand, you are getting a loud rushing sound every time you brake, then this is brake static. This effect is most prominent on hot dry days and is cured only by fitting a special kit, which is quite expensive.

In conclusion, it is pointed out that it is relatively easy, and therefore cheap, to eliminate 95 per cent of all noises, but to eliminate the final 5 per cent is time and money consuming. It is up to the individual to decide if it is worth it. Please remember also, that you will not get concert hall performance from a cheap radio.

Finally, at the beginning of this Section are mentioned tape players; these are not usually affected by interference but in a very bad case, the best remedies are the first three suggestions plus using a 3 to 5 amp choke in the 'live' line, and in incurable cases screen the live and speaker wires.

Note: *If your car is fitted with electronic ignition, then it is not recommended that either the spark plug resistors or the ignition coil capacitor be fitted as these may damage the system. Most electronic ignition units have built-in suppression and should, therefore, not cause interference.*

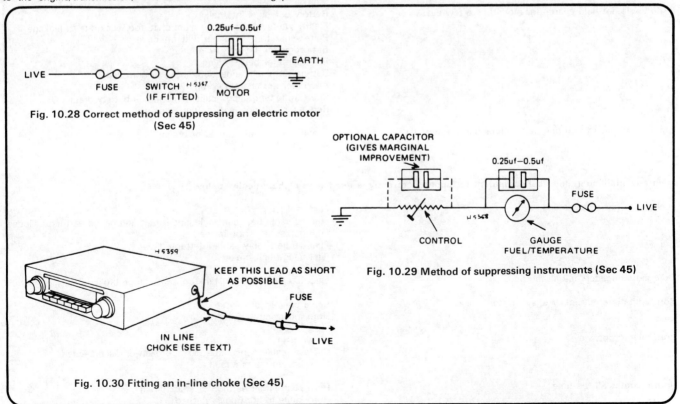

Fig. 10.28 Correct method of suppressing an electric motor (Sec 45)

Fig. 10.29 Method of suppressing instruments (Sec 45)

Fig. 10.30 Fitting an in-line choke (Sec 45)

46 Fault diagnosis – electrical system

Symptom	Reason(s)
No voltage at starter motor	Battery discharged Battery defective internally Battery terminal leads loose or earth lead not securely attached to body Loose or broken connections in starter motor circuit Starter motor switch or solenoid faulty
Voltage at starter motor: faulty motor	Starter brushes badly worn, sticking, or brush wires loose Commutator dirty, worn or burnt Starter motor armature faulty Field coils earthed
Electrical defects	Battery in discharged condition Starter brushes badly worn, sticking, or brush wires loose Loose wires in starter motor circuit
Mechanical damage	Pinion or flywheel gear teeth broken or worn
Lack of attention or mechanical damage	Pinion or flywheel gear teeth broken or worn Starter motor retaining bolts loose
Wear or damage	Battery defective internally Electrolyte level too low or electrolyte too weak due to leakage Plate separators no longer fully effective Battery plates severely sulphated
Insufficient current flow to keep battery charged	Fanbelt slipping Battery terminal connections loose or corroded Alternator not charging properly Short in lighting circuit causing continual battery drain Regulator unit not working correctly
Alternator not charging*	Fanbelt loose and slipping, or broken Brushes worn, sticking, broken or dirty Brush springs weak or broken

If all appears to be well but the alternator is still not charging, take the car to an automobile electrician for checking of the alternator and regulator.

Battery will not hold charge for more than a few days	Battery defective internally Electrolyte level too low or electrolyte too weak due to leakage Plate separators no longer fully effective Battery plates severely sulphated Fan/alternator belt slipping Battery terminal connections loose or corroded Alternator not charging properly Short in lighting circuit causing continual battery drain Regulator unit not working correctly
Ignition light fails to go out, battery runs flat in a few days	Fanbelt loose and slipping or broken Alternator faulty

Failure of individual electrical equipment to function correctly is dealt with alphabetically, below

Fuel gauge gives no reading	Fuel tank empty! Electric cable between tank sender unit and gauge earthed or loose Fuel gauge case not earthed Fuel gauge supply cable interrupted Fuel gauge unit broken
Fuel gauge registers full all the time	Electric cable between tank unit and gauge broken or disconnected
Horn emits intermittent or unsatisfactory noise	Cable connections loose Horn incorrectly adjusted
Horn fails to operate	Blown fuse Cable or cable connection loose, broken or disconnected Horn has an internal fault
Horn operates all the time	Horn push either earthed or stuck down Horn cable to horn push earthed

Symptom	Reason(s)
Instrument readings erratic	Voltage stabiliser faulty
Lights come on but fade out	If engine not running battery discharged
Lights do not come on	If engine not running, battery discharged Light bulb filament burnt out or bulbs broken Wire connections loose, disconnected or broken Light switch shorting or otherwise faulty
Lights give very poor illumination	Lamp glasses dirty Reflector tarnished or dirty Lamps badly out of adjustment Incorrect bulb with too low wattage fitted Existing bulbs old and badly discoloured Electrical wiring too thin not allowing full current to pass
Wiper motor fails to work	Blown fuse Wire connections loose, disconnected or broken Brushes badly worn Armature worn or faulty Field coils faulty
Wiper motor works but wiper blades remain static	Linkage disengaged or faulty Drive spindle damaged or worn Wiper motor gearbox parts badly worn
Wiper motor works slowly and takes little current	Brushes badly worn Commutator dirty, greasy or burnt Armature badly worn or faulty
Wiper motor works very slowly and takes excessive current	Commutator dirty, greasy or burnt Drive to spindles too bent or unlubricated Drive spindle binding or damaged Armature bearings dry or unaligned Armature badly worn or faulty

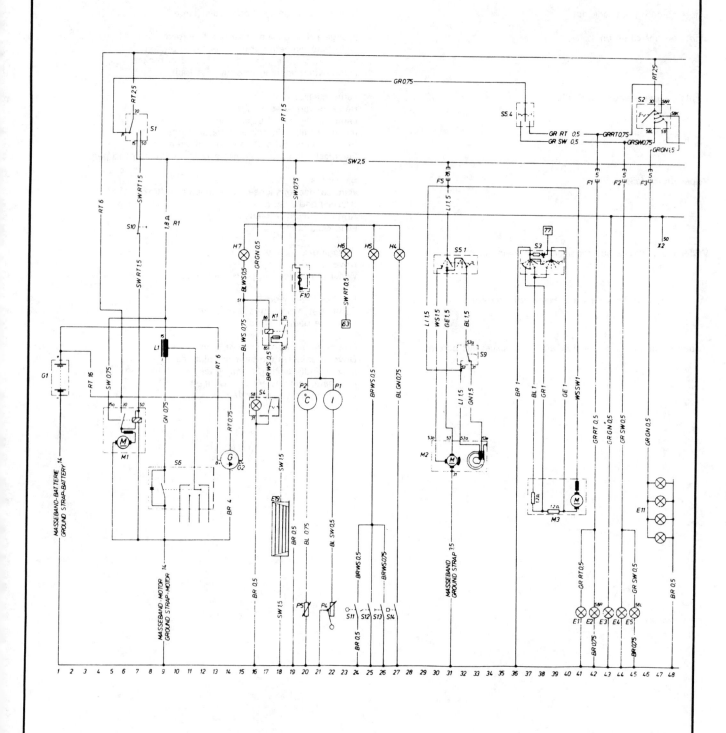

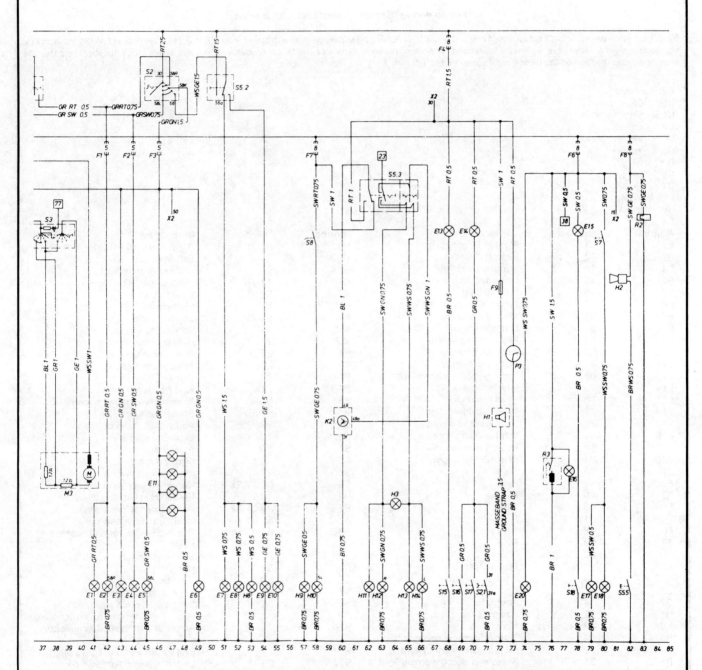

Fig. 10.31 Wiring diagram (schematic) – all models 1978 to 1982

This diagram is continued in Chapter 13

Key to wiring diagram (schematic) – all models

Note that each wire is identified by either one or two sets of letter codes followed by a number – eg GE WS 1.5. The first set of letters indicates the basic colour (in this case, yellow). The second set (where present) indicates the tracer colour (in this case, white). The number indicates the area of a cross-section of the wire in mm² (in this case 1.5 mm²)

Colour code

BL	Blue
HLB	Light Blue
BR	Brown
LI	Violet
GE	Yellow
GR	Grey
GN	Green
RT	Red
WS	White
SW	Black

Number	Location	Component	Number	Location	Component
E1	41	Right sidelight	H12	63	Right rear turn indicator
E2	42	Right tail light	H13	65	Left front turn indicator
E3	43	Number plate light	H14	66	Left rear turn indicator
E4	44	Left sidelight	K1	17,18	Heated rear window relay
E5	45	Left tail light	K2	60	Flasher unit
E6	49	Engine compartment light	L1	9	Ignition coil
E7	51	Right main beam	M1	5,6,7	Starter motor
E8	52	Left main beam	M2	31	Windscreen wiper motor
E9	54	Right dipped beam	M3	37,38,39,40	Heater blower motor
E10	55	Left dipped beam	P1	22	Fuel gauge tank unit
E11	46,48	Instrument lights	P2	20	Temperature gauge
E13	68	Luggage compartment light	P3	73	Clock
E14	70	Interior light	P4	21	Fuel gauge
E15	78	Glove box light	P5	20	Temperature gauge transmitter
E16	77	Cigarette lighter light	R1	9	Ballast resistor cable
E17	79	Right reversing light	R2	83	Automatic choke pre-heater
E18	80	Left reversing light	R3	76	Cigarette lighter
E19	18	Heated rear window	S1	6,7	Starter switch
E20	74	Selector lever light	S2	46	Light switch
F1	42	Fuse	S2.1	71	Interior light switch
F2	44	Fuse	S3	36,37,38,39	Heater blower switch
F3	46	Fuse	S4	16,17	Heated rear window switch
F4	68	Fuse	S5.1	30,31,32	Windscreen wiper switch
F5	31	Fuse	S5.2	50,51	Headlight dipper switch
F6	78	Fuse	S5.3	62,63,65	Direction indicator and flasher
F7	58	Fuse			switch
F8	82	Fuse	S5.4	36,37	Sidelight switch
F9	72	Fuse holder	S5.5	82	Horn switch
F10	19	Voltage stabilizer	S6	9,11	Distributor
G1	1	Battery	S7	80	Reversing light switch
G2	14	Alternator	S8	58	Stop light switch
H1	72	Radio	S9	32	Wiper unit foot control switch
H2	82	Horn	S10	7	Automatic transmission inhibitor
H3	64	Turn indicator warning light			switch
H4	27	Oil pressure warning light	S11	24	Brake fluid warning light switch
H5	25	Brake and clutch warning light	S12	25	Clutch warning light switch
H6	23	Hazard flasher warning light	S13	26	Handbrake warning light switch
H7	15	Charging indicator light	S14	27	Oil pressure switch
H8	53	Main beam warning light	S15	68	Luggage compartment light switch
H9	57	Right stop light	S16	69	Right door pillar switch
H10	58	Left stop light	S17	70	Left door pillar switch
H11	62	Right front turn indicator	S18	78	Glove box light switch

Chapter 11 Suspension and steering

For modifications, and information applicable to later models, see Supplement at end of manual

Contents

Specifications

Front suspension

Type .... Independent, MacPherson strut
Lateral control .... Track control arms
Longitudinal control .... Tie-bar
Shock absorbers .... Hydraulic, telescopic

Front wheel bearing lubricant type .... Multi-purpose lithium based grease (Duckhams LB 10)

Rear suspension

Type .... Trailing arm, coil spring, Panhard rod and anti-roll bar
Shock absorbers .... Hydraulic telescopic

Steering gear (standard)

Type .... Recirculating ball
Steering wheel turns (lock to lock) 4
Turning circle .... 10.7 metres (35.4 ft)
Lubricant type .... Gear oil, viscosity SAE 90 (Duckhams Hypoid 90S)
Lubricant capacity .... 0.4 litres (0.7 Imp pints)

Power assisted steering gear

Type .... ZF recirculating ball
Steering wheel turns (lock to lock) 4
Fluid type .... Dexron II type ATF (Duckhams D-Matic)
Fluid capacity .... 1.0 litres (1.75 Imp pints)

Front wheel alignment (unladen)

Camber .... -0°15' to +0°45'
Camber-max difference (side to side) .... 1°0'
Castor:
    Saloon .... +1°15' to +3°
    Estate .... +0°45' to +2°30'
Castor-max difference (side to side) .... 1°0'
Toe-in .... 2.5 to 4.5 mm (0.098 to 0.177 in)

Tyres

Size:
    Standard .... 175 SR 14
    Optional .... 185/70 SR 14

Tyre pressures

	Front	Rear
Saloon:		
Load up to 3 persons	26 lbf/in² (1.8 Bar)	26 lbf/in² (1.8 Bar)
Load exceeding 3 persons	29 lbf/in² (2.0 Bar)	32 lbf/in² (2.2 Bar)
Estate:		
Load up to 3 persons	26 lbf/in² (1.8 Bar)	29 lbf/in² (2.0 Bar)
Load exceeding 3 persons	26 lbf/in² (1.8 Bar)	37 lbf/in² (2.5 Bar)
Maximum loading	29 lbf/in² (2.0 Bar)	40 lbf/in² (2.8 Bar)

Torque wrench settings

	Nm	lbf ft
Front crossmember-to-chassis bolts	50	37
Engine mountings-to-crossmember	65	48
Track control arm-to-crossmember	70	52
Tie-bar-to-track control arm	80	59
Tie-bar-to-crossmember	80	59
Track control arm-to-Macpherson strut	70	52
MacPherson strut upper mountings-to-chassis	25	18
Front shock absorber-to-upper mounting	70	52
Shock absorber cartridge locking ring	200	147
Brake caliper-to-MacPherson strut	95	70
Brake disc-to-wheel hub	45	33
Track rod end castellated nut	50	37
Anti-roll bar front mounting plates	20	15
Wheel nuts	90	66
Rear upper control arm-to-chassis	65	48
Rear upper control arm-to-axle	65	48
Rear lower control arm-to-chassis	105	77
Rear lower control arm-to-axle	105	77
Anti-roll bar-to-upper control arm	15	11
Panhard rod-to-axle	60	44
Panhard rod-to- chassis	105	77
Shock absorber-to-rear axle (not estate car)	45	33
Shock absorber-to-rear axle (estate car only)	23	17
Propeller shaft rear mounting U-bolts	12	9
Steering box adjusting screw locknut	40	30
Steering box drop arm nut	160	118
Steering box-to-body	40	30
Steering box-to-pedal suspension bracket	20	15
Bearing adjustment cap lockring	120	89
Steering wheel nut	15	11
Steering box cover bolts	20	15

1 General description

The independent front suspension is of the MacPherson strut type, each strut unit containing a telescopic shock absorber cartridge, surrounded at the top by a coil spring.

The upper end of each strut is secured to the wing valance in the engine compartment by a rubber mounting, while the lower end is connected to a track control arm via a renewable balljoint. The front stub axle, which carries the wheel hub and brake disc, is forged integrally with the suspension strut, as are the steering arms and brake caliper mounting flanges.

Fore and aft movement of the suspension strut is controlled by a tie-bar, and an anti-roll bar interconnects each track control arm to reduce excess body roll when cornering.

A front crossmember is used to locate the tie-bar and track control arm inner mounting, and also carries the engine mounting brackets.

The steering gear is of the recirculating ball type. The steering box, which is bolted to the chassis member, is connected to an upper column assembly via a flexible coupling. The upper column is energy absorbing and is designed to progressively collapse on impact.

The steering arms at the base of each MacPherson strut are connected via balljoints to the steering track rods. The other end of each trackrod is attached via a balljoint to a drag link, while the other end is supported by an idler assembly. Power assistance is available as an option.

Basically, the front suspension geometry is preset during manufacture and cannot be altered, the only adjustment possible being the toe-in of the front wheels. It is, however, possible to reposition the MacPherson strut top mounting in either of two positions, thus providing two additional settings of camber and castor angle.

At the rear, the axle is located by four trailing links, while suspension is by coil springs and telescopic shock absorbers. An anti-

roll bar is also provided.

2 Maintenance and inspection

1 At regular intervals, inspect the condition of all flexible gaiters, balljoint dust excluders and rubber suspension bushes. Renew any that have split or deteriorated, as described in the appropriate Sections of this Chapter.

2 At the same time, check for any wear or excess play in the suspension and steering balljoints and linkages. Ensure the hub bearings are correctly adjusted and check the torque of all nuts and bolts on the suspension and steering components are in accordance with those listed in the Specifications.

3 It is also a good idea to have the front wheel alignment (toe-in) checked, and if necessary, reset at regular intervals. Refer to Section 20.

3 Front hub bearings – adjustment

1 To check the condition and adjustment of the hub bearings, apply the handbrake, jack up the front of the car and support it on firmly based axle stands. Grasp the roadwheel at the '12 o'clock' and '6 o'clock' positions and check for any rocking movement in the wheel hub. Watch carefully for any movement in the steering gear or suspension joints, which can easily be mistaken for hub movement.

2 If a front wheel hub has excessive movement, this is adjusted by removing the hub cap and then tapping and levering the dust cap from the centre of the hub.

3 Extract the split pin from the castellated nut and, if a torque wrench is available, tighten the nut to 25 Nm (18 lbf ft). Then back off the nut by three slots (approximately 90°). This will give the required

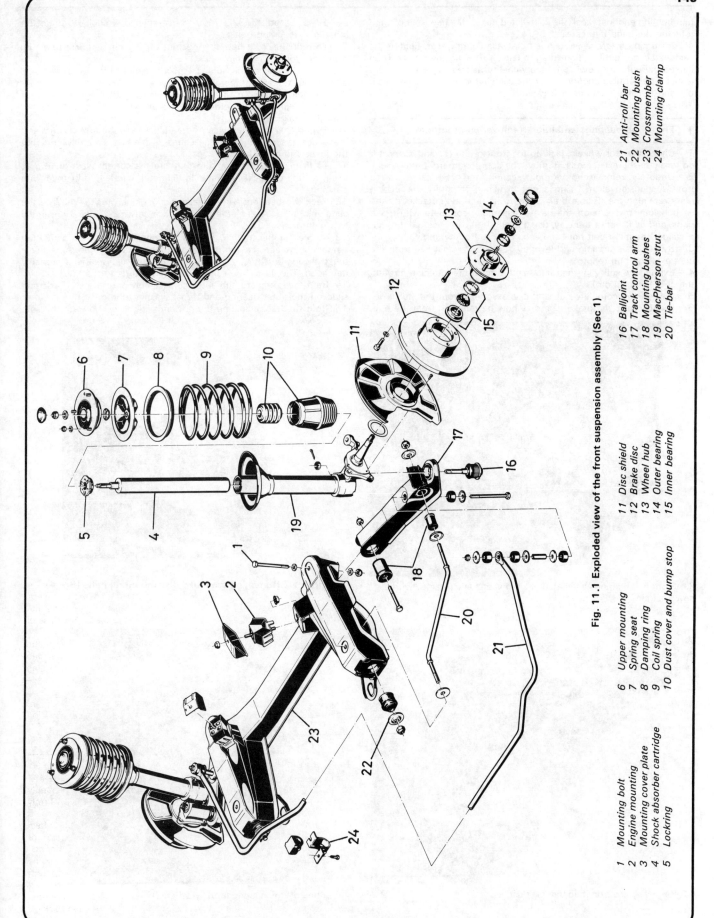

Fig. 11.1 Exploded view of the front suspension assembly (Sec 1)

1 Mounting bolt
2 Engine mounting
3 Mounting cover plate
4 Shock absorber cartridge
5 Lockring

6 Upper mounting
7 Spring seat
8 Damping ring
9 Coil spring
10 Dust cover and bump stop

11 Disc shield
12 Brake disc
13 Wheel hub
14 Outer bearing
15 Inner bearing

16 Balljoint
17 Track control arm
18 Mounting bushes
19 MacPherson strut
20 Tie-bar

21 Anti-roll bar
22 Mounting bush
23 Crossmember
24 Mounting clamp

hub bearing endfloat. Lock the castellated nut with a new split pin and refit the dust and hub caps.

4   Assuming a torque wrench is not available, however, tighten the castellated nut until a slight drag is felt on rotating the wheel. Then loosen the nut very slowly until the wheel turns freely again and there is just a perceptible endfloat. Lock the castellated nut with a new split pin and refit the dust and hub caps (photo).

4   Front hub bearings and hub – removal and refitting

1   Chock the rear wheels, jack up the front of the car and support it on firmly based axle stands. Remove the appropriate front roadwheel.
2   Undo and remove the two bolts securing the brake caliper to the front suspension strut. Using a pair of pliers, withdraw the locking plate retaining the flexible brake hose to its mounting bracket on the suspension strut. Lift off the caliper assembly, complete with brake pads, and tie it out of the way, using a length of wire inserted through a caliper retaining bolt hole and secured to a front spring coil.
3   By judicious tapping and levering, remove the dust cap from the centre of the hub (photo).
4   Extract the split pin, then undo and remove the retaining nut and thrust washer (photo).
5   Pull off the complete hub and disc assembly from the stub axle.
6   If necessary, the brake disc may now be removed from the hub,

using special tool KM322 (M10 twelve-splined wrench) to undo the brake disc retaining bolts.
7   To refit the front hub bearings, lift off the outer tapered bearing from the front of the hub.
8   From the rear of the hub assembly, prise out the hub grease seal and lift out the inner tapered bearing.
9   Carefully clean out the hub and wash the bearings in petrol or paraffin, making sure no grease or oil is allowed to come into contact with the brake disc.
10   Support the hub in a vice or on a block of wood and, using a soft metal drift inserted through the centre of the hub, carefully drive out the inner and outer bearing cups.
11   To fit new cups, make sure they are the correct way round and, using a tube or socket of suitable diameter, carefully drift them into position.
12   Pack the bearings with grease working the grease well into the cage and rollers. Also fill the hollow space between the bearings in the hub with grease.
13   To reassemble the hub, first fit the inner bearing, then gently tap a new hub grease seal into position on the rear of the hub. A new seal must always be fitted, as during removal the old seal was probably damaged. The lip on the seal must face inwards to the hub.
14   Refit the complete hub and disc assembly onto the stub axle and slide on the outer bearing and thrust washer (photo).
15   Refit the hub, adjusting the nut finger tight; do not refit the split

3.4 Front hub bearing castellated nut in position and retained with a new split pin

Fig. 11.2 Removing the brake disc mounting bolts (Sec 4)

4.3 Removing the front hub bearing dust cap

4.4 Lifting off the bearing thrust washer

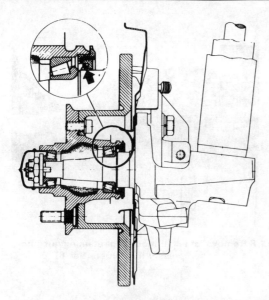

Fig. 11.3 Correctly assembled front hub bearings and oil seal (arrowed) (Sec 4)

Fig. 11.4 Using a balljoint separator to remove the track rod end from the steering arm (Sec 5)

4.14 Refitting the outer bearing

Fig. 11.5 Front anti-roll bar and bushes (arrowed) (Sec 5)

pin or dust cap at this stage.

16 Refit the brake caliper using the reverse sequence to removal. Tighten the retaining bolts to the torque figure given in the Specifications.

17 Refit the roadwheel, then adjust the front hub bearings as described in Section 3.

5 Front suspension strut – removal and refitting

1 Chock the rear wheels, jack up the front of the car and support it on firmly based axle stands. Mark the relationship of the front wheel to the wheel studs and remove the appropriate front roadwheel.

2 Refer to Section 4, paragraph 2, and remove the brake caliper.

3 Extract the split pin, then undo and remove the castellated nut securing the track rod end to the steering arm. The track rod end is a taper fit in the steering arm and if possible, a universal balljoint separator, or special tool KM260, should be used to part the two components. It is usually possible, however, to break the taper fit with a few sharp hammer blows. To do this, refit the castellated nut one turn (to protect the threads), then sharply strike the end of the steering arm with a medium hammer. When the taper is free, remove the nut

and lift off the track rod end.

4 Undo and remove the nut securing the anti-roll bar and mounting bushes to the long locating bolt on the lower suspension arm. Hold the bolt head from below with a socket and extension, to stop it turning while the nut is undone. Lift off the anti-roll bar, bushes, and distance sleeve, then withraw the long bolt from below.

5 Extract the split pin, then undo and remove the castellated nut securing the suspension strut to the lower arm balljoint. This joint is a taper fit in the suspension leg and is removed in the same manner as the trackrod end, using special tool KM333. If this tool is not available, it is possible to separate the joint by striking the suspension leg around the balljoint shank, using the method described in paragraph 3.

6 When the joint has separated, use a sturdy bar to lever the lower suspension arm down sufficiently to withdraw the balljoint shank from the suspension leg.

7 Working under the bonnet, note the position of the mark on the spring strut tower in relationship to the mark on the suspension leg upper mounting. The mounting may be fitted in any one of three positions; obviously, it must be refitted in the same position from which is was removed, otherwise the suspension geometry will be altered.

8 With the position of the mounting duly noted, undo and remove the three retaining nuts, then withdraw the complete unit downwards and off the car.

9 Refitting is a direct reversal of the removal sequence. Tighten all mountings to the torque wrench settings given in the Specifications, and use new split pins in the suspension arm and track rod end balljoint castellated nuts.

Fig. 11.6 Levering the balljoint from the suspension strut using strong bar (arrowed) (Sec 5)

Fig. 11.8 Removal of upper mounting retaining nut – note spring compressor in position (Sec 6)

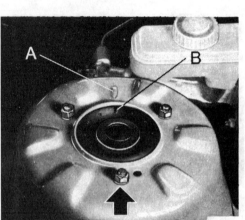

Fig. 11.7 Correct location of upper mounting with notch 'A' in line with mark 'B' – arrow shows one of securing nuts (Sec 5)

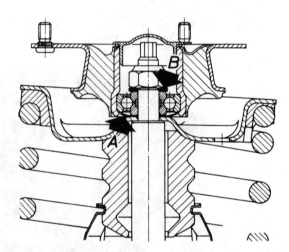

Fig. 11.9 Dished washer 'A' and thrust washer 'B' correctly positioned (Sec 6)

6 Front suspension strut upper mounting – removal and refitting

1   It is difficult to work on the front suspension without one or two special tools, the most important of which being a compressor for the front roadspring, special tool KM329. If difficulty is experienced in obtaining this tool from your local dealer, other garages in your area should carry similar coil spring compressors; MacPherson strut front suspension is quite popular and is used on a wide range of vehicles. This tool (or a similar compressor) is vital, and any attempt to dismantle the units without it may result in personal injury.
2   Proceed by removing the complete front suspension strut, as described in Section 5.
3   Compress the spring, using special tool KM329 or a suitable coil spring compressor, until there is no spring tension on the upper spring seat or upper mounting.
4   Lift off the dust cap, then undo and remove the piston retaining nut and thrust washer.
5   Lift off the upper mounting and dished washer from the spring seat.
6   The mounting is a sealed assembly and cannot be dismantled. If damaged or worn, the unit must therefore be renewed.
7   Begin reassembly by placing the dished washer in position on the spring upper retaining plate, with the dished edge upwards.
8   Place the upper mounting in position over the piston rod. Refit the thrust washer and retaining nut, tightening the nut to the torque figure

given in the Specifications. Refit the dust cap.
9   Release the spring compressor and refit the suspension strut to the car, as described in Section 5.

7 Front coil spring – removal and refitting

1   Remove the front suspension strut as described in Section 5, and the suspension strut upper mounting as described in Section 6.
2   Lift off the upper spring seat and damping ring from the top of the coil spring.
3   Release the spring compressor and withdraw the spring off the suspension strut.
4   If a new spring is being fitted, check carefully that it is of the same rating as the spring it replaces. Spring identification is by a letter stamped on the spring. Note also that springs of different rating are used either side and are therefore not interchangeable. *It is recommended that springs are changed in pairs; never individually.*
5   Begin reassembly by compressing the spring, using the spring compressors.
6   Place the spring in position on the suspension strut, locating the projecting end of the lower coil in the wide seat of the spring carrier plate.
7   Mount the damping ring to the top of the spring, then place the spring upper seat in position with the small hole facing away from the stub axle.

Fig. 11.10 Projecting end of coil spring locates in wide seat of carrier plate (arrowed) (Sec 7)

Fig. 11.11 Small hole in spring seat must face away from stub axle (Sec 7)

Fig. 11.12 Removing the shock absorber lockring (Sec 8)

9.2 Anti-roll bar mounting bolt on suspension arm

8   Refit the suspension strut upper mounting as described in Section 6, then refit the complete strut to the car, as described in Section 5.

8   Front shock absorbers – removal and refitting

1   Each front shock absorber is a telescopic cartridge contained within the front suspension strut. Therefore, should fluid leakage become apparent around the piston (or if the shock absorber is losing its damping capabilities), renewal is simply a matter of renewing the cartridge rather than fitting a complete front strut.
2   To provide access to the cartridge, the suspension strut must be removed from the car as described in Section 5, and the upper mounting removed as described in Section 6.
3   Lift off the spring upper seat and damping ring, as detailed in Section 7.
4   Withdraw the shock absorber dust cover and bump stop rubber, if fitted, from the end of the piston.
5   Using a large socket or box spanner, undo and remove the retaining lockring securing the cartridge to the suspension strut.
6   Lift out the cartridge from the centre of the strut.
7   Refitting is the reverse sequence to removal, bearing in mind the following points:

(a) Always use a new shock absorber lockring tightened to the torque figure given in the Specifications.
(b) New lockrings are coated in a wax sealer which must not be wiped off when fitting

(c) Refit the spring damping ring and seat as described in Section 7
(d) Refit the upper mounting as described in Section 5

9   Front anti-roll bar – removal and refitting

1   Chock the rear wheels, jack up the front of the car and support it on firmly based axle stands.
2   Undo and remove the nut securing the anti-roll bar and bushes to the long mounting bolt on each lower suspension arm. Use a socket and extension bar to hold the bolt from underneath while the nut is undone (photo).
3   Lift off the rubber bushes and cups, then withdraw each end of the anti-roll bar from the mounting bolt.
4   Undo and remove the two bolts securing the two mounting brackets to the left and right chassis side-members, then lower the anti-roll bar to the ground.
5   The mounting bushes should be carefully inspected and, if necessary, renewed. The bushes in the chassis mounting brackets are fitted with their slots facing forward, while the anti-roll bar to suspension arm bushes are fitted with their necks located in the anti-roll bar eye and suspension arm mounting hole.
6   Refitting the anti-roll bar is the reverse sequence to removal. When tightening the mounting bolt, ensure that the bushes are compressed to the dimension shown in Fig. 11.15.

Fig. 11.13 Anti-roll bar mounting bolt and bushes (arrowed)
(Sec 9)

Fig. 11.14 Anti-roll bar front mounting bushes fitted with slots
(arrowed) facing forward (Sec 9)

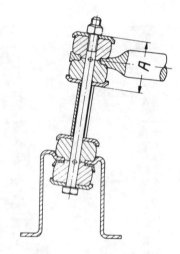

Fig. 11.15 Cross-section of anti-roll bar mounting – dimension 'A'
= 40.64 mm (1.6 in) (Sec 9)

Fig. 11.16 Suspension arm inner mounting and tie-bar mounting
(arrowed) (Sec 10)

10 Track control arm (suspension arm) – removal and refitting

1   Chock the rear wheels, jack up the front of the car and support it
on firmly based axle stands. Mark the relationship of the front wheel
to the wheel studs and remove the front roadwheel.
2   Undo and remove the nut securing the anti-roll bar and bushes to
the long suspension arm mounting bolt. Use a socket and extension
bar to hold the bolt from underneath while the nut is undone. Lift off
the anti-roll bar and bushes, then withdraw the bolt downwards and
off the suspension arm.
3   Undo and remove the nut and bolt securing the suspension arm
inner mounting to the crossmember.
4   Undo and remove the nut and thrust washer securing the tie-bar
to the suspension arm.
5   Withdraw the suspension arm from its location in the
crossmember and move it rearwards to disengage the tie-bar.
6   Using the method described in Section 5, paragraph 5, separate
the balljoint from the suspension strut and lift the suspension arm from
the car.
7   The bushes in the arm may be removed by drawing them out,
using a tube of suitable diameter, long bolt and nut and assorted flat
washers. Alternatively, the bush may be pressed out using a vice,
socket or tube and distance piece. New bushes are fitted in the same
manner. The tie-bar mounting bush may be lubricated in soapy water
to facilitate fitting; however the suspension arm mounting bush must

be fitted dry.
8   To refit the arm, first assemble the suspension arm balljoint to the
base of the suspension strut. Refit the nut and tighten it to the
specified torque. Secure with a new split pin.
9   Place the suspension arm so that it locates correctly over the tie-
bar and refit the thrust washer and locknut finger tight only at this
stage.
10   Position the inner mounting in its location in the crossmember and
secure with the pivot bolt inserted from the front. Refit the nut but do
not fully tighten at this stage.
11   Jack up the suspension arm until it is in an approximately
horizontal position. Now tighten the tie-bar and suspension arm
mounting bolts to the torque figure given in the Specifications at the
beginning of this Chapter.
12   Lower the jack and place the anti-roll bar mounting bolt and
bushes in position on the suspension arm. Refit the distance sleeve,
upper bushes and anti-roll bar, secure the assembly with the locknut,
tightened until the bushes are compressed to the dimension shown in
Fig. 11.15.
13   Refit the roadwheel in its original position and lower the car to
the ground.

11 Track control arm (suspension arm) balljoint – removal and refitting

1   It is permissible to renew the balljoint in an original suspension

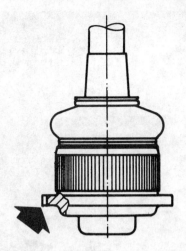

Fig. 11.17 Suspension arm balljoint identification notch (Sec 11)

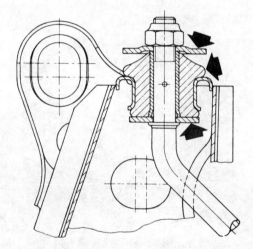

Fig. 11.18 Cross-section showing correct location of tie-bar front mounting bush and thrust washers (Sec 12)

12.2 Tie-bar front mounting in the suspension crossmember

arm once only. Should the joint require renewal a second time, it will be necessary to obtain a new suspension arm complete with factory fitted balljoint. Balljoints supplied separately have an identification notch on their lower face, while joints supplied already fitted in the suspension arm are unmarked. Therefore, if the balljoint does not have an identification notch it may be renewed separately. If a notch is present a complete suspension arm is required.

2   Begin by removing the suspension arm as described in Section 10.
3   The balljoint is splined externally and is an interference fit in the suspension arm. The only satisfactory method of removing and refitting the balljoint is with a hydraulic press. Most garages have these facilities and should be able to renew the joint for you.
4   With the new balljoint in place, refit the arm to the car as described in Section 10.

12 Tie-bar and bushes – removal and refitting

1   To remove the tiebar, first withdraw the suspension arm using the procedure described in Section 10, paragraphs 1 to 5 inclusive.
2   With the suspension arm withdrawn from the tie-bar rear mounting, undo and remove the locknut and thrust pad securing the tie-bar to its mounting in the crossmember (photo).
3   Slide the tie-bar rearwards and downwards, and withdraw it from under the car.
4   Examine the rubber mounting in the crossmember for distortion, damage or cracking of the rubber. If renewal is necessary, draw the bush out toward the front of the car using a tube of suitable diameter, long bolt, nut and flat washers.
5   Lubricate a new bush in soapy water and draw it into place from the front. Ensure the bush is fitted with its larger shoulder facing forward.
6   The tie-bar rear mounting in the suspension arm is renewed in the same manner, using the procedure described in Section 10.
7   Place the tie-bar in position on the front mounting, ensuring that the thrust washers are correctly positioned. Refit the locknut and tighten it to the specified torque.
8   Refit the suspension arm using the procedure described in Section 10, paragraphs 9 to 13 inclusive.

13 Front crossmember – removal and refitting

1   Chock the rear wheels and jack up the front of the car, supporting it on firmly based axle stands. Position the stands along the chassis side-members, ensuring that they are clear of the crossmember.
2   Undo and remove the pivot bolts and locknuts securing the two suspension arms to the crossmember. Pull the two suspension arms down and out of their locations in the crossmember.
3   Undo and remove the two tie-bar front mounting locknuts and thrust washers. Withdraw the tie-bars rearwards from their rubber bushes.
4   Place a block of wood between a suitable jack and the engine sump, then just take the weight of the engine.
5   Undo and remove the two locknuts securing the left and right front engine mountings.
6   Support the crossmember on a jack or blocks, then undo and remove the two long bolts and locknuts each side securing the crossmember to the chassis side-members.
7   Carefully lower the crossmember to the ground and slide it out from underneath the car.
8   Refitting is the reverse sequence to removal, bearing in mind the following points:

(a)   *Tighten all mounting bolts to the torque figures given in the Specifications*
(b)   *With the suspension arm and tie-bar refitted, jack up the arm until it is approximately horizontal and fully tighten the mounting bolts with the arm in this position*

14 Rear spring – removal and refitting

1   Chock the front wheels, jack up the rear of the car and support it on firmly based axle stands positioned along the chassis side-members.

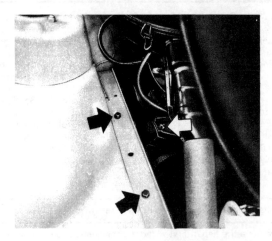

Fig. 11.19 Crossmember to chassis and engine mounting bolts
(Sec 13)

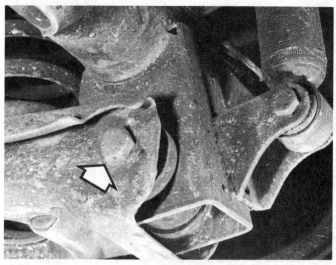

14.2 Lower control arm rear mounting bolt (arrowed)

2   Slacken the lower control arm mounting bolts at the rear axle and
chassis mounting brackets (photo).
3   Place a jack beneath the lower control arm, adjacent to the front
mounting, and just take the weight of the arm.
4   Undo the locknut and remove the front mounting bolt (photo). If
necessary, use a stout bar as a lever and move the control arm forward
slightly, to allow the bolt to be removed,
5   Slowly, lower the jack and ease out the control arm from its
location in the mounting bracket.
6   When sufficient clearance exists, withdraw the handbrake cable
from its retaining clip on the control arm, by slightly bending up the
clip.
7   Fully lower the jack and control arm, then lift out the rear spring.
8   To refit the spring, place it in position on the lower control arm.
Raise the jack slightly and locate the spring in its upper mounting
(photo).
9   Raise the jack until the control arm is in position in the front
mounting.
10   Lever the arm forward until the holes in the control arm bush and
mounting bracket are in line, then refit the bolt and locknut. Do not
tighten the locknut at this stage.
11   Reposition the handbrake cable and bend over the retaining clip.
12   Lower the car to the ground and, with the full weight of the car on
its wheels, tighten the lower control arm mounting bolts at the rear
axle and chassis bracket to the specified torque.

14.4 Lower control arm front mounting bolt

15 Rear suspension lower control arm – removal and refitting

1   Remove the rear spring as described in Section 14.
2   Undo and remove the retaining bolt and locknut securing the
control arm to the rear axle bracket.
3   Withdraw the control arm from underneath the car.
4   Should it be necessary to renew the control arm front mounting
bushes, these may be removed by using a piece of tube about 76 mm
(3 in) long and of suitable diameter, a long bolt and nut and packing
washers, and drawing out the old bushes.
5   Fitting new bushes is the reverse procedure as was used for
removal. Lubricate the bushes in soapy water to facilitate fitting and
ensure that they are correctly orientated as shown in Fig. 11.21.
6   The bushes in the rear axle mounting bracket may be refitted using
the same procedure as for the control arm. Draw the bushes out
toward the centre of the car, and when refitting, ensure that the rubber
in the bush and the marking on the axle bracket are offset by 90°.
7   To refit the lower control arm, place the arm in position on the rear
axle bracket and secure it with the mounting bolt and locknut. Do not
fully tighten the locknut at this stage.
8   Refit the rear spring, using the procedure described in Section 14,
paragraphs 8 to 12 inclusive.

14.8 Rear spring tang must be in contact with stop on upper seat
when fitted

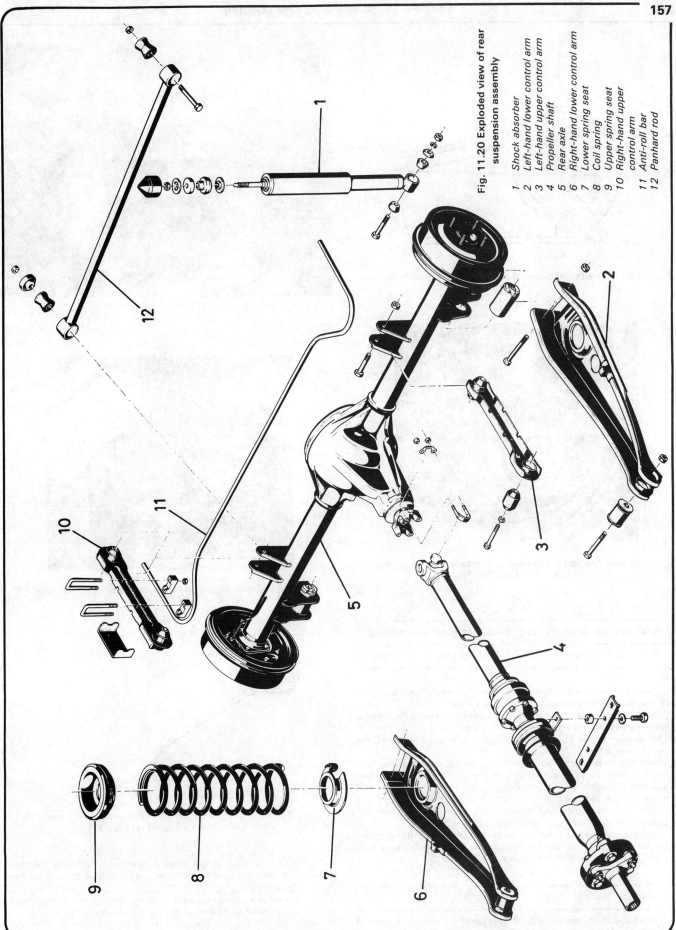

Fig. 11.20 Exploded view of rear suspension assembly

1 Shock absorber
2 Left-hand lower control arm
3 Left-hand upper control arm
4 Propeller shaft
5 Rear axle
6 Right-hand lower control arm
7 Lower spring seat
8 Coil spring
9 Upper spring seat
10 Right-hand upper control arm
11 Anti-roll bar
12 Panhard rod

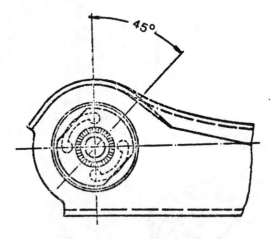

Fig. 11.21 Correct orientation of lower control arm front bushes (Sec 15)

16.2 Anti-roll bar mounting U-bolts on upper control arm

Fig. 11.22 Axle bracket bushes correctly located – note alignment mark (arrowed) (Sec 15)

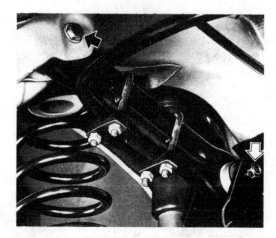

Fig. 11.23 Upper control arm mounting bolts (arrowed) (Sec 16)

16 Rear suspension upper control arm – removal and refitting

1   Chock the front wheels, jack up the rear of the car and support it on firmly based axle stands positioned along the chassis side members.

2   Undo and remove the four locknuts and two U-bolts securing the rear anti-roll bar to the upper control arm (photo).

3   Place a jack under the rear axle and raise the axle sufficiently to remove all tension from the upper control arm.

4   Undo and remove the retaining bolts and locknuts, then lift off the upper control arm.

5   Should it be necessary to renew the rubber mounting bushes, they may be removed by using a piece of tube about 76 mm (3 in) long and of suitable diameter, a long bolt and nut, and packing washers, and drawing out the old bushes.

6   New bushes may be fitted using the reverse procedure to removal. Lubricate the new bushes in soapy water prior to refitting.

7   Refitting the upper control arm is the reverse of the removal procedure; however, do not fully tighten the retaining locknuts until the weight of the car is on its wheels.

17 Rear anti-roll bar – removal and refitting

1   Chock the front wheels, jack up the rear of the car and support it on firmly based axle stands.

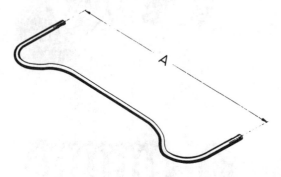

Fig. 11.24 Width of anti-roll bar; dimension 'A' must equal 731 $\pm$ 1 mm (28.78 $\pm$ 0.04 in) (Sec 17)

2   Undo and remove the four locknuts and two U-bolts securing the anti-roll bar to each upper control arm, then withdraw the anti-roll bar from under the car.

3   Before refitting the bar, check it is not distorted in any way and that its width is equal to that shown in dimension A, Fig. 11.24.

4   Refitting the anti-roll bar is a straightforward reversal of the removal procedure.

Fig. 11.25 Fitting Panhard rod mounting bushes (Sec 18)

18 Panhard rod – removal and refitting

1   The Panhard rod is located between a chassis anchorage bracket and a mounting stud on the right-hand side of the rear axle.
2   To remove the Panhard rod, chock the front wheels, jack up the rear of the car and support it on firmly based axle stands.
3   Undo and remove the mounting bolt and locknut securing the Panhard rod to the chassis bracket (photo).
4   Undo and remove the locknut and protective cap from the rear axle mounting stud. On estate cars, access to the locknut is gained by carefully bending back the protective cover.
5   Withdraw the Panhard rod from the chassis bracket and axle mounting stud, then lift it out from under the car.
6   If necessary, the rubber mounting bushes may be drawn out, using a tube of suitable length and diameter, a long bolt and nut and spacing washers.
7   Lubricate the new bushes in soapy water and press them into the Panhard rod by hand.
8   Refitting is the straightforward reverse of the removal procedure. With the Panhard rod refitted, ensure that on estate cars, the protective cap over the rear axle mounting nut is positioned as shown in Fig. 11.26.

19 Rear shock absorbers – removal, testing and refitting

1   Chock the front wheels, jack up the rear of the car and support it on firmly based axle stands, placed beneath the rear axle.
2   From inside the luggage compartment, lift off the protective cap and undo and remove the locknut(s), thrust washer and rubber bush.
3   Working beneath the car, undo and remove the locknut and lower mounting bolt, then lift off the shock absorber (photo).
4   Examine the shock absorber for signs of damage to the body, distorted piston rod or hydraulic leakage and if evident, renew the unit.
5   Hold the shock absorber in a vertical position and fully extend the piston. Apply firm pressure to the piston and push it back into the shock absorber body. An equal resistance should be felt during the full length of piston travel, with no trace of binding or tight spots. If this is not the case, the unit must be renewed.
6   Refitting the shock absorber is the reverse sequence to removal. When tightening the upper mounting locknut, the distance between the top face of the upper nut and the end of the mounting stud must be set as shown in Fig. 11.27.

18.3 Panhard rod mounting, locknut and protective cap on rear axle

20 Front wheel alignment and steering angles

1   Accurate front wheel alignment is essential to provide positive steering and prevent excessive tyre wear. Before considering the

Fig. 11.26 Panhard rod mounting cap fitted to estate cars –
dimension A = 19 mm (0.75 in) (Sec 18)

19.3 Shock absorber lower mounting (arrowed)

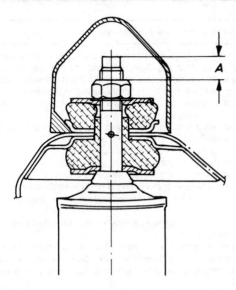

Fig. 11.27 Cross-section of shock absorber upper mounting (Sec 19)

Dimension A = Saloon: 9.5 mm (0.37 in)
Saloon with 'SR' equipment: 6.0 mm (0.24 in)
Estate and van: 12 mm (0.47 in)

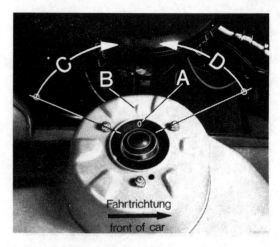

Fig. 11.28 MacPherson strut upper mounting positions (Sec 20)

Notch 'A' and 'B' in line = initial factory setting
Notch 'A' repositioned in direction 'C' causes − 0°30' castor change
Notch 'A' repositioned in direction 'D' causes + 0°30' castor change

20.8 Suspension strut upper mounting studs (A) and alignment mark (B) for castor angle factory setting

steering/suspension geometry, check the tyres are correctly inflated, the front wheels are not buckled, the hub bearings are not worn or incorrectly adjusted, and the steering linkage is in good order, without slackness or wear at the joints.

2   Wheel alignment consists of four factors: *Camber* is the angle at which the front wheels are set from the vertical when viewed from the front of the car. 'Positive camber' is the amount (in degrees) that the wheels are tilted outward at the top from the vertical. *Castor* is the angle between the steering axis and a vertical line when viewed from each side of the car 'Positive castor' is when the steering axis is inclined rearward. *Steering axis inclination* is the angle (when viewed from the front of the car) between the vertical and an imaginary line drawn between the MacPherson strut upper mounting and lower suspension arm balljoint. *Toe-in setting* is the amount by which the distance between the front inside edges of the roadwheels (measured at hub height) differs from the diametrically opposite distance measured between the rear inside edges of the front roadwheels.

3   Due to the need for special gauges, it is not normally within the scope of the home mechanic to check and adjust any steering angle except toe-in. Where suitable equipment can be borrowed, however, adjustments can be carried out in the following way, setting the tolerances to those given in the Specifications.

4   Before carrying out any measurements or adjustments, place the car on level ground, tyres correctly inflated and the front roadwheels set in the 'straight ahead' position. Make sure all suspension and steering components are securely attached and without wear in the moving parts.

5   *Camber and castor adjustment:* By altering the position of the MacPherson strut upper mounting to either of two positions off the initial factory setting, an increase in camber and a corresponding change in castor will occur (see Fig. 11.28). This adjustment should only be carried out when the measured camber angle of the car is outside the maximum permissible *negative* camber angle value as shown in the Specifications. Repositioning the mounting 120° to the front (direction 'C' in Fig. 11.28) will cause a castor change of −0°30'. Repositioning the mounting 120° to the rear (direction 'D' in Fig. 11.28) will cause a castor change of +0°30'. In both cases, the camber angle will increase by +1°.

6   To adjust the position of the upper mounting, jack up the front of the car and support it on firmly based axle stands.

7   Place a jack beneath the lower suspension arm and just take the weight of the arm and MacPherson strut.

8   Undo the three mounting nuts and lower the jack slightly, until the three studs are just clear of their mounting holes (photo).

9   Rotate the upper mounting 120° in the desired direction, raise the

jack slightly and engage the mounting studs in their respective locations.

10   Tighten the nuts to the specified torque and lower the car to the ground. Before rechecking the new settings, bounce the front of the car to settle the suspension and push the car back one car length and then forward.

11   *Toe-in adjustment:* To adjust the toe-in (which must always be carried out after adjustment of the camber/castor angle), make or obtain a toe-in gauge. One can be made up from a length of tubing or bar, cranked to clear the sump, clutch or torque converter bellhousing and having a screw and locknut at one end.

12   Use this gauge to measure the distance between the two inner wheel rims (at hub height and at the rear of the roadwheels).

13   Push or pull the car to rotate the roadwheels through 180° (half a turn), then measure the distance between the inner wheel rims (at hub height and at the front of the roadwheels). This last measurement will differ from the first by the amount specified in the Specifications, and represents the correct toe-in setting of the front wheels.

14   Where the toe-in is found to be incorrect, slacken the two locking clamps on each track rod (photo).

15   Turn each track rod by not more than one quarter of a turn at a time, then recheck the toe-in setting. When the adjustment is correct, tighten the two clamps on each track rod.

20.14 Track rod adjustment locking clamps

16 It is important always to adjust each track rod equally. Where new components have been fitted, adjust the length of each track rod so that they are equal and the front roadwheels are in approximately the 'straight ahead' position, before commencing a final setting with the gauge.

21 Steering wheel – removal and refitting

1   Disconnect the battery earth terminal.
2   Using a small screwdriver, carefully prise out the horn button from the centre of the steering wheel, followed by the horn button outer case, if this stays behind in the wheel.
3   Bend back the locktab, then undo and remove the steering wheel retaining nut, using a socket and extension bar.
4   Turn the steering wheel until the roadwheels are in the 'straight ahead' position and the steering wheel spokes are symmetrical and angled downwards.
5   Using a suitable puller, draw the steering wheel off the steering shaft. A useful puller can be made using a flat strip of metal, two long bolts, nuts and washers (photos); it will be necessary to remove the column surround. *Under no circumstances should force or any sharp blows be applied to the steering wheel; damage to the collapsible structure of the outer column and steering shaft may result.*
6   When the steering wheel is removed, take care not to damage the turn signal cancellation pin and horn slip ring wire, protruding from the base of the wheel (photo).

Fig. 11.29 Removal of steering wheel horn button (Sec 21)

21.5a A simple steering wheel puller made up from a flat strip of steel, two bolts, washers and nuts

21.5b The puller in position on the steering wheel

Fig. 11.30 Using a puller to remove steering wheel (Sec 21)

21.5c Removing the steering wheel from the shaft

21.6 Turn signal cancelling pin and horn slip ring contact at the rear of the steering wheel

22.2 Steering shaft flexible coupling and pinch bolt

Fig. 11.31 Lower trim panel retaining button (arrowed) (Sec 22)

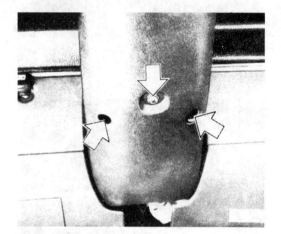

Fig. 11.32 Column shroud retaining screws (Sec 22)

Fig. 11.33 Column lower bracket mounting bolt (Sec 22)

Fig. 11.34 Location of the cable harness block connectors (Sec 22)

7   Refitting the steering wheel is the reverse sequence to removal. Ensure that, with the roadwheels in the 'straight ahead' position, the steering wheel spokes are symmetrical and the retaining nut is tightened to the specified torque.

22 Steering upper column assembly – removal and refitting

1   Disconnect the battery earth terminal.
2   Working under the bonnet, undo and remove the pinch bolt securing the steering shaft to the flexible coupling at the base of the column (photo).
3   From inside the car, prise out the five plastic retaining buttons and

lift off the kick panel from under the dash.
4   Undo and remove the three screws, then lift off the two halves of the steering column shroud.
5   Remove the cruise control switch lever from the right-hand side of the steering column (if fitted) and the heater duct from under the dash.
6   Undo and remove the bolt securing the steering column lower bracket to the pedal box.
7   Disconnect the three cable harness block connectors.
8   Undo and remove the two nuts securing the upper mounting bracket to the base of the dashboard (Fig. 11.36).
9   Supporting the weight of the column assembly, disengage the steering shaft and column from the flexible coupling and the grommet from the bulkhead, then carefully withdraw the complete column

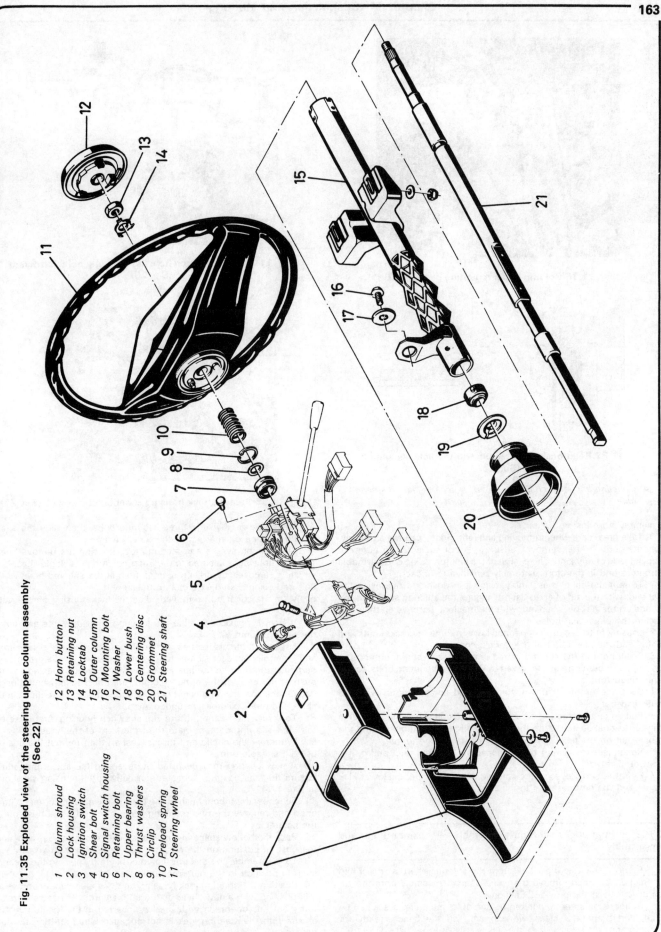

Fig. 11.35 Exploded view of the steering upper column assembly (Sec 22)

1 Column shroud
2 Lock housing
3 Ignition switch
4 Shear bolt
5 Signal switch housing
6 Retaining bolt
7 Upper bearing
8 Thrust washers
9 Circlip
10 Preload spring
11 Steering wheel
12 Horn button
13 Retaining nut
14 Locktab
15 Outer column
16 Mounting bolt
17 Washer
18 Lower bush
19 Centering disc
20 Grommet
21 Steering shaft

Fig. 11.36 Column upper mounting nuts (Sec 22)

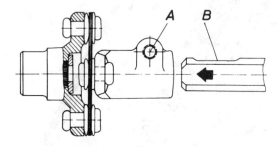

Fig. 11.37 Relationship of steering shaft to flexible coupling
(Sec 22)

A Coupling flange pinch bolt   B Machined flat on steering
   hole   shaft

Fig. 11.38 Signal switch housing retaining bolts (arrowed)
(Sec 23)

Fig. 11.39 Steering lock housing shear bolt (arrowed) (Sec 23)

assembly from inside the car.

10 Take great care when removing and refitting the column assembly; when storing it after removal, ensure it is not subjected to bump or shock loads of any kind. The design of the column is one of deformable structure and is therefore extremely sensitive to impact.

11 To refit the column assembly, place it in position from inside the car and, with the aid of an assistant, engage the steering shaft into the flange on the flexible coupling, with the machined groove on the shaft facing the pinch bolt holes.

12 Loosely fit the column upper and lower mounting bracket nuts and bolts, and the pinch bolt at the flexible coupling.

13 Ensuring that the column is free from stress or strain, tighten the two upper mounting nuts, followed by the lower mounting bolts, to the prescribed torque.

14 Slide the grommet down the shaft and engage its lip with the bulkhead flange.

15 Pull up on the steering wheel until the steering shaft stop contacts the turn signal switch. With the shaft held in this position, tighten the pinch bolt on the flexible coupling to the prescribed torque.

16 Reconnect the wiring block connectors, heating duct and cruise control, if fitted.

17 Refit the two halves of the steering column shroud, the lower kick panel and the battery earth terminal.

23 Steering upper column assembly – dismantling and reassembly

1 Remove the steering wheel from the steering shaft, as described in Section 21, then remove the upper column assembly from the car as described in the previous Section.

2 Support the steering column by one of its mounting brackets in a vice, and prepare a clean working area on the bench, ready for dismantling.

3 Undo and remove the three securing bolts, then slide the signal switch housing off the end of the outer column.

4 The ignition switch and steering lock housing are removed next. The lock housing is secured to the outer column by a single shear bolt, which is removed by drilling a small hole in the sheared head of the bolt and using a stud extractor to unscrew it.

5 With the shear bolt removed, slide the lock housing off the outer column.

6 It is now possible to slide the steering shaft upwards and out of the outer column.

7 Lay out all the dismantled components in the order of disassembly and carefully inspect them for wear, damage or distortion. Pay particular attention to the bearing in the signal switch housing and the bush at the base of the outer column. Roll the steering shaft along a flat surface and ensure it is not bent, and the collapsible sections in the shaft and outer column are undamaged.

8 To screw the bearing in the signal switch housing, first prise out the horn slip ring contact plate from the front of the housing.

9 Withdraw the circlip and thrust washer, then tap out the bearing using a suitable drift.

10 A new bearing may be fitted by reversing the above procedure. Ensure that the bearing is located correctly in the housing, as shown in Fig. 11.41.

11 To renew the rubber bush at the base of the steering outer column, undo and remove the two retaining screws and prise the bush out of the column.

12 Pack the hollow space in a new bush with rubber grease and place the bush in position on the column. Secure it with the two screws.

13 To reassemble the steering column, begin by placing the steering shaft in position in the outer column.

14 Position the steering lock housing on the upper column and retain it in position with a new shear bolt, tightened until the head shears off. Carry out this operation with the key inserted in the ignition switch; ensure that the steering lock is not engaged when refitting the lock housing.

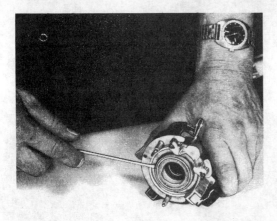

Fig. 11.40 Removing the horn slip ring contact plate (Sec 23)

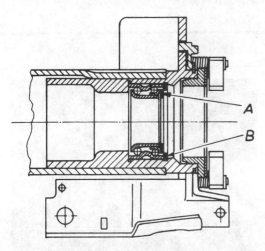

Fig. 11.41 Cross-section of signal switch housing and upper bearing (Sec 23)

A Thrust washer   B Circlip

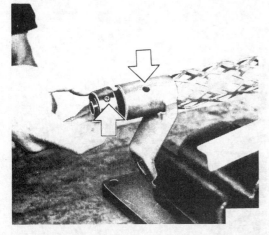

Fig. 11.42 Refitting the lower bush to the outer column (Sec 23)

15 Refit the signal switch housing to the top of the steering column and secure it in place with the three retaining bolts.
16 Refit the assembled column in the car following the procedure described in Section 22, then refit the steering wheel as described in Section 21.

24 Steering box – removal and refitting

1 Chock the rear wheels, jack up the front of the car and support it on firmly based axle stands.
2 Disconnect the battery earth terminal.
3 Working in the engine compartment, undo and remove the pinch bolt securing the steering shaft to the flexible coupling at the base of the column.
4 From inside the car, undo and remove the three screws, then lift off the two halves of the steering column shroud.
5 Undo and remove the three bolts securing the turn signal switch to the upper column.
6 Pull the steering shaft, complete with steering wheel and turn signal switch, upwards until the shaft disengages from the flange on the flexible coupling. Disconnect the windscreen washer hoses and starter motor cable.
7 From underneath the car, undo and remove the nut and spring washer securing the steering arm to the steering box shaft (photo).
8 Using a centre punch, mark the relationship of the steering arm to the shaft to ensure refitment in the same position.
9 Using a universal puller, draw the steering arm off the steering shaft.
10 Undo and remove the three long bolts, washers and nuts securing the steering box to the chassis member (photo) and the nut and washers securing the steering box to the wheel well.
11 Carefully withdraw the steering box upwards and out of the engine compartment.
12 To refit the steering box, locate the unit in position on the chassis member and refit the mounting bolts and nuts, but do not fully tighten them at this stage.
13 With the aid of an assistant, slide the steering shaft down the column and engage the end of the shaft with the flange on the flexible coupling. Ensure that the machined groove on the steering shaft is adjacent to the pinch bolt holes on the coupling flange.
14 Loosely refit the pinch bolt to the coupling flange.
15 Locate the turn signal switch in position on the upper column, and secure it with the three bolts, tightened to the specified torque.
16 Pull up on the steering wheel, until the stop on the steering shaft is against the signal switch. With the shaft held in this position, tighten the pinch bolt on the flexible coupling flange.
17 Fully tighten the steering box mountings to the specified torque.
18 Set the front wheels to the 'straight ahead' position and centralise the steering gear: turn the steering wheel from lock to lock and stop half way, ensuring the steering wheel spokes are symmetrical and angled downward.
19 Align the previously made marks and refit the steering arm to the steering box shaft. Secure it with the nut and spring washer tightened to the specified torque.
20 Refit the two halves of the steering column shroud and battery earth terminal connection. Refit the starter motor cable and windscreen washer hoses.
21 Lower the car to the ground, then check and if necessary top-up the steering box oil level.

25 Steering box – overhaul

1 Due to the complexity of the steering box, the task of overhaul may be beyond the scope of many diy motorists. Read through the Section before commencing any work, and if not considered feasible, entrust the work to your local vehicle main dealer.
2 Begin by removing the steering box from the car, as described in Section 24.
3 Prepare a clean, uncluttered workng surface on the bench and have at the ready a number of small containers to store the various parts as they are removed, particularly the small steel balls, which are easily lost.
4 Clamp the steering box mounting flange in a vice and, using an Allen key, undo and remove the bolt securing the flexible coupling to the worm shaft.
5 Using a small puller, draw the flexible coupling off the shaft.
6 Undo and remove the adjusting screw locknut from the steering box cover, and the four cover retaining bolts and washers.
7 Place a suitable container of approximately 0.5 litres (1 Imp pint) capacity beneath the steering box. Carefully, lift off the steering box

24.7 Steering drop arm retaining bolt

24.10 Location of steering box to chassis mountings

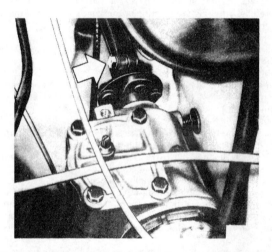

Fig. 11.43 Flexible coupling pinch bolt (arrowed) (Sec 24)

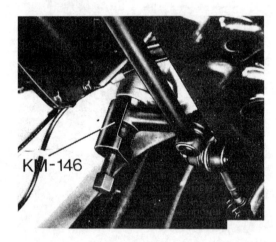

Fig. 11.44 Using a puller to remove the steering arm (Sec 24)

Fig. 11.45 Steering box to wheel well retaining nut (arrowed)
(Sec 24)

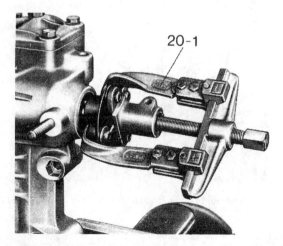

Fig. 11.46 Using a puller to remove the flexible coupling (Sec 25)

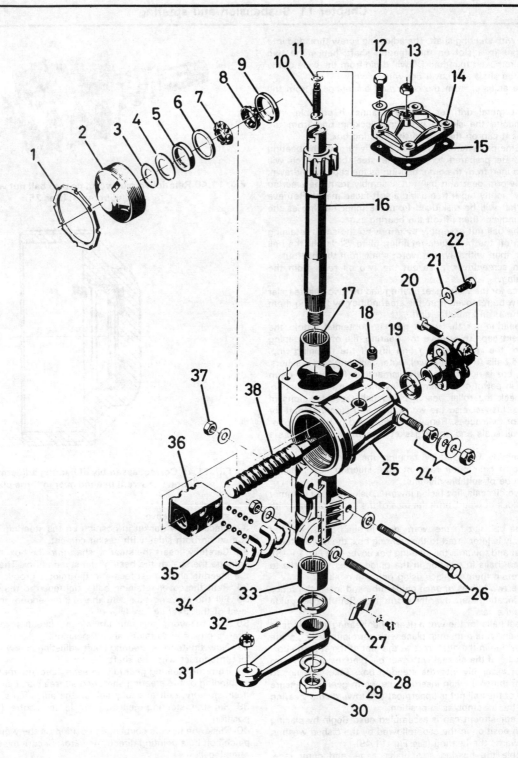

Fig. 11.47 Exploded view of steering box assembly (Sec 25)

1	Locking ring	11	Washer	21	Washer	30	Retaining nut
2	Bearing adjustment cap	12	Retaining bolt	22	Coupling retaining bolt	31	Castellated nut
3	Flat washer	13	Adjusting screw locknut	23	Flexible coupling	32	Oil seal
4	Dished washer	14	Steering box cover	24	Mounting nuts	33	Roller bearing
5	Outer race	15	Gasket	25	Steering box housing	34	Ball guide tubes
6	Retaining ring	16	Steering shaft	26	Mounting bolts	35	Worm balls
7	Bearing cage (outer)	17	Roller bearing	27	Ball guide retaining plate	36	Ball nut
8	Bearing cage (inner)	18	Filler plug	28	Steering arm	37	Mounting nut
9	Outer race	19	Oil seal	29	Lockwasher	38	Worm gear
10	Adjusting screw	20	Pinch bolt				

cover, complete with steering shaft. The adjusting screw threaded into the cover engages in a slot on the steering shaft; hence the two components are removed together. Oil will drain from the base of the steering box as the shaft and cover are withdrawn.

8   Unscrew the adjuster from the cover and disengage it from the steering shaft.

9   Using a soft metal drift, or suitable spanner if possible, very carefully tap undone the slotted octagonal locking ring from the bearing adjustment cap on the side of the steering box.

10 Using the same procedure, undo and carefully remove the bearing adjustment cap. Be prepared to catch the steel balls, which will probably be dislodged from the outer bearing as the cap is withdrawn.

11 Lift out the worm gear and ball nut assembly from the steering box. If necessary, gently tap it free using a soft-faced mallet. Retrieve the steel balls that will be dislodged from the inner bearing as the worm gear is removed, then lift off the bearing cage.

12 Dismantle the ball nut assembly by removing the small retaining screw and lifting off the ball guide retaining plate. Slide out the ball guides and balls, then withdraw the worm shaft from the ball nut.

13 Using a thin screwdriver, prise out the two oil seals from the steering box casing.

14 The outer race for the worm gear bearing and the two needle roller bearings may now be removed from the steering box by tapping them out, using a hammer and suitable drift.

15 The outer bearing for the worm gear is contained within the bearing adjustment cap. To remove the bearing, file off the peening burrs that secure the retaining ring and lift off the retaining ring, bearing cage and balls (if still in place), outer race and two washers.

16 The steering box is now completely dismantled. Thoroughly clean the components in petrol or paraffin and lay them out for inspection.

17 Carefully, check the roller bearings and ball races for signs of pitting or scoring. Inspect also the worm gear and steering shaft for wear or scoring of their faces. Renew any damaged or worn components. The two oil seals and cover gasket should be renewed as a matter of course.

18 Begin reassembly by carefully tapping the two needle roller bearings and worm gear outer race into the steering box housing, using a drift or tube of suitable diameter.

19 Tap in the two oil seals, lips facing inwards, using a small hammer and interposed block of wood, until the face of the seals are flush with the housing.

20 Assemble the ball nut to the worm gear in such a fashion that when the assembly is later fitted to the steering box, the narrow tooth will be uppermost and towards the steering box cover (see Fig. 11.48).

21 Place the steel balls in position in the guide tubes, nine balls to each tube, and retain them in place using petroleum jelly.

22 Assemble the two halves of each guide tube and insert the tubes into the ball nut, locating them over the worm gear. Refit the ball guide retaining plate and screw.

23 Place the steel balls for the worm gear inner bearing in position in the bearing cage and retain them in place with petroleum jelly. Locate the bearing in position in the outer race at the rear of the steering box.

24 Lubricate the lip of the oil seal with gear oil, then insert the worm gear and ball nut assembly into the steering box. Take care not to damage the lip of the seal when inserting the worm gear, and ensure the narrow tooth of the ball nut is uppermost and towards the steering box cover when the assembly is in position.

25 The bearing adjustment cap is assembled next. Begin by placing the flat washer in position in the cap, followed by the dished washer, with the dish towards the bearing (see Fig. 11.49).

26 Next, assemble the bearing steel balls, cage, and outer race, retaining the balls in position with petroleum jelly.

27 Locate the bearing in the cap, followed by the retaining ring. Secure the ring in position by peening over the edge of the bearing cap flange, in three places around its circumference, using a small punch. The bearing must turn freely with the retaining ring peened over.

28 Refit the bearing cap to the steering box, while at the same time rotating the worm gear back and forth to centralise the bearings. Tighten the bearing cap until it is only just possible to turn the worm gear by hand. Now back off the bearing cap until the worm gear turns easily, but without any trace of endfloat.

29 Now refit and fully tighten the bearing cap locking ring.

30 Turn the worm gear until the ball nut assembly is central on the gear.

31 Place the steering shaft adjusting screw and washer into position in the groove of the steering shaft, then screw the adjusting screw into

Fig. 11.48 Relationship of worm gear to ball nut with narrow tooth 'A' uppermost (Sec 25)

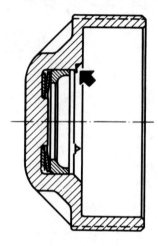

Fig. 11.49 Correct assembly of bearing adjustment cap with flange (arrowed) peened over in three places (Sec 25)

the steering box cover.

32 Place a new gasket in position on the steering box cover flange, coated on both sides with gasket cement.

33 Carefully, insert the steering shaft into the box, taking care not to damage the seal at the base of the steering box. The middle tooth on the steering shaft must locate in the middle groove of the ball nut.

34 Refit the cover retaining bolts, tightened to the specified torque.

35 Fill the steering box with the recommended grade of oil to the level of the steering box filler plug.

36 Turn the worm gear one turn in either direction so that the steering gear is out of its 'straight ahead' position.

37 Now tighten the steering shaft adjusting screw until the screw is just in contact with the shaft.

38 Turn the steering gear fully in each direction, making sure there is no binding of the steering shaft and all free play has been eliminated. If satisfactory, refit and fully tighten the adjusting screw locknut.

39 Set the steering gear exactly in its centre ('straight ahead') position.

40 Place the flexible coupling in position on the worm shaft, with the pinch bolt hole pointing directly upwards. Secure the coupling with the retaining bolt.

41 The steering box is now ready for refitting into the car, as described in Section 24.

26 Track rod end balljoints – testing and renewal

1   Chock the rear wheels, jack up the front of the car and support it on firmly based axle stands.

2   Inspect the condition of the track-rod end balljoint dust-excluding rubber boots. If they are split, the complete joint will have to be renewed; the boots are not supplied separately.

3   The balljoints are spring-loaded with nylon seats and require no lubrication.

4   If any free movement can be felt when the trackrod is gripped and moved up and down, or from side to side, then the balljoint is worn and

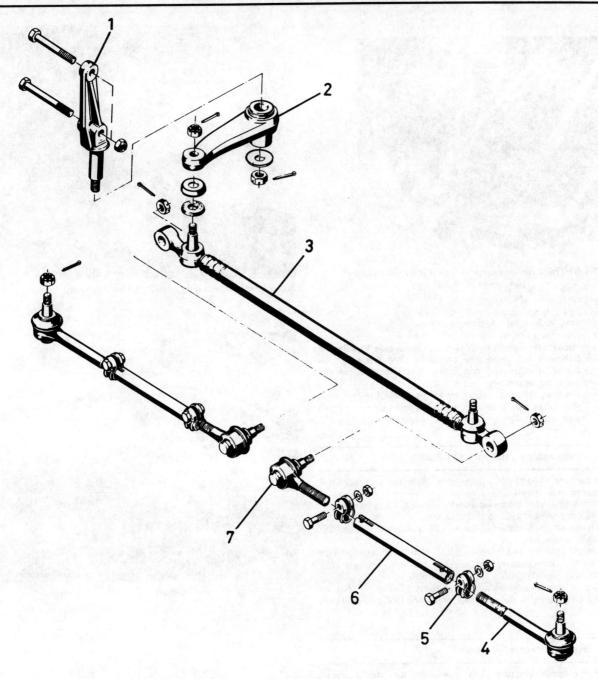

Fig. 11.50 Exploded view of steering linkage (left-hand drive vehicle illustrated) (Sec 26)

1 Idler arm bracket	3 Drag link	5 Locking clamp	7 Track rod end (inner)
2 Idler arm	4 Trackrod end (outer)	6 Track rod	

must be renewed.

5   To renew the track rod end inner or outer balljoints, extract the split pin, then undo and remove the castle nut securing the balljoint to the steering arm or drag link.

6   Separate the taper seat of the balljoint to the steering arm or drag link using a universal balljoint separator. If a separator is not available, refit the castellated nut one turn and strike the flange of the steering arm or drag link with a medium hammer. A few sharp blows should free the taper and allow removal of the joint.

7   Slacken the locking clamp around the track rod and, after making a note of the number of exposed threads, unscrew and remove the balljoint. **Note**: *The inner balljoint has a right-hand thread, while the outer balljoint, identified by a nub on the base of the joint, has a left-hand thread.*

8   Screw a new balljoint onto the track rod until the same number of

threads are exposed as were previously noted.

9   Refit the balljoint taper seat to the steering arm or drag link and secure with the castle nut and a new split pin.

10 Check, and if necessary, reset the front wheel alignment as described in Section 20.

27 Drag link – removal and refitting

1   Chock the rear wheels, jack up the front of the car and support it on firmly based axle stands.

2   Extract the split pins, then undo and remove the castellated nuts from the two track rod end inner balljoints and the two drag link balljoints.

3   Separate the track rod end and drag link balljoint tapers, using the

Fig. 11.51 Track rod end outer balljoint identification nub
(arrowed) (Sec 26)

28.4a Idler arm retaining castellated nut (arrowed) ...

method described in Section 26, paragraph 6.
4   Withdraw the drag link from underneath the car.
5   Carefully, inspect the balljoints for wear or excess side-to-side free
play. If the balljoints are worn, the complete drag link must be
renewed. Only the plastic caps and foam dust excluders on the
balljoints are supplied separately.
6   Refitting the drag link is a straightforward reversal of the removal
procedure. Tighten the castellated nuts to the specified torque and use
new split pins to retain them.

28 Idler arm assembly – removal and refitting

1   Chock the rear wheels, jack up the front of the car and support it
on firmly based axle stands.
2   Extract the split pin, then undo and remove the castellated nut
securing the drag link balljoint to the idler arm.
3   Using the method described in Section 26, paragraph 6, separate
the balljoint from the idler arm.
4   Remove the split pin and castellated nut, then lift the idler arm off
the idler bracket. If necessary, the bracket may be removed after
undoing the two mounting nuts and bolts (photos).
5   Refitting is the reverse sequence to removal. Ensure that all
mountings are tightened to the specified torque and that new split pins
are used.

28.4b ... and idler arm bracket retaining bolts (arrowed)

29 Power assisted steering – general

Due to the complex nature of the power assisted steering gear,
overhaul is beyond the scope of the diy motorist. The relevant sections
of this manual are therefore limited to the removal and refitting
instructions of the various components.
As overhaul of the power assisted steering gear is also considered
to be beyond the scope of the vehicle manufacturer's Dealer Service
Department, the best course of action, should a fault develop, is to
obtain a factory exchange unit or entrust the work to a power steering
specialist.

30 Power assisted steering drivebelt - removal, refitting and adjustment

1   Remove the air cleaner pre-heating hose.
2   Slacken off the pump-to-bracket front mounting bolt and the rear
upper mounting bolt and nut.
3   Push the pump body inwards as far as it will go, then lift the
drivebelt off the pump and crankshaft pulleys.
4   Place a new belt in position over the two pulleys.
5   Using a stout bar as a lever, move the pump away from the engine

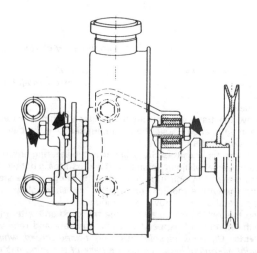

Fig. 11.52 Power steering pump mountings (Sec 30)

until there is approximately 12.7 mm (0.5 in) deflection, using light finger pressure on the belt, midway between the two pulleys.

6   Holding the pump in this position, tighten the three mountings and recheck the belt tension.

7   Refit the air cleaner pre-heating hose.

31 Power assisted steering – bleeding

1   The power assisted steering system will only need bleeding in the event of air being introduced into the system, eg where pipes have been disconnected or where a leakage has occurred. To bleed the system, proceed as described in the following paragraphs.

2   Remove the filler cap from the power assisted steering pump integral reservoir, and fill the reservoir to the top of the filler neck with the specified type of fluid. During the subsequent operations, the fluid reservoir must not be allowed to run dry.

3   Start the engine, then immediately stop it and top-up the fluid level to the lower dipstick mark. Repeat this procedure several times until the level in the reservoir remains constant.

4   Remove the dust cap from the bleed nipple on the steering box cover. Connect one end of a length of plastic tube to the bleed nipple, ensuring that it is a snug fit. Insert the other end of the tube in a clean glass jar.

5   Start the engine and allow it to idle. Open the bleed nipple and observe the emerging fluid.

6   When fluid, free from air bubbles, is discharged, close the bleed nipple and top-up the reservoir.

7   With the engine still idling, turn the steering wheel approximately one eighth of a turn to the left and right two or three times, then from lock to lock twice.

8   The bleeding operation is now complete. Switch off the engine and top-up the fluid reservoir to the appropriate mark. Remove the bleed tube and refit the bleed nipple dust cap.

32 Power assisted steering pump – removal and refitting

1   From underneath the car, disconnect the two fluid pressure and return hoses from the rear of the pump and allow the fluid to drain into a suitable container. If it is necessary to jack the car up, be sure it is well supported on axle stands. Tape over the hose ends to prevent dirt ingress.

2   Drain the cooling system as described in Chapter 2, then remove the radiator bottom hose.

3   Remove the air cleaner pre-heating hose.

4   Slacken the bolts securing the pump to its mounting brackets, push the pump inwards and lift the drivebelt off the pulley.

5   Undo and remove the bolts securing the rear mounting bracket to the engine block, and the pump to the front mounting bracket, then withdraw the pump from the engine.

6   Refitting the power assisted steering pump in the reverse sequence to removal, bearing in mind the following points:

   (a) Adjust the drivebelt tension as described in Section 30
   (b) Ensure that the hydraulic hose unions are scrupulously clean before refitting, then bleed the power steering system as described in Section 31
   (c) Refill the cooling system, referring to Chapter 2 if necessary

33 Power assisted steering gear – removal and refitting

1   Chock the rear wheels, jack up the front of the car and support it on firmly based axle stands.

2   Carefully ease out the five plastic retaining buttons, and withdraw the trim panel from beneath the dashboard.

3   Prise up the rubber grommet from the base of the steering column and slide it upwards along the column.

4   Undo and remove the pinch bolt securing the steering shaft to the flexible coupling.

5   Working in the engine compartment, wipe clean the area around the hydraulic unions on the steering gear. Remove the windscreen washer reservoir and disconnect the starter cable.

6   Undo and remove the two hydraulic unions, allowing the fluid to drain into a suitable container placed beneath the car. Take care not to

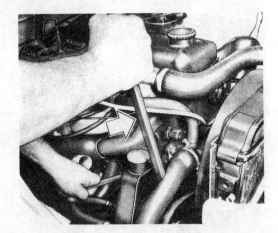

Fig. 11.53 Adjusting the power steering belt tension using bar (arrowed) as lever (Sec 30)

Fig. 11.54 Power steering pump hydraulic hose attachments (Sec 32)

Fig. 11.55 Power steering pump attachment points (arrowed) (Sec 32)

Fig. 11.56 Power steering flexible coupling pinch bolt and rubber grommet (Sec 33)

Fig. 11.57 Power steering gear mountings (Sec 33)

10 Undo and remove the three long bolts and nuts securing the steering gear to the chassis side-member.

11 Undo and remove the short bolt and forked shim securing the steering gear to the wheel well.

12 Carefully, withdraw the steering gear downward, to disengage the flexible coupling from the steering wheel so the spokes are symmetrical and angled downwards.

13 To refit the steering gear, first position the steering wheel so the spokes are symmetrical and angled downwards.

14 Set the steering gear in its midway position, with the pinch bolt holes in the flexible coupling pointing directly upwards.

15 Engage the flexible coupling flange with the steering shaft and loosely refit the three mounting bolts and nuts.

16 Loosely refit the short mounting bolt and forked shim.

17 Refit the pinch bolt to the flexible coupling and tighten the bolt to the specified torque.

18 Slide the steering column grommet down the column and locate it in the retaining lip. Refit the trim panel under the dash.

19 Ensuring that the steering gear is not under tension, fully tighten the mounting bolts to the specified torque.

20 With the front wheels in the 'straight ahead' position, the steering gear centered with the spokes on the steering wheel symmetrical and angled downwards, refit the steering arm to the shaft, aligning the mark made previously.

21 Refit the steering arm retaining nut and spring washer, tightening them to the specified torque.

22 Ensure that the hydraulic unions are scrupulously clean and refit them to the steering gear, tightening them to the specified torque. Refit the starter motor cable and windscreen washer reservoir.

23 Refitting is now completed and the system must be bled as described in Section 31.

34 Wheels and tyres

1 Check the tyre pressures weekly, when the tyres are cold.

2 Frequently inspect the tyre walls and treads for damage and pick out any large stones which have become trapped in the tread pattern.

3 If the wheels and tyres have been balanced on the car, they should not be moved to a different axle position. If they have been balanced off the car then, in the interests of extending tread life, they can be moved between front and rear on the same side of the car and the spare incorporated in the rotational pattern.

4 Never mix tyres of different construction, or very dissimilar tread patterns.

5 Always keep the roadwheels tightened to the specified torque and if the bolt holes become elongated or flattened, renew the wheel.

6 Occasionally, clean the inner faces of the roadwheels and is there is any sign of rust or corrosion, paint them with metal preservative paint. **Note**: *Corrosion on aluminium alloy wheels may be evidence of a more serious problem which could lead to wheel failure. If corrosion is evident, consult your dealer for advice.*

7 Before removing a roadwheel which has been balanced on the car, always mark one wheel stud and bolt hole, so that the roadwheel may be refitted in the same relative position, to maintain the balance.

lose the two sealing washers from each union as it is removed from the steering gear. Plug or tape over the hoses to prevent dirt ingress.

7 From beneath the car, undo and remove the nut and spring washer securing the steering arm to the steering shaft.

8 Using a centre punch, mark the relationship of the steering arm to the shaft to ensure refitment in the same position.

9 Using a universal puller, draw the steering arm off the steering shaft.

35 Fault diagnosis – suspension and steering

Symptom	Reason(s)
Excess free play felt at steering wheel	Steering box adjustment incorrect Wear in steering box internal components Wear in steering linkage
Vehicle difficult to steer in a consistent straight line – wandering	As above Wheel alignment incorrect Worn steering balljoints Front hub bearings loose or worn
Steering stiff and heavy	Wheel alignment incorrect Insufficient steering box lubricant Bent or distorted upper column or steering shaft Partial seizure of one or more steering or suspension joints Incorrect tyre pressures Broken or incorrectly adjusted power assisted steering drivebelt Faulty power steering pump
Excessive noise from steering gear (power assisted steering only)	Drivebelt slipping Insufficient hydraulic fluid in reservoir Worn or faulty power steering pump
Wheel wobble and vibration	Roadwheels out of balance Roadwheels buckled *See also 'Fault diagnosis – propeller shaft' and 'Fault diagnosis – rear axle'*
Excessive pitching and rolling on corners and during braking	Weak or ineffective shock absorbers Weak or broken coil springs Broken or worn anti-roll bar on mountings
Excessive tyre wear	Incorrect tyre pressures Incorrect front wheel alignment Wear in suspension or steering linkages

Chapter 12 Bodywork and fittings

For modifications, and information applicable to later models, see Supplement at end of manual

Contents

1 General description

The vehicle body structure is a welded fabrication of many individual shaped panels to form a 'monocoque' bodyshell. Certain areas are strengthened locally to provide for suspension system, steering system, engine support anchorages and transmission. The resultant structure is very strong and rigid.

It is as well to remember that monocoque structures have no discreet load paths and all metal is stressed to an extent. It is essential therefore to maintain the whole bodyshell both top and underside., inside and outside, clean and corrosion free. Every effort should be made to keep the underside of the car as clear of mud and dirt accumulations as possible. If you were fortunate enough to acquire a new car then it is advisable to have it rustproofed and undersealed at one of the specialist workshops who guarantee their work.

2 Maintenance – bodywork and underframe

The general condition of a vehicle's bodywork is the one thing that significantly affects its value. Maintenance is easy but needs to be regular. Neglect, particularly after minor damage, can lead quickly to further deterioration and costly repair bills. It is important also to keep watch on those parts of the vehicle not immediately visible, for instance the underside, inside all the wheel arches and the lower part of the engine compartment.

The basic maintenance routine for the bodywork is washing – preferably with a lot of water, from a hose. This will remove all the loose solids which may have stuck to the vehicle. It is important to flush these off in such a way as to prevent grit from scratching the finish. The wheel arches and underframe need washing in the same way to remove any accumulated mud which will retain moisture and tend to encourage rust. Paradoxically enough, the best time to clean the underframe and wheel arches is in wet weather when the mud is thoroughly wet and soft. In very wet weather the underframe is usually cleaned of large accumulations automatically and this is a good time for inspection.

Periodically, except on vehicles with a wax-based underbody protective coating, it is a good idea to have the whole of the underframe of the vehicle steam cleaned, engine compartment included, so that a thorough inspection can be carried out to see what minor repairs and renovations are necessary. Steam cleaning is available at many garages and is necessary for removal of the accumulation of oily grime which sometimes is allowed to become thick in certain areas. If steam cleaning facilities are not available, there are one or two excellent grease solvents available such as Holts Engine Cleaner or Holts Foambrite which can be brush applied. The dirt can then be simply hosed off. Note that these methods should not be used on vehicles with wax-based underbody protective coating or the coating will be removed. Such vehicles should be inspected annually, preferably just prior to winter, when the underbody should be washed down and any damage to the wax coating repaired using Holts Undershield. Ideally, a completely fresh coat should be applied. It would also be worth considering the use of such wax-based protection for injection into door panels, sills, box sections, etc, as an additional safeguard against rust damage where such protection is not provided by the vehicle manufacturer.

After washing paintwork, wipe off with a chamois leather to give an unspotted clear finish. A coat of clear protective wax polish, like the many excellent Turtle Wax polishes, will give added protection against chemical pollutants in the air. If the paintwork sheen has dulled or oxidised, use a cleaner/polisher combination such as Turtle Extra to restore the brilliance of the shine. This requires a little effort, but such dulling is usually caused because regular washing has been neglected. Care needs to be taken with metallic paintwork, as special non-abrasive cleaner/polisher is required to avoid damage to the finish. Always check that the door and ventilator opening drain holes and pipes are completely clear so that water can be drained out. Bright work should be treated in the same way as paint work. Windscreens and windows can be kept clear of the smeary film which often appears, by the use of a proprietary glass cleaner like Holts Mixra. Never use any form of wax or other body or chromium polish on glass.

3 Maintenance – upholstery and carpets

Mats and carpets should be brushed or vacuum cleaned regularly to keep them free of grit. If they are badly stained remove them from the vehicle for scrubbing or sponging and make quite sure they are dry before refitting. Seats and interior trim panels can be kept clean by wiping with a damp cloth and Turtle Wax Carisma. If they do become stained (which can be more apparent on light coloured upholstery) use a little liquid detergent and a soft nail brush to scour the grime out of the grain of the material. Do not forget to keep the headlining clean in the same way as the upholstery. When using liquid cleaners inside the vehicle do not over-wet the surfaces being cleaned. Excessive damp could get into the seams and padded interior causing stains, offensive odours or even rot. If the inside of the vehicle gets wet accidentally it is worthwhile taking some trouble to dry it out properly, particularly where carpets are involved. *Do not leave oil or electric heaters inside the vehicle for this purpose.*

4 Minor body damage – repair

The colour bodywork repair photographic sequences between pages 32 and 33 illustrate the operations detailed in the following sub-sections.

Note: *For more detailed information about bodywork repair, the Haynes Publishing Group publish a book by Lindsay Porter called The Car Bodywork Repair Manual. This incorporates information on such aspects as rust treatment, painting and glass fibre repairs, as well as details on more ambitious repairs involving welding and panel beating.*

Repair of minor scratches in bodywork

If the scratch is very superficial, and does not penetrate to the metal of the bodywork, repair is very simple. Lightly rub the area of the scratch with a paintwork renovator like Turtle Wax New Color Back, or a very fine cutting paste like Holts Body + Plus Rubbing Compound, to remove loose paint from the scratch and to clear the surrounding bodywork of wax polish. Rinse the area with clean water.

Apply touch-up paint, such as Holts Dupli-Color Color Touch or a paint film like Holts Autofilm, to the scratch using a fine paint brush;

continue to apply fine layers of paint until the surface of the paint in the scratch is level with the surrounding paintwork. Allow the new paint at least two weeks to harden: then blend it into the surrounding paintwork by rubbing the scratch area with a paintwork renovator or a very fine cutting paste, such as Holts Body + Plus Rubbing Compound or Turtle Wax New Color Back. Finally, apply wax polish from one of the Turtle Wax range of wax polishes.

Where the scratch has penetrated right through to the metal of the bodywork, causing the metal to rust, a different repair technique is required. Remove any loose rust from the bottom of the scratch with a penknife, then apply rust inhibiting paint, such as Turtle Wax Rust Master, to prevent the formation of rust in the future. Using a rubber or nylon applicator fill the scratch with bodystopper paste like Holts Body + Plus Knifing Putty. If required, this paste can be mixed with cellulose thinners, such as Holts Body + Plus Cellulose Thinners, to provide a very thin paste which is ideal for filling narrow scratches. Before the stopper-paste in the scratch hardens, wrap a piece of smooth cotton rag around the top of a finger. Dip the finger in cellulose thinners, such as Holts Body + Plus Cellulose Thinners, and then quickly sweep it across the surface of the stopper-paste in the scratch; this will ensure that the surface of the stopper-paste is slightly hollowed. The scratch can now be painted over as described earlier in this Section.

Repair of dents in bodywork

When deep denting of the vehicle's bodywork has taken place, the first task is to pull the dent out, until the affected bodywork almost attains its original shape. There is little point in trying to restore the original shape completely, as the metal in the damaged area will have stretched on impact and cannot be reshaped fully to its original contour. It is better to bring the level of the dent up to a point which is about ⅛ in (3 mm) below the level of the surrounding bodywork. In cases where the dent is very shallow anyway, it is not worth trying to pull it out at all. If the underside of the dent is accessible, it can be hammered out gently from behind, using a mallet with a wooden or plastic head. Whilst doing this, hold a suitable block of wood firmly against the outside of the panel to absorb the impact from the hammer blows and thus prevent a large area of the bodywork from being 'belled-out'.

Should the dent be in a section of the bodywork which has a double skin or some other factor making it inaccessible from behind, a different technique is called for. Drill several small holes through the metal inside the area – particularly in the deeper section. Then screw long self-tapping screws into the holes just sufficiently for them to gain a good purchase in the metal. Now the dent can be pulled out by pulling on the protruding heads of the screws with a pair of pliers.

The next stage of the repair is the removal of the paint from the damaged area, and from an inch or so of the surrounding 'sound' bodywork. This is accomplished most easily by using a wire brush or abrasive pad on a power drill, although it can be done just as effectively by hand using sheets of abrasive paper. To complete the preparation for filling, score the surface of the bare metal with a screwdriver or the tang of a file, or alternatively, drill small holes in the affected area. This will provide a really good 'key' for the filler paste.

To complete the repair see the Section on filling and re-spraying.

Repair of rust holes or gashes in bodywork

Remove all paint from the affected area and from an inch or so of the surrounding 'sound' bodywork, using an abrasive pad or a wire brush on a power drill. If these are not available a few sheets of abrasive paper will do the job just as effectively. With the paint removed you will be able to gauge the severity of the corrosion and therefore decide whether to renew the whole panel (if this is possible) or to repair the affected area. New body panels are not as expensive as most people think and it is often quicker and more satisfactory to fit a new panel than to attempt to repair large areas of corrosion.

Remove all fittings from the affected area except those which will act as a guide to the original shape of the damaged bodywork (eg headlamp shells etc). Then, using tin snips or a hacksaw blade, remove all loose metal and any other metal badly affected by corrosion. Hammer the edges of the hole inwards in order to create a slight depression for the filler paste.

Wire brush the affected area to remove the powdery rust from the surface of the remaining metal. Paint the affected area with rust inhibiting paint like Turtle Wax Rust Master; if the back of the rusted area is accessible treat this also.

Before filling can take place it will be necessary to block the hole in

some way. This can be achieved by the use of aluminium or plastic mesh, or aluminium tape.

Aluminium or plastic mesh or glass fibre matting, such as the Holts Body + Plus Glass Fibre Matting, is probably the best material to use for a large hole. Cut a piece to the approximate size and shape of the hole to be filled, then position it in the hole so that its edges are below the level of the surrounding bodywork. It can be retained in position by several blobs of filler paste around its periphery.

Aluminium tape should be used for small or very narrow holes. Pull a piece off the roll and trim it to the approximate size and shape required, then pull off the backing paper (if used) and stick the tape over the hole; it can be overlapped if the thickness of one piece is insufficient. Burnish down the edges of the tape with the handle of a screwdriver or similar, to ensure that the tape is securely attached to the metal underneath.

Bodywork repairs – filling and re-spraying

Before using this Section, see the Sections on dent, deep scratch, rust holes and gash repairs.

Many types of bodyfiller are available, but generally speaking those proprietary kits which contain a tin of filler paste and a tube of resin hardener are best for this type of repair, like Holts Body + Plus or Holts No Mix which can be used directly from the tube. A wide, flexible plastic or nylon applicator will be found invaluable for imparting a smooth and well contoured finish to the surface of the filler.

Mix up a little filler on a clean piece of card or board – measure the hardener carefully (follow the maker's instructions on the pack) otherwise the filler will set too rapidly or too slowly. Alternatively, Holts No Mix can be used straight from the tube without mixing, but daylight is required to cure it. Using the applicator apply the filler paste to the prepared area; draw the applicator across the surface of the filler to achieve the correct contour and to level the filler surface. As soon as a contour that approximates to the correct one is achieved, stop working the paste – if you carry on too long the paste will become sticky and begin to 'pick up' on the applicator. Continue to add thin layers of filler paste at twenty-minute intervals until the level of the filler is just proud of the surrounding bodywork.

Once the filler has hardened, excess can be removed using a metal plane or file. From then on, progressively finer grades of abrasive paper should be used, starting with a 40 grade production paper and finishing with 400 grade wet-and-dry paper. Always wrap the abrasive paper around a flat rubber, cork, or wooden block – otherwise the surface of the filler will not be completely flat. During the smoothing of the filler surface the wet-and-dry paper should be periodically rinsed in water. This will ensure that a very smooth finish is imparted to the filler at the final stage.

At this stage the 'dent' should be surrounded by a ring of bare metal, which in turn should be encircled by the finely 'feathered' edge of the good paintwork. Rinse the repair area with clean water, until all of the dust produced by the rubbing-down operation has gone.

Spray the whole repair area with a light coat of primer, either Holts Body + Plus Grey or Red Oxide Primer – this will show up any imperfections in the surface of the filler. Repair these imperfections with fresh filler paste or bodystopper, and once more smooth the surface with abrasive paper. If bodystopper is used, it can be mixed with cellulose thinners to form a really thin paste which is ideal for filling small holes. Repeat this spray and repair procedure until you are satisfied that the surface of the filler, and the feathered edge of the paintwork are perfect. Clean the repair area with clean water and allow to dry fully.

The repair area is now ready for final spraying. Paint spraying must be carried out in a warm, dry, windless and dust free atmosphere. This condition can be created artificially if you have access to a large indoor working area, but if you are forced to work in the open, you will have to pick your day very carefully. If you are working indoors, dousing the floor in the work area with water will help to settle the dust which would otherwise be in the atmosphere. If the repair area is confined to one body panel, mask off the surrounding panels; this will help to minimise the effects of a slight mis-match in paint colours. Bodywork fittings (eg chrome strips, door handles etc) will also need to be masked off. Use genuine masking tape and several thicknesses of newspaper for the masking operations.

Before commencing to spray, agitate the aerosol can thoroughly, then spray a test area (an old tin, or similar) until the technique is mastered. Cover the repair area with a thick coat of primer; the thickness should be built up using several thin layers of paint rather than one thick one. Using 400 grade wet-and-dry paper, rub down the surface of the primer until it is really smooth. While doing this, the work area should be thoroughly doused with water, and the wet-and-dry paper periodically rinsed in water. Allow to dry before spraying on more paint.

Spray on the top coat using Holts Dupli-Color Autospray, again building up the thickness by using several thin layers of paint. Start spraying in the centre of the repair area and then work outwards, with a side-to-side motion, until the whole repair area and about 2 inches of the surrounding original paintwork is covered. Remove all masking material 10 to 15 minutes after spraying on the final coat of paint.

Allow the new paint at least two weeks to harden, then, using a paintwork renovator or a very fine cutting paste such as Turtle Wax New Color Back or Holts Body + Plus Rubbing Compound, blend the edges of the paint into the existing paintwork. Finally, apply wax polish.

5   Major body damage – repair

1   Because the body is built on the monocoque principle, major damage must be repaired by a competent body repairer with the necessary jigs and equipment.
2   In the event of a crash that resulted in buckling of body panels, or damage to the roadwheels, the car must be taken to a GM dealer or body repairer where the bodyshell and suspension alignment may be checked.
3   Bodyshell and/or suspension misalignment will cause excessive wear of the tyres, steering system and possibly transmission. The handling of the car will also be affected adversely.

6   Hinges, door catches and locks – maintenance

1   Oil the hinges of the bonnet, boot and doors with a drop or two of light oil, periodically. A good time is after the car has been washed.
2   Oil the bonnet release catch pivot pin and the safety catch pivot pin, periodically.
3   Do not over-lubricate door latches and strikers. Normally, a little oil on the end of the rotary pinion spindle and a thin smear of high melting point grease on the striker pinion teeth and shoe spring plunger are adequate. Make sure that before lubrication, they are wiped thoroughly clean and correctly adjusted.

7   Doors – tracing rattles and rectification

1   Check the door is not loose at the hinges and the latch is holding it firmly in position. Check also that the door lines up with the aperture in the body.
2   If the hinges are loose or the door is out of alignment it will be necessary to detach it from the hinges as described in Section 8.
3   If the latch is holding the door correctly, it should be possible to press the door inwards fractionally against the rubber weatherstrip. If not, adjust the striker plate as described in Section 9.
4   Other rattles from the door would be caused by wear or looseness in the window winder, the glass channels and sill strips, or the door handles and remote control arm all of which are described in following Sections.

8   Door hinges – pin removal and setting

1   The two halves of the door hinges are welded to the door and frame respectively.
2   To detach the doors, first drill or grind out the pivot rivet from the door check link.
3   Remove the sealing plugs from the hinge roll pins and drive the pins out using a suitably sized punch. If difficulty is experienced, a special cable-type extracting tool is available from your GM dealer. Get someone to support the weight of the door while the pins are being withdrawn.
4   When fitting the hinge pins, tap them in as shown in Fig. 12.1, before hanging the door.
5   As the door hinge plates are welded to both the door pillar and the door frame, no adjustment for incorrect door alignment can be carried out other than by prising the pillar hinge plates, using an adjustable wrench. This should be done very carefully and only a fraction at a time before rechecking the alignment.
6   Wear in the hinge pin holes will cause a door to drop and if the condition cannot be remedied by drilling and fitting oversize pins, then new hinge plates will have to be fitted.

9   Door latch striker – adjustment

1   When the door is shut, the panel should be flush with the

Fig. 12.1 Locating hinge pins in hinges prior to fitting doors (Sec 8)

9.1 Door striker position adjusted after slackening striker using an Allen key

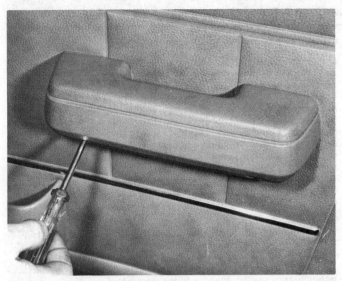

10.6 Removing the interior door handle

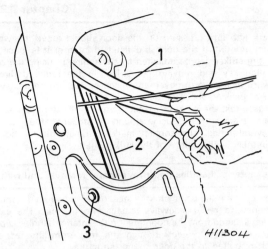

Fig. 12.2 Withdrawing the window rear channel rubber from the lower guide track (Sec 11)

1   Rubber   3   Retaining screw
2   Guide track

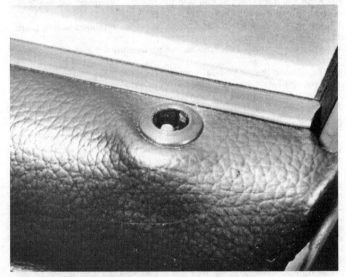

10.8 Interior lock operating rod with lock button removed

10.11 Refitting the interior window winder handle

11.7 Front door lock assembly and retaining screws

11.20 Front outer door handle assembly

bodywork and firm pressure on the door should move it inwards a fractional amount. If the door is difficult to latch or it is loose when closed, the striker can be adjusted by slackening it, using the correct sized Allen key and moving the striker in the required direction. Downward or rearward movement of the striker can be achieved by the use of packing washers (photo).

2   To ascertain the point of contact between the door lock fork and the striker, place some plasticine around the striker shaft and close the door several times. The contact mark in the plasticine should be approximately in the centre of the striker shaft.

10 Door interior handles and trim panel – removal and refitting

1   The doors are the usual pressed steel panel construction, specially strengthened to resist sideways impact into the car. The exterior fittings are secured from the door interior: the interior handles clip onto the spindles which project through the trim from the respective mechanism, bolted to the door interior structure.

2   To gain access to any component attached to the door, begin by removing the interior facing fittings and trim.

3   Make a note of the position of the window winder handle on the interior face, with the window open, so that it can be refitted in its original position.

4   Depress the bezel around the handle spindle, and with a piece of piano wire fashioned into a small hook, pull the wire clip retaining the handle on the splined end of the spindle out of its slots.

5   The handle and bezel can now be removed from the spindle.

6   The door handle/armrest is secured by two screws. Once these are undone and removed, the handle may be lifted from the door (photo).

7   Using a small screwdriver, carefully prise off the interior door latch escutcheon from its location in the trim panel.

8   Next, unscrw the interior lock button from its operating rod (photo).

9   Having removed all the handles and fittings, the trim panel may be prised from the door structure. Use a wide-bladed scrwdriver or flat strip of metal; insert it between the trim panel and the door. Lever the trim panel very carefully away from the door. This action will release the panel retaining buttons. The panel can then be lifted up and off the door.

10 With the trim panel removed, access to the door internal components is gained by carefully peeling back the water deflection sheet.

11 Refitting the trim panel is the reverse sequence to removal bearing in mind the following points:

   (a) *Make sure the water deflection sheet is in place and the window handle spring is correctly positioned before refitting the trim panel*

   (b) *When refitting the window winder handle, place the wire retaining clip on the handle first, then firmly push the handle onto the spindle (photo)*

11 Door exterior fittings – removal and refitting

1   All the exterior fittings are secured in position by screws and clips which pass through from the inside of the door.

2   Remove the interior handles and trim panel (as described in Section 10) to gain access to the relevent attachments. The exterior

fittings can now be removed as follows.

Door lock assembly – front

3   Temporarily place the winder handle on the spindle and raise the window fully.

4   Carefully withdraw the window rear channel rubber from the lower guide track.

5   Undo and remove the retaining screw and withdraw the lower guide track from the door.

6   Prise off the retaining clips and remove the operating rod from the lock barrel and the interior latch operating rod and interior button operating rod from the door lock assembly.

7   Now undo and remove the three retaining screws, and lift out the lock assembly through the aperture in the door panel (photo).

8   Refitting is the reverse of the removal procedure.

Door lock assembly – rear

9   Temporarily refit the winder handle and raise the window fully.

10 Prise off the retaining clips and remove the three operating rods from the lock assembly.

11 Undo and remove the three retaining screws, then lift out the lock assembly through the aperture in the door panel.

12 Refitting is the reverse sequence to removal.

Lock cylinder – front

13 Prise off the retaining clip and lift the operating rod off the lock cylinder transfer lever.

14 Using a wide-bladed screwdriver, slide the retaining spring plate off the lock cylinder.

15 The lock cylinder can now be withdrawn from the outside of the door.

16 To remove the lock barrel from the cylinder, insert the ignition key into the barrel, prise off the transfer lever using a wide-bladed screwdriver, and lift out the barrel.

17 Refitting the assembly is the reverse of the removal sequence.

Outer door handle – front

18 With the window winder handle temporarily fitted, raise the window fully.

19 Prise up the retaining clip and disconnect the handle operating rod at the handle.

20 The two retaining nuts and washers can now be undone and removed, and the handle lifted off the outside of the door (photo).

21 Refit the handle, following the reverse of the removal procedure.

Outer door handle – rear

22 To gain access to the rear handle retaining nuts, first remove the lock assembly as described earlier in this Section.

23 With the lock assembly removed, undo and remove the two retaining nuts and washers, then lift the handle off the outside of the door/

24 Refitting is the reverse of the above procedure.

12 Front door window operating mechanism – removal and refitting

1   Remove the door handles and trim panel as described in Section 10.

2   Temporarily refit the window winder handle and raise the window fully. Retain the window in this position, using a thin wooden wedge

12.3 Front window adjustment track bolts (arrowed)

12.4 Window operating mechanism retaining bolts (arrowed)

12.5 Front window lower channel and rollers

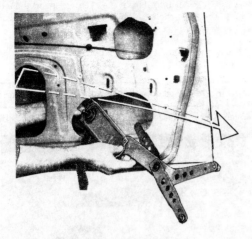

Fig. 12.3 Removing the front door window operating mechanism (Sec 12)

Fig. 12.6 Correct positioning of rear window crank gear prior to refitting cables (Sec 13) Cable eye (X) positioned as shown, cable end (Z) at inside of crank gear

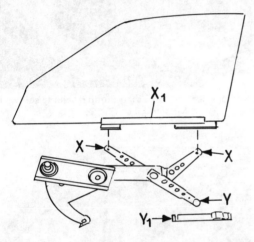

Fig. 12.4 Front door window operating mechanism components (Sec 12)

X   Lift rollers
Y   Guide roller

X^I Window guide rails
Y^I Adjustment rail

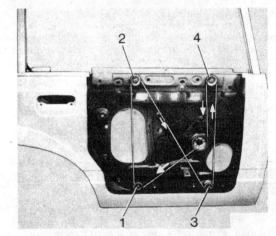

Fig. 12.7 Refitting the rear window operating cable (Sec 13)

1   Tension pulley
2   Top rear guide pulley

3   Bottom front guide pulley
4   Top front guide pulley

Fig. 12.5 Rear door window tension pulley retaining bolts (A) and crank mechanism retaining bolts (B) (Sec 13)

Fig. 12.8 Refitting the rear window operating cable to the crank gear (Sec 13)

1   Starting position of cable
W   Finishing position of cable

C   Tensioning pulley

inserted between the glass and the top edge of the door.

3 Undo and remove the two window adjustment track bolts (photo).

4 Next, undo and remove the four bolts securing the window operating mechanism to the door (photo).

5 Disengage the rollers on the operating mechanism from the lower channel in the window (photo)., then manipulate the mechanism and withdraw it through the rear lower door aperture (Figs. 12.3 and 12.4).

6 Refitting is the reverse of the removal sequence.

13 Rear door window operating mechanism – removal and refitting

1 Remove the interior handles and door trim panel as described in Section 10.

2 Before removing the operating mechanism and cables, it is necessary to remove the window glass, as described in Section 15.

3 With the window removed, refer to Fig. 12.5 and slacken the tension pulley retaining bolts.

4 The pulley can now be moved upwards and the cable lifted off.

5 Lift the cable off the other three pulleys, then undo and remove the three crank mechanism retaining bolts.

6 Withdraw the crank mechanism, complete with cables, through the door aperture.

7 To refit the mechanism, begin by refitting the crank mechanism and retaining bolts.

8 Refer to Fig. 12.6 and position the crank gear as shown.

9 Now feed the cable over the tension pulley, the top rear guide pulley, bottom front guide pulley and then the top front guide pulley.

10 The remaining slackness in the cable is taken up by winding it onto the crank gear, starting at the outside groove and working toward the gear teeth, as shown in Fig. 12.8.

11 Now tension the cable, by means of the tensioning pulley, and tighten the retaining bolts.

12 Check for correct operation of the operating mechanism, then refit the window glass and trim panel.

14 Front door window glass – removal and refitting

1 Remove the door interior trim panel as described in Section 10.

2 Remove the window operating mechanism as described in Section 12.

3 Now hold the window in both hands, lower it down at the front and lift it out of the door at an angle, rear top cover uppermost.

4 Refitting the window is the reverse sequence to removal.

15 Rear door window glass – removal and refitting

1 Begin by removing the inner trim panel as described in Section 10.

2 Fully lower the window, then undo and remove the screws securing the window clamps to the operating cables.

3 Refer to Fig. 12.10, and undo and remove the window guide channel retaining screws and nuts at the points shown. Now undo and remove the lower retaining stud, which is also the adjustment screw, from the guide channel. The channel can now be removed from the door.

4 The window can now be removed upwards and inwards at an angle from the door frame.

5 If required, the fixed rear quarter window may be withdrawn now by pulling it forward out of its rubber surround.

6 Refitting is the reverse sequence to removal. Before tightening the screws securing the window clamps to the operating cables, turn the operating mechanism, by means of the handle, to its upper stop, ie right door handle anti-clockwise, left door handle clockwise. Now turn the handle back two and a half turns. With the window glass at its bottom stop, the clamps can now be tightened.

16 Luggage compartment lock and lock cylinder – removal and refitting

1 Open the luggage compartment lid, then undo and remove the two screws securing the lock to the lid. Lift off the lock (photo).

2 Using a screwdriver, slide the lock cylinder retaining clip sideways and off the cylinder.

3 The lock cylinder can now be lifted off the outside of the luggage compartment lid.

4 To separate the lock barrel from the cylinder, insert the ignition key into the lock, prise up the retaining circlip using a screwdriver and withdraw the key and lock barrel.

5 Refitting is the reverse sequence to removal.

6 If necessary, adjust the boot lid for correct closure by adjusting the striker bracket (photo).

17 Bonnet and luggage compartment lid – removal and refitting

1 Removal of both these items is simply a matter of undoing and

Fig. 12.9 Rear door window cable clamp retaining screws (A) and window glass (Z) (Sec 15)

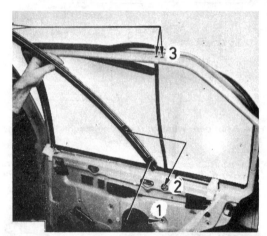

Fig. 12.10 Removing the rear window guide channel (Sec 15)

1 Lower retaining stud   *3 Upper fixings*
2 Centre fixing

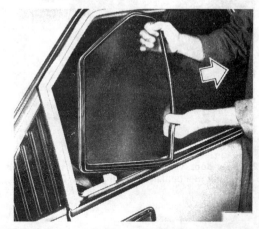

Fig. 12.11 Lifting out the fixed rear quarter window (Sec 15)

16.1 Luggage compartment lock assembly

16.6 Luggage compartment lock striker bracket

17.1 Bonnet hinge retaining bolts

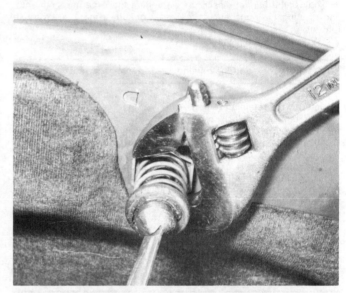

18.7 Adjusting the bonnet lock engagement tongue

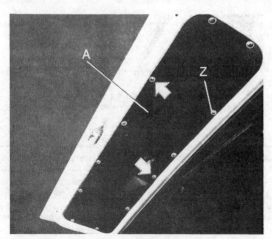

Fig. 12.12 Tailgate trim panel (A) and retaining buttons (Z)
(Sec 19)

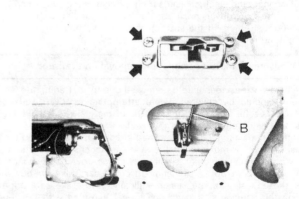

Fig. 12.13 Tailgate lock retaining screws (arrowed) and operating
rod (B) (Sec 19)

removing the retaining bolts and lifting off (photo).
2   Mark the hinge outline before removing the retaining bolts, to ensure correct alignment upon refitment; engage the help of a second person to avoid scratching the paintwork during removal and refitting.
3   In the case of the bonnet, the illuminating light electrical connection must first be disconnected before the panel can be lifted off.

18 Bonnet release cable – removal and refitting

1   Open the bonnet, and undo and remove the bolt and bonnet cable retaining plate adjacent to the lock mechanism.
2   Disconnect the end of the inner cable from the lock mechanism and release the outer cable from the retaining clips in the engine compartment.
3   From inside the car, position the cable so that it can be slid through the cut-out and withdrawn from the release handle.
4   Now pull the complete cable through the bulkhead grommet and into the engine compartment.
5   The cable can now be withdrawn from the car.
6   Refitting is the reverse sequence to removal. Adjust the cable to take up any free play, by altering its position in the cable retaining plate.
7   Adjust the bonnet closure by slackening the large hexagonal nut and rotating the engagement tongue in or out, using a screwdriver (photo).
8   When set, tighten the locknut.

19 Tailgate lock and lock cylinder – removal and refitting

1   Open the tailgate and remove the interior trim panel, by carefully prising out the retaining buttons.
2   To remove the lock, prise off the retaining clip and slide the operating rod out of the lever on the lock cylinder.
3   Undo and remove the four retaining screws to withdraw the lock assembly.
4   To remove the lock cylinder, first undo and remove the two retaining screws, then lift off the outer handle.
5   Undo and remove the actuation linkage adjusting screw from the rear of the lock cylinder linkage.
6   Using a screwdriver, remove the lock cylinder slotted retaining nut, by turning it to the right.
7   Now lift away the cylinder from the outside of the tailgate.
8   To separate the lock barrel from the lock cylinder, extract the retaining circlip and lift out the lock barrel, washer and spring.
9   Refitting is the reverse sequence to removal.

20 Tailgate support struts – removal and refitting

1   Open the tailgate, and have at the ready a length of wood to support it when the struts are removed.
2   Disconnect the electrical leads from the end of the support struts.
3   Using a screwdriver, prise out the lock wedges at each support strut mounting, then lift the strut off the ball end mounting.
4   Refitting is the reverse sequence to removal.

21 Windscreen and rear window – removal and refitting

1   Where a windscreen is to be removed due to shattering, the facia air vents should be covered before attempting removal. Adhesive sheeting is useful to stick to the outside of the glass to enable large areas of crystallised glass to be removed.
2   Where the screen is to be removed intact or is of laminated type, an assistant will be required. First release the rubber surround from the bodywork by running a blunt, small screwdriver around and under the rubber weatherstrip both inside and outside the car. This operation will break the adhesion of the sealer originally used. Take care not to damage the paintwork or catch the rubber surround with a screwdriver. Remove the windscreen wiper arms and interior mirror and place a protective cover on the bonnet.
3   Have your assistant push the inner lip of the rubber surround off the flange of the windscreen body aperture. Once the rubber surround starts to peel off the flange, the screen may be forced gently outwards by careful hand pressure. The second person should support and remove the screen complete with rubber surround and metal beading

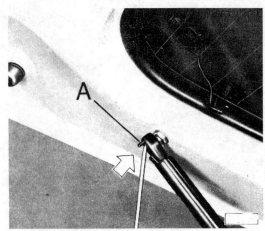

Fig. 12.14 Prising out the tailgate strut lock wedges (A) (Sec 20)

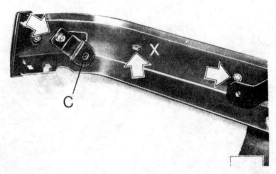

Fig. 12.15 Bumps brackets (C), trim retaining clips (X) and studs (arrowed) (Sec 22)

as it comes out.
4   Remove the bright moulding from the rubber surround.
5   Before fitting a windscreen, ensure that the rubber surround is completely free from old sealant and glass fragments, and has not hardened or cracked. Fit the rubber surround to the glass and apply a bead of suitable sealant between the glass outer edge and sealing strip.
6   Clean old sealant from the bodyflange.
7   Cut a piece of strong cord, greater in length than the periphery of the glass, and insert it into the body flange locating channel of the rubber surround.
8   Apply a thin bead of sealant to the face of the rubber channel which will eventually mate with the body.
9   Offer the windscreen to the body aperture and pass the ends of the cord, previously fitted and located at bottom centre, into the vehicle interior.
10   Press the windscreen into place; at the same time, have an assistant pull the cords to engage the lip of the rubber channel over the body flange.
11   Remove any excess sealant with a paraffin soaked rag.
12   Refit the bright moulding to the rubber surround. A special tool will facilitate this operation, but take care not to tear the lips of the rubber.

22 Bumpers and exterior bright trim – removal and refitting

1   All bumpers and overriders are bolt-on assemblies. Removal is straightforward, but the nuts and bolt threads will probably require penetrating oil because they are invariably rusted.
2   The protective rubber strips on the front and rear bumpers are retained in place by spring clips and studs (Fig. 12.15). The bumper must be removed from the car before the strips can be removed.
3   The body trim both internally and externally is of very simple construction. Its removal is obvious in each case. If a screw is not visible then it is either a push-on, or slide-on fit. Check each part – never force anything.

24.3a The plastic trim buttons covering the centre console retaining screws

24.3b Centre console front, ...

24.3c ... centre ...

24.3d ... and rear retaining screws

Fig. 12.16 Prising out the central fresh air vent (Sec 25)

Fig. 12.17 Removing the side demister vents (Sec 25)

23 Sliding roof – removal, refitting and adjustment

It is strongly recommended that, if any service attention is required on the sliding roof assembly, this be left to the specialist due to knowledge and experience necessary to effect a satisfactory repair.

24 Centre console – removal and refitting

1   Lift up the gear lever upper rubber boot and slide it up the lever to the knob. On vehicles equipped with automatic transmission, undo and remove the three securing screws, then lift off the selector lever cover.
2   If an optional switch panel is fitted to the console, prise it out using a screwdriver, and disconnect the wiring multi-plug.
3   Lift up the trim buttons covering the centre console securing screws (photo), then undo and remove the screws (photos).
4   Now lift off the console and carefully slide it over the gear lever and upper rubber boot.
5   Refitting is the reverse sequence to removal.

25 Centre fresh air and side demister vents – removal and refitting

1   To remove the fresh air vents from the centre of the dash panel,

insert a thin screwdriver at the top or bottom centre of the vent and prise outward.
2   The side demister vents are withdrawn in a similar fashion. Prise the top vent out, using a screwdriver inserted at the side of the vent, and at the top for the lower vent.
3   To refit the vents, simply push them into place in their respective housings.

26 Dashboard crash padding – removal and refitting

1   Open the bonnet and disconnect the battery earth terminal.
2   Remove the central fresh air and side defroster vents, as described in Section 25.
3   Prise out the retaining buttons and remove the lower trim panel from the passenger footwell.
4   Undo and remove the retaining screws, then remove the left-hand side lower dash panel, complete with glove box.
5   Undo and remove the three retaining screws then lift off the steering column upper and lower shrouds.
6   Undo and remove the retaining screws, then lift away the dashboard facing between the steering column and heater air distributor housing.
7   Prise out the headlight switch and disconnect the wiring multi-plug. Now undo and remove the retaining screws, and lift off right-hand side dashboard facing.

Fig. 12.18 Location of lower dash panel and glove box retaining screws (Sec 26)

Fig. 12.19 Dashboard facing (M) retaining screw locations (arrowed) (Sec 26)

Fig. 12.20 Dashboard side facing retaining screw locations (arrowed) (Sec 26)

Fig. 12.21 Vent ducts (L) and switch panel securing screws (arrowed) (Sec 26)

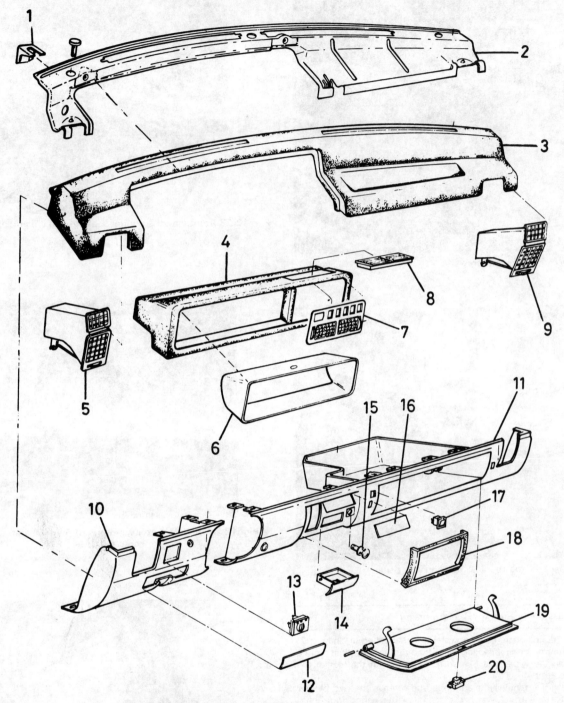

Fig. 12.22 Exploded view of the dashboard components (Sec 26)

1	Bracket
2	Inner panel
3	Dashboard crash padding
4	Instrument panel crash padding
5	Left-hand demister vent
6	Instrument panel surround
7	Central switch and vent panel
8	Upper vent grille
9	Right-hand side demister vent
10	Dashboard facing
11	Lower dash panel
12	Cover
13	Light switch
14	Ashtray
15	Cigarette lighter
16	Radio facing (if fitted)
17	Switch
18	Rubber surround
19	Glove box lid
20	Glove box lock

8 Prise out the two outer switches from their locations in the centre of the switch panel. Make a note of the positions of the electrical connections, then disconnect the connections and remove the switches.

9 Now undo and remove the retaining screws and withdraw the central switch and fresh air vent panel (photos).

10 Refer to Chapter 10 and remove the instrument panel.

11 The screws securing the instrument panel crash padding can now be removed and the padding lifted away.

12 Remove the dashboard crash padding from the three angle bracket mountings and lift it carefully off and out of the car.

13 Refitting the crash padding follows the reverse sequence to removal.

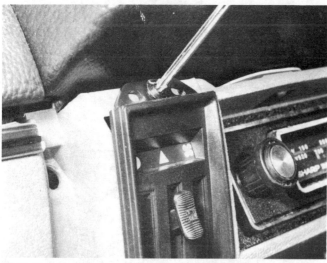

26.9a Remove the retaining screws ...

Fig. 12.23 Removing the bonnet sealing strip (A) and plastic grille panel (B) (Sec 27)

26.9b ... and lift out the heater switch and vent panel

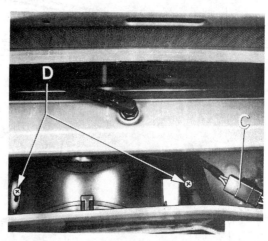

Fig. 12.24 Blower motor wiring multi-plug (C) and retaining screws (D) (Sec 27)

27 Heater assembly – removal and refitting

1   Begin by draining the cooling system, as described in Chapter 2.
2   Lift off the rear bonnet sealing strip, then remove the plastic grille panel covering the wiper and heater blower motor at the rear of the engine compartment.
3   With the grille panel removed, undo and remove the two blower motor cover retaining screws, and disconnect the wiring multi-plug connector for the motor.
4   Slacken the retaining clips and remove the two heater hoses from the heater core outlets. Plug the ends of the heater core outlets to prevent coolant water spilling into the car should the core be tipped up inadvertently during removal.
5   Working inside the car, remove the centre console as described in Section 24.
6   Undo and remove the retaining screws, then remove the air distributor housing lower facing.
7   Next, pull off the padded rubber surround from the air distributor housing (photo).
8   Slacken the heater control unit operating lever setscrews, undo and remove the control unit retaining screws and withdraw the unit forward and out of the air distributor housing. Make a careful note of the wiring positions at the rear of the control unit and disconnect the wires. Now lift away the unit.

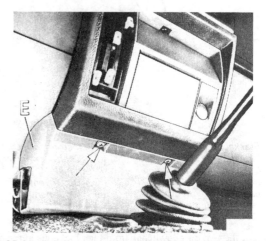

Fig. 12.25 Air distributor housing lower facing (E) retaining screws (arrowed) (Sec 27)

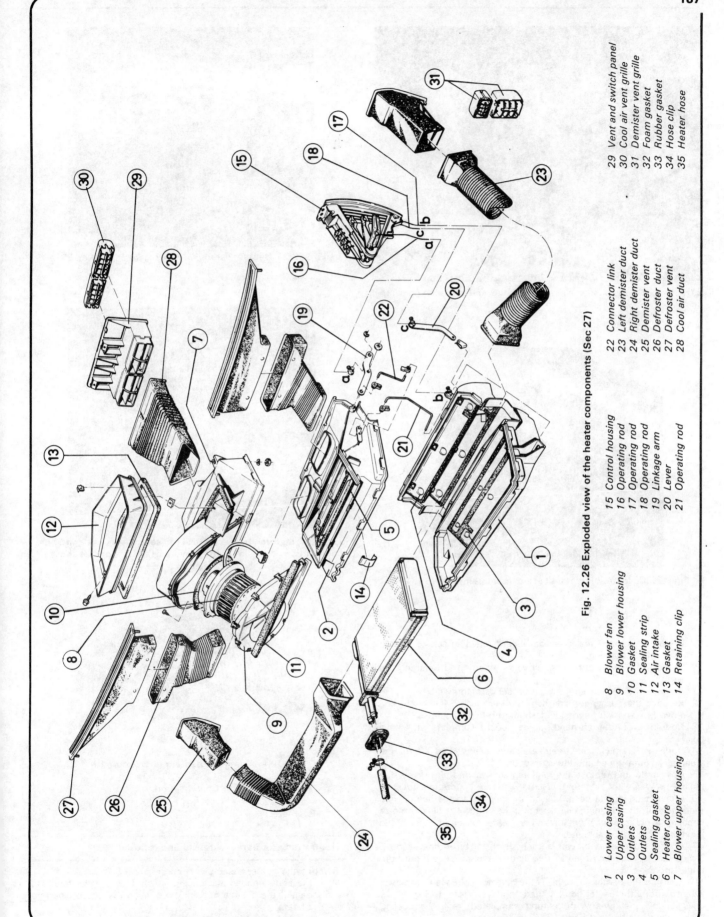

Fig. 12.26 Exploded view of the heater components (Sec 27)

1 Lower casing
2 Upper casing
3 Outlets
4 Outlets
5 Sealing gasket
6 Heater core
7 Blower upper housing

8 Blower fan
9 Blower lower housing
10 Gasket
11 Sealing strip
12 Air intake
13 Gasket
14 Retaining clip

15 Control housing
16 Operating rod
17 Operating rod
18 Operating rod
19 Linkage arm
20 Lever
21 Operating rod

22 Connector link
23 Left demister duct
24 Right demister duct
25 Demister vent
26 Defroster duct
27 Defroster vent
28 Cool air duct

29 Vent and switch panel
30 Cool air vent grille
31 Demister vent grille
32 Foam gasket
33 Rubber gasket
34 Hose clip
35 Heater hose

27.7 Removing the padded surround from the air distribution housing

Fig. 12.27 Heater assembly retaining clips (N) (Sec 27)

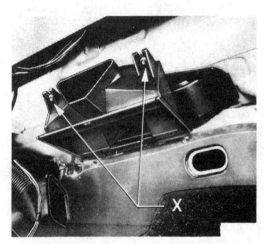

Fig. 12.28 Heater blower unit attachment points (X) (Sec 27)

Fig. 12.29 The three heater control rod setscrews (1, 2 and 3) are tightened with the operating levers (H) positioned as shown (Sec 27)

9   Undo and remove the lower dashboard retaining screw, located above the radio opening.
10   Remove the two centre fresh air vents, referring to Section 25 if necessary.
11   Remove the trim panel from the passengers' footwell.
12   Remove the passenger side demister vent (see Section 25) and the glove box and left-hand side dashboard retaining screws.
13   Now lift away the left-hand side dashboard, complete with glove box.
14   Undo and remove the three retaining screws then lift off the steering column upper and lower shrouds.
15   Now undo and remove the retaining screws, and lift off the side facing between the steering column and air distributor housing.
16   Working under the dash, pull off the ducting to the heater unit, then prise off the retaining clips securing the unit to the blower motor housing. Now carefully withdraw the heater assembly out of its location under the dashboard.
17   The separate heater blower motor housing can be withdrawn now, if required, by removing the securing screws and lowering it out from under the dash.
18   Refitting the heater assembly is the reverse sequence to removal. When refitting the heater control operating levers, refer to Fig. 12.29 and adjust as shown. With refitting completed, refill the cooling system as described in Chapter 2.

Fig. 12.30 Removing the heater radiator core (Sec 28)

X   Operating rod

28 Heater radiator core – removal and refitting

1   Remove the heater assembly as described in Section 27.
2   With the unit removed and on the bench, prise off the retaining clips, disconnect the linkage operating rod, open the unit casing and lift out the heater core.
3   Refitting is the reverse sequence to removal.

29 Heater blower motor – removal and refitting

1   Remove the heater assembly and blower motor housing, as described in Section 29.

2   Prise off the retaining clips and lift off the blower motor cover.
3   Undo and remove the retaining screws and withdraw the blower motor from the housing.
4   Refitting is the reverse sequence to removal.

Chapter 13 Supplement:
Revisions and information on later models

Contents

1 Introduction

This Supplement contains information which is additional to, or a revision of, material in the preceding Chapters. The Sections in this Supplement follow the same order as the Chapters to which they relate. The Specifications are all grouped together for convenience but follow Chapter order.

It is recommended that before any particular operation is undertaken, reference be made to the appropriate Section(s) of the Supplement. In this way, any changes to procedure or components can be noted before referring to the main Chapters.

Not all items described or mentioned in the Chapter are necessarily available on vehicles intended for the UK market.

2 Specifications

The Specifications below are supplementary to, or revisions of, those at the beginning of the preceding Chapters.

1.8 ohc engine
General

Type	Four cylinder in-line, overhead camshaft	
	18N	**18S**
Bore	84.8 mm (3.34 in)	84.8 mm (3.34 in)
Stroke	79.5 mm (3.13 in)	79.5 mm (3.13 in)
Displacement	1796 cc (109.5 cu in)	1796 cc (109.5 cu in)
Max bhp	75 at 5400 rpm	90 at 5400 rpm
Max torque	135 Nm (99.5 lbf ft) at 3000 rpm	143 Nm (105.5 lbf ft) at 3000 to 3400 rpm
Compression ratio	8.2 : 1	9.2 : 1
Firing order	1-3-4-2	1-3-4-2
No 1 cylinder location	Timing belt cover end	Timing belt cover end

Note: *Engine designations are: N – low compression, S – carburettor*

Lubrication system

Oil capacity:	
With filter change	3.75 litres (6.6 Imp pints)
Without filter change	3.5 litres (6.2 Imp pints)
Dipstick MIN to MAX quantity	1.0 litres (1.8 Imp pints)
Oil pressure at idle with engine at operating temperature	1.5 bar (22 lbf/in²)
Oil filter	Champion G102

Cylinder block (crankcase)

Material	Cast-iron
Maximum cylinder bore out-of-round	0.013 mm
Maximum permissible taper	0.013 mm
Maximum rebore oversize	0.5 mm

Crankshaft

Number of main bearings	5
Main bearing journal diameter	57.982 to 57.995 mm
Crankpin diameter	48.971 to 48.987 mm
Undersizes	0.25 and 0.50 mm
Endfloat	0.07 to 0.3 mm
Main bearing running clearance	0.015 to 0.04 mm
Big-end running clearance	0.019 to 0.063 mm
Big-end side-play	0.07 to 0.24 mm

Camshaft

Identification code	C
Endfloat	0.04 to 0.14 mm
Cam lift	6.12 mm
Camshaft journal diameters:	
No 1	42.455 to 42.470 mm
No 2	42.705 to 42.720 mm
No 3	42.955 to 42.970 mm
No 4	43.205 to 43.220 mm
No 5	43.455 to 43.370 mm
Camshaft bearing (direct in housing) diameters:	
No 1	42.500 to 42.525 mm
No 2	42.750 to 42.775 mm
No 3	43.000 to 43.025 mm
No 4	43.250 to 43.275 mm
No 5	43.500 to 43.525 mm

Pistons and rings

Type	Alloy, recessed head
Piston-to-bore clearance	0.02 mm
Number of piston rings	2 compression, 1 oil control
Ring end gap:	
Compression	0.3 to 0.5 mm
Oil control (rail)	0.40 to 1.40 mm
Ring gap offset	180°
Gudgeon pin:	
Length	70.0 mm
Diameter	23.0 mm
Fit	Interference in connecting rod
Clearance in piston	0.011 to 0.014 mm

Cylinder head

Material	Light alloy
Maximum permissible distortion of sealing face	0.025 mm
Overall height of cylinder head	95.75 to 96.25 mm
Valve seat width:	
Inlet	1.3 to 1.4 mm
Exhaust	1.7 to 1.8 mm

Valves

Valve clearance	Automatic by hydraulic valve lifters (cam followers)
Valve stem-to-guide clearance:	
Inlet	0.015 to 0.042 mm
Exhaust	0.03 to 0.06 mm
Valve seat angle	44°
Valve guide installed height	80.95 to 81.85 mm
Valve stem diameter:	
Inlet	7.795 to 7.985 mm
Exhaust	7.957 to 7.970 mm
Oversizes	0.075, 0.150, 0.250 mm
Valve guide bore (standard)	8.000 to 8.017 mm

Flywheel

Maximum thickness reduction at clutch disc and pressure plate cover contact surfaces	0.3 mm

Oil pump

Tooth play (gear to gear)	0.1 to 0.2 mm
Gear endfloat	0.03 to 0.1 mm

Torque wrench settings

	Nm	lbf ft
Flywheel (or driveplate) to crankshaft	60	44
Main bearing cap bolts	80	59
Oil pump mounting bolts	6	4
Oil pump relief valve cap	30	22
Alternator bracket bolts	40	30
Big-end cap bolts	50	37
Sump pan bolts	5	4
Cylinder head bolts:		
Stage 1	25	18
Stage 2	Turn bolt through 60°	
Stage 3	Turn bolt through 60°	
Stage 4	Turn bolt through 60°	
Stage 5	Tighten a further 30° to 50° after warm-up	

Camshaft sprocket bolt	45	33
Torsional damper bolt	60	44
Starter motor bolts	45	33
Manifold bolts and nuts	22	16
Engine mounting bracket to crankcase	50	37
Engine mounting bracket to transmission	30	22
Engine mountings to bodyframe	40	30
Oil pressure switch	30	22
Oil drain plug	45	33

2.0 CIH engine
General

	20N	20E
Max bhp	90 at 5200 rpm	110 at 5400 rpm
Max torque	145 Nm (107 lbf ft)	163 Nm (120 lbf ft)
	at 3000 to 3800 rpm	at 3000 rpm
Compression ratio	8.0 : 1	9.4 : 1

Note: *Engine desginations are: E – fuel injection, N – low compression*

2.2 CIH engine
As 2.0 CIH engine with the following exceptions

General

Bore	95.0 mm (3.74 in)
Stroke	77.5 mm (3.05 in)
Displacement	2197 cc (134 cu in)
Maximum power (DIN)	85 kW (115 bhp) at 4800 rpm
Maximum torque (DIN)	182 Nm (135 lbf ft) at 2800 rpm
Compression ratio	9.4 : 1

Valves

Valve timing:	
Inlet valve:	
Opens	28° BTDC
Closes	77° ABDC
Exhaust valve:	
Opens	66° BTDC
Closes	39° ABDC
Inlet valve head diameter	45.0 mm
Exhaust valve head diameter	40.0 mm
Valve seat angle	45°
Valve head edge angle	46°

Camshaft

Cam lift	6.860 mm

Crankshaft

Main bearing and big-end bearing undersizes ...	0.25 and 0.5 mm

Pistons

Piston ring thickness:	
Top compression	1.728 to 1.740 mm
Second compression	1.478 to 1.490 mm
Oil control	3.475 to 3.490 mm
End gap (compression)	0.30 to 0.60 mm

Torque wrench settings

	Nm	lbf ft
Crankshaft vibration damper:		
M12 bolts (new)	155	114
M14 bolts	220	162
Crankshaft pulley bolt	120	89
Engine front mounting bracket to cylinder block ...	40	30
Engine rear mounting to transmission	30	22
Engine front mounting bracket to damping pad ...	40	30

Cooling system (1.8 ohc engine)
System type

System type	Pressurised, 'no-loss', with remote expansion tank. Coolant pump driven by toothed timing belt

Thermostat

Opening temperature	91°C (196°F)
Fully open temperature	103°C (217°F)
Marking	91°C (196°F)

Expansion tank cap
Colour .... Blue or yellow
Opening pressure:
    Blue .... 1.20 to 1.35 bar (17.4 to 19.6 lbf/in²)
    Yellow .... 1.02 to 1.15 bar (14.8 to 16.7 lbf/in²)

Coolant capacity
Manual transmission models .... 6.8 litres (12.0 pints)
Automatic transmission models .... 6.7 litres (11.8 pints)

Torque wrench settings

	Nm	lbf ft
Coolant pump bolts	25	18
Thermostat housing bolts	15	11
Temperature sender in manifold	10	7

Cooling system (2.2 CIH engine)
As 2.0 CIH engine with the following exceptions

Coolant capacity
Manual transmission models .... 10.2 litres (17.9 pints)
Automatic transmission models .... 10.1 litres (17.8 pints)

Fuel and exhaust systems (1.8 ohc engine)

Air cleaner element
1.8 litre carburettor engine .... Champion U512
1.8 litre fuel injection engine .... Champion U511

Fuel pump
Type .... Mechanical drive from camshaft
Delivery pressure .... 25 to 36 kPa (3.6 to 5.2 lbf/in²)

Carburettor
Carburettor type .... GM Varajet II
Choke type .... Automatic
Carburettor No .... 96 002 109 or 96 002 110
Choke valve gaps (see text):
    A .... 3.7 to 4.3 mm (0.15 to 0.17 in)
    B .... 2.7 to 3.3 mm (0.11 to 0.13 in)
    C .... 9.5 to 10.5 mm (0.37 to 0.41 in)
Choke cover adjustment .... Middle mark
Main jet:
    Identification 195
    Stage I .... 1.95 mm (0.077 in)
    Stage II .... 3.2 mm (0.13 in)
Jet needle:
    Identification .... G
    Stage II .... 2.2 mm (0.08 in)
Float needle valve:
    Identification 30886
    Seating .... One groove – 1.93 mm (0.076 in)
Vacuum unit dashpot/delay valve 96 001 122
Vacuum unit 0.1124
Air valve play .... 0.1 to 0.3 mm (0.004 to 0.012 in)
Float adjustment .... 4.5 to 6.5 mm (0.18 to 0.26 in)
Idle jet (fully inserted) .... 0.65 mm (0.026 in)
Idle speed .... 800 to 850 rpm
Fast idle speed .... 2000 ± 50 rpm
Ignition vacuum at idle .... 0 to 2.0 kPa (0 to 0.28 lbf/in²)
Exhaust gas CO content at idle .... 0.5 to 1.5%

Torque wrench settings

	Nm	lbf ft
Fuel pump	15	11
Carburettor mounting nuts	15	11

Fuel and exhaust systems (2.0 CIH engine)
Carburettor
Type .... Zenith 35/40 INAT
Auxiliary system .... Additional idling mixture
Float needle valve .... 2 mm (0.08 in)
Float needle valve washer .... 1 mm (0.04 in)
Exhaust CO content at idling speed .... 1.5 to 2.5%
Fast idling speed (engine hot) .... 2700 rpm
Float chamber vent valve setting .... 1.5/1.8 mm (0.06/0.07 in)
Throttle valve gap (secondary barrel) .... 0.5 mm (0.02 in)
Choke valve gap .... 2.7 to 2.9 mm (0.10 to 0.11 in)
Idling speed (engine hot) .... 800 to 850 rpm

	Primary	Secondary
Venturi diameter	22 mm (0.87 in)	32 mm (1.26 in)
Mixture outlet	3.1	3.1
Main jet	X 110	X 170
Air correction jet	160	100
Emulsion tube	9S	4K
Idling jet	52.5	–
Progression jet	–	55
Progression air jet	–	1.0
Injector tube	50	50
Enrichment (main jet system)	40	–
Additional idling fuel jet	45	–
Additional idling mixture jet	50	–

Fuel injection

Engine type	20E
System type	Bosch LE Jetronic
Idle speed	850 to 900 rpm
Exhaust gas CO content at idle	0.5% maximum

Torque wrench setting

	Nm	lbf ft
Fuel injectors	32	24

Fuel and exhaust systems (2.2 CIH engine)
As 2.0 CIH engine with the following exceptions

General

Engine type	22E
System type	Bosch LE Jetronic with idle air control system
Idle speed:	
Manual transmission	775 to 825 rpm
Automatic	675 to 725 rpm

Air cleaner element

Champion U502

Ignition system
General

System type (later models)	Electronic (breakerless), Bosch or AC Delco
Firing order	1-3-4-2

Distributor (breakerless)

Direction of rotation (viewed from top of cap):	
1.8 ohc	Anti-clockwise
2.0 and 2.2 CIH	Clockwise
Dwell angle	Electronically controlled
Rotor resistance	1000 ohms approx

Ignition timing

1.8 ohc engine	10° BTDC at idle
2.2 CIH engine	10° BTDC at idle

Ignition coil (electronic ignition)

Type	Bosch KW12V or equivalent
Primary resistance	0.6 to 0.9 ohms

Spark plugs

Make and type:	
1.8 ohc	Champion RN7YCC or RN7YC
2.0 and 2.2 CIH	Champion RL82YCC or RL82YC
Electrode gap:	
RN7YCC and RL82YCC spark plugs	0.8 mm (0.032 in)
RN7YC and RL82YC spark plugs	0.7 mm (0.028 in)

HT leads

1.8 ohc, 2.0 fuel injection (1982 on)	Champion CLS 13
2.0 carburettor (1980 on) and 2.2 fuel injection (1984 on)	Champion CLS 5

Torque wrench settings

	Nm	lbf ft
Spark plugs (1.8 ohc)	20	15
Distributor clamp nuts	22	16

Clutch
Clutch disc diameter

18S engine	203.2 mm (8.0 in)
20S engine	203.2 mm (8.0 in)
20E engine	215.9 mm (8.5 in)
22E engine	228.6 mm (9.0 in)

Overdrive unit
Type .... Laycock-de Normanville

Gearbox mainshaft
Diameter of oil transfer .... 24.485 to 24.511 mm (0.9840 to 0.9650 in)
Inside diameter of main case at oil transfer .... 24.536 to 24.561 mm (0.9660 to 0.9670 in)
Diameter at sunwheel .... 23.901 to 23.951 mm (0.9410 to 0.9430 in)
Inside diameter of sunwheel bush (where fitted) .... 24.052 to 24.103 mm (0.9470 to 0.9490 in)
Diameter at mainshaft spigot .... 14.274 to 14.288 mm (0.5620 to 0.5625 in)
Inside diameter at spigot bearing .... 14.294 to 14.320 mm (0.5628 to 0.5638 in)

Operating pistons
Operating piston diameter .... 31.7297 to 31.7424 mm (1.2492 to 1.2497 in)
Operating piston bore diameter .... 31.7500 to 31.7805 mm (1.2500 to 1.2512 in)

Pump
Pump plunger diameter .... 12.6898 to 12.7000 mm (0.4996 to 0.5000 in)
Pump body bore .... 12.7076 to 12.7228 mm (0.5003 to 0.5009 in)

Relief valve
Outside diameter of relief valve piston .... 6.3398 to 6.3449 mm (0.2496 to 0.2498 in)
Inside diameter of relief valve body .... 6.3500 to 6.3627 mm (0.2500 to 0.2505 in)
Outside diameter of dashpot piston .... 23.7990 to 23.8066 mm (0.9370 to 0.9373 in)
Inside diameter of dashpot sleeve .... 23.8125 to 23.8377 mm (0.9375 to 0.9385 in)

Speedometer pinion
Outside diameter of speedometer pinion .... 7.8867 to 7.9004 mm (0.3105 to 0.3110 in)
Inside diameter of speedometer bearing .... 7.9240 to 7.9629 mm (0.3120 to 0.3135 in)

Sliding member
Travel from direct drive to overdrive (measured at bridge
pieces) .... 1.2954 to 2.5400 mm (0.0510 to 0.1000 in)

Hydraulic system residual pressure .... 1.4 bar (20 lbf/in²)

Torque wrench settings

	Nm	lbf ft
Pump non-return valve to main casing	22	16
Pressure filter base plug	22	16
Speedometer drivegear retaining nut	68 to 81	50 to 60
Coupling flange securing nut	109 to 176	80 to 130
Relief valve base plug	22	16

Manual gearbox (4-speed)

Gear ratios

	Pre-1983 models	Post-1983 models
First	3.640 : 1	4.016 : 1
Second	2.120 : 1	2.147 : 1
Third	1.336 : 1	1.318 : 1
Fourth	1.000 : 1	1.000 : 1
Overdrive (where fitted)	0.778 : 1	–
Reverse	3.522 : 1	3.765 : 1

Manual gearbox (5-speed)
Gearbox type 240

Gear ratios
First .... 3.717 : 1
Second .... 2.019 : 1
Third .... 1.316 : 1
Fourth .... 1.000 : 1
Fifth .... 0.804 : 1
Reverse .... 3.445 : 1

Assembly tolerances
Reverse idler gear pinion-to-plate clearance .... 0.1 mm (0.004 in)
Fifth gear pinion-to-retaining nut clearance .... 0.05 to 0.10 mm (0.002 to 0.004 in)
Mainshaft bearing spacer thicknesses .... 0.3, 0.4 and 0.5 mm (0.012, 0.016 and 0.020 in)
Input shaft bearing spacer thicknesses .... 2.3, 2.4, 2.5 and 2.6 mm (0.091, 0.094, 0.098 and 0.102 in)
Clutch release bearing guide:
    Spacer thicknesses .... 1.3, 1.4 and 1.5 mm (0.051, 0.055 and 0.059 in)
    Maximum axial play .... 0.05 mm (0.002 in)
Selector fork end minimum thickness .... 4.90 to 4.96 mm (0.19 to 0.20 in)
Synchroniser ring-to-pinion teeth clearance:
    Used ring .... 1.0 mm (0.04 in) minimum
    New ring .... 1.0 to 1.5 mm (0.04 to 0.06 in)

Lubricant type/specification .... GM special oil 90 006 326 (Duckhams Hypoid 75W/90S)

Torque wrench settings

	Nm	lbf ft
Support plate mounting bolt	25	18
Selector rail end support bolt	25	18
Fifth gear detent plug	60	44
Reverse idler shaft bolts	25	18
Reverse idler gear plate bolt	25	18
Casing bolts	25	18
Clutch release guide bolts	10	7

Rear axle (later models)
Final drive ratio

	Manual	Automatic
18S engine	3.70 : 1	3.45 : 1
20S engine	3.70 : 1	3.45 : 1
22E engine	3.45 : 1	3.27 : 1

Braking system
Front brakes (floating caliper)
Discs:
  Diameter .... 246 mm (9.7 in)
  Thickness:
    Models without ABS .... 12.7 mm (0.50 in)
    Models with ABS (ventilated) .... 23.0 mm (0.91 in)
  Minimum thickness after refinishing:
    Models without ABS .... 11.7 mm (0.46 in)
    Models with ABS (ventilated) .... 22.0 mm (0.87 in)
  Maximum run-out .... 0.01 mm (0.0004 in)
Pads:
  Overall thickness including backing plate .... 15.5 to 15.9 mm (0.61 to 0.63 in)
  Wear limit .... 7.0 mm (0.28 in)
Caliper piston diameter .... 48.0 mm (1.89 in)
Master cylinder:
  Bore .... 20.64 mm ((0.813 in)
  Piston diameter .... 20.58 mm (0.810 in)

Rear brakes
Maximum permissible drum scoring depth .... 0.4 mm (0.016 in)
Handbrake adjustment (1984 on):
  Shoe lever cam-to-brake shoe arm clearance .... 3 mm (0.12 in)

Torque wrench settings
Discs and floating caliper

	Nm	lbf ft
Master cylinder stop bolt	6	4
Pressure regulator to master cylinder	40	30
Caliper mounting bolts	95	70
Caliper banjo union hollow bolt	25	18
Hydraulic pipeline union nuts	11	8
Roadwheel speed sensor (ABS)	8	6
Hydraulic modulator (ABS)	10	7

Disc and twin piston caliper

	Nm	lbf ft
Disc securing bolts (splined)	45	33

Electrical system
Light bulbs
Long range headlight .... 55 W Halogen
Engine compartment lamp .... 10 W
Luggage boot or area lamps .... 10 W
Map reading lamp .... 5 W
Cigar lighter and ashtray lamps .... 1.2 W

Fuse (later models – typical)

Fuse No	Rating (A)	Circuits protected
1	7.5	Side/tail lights (RH)
2	7.5	Side/tail lights (LH)
3	7.5	Number plate light, instrument/switch illumination, engine bay light, headlight wash/wipe relay, buzzer
4	15	Hazard warning lights, load area light, interior lights, radio
5	25	Wipers (front and rear), washer pump delay relay, horn and relay, parking light relay, cooling fan relay
6	20	Cigarette lighter, glovebox light, reversing light, foglamp relay, tailgate/boot lid release, clock and light switch illumination, mirror heating and adjustment, trip computer, central locking
7	10	Stop-lights, direction indicators, cruise control, torque converter clutch

8	25	Heater fan, carburettor heater, instrumentation, automatic level control, idle speed increase system, cooling fan, air conditioning
9	20	Trailer socket (terminal 30)
10	15	Fuel injection system
11	20	Heated rear window
12	20*	Sunroof
13	10	Main beam (LH)
14	10	Main beam (RH)
15	15	Additional headlights
16	10	Dipped beam (LH)
17	10	Dipped beam (RH), rear foglamp
18	15	Front foglamp

Can be uprated to 25 amps if persistent blowing occurs

Suspension and steering
Tyres
Size:

	Standard	Optional
18S Saloon (manual and automatic)	175 SR 14 – 88S	185/70 SR 14 – 86S
20S Saloon (manual)	175 HR 14 – 88H	185/70 HR 14 – 86H
20S Saloon (automatic)	175 SR 14 – 88S	185/70 SR 14 – 86S
20E Saloon (manual and automatic)	175 HR 14 – 88H	185/70 HR 14 – 86H
20S Estate (manual and automatic)	175 SR 14 – 88S	–
20E Estate (manual)	175 HR 14 – 88H	–
20E Estate (automatic)	175 SR 14 – 88S	–
22E (manual and automatic)	185/70 HR 14 – 86H	–

Torque wrench settings

	Nm	lbf ft
Front crossmember securing bolts (fine thread)	90	66
Level control system pipeline unions	5	4

General weights and dimensions (later models)
Dimensions

	Saloon	Estate
Overall length	4652 mm (183 in)	4678 mm (184 in)
Overall width	1726 mm (68 in)	1720 mm (68 in)
Overall height (unladen)	1420 mm (56 in)	1470 mm (58 in)

Kerb weights

	Manual	Automatic
18S	1115 kg (2458 lb)	1135 kg (2502 lb)
20S	1135 kg (2502 lb)	1150 kg (2535 lb)
22E	1165 kg (2568 lb)	1180 kg (2601 lb)

3 Trailer/caravan towing

When towing, avoid overloading the trailer as this will place an unacceptable strain on the vehicle bodyshell and transmission. Refer to the following table for the maximum permissible loads shown in kg (lb). These are standard trailer weights for gradients up to 12%:

Engine	Transmission	Without brakes	With brakes
18S	Manual	535 (1069)	1000 (2205)
	Automatic	535 (1069)	1500 (3307) Saloon
			1300 (2865) Estate
20S	Manual	535 (1069)	1250 (2655)
	Automatic	535 (1069)	1350 (2975) Saloon
			1250 (2655) Estate
20E	Manual	535 (1069)	1250 (2655)
	Automatic	535 (1069)	1500 (3307) Saloon
			1350 (2975) Estate
22E	Manual	535 (1069)	1500 (3307)
	Automatic	535 (1069)	1500 (3307)

4 Routine maintenance

1 The maintenance schedule at the beginning of this manual is still relevant but note the following reservations, where applicable.
2 When checking the fanbelt tension (6000 mile intervals), note the information given in Section 9 of this Chapter.
3 As part of the weekly check, examine the pipelines and connections of the fuel system for signs of leakage or chafing against other components.
4 On carburettor models, check the throttle operating cable for freedom of movement at the 6000 mile interval.
5 From 1981, GM recommend renewal of the fuel filter element fitted to the Varajet II carburettor, instead of filter cleaning, at the 12 000 mile interval.
6 Air filter renewal at the 12 000 mile interval also applies to the filter element fitted to fuel injection models. For details of element renewal, refer to Section 10 of this Chapter.
7 At every 12 000 mile interval, renew the micro-filter contained in the fuel system of vehicles fitted with fuel injection. Details of filter renewal can be found in Section 10 of this Chapter.
8 Where the vehicle is fitted with electronic ignition, ignore all references to contact breaker points. Instead, refer to Section 11 of this Chapter and examine the component parts of the system for obvious signs of damage or deterioration. Separate any wiring connections and examine them for moisture, contamination or corrosion, cleaning each connection as necessary.
9 On vehicles fitted with 5-speed manual transmission, refer to the accompanying photograph when checking gearbox oil level (6000 mile intervals). Refer to *Recommended lubricants and fluids* at the beginning of this manual and use only the special oil stated.
10 On vehicles fitted with the Delco 'freedom battery' refer to Section 18 of this Chapter.

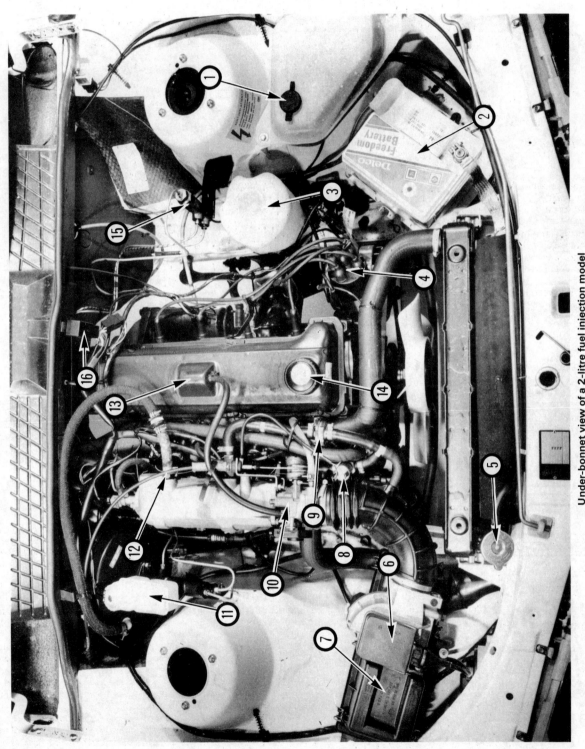

Under-bonnet view of a 2-litre fuel injection model

1 Coolant expansion tank
2 Battery
3 Washer reservoir
4 Distributor

5 Radiator pressure cap
6 Airflow meter
7 Air cleaner

8 Secondary air valve
9 Auxiliary air valve
10 Throttle valve housing

11 Brake fluid reservoir
12 Brake servo connection
13 Crankcase ventilation connection

14 Oil filler cap
15 Brake pressure control valve
16 Fuel injection control relay

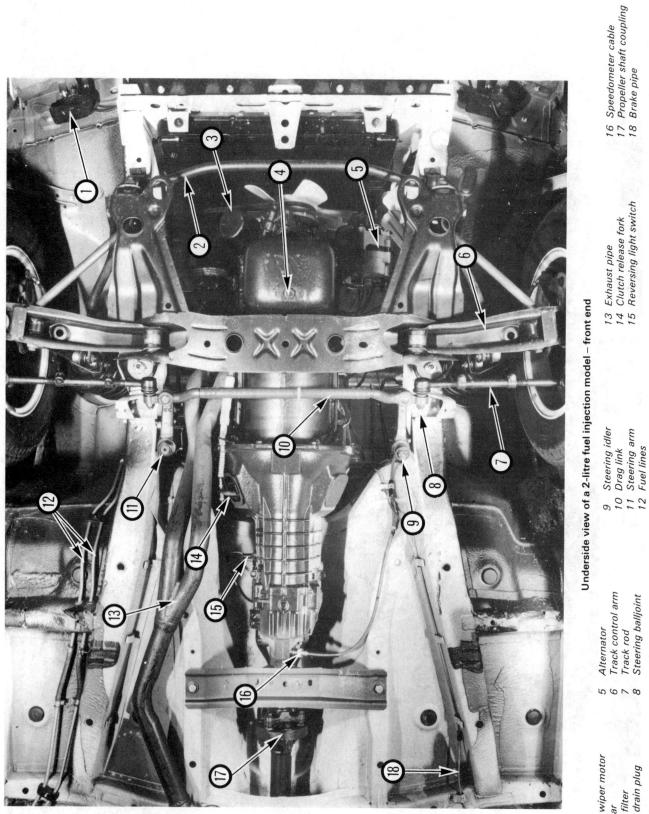

Underside view of a 2-litre fuel injection model – front end

1 Headlight wiper motor
2 Anti-roll bar
3 Engine oil filter
4 Engine oil drain plug

5 Alternator
6 Track control arm
7 Track rod
8 Steering balljoint

9 Steering idler
10 Drag link
11 Steering arm
12 Fuel lines

13 Exhaust pipe
14 Clutch release fork
15 Reversing light switch

16 Speedometer cable
17 Propeller shaft coupling
18 Brake pipe

Underside view of a 2-litre fuel injection model – rear end

1 Fuel filter
2 Handbrake cables
3 Brake pipe
4 Propeller shaft
5 Intermediate silencer
6 Lower control arm
7 Shock absorber mounting
8 Panhard rod
9 Resonator
10 Fuel tank
11 Fuel pump
12 Fuel return hose
13 Rear axle
14 Brake flexible hose
15 Anti-roll bar
16 Counterbalance weights
17 Brake 3-way union

4.9 5-speed gearbox oil filler/level plug

5 Engine – general

Engine removal

1 On later models, some difficulty may be experienced when attempting to disconnect the bonnet light prior to bonnet removal. Where the electrical lead is permanently sealed and fixed at both ends, cut it at a convenient point along its length and fit a waterproof quick release connector.

2 Disconnect the battery before cutting the lead. On completion of bonnet refitting, check the lead is securely taped in position.

Engine front mountings

3 From 1982, the rubber block mountings have been replaced with glycol-filled components which reduce the transmission of engine noise and vibration.

Engine identification

4 The engine number reveals much information. Refer to Fig. 13.1 for further details.

2.2 litre CIH engine

5 In late 1984 a fuel injected 2.2 litre CIH engine was introduced to replace the fuel injected 2.0 litre version.

6 The 2.0 and 2.2 litre engines only vary in basic specification; all procedures for the 2.0 CIH engine apply to the 2.2 version.

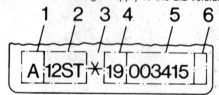

Fig. 13.1 Typical engine identification number (Sec 5)

1	Export market code:	3 Star – suitable for operation
	A Austria,	on low-lead fuel
	S Sweden/Switzerland	4 Manufacturing plant
2	Displacement (litres):N	number
	Low compression, S high	5 Engine serial number
	compression, T Power	6 Blank
	output variation	

6 Engine – 1.8 litre ohc, overhaul

PART A: General and tasks possible *in situ*

General description

1 The engine is of four-cylinder, overhead camshaft type. The cylinder head is of light alloy construction while the cylinder block is of cast-iron. The cylinder head is of crossflow design. The crankshaft runs in five main bearings. The camshaft is supported in non-renewable bearings and is driven by a toothed belt from a sprocket on the crankshaft.

2 Valve adjustment is not required as the valve lifters (cam followers) are of the hydraulic self-adjusting type. A torsional damper is fitted to the crankshaft front end.

Main operations possible with engine in car

3 The following operations may be carried out without having to remove the engine from the vehicle:

    (a)   *Removal and refitting of oil pressure regulator valve*
    (b)   *Renewal of camshaft drivebelt*
    (c)   *Removal and refitting of cylinder head*
    (d)   *Removal and refitting of camshaft housing*
    (e)   *Removal and refitting of camshaft*
    (f)   *Removal and refitting of sump*
    (g)   *Removal and refitting of oil pump*
    (h)   *Removal and refitting of pistons/connecting rods*
    (i)   *Removal and refitting of flywheel (transmission detached)*
    (j)   *Renewal of crankshaft front oil seal*
    (k)   *Renewal of crankshaft rear oil seal (transmission detached)*
    (l)   *Renewal of engine/transmission mountings*
    (m)   *Removal and refitting of ancillary components (coolant pump, fuel pump, manifolds, distributor etc)*

Oil pressure regulator valve – removal and refitting

4 From just to the rear of the crankshaft pulley, unscrew the pressure regulator valve plug and extract the spring and plunger.

5 Renew the spring if it is distorted or weak (compare it with a new one if possible).

6 If the plunger is scored, renew it.

7 Clean out the plunger hole and reassemble.

Camshaft drivebelt – renewal

8 Unscrew and remove the drivebelt cover, removing cooling system components as necessary.

9 Using a socket spanner on the crankshaft pulley bolt, turn the crankshaft until No 1 piston is rising on its compression stroke. The notch in the rim of the crankshaft pulley should be aligned with the timing pointer and represents ignition timing at the specified degrees BTDC, **not** TDC which is not marked on these engines. The camshaft sprocket mark will be in alignment with the mark on the belt cover backplate (photo).

10 Remove the alternator drivebelt, the crankshaft torsional damper and the distributor (see Section 11). Remove the distributor drivebelt.

11 Drain the cooling system.

12 Release the coolant pump mounting bolts just enough to be able to swivel the pump and to release the tension of the drivebelt.

6A.9 Camshaft sprocket timing marks

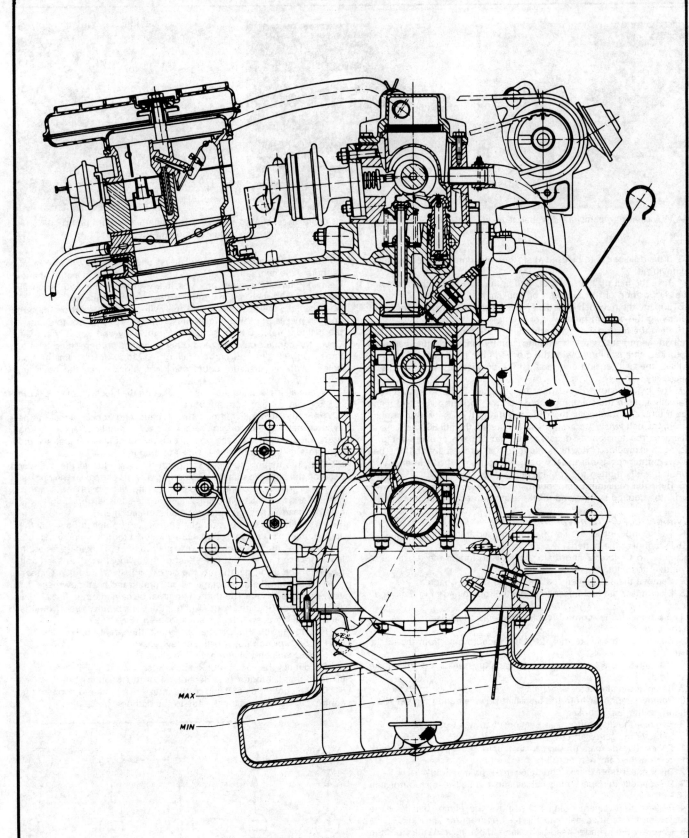

MAX

MIN

Fig. 13.2 Sectional view of 18S ohc engine (Sec 6)

6A.17A Checking camshaft drivebelt tension

6A.17B Adjusting camshaft drivebelt tension

6A.17C Tightening a coolant pump bolt after tensioning the drivebelt

13 If the drivebelt is to be used again, note its running direction before removing it.

14 Take the belt off the sprockets and fit the new one without moving the set position of the camshaft or crankshaft.

15 Engage the new belt over the sprockets and apply some tension by removing the coolant pump.

16 Refit the torsional damper and then check that the pulley notch is still in alignment with the timing pointer and that the camshaft sprocket mark is aligned with the groove in the plate behind it. If not, release the belt tension and readjust the position of the sprockets as necessary.

17 The belt tension should now be adjusted in the following way. Partially tighten the clamping screws on the coolant pump and using the thumb and forefinger, twist the belt through 90°. If with moderate effort, the belt twists too easily or will not reach the full 90°, increase or decrease the tension as necessary by moving the coolant pump; a hexagon is moulded into the pump to turn it with a spanner. If the belt is overtightened, it will usually be heard to hum when the engine is running. Fully tighten the coolant pump bolts (photos).

18 Refit the remaining components in the reverse order to removal. Refill the cooling system and reset the ignition timing on completion.

Cylinder head – removal and refitting

19 The cylinder head should only be removed from a cold engine.

20 Disconnect the battery.

21 Refer to Chapter 2 and drain the coolant. Ignore the reference to cylinder block draining.

22 Remove the air cleaner, see Section 10 of this Chapter.

23 Disconnect the fuel hoses from the fuel pump and plug their open ends.

24 Disconnect the control cables and electrical leads from the carburettor.

25 Disconnect the heater hose and the vacuum pipe from the intake manifold.

26 Disconnect the lead from the temperature sensor on the intake manifold.

27 Remove the alternator drivebelt.

28 Remove the cover from the camshaft drivebelt and then set No 1 piston on the firing stroke.

29 Remove the distributor (see Section 11 of this Chapter).

30 Remove the camshaft cover.

31 Check that the mark on the camshaft sprocket is in alignment with the one on the camshaft housing.

32 Disconnect the exhaust downpipe from the manifold.

33 Disconnect the spark plug cables and the coil-to-distributor cap HT lead.

34 Release the coolant pump bolts, move the pump to relieve the tension on the toothed belt and slip the belt from the sprockets.

35 Unscrew the cylinder head bolts and remove them. Work from the outside to inside in a spiral pattern, unscrewing them first by a quarter turn, and then by half a turn each time.

36 Lift off the camshaft housing. This is located on dowels. Lift straight upwards.

37 Lift off the cylinder head. If it is stuck, tap it gently with a plastic-faced hammer.

38 Peel away the cylinder head gasket and discard it.

39 Remove the rocker arms and thrust pads from the cylinder head. Withdraw the hydraulic valve lifters and immerse them in a container of clean engine oil to avoid any possibility of them draining. Keep all components in their original order if they are to be refitted.

40 Clean the cylinder block and the cylinder head free from carbon and old pieces of gasket by careful scraping. Take care not to damage the cylinder head, which is made of light alloy and is easily scored. Cover the coolant passages and other openings with masking tape or rag to prevent dirt and carbon falling in. Mop out oil from the bolt holes; hydraulic pressure could crack the block when the bolts are screwed in if oil is left in the holes.

41 When all is clean, locate a new gasket on the block so that the word 'OBEN' can be read from above.

42 Refit the hydraulic lifters, thrust pads and rocker arms to the cylinder head in their original order. If new hydraulic lifters are being used, initially immerse each one in a container of clean engine oil and compress it (by hand) several times to charge it.

43 With the mating surfaces scrupulously clean, locate the cylinder head on the block so that the positioning dowels engage in their holes.

44 Apply jointing compound to the mating flanges of the cylinder head and the camshaft housing and refit the camshaft housing to the cylinder head (camshaft sprocket marks in alignment).

45 The cylinder head bolts on ohc engines are tightened down by the angular method, as opposed to a conventional torque wrench method. This involves turning each bolt an equal number of degrees, resulting in a more even 'holding down' effect of the cylinder head, as each bolt travels in the same depth into the block. However, a torque wrench must be used in the initial stage when settling the head down against valve spring pressure. The tightening must be carried out in five stages as given in the Specifications. Tighten the bolts progressively from the centre working outwards in a spiral pattern (Fig. 13.3).

46 Fit and tension the camshaft drivebelt, then, refit the belt cover.

47 Fit the camshaft cover using a new gasket.

48 Fit and tension the alternator drivebelt.

49 Reconnect the vacuum pipe and heater hose.

50 Refit the distributor (see Section 11 of this Chapter).

51 Fit the coolant pipe clamp to the intake manifold and connect the control cables and electrical leads to the carburettor.

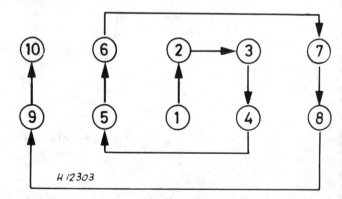

H 12303

Fig. 13.3 Cylinder head bolt tightening sequence (Sec 6)

52 Reconnect the fuel pipes to the pump.
53 Connect the exhaust pipe to the manifold.
54 Connect the lead to the temperature sensor on the intake manifold.
55 Fill the cooling system and bleed it as described in Chapter 2.
56 Reconnect the battery.
57 Fit the air cleaner.

Camshaft housing and camshaft – dismantling and reassembly

Refer also to Section 7
58 With the camshaft housing removed from the cylinder head as previously described, make sure that the distributor and fuel pump are withdrawn.
59 Fit an open-ended spanner to the flats on the camshaft. Hold the camshaft and unscrew the camshaft sprocket retaining bolt. Pull off the sprocket.
60 At the opposite end of the camshaft housing, use an Allen key to unscrew the two screws which retain the camshaft retaining plate.
61 Withdraw the retaining plate.
62 Remove the camshaft carefully out of the rear end of the camshaft housing taking care not to damage the camshaft bearing surfaces.
63 Before refitting the camshaft, oil the bearings.
64 Fit the camshaft retaining plate with fixing screws and then check the camshaft endfloat. If it exceeds the specified limit, renew the retaining plate.
65 Refit the camshaft sprocket. Hold the camshaft steady and tighten the sprocket timing bolt to the specified torque.

Sump – removal and refitting

66 It is necessary to lift the front of the engine slightly to effect sump removal.
67 Unscrew the top securing nut of both engine front mountings and disconnect the engine earth cable.
68 Position an engine lifting hoist so that its hook is engaged with the eye forward of the cylinder head.
69 Drain the engine oil.
70 Remove the sump securing bolts. Lift the engine just enough to allow sump removal, taking care not to strain any connections.
71 Remove the old sump gasket and clean both mating surfaces.
72 To refit the sump, apply jointing compound to the mating surface corners. Smear each side of the new gasket with grease and press it onto the cylinder block. Coat the threads of each bolt with locking compound, position the sump and fit and tighten the bolts.
73 Lower the engine back onto its mountings. Secure the mountings and reconnect the earth cable. Refill the engine with oil.

Oil pump – removal and refitting

74 Remove the camshaft drivebelt as previously described. Remove the belt cover backplate.
75 Using two screwdrivers as levers, prise off the belt sprocket from the front end of the crankshaft. Remove the Woodruff key.
76 Remove the sump as previously described.
77 Remove the oil pump pick-up pipe and strainer.
78 Unbolt the oil pump from the cylinder block and remove it.
79 Refer to Part B, paragraphs 22 to 27, for details of oil pump overhaul.
80 Before refitting the oil pump, steps must be taken to protect the seal lips from damage or turning back on the shoulder at the front end of the crankshaft. To do this, grease the seal lips and then bind tape around the crankshaft to form a gentle taper. Locate a new gasket.
81 Refit the oil pump and unwind and remove the tape.
82 Tighten the bolts to the specified torque and fit the Woodruff key and belt sprocket.
83 Refit the pick-up pipe and strainer, the sump, the drivebelt and its cover as previously described.
84 Refit the crankshaft pulley and the drivebelt and fill the engine with oil.

Pistons and connecting rods – removal and refitting

85 Remove the cylinder head and sump.
86 Remove the oil pump pick-up pipe and strainer.
87 Remove the pistons and connecting rods as described in Chapter 1, Section 15. Make alignment marks for use when refitting.
88 Refit the pistons and connecting rods as described in Chapter 1, Section 42; note that the piston orientation marks are not on the crown but on the underside (photo).

Fig. 13.4 Camshaft retaining plate screws (arrowed) (Sec 6)

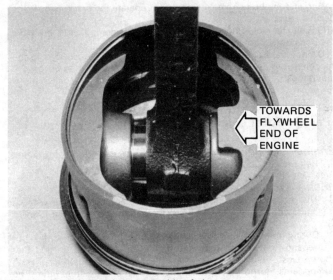

6A.88 Orientation mark on underside of piston

89 Refit the big-end bearing caps as described in Chapter 1, Section 43, referring to the Specifications at the beginning of this Chapter for the torque wrench setting.
90 Refit the oil pump pick-up pipe and strainer, the cylinder head and the sump.

Flywheel – removal and refitting

91 Refer to Chapter 5 and remove the clutch assembly.
92 Although the flywheel bolt holes are offset so that it can only be fitted in one position, it will make fitting easier if the flywheel-to-crankshaft flange alignment is marked before removal.
93 Jam the flywheel starter ring gear and using a ring spanner or socket, unscrew the bolts from the flywheel. As the heads of these bolts are very shallow, if a chamfered type of socket is being used, it is best to grind it to ensure more positive engagement.
94 Remove the flywheel.
95 Refit by reversing the removal operations, but apply thread locking compound to the bolts and tighten them to the correct torque.

Crankshaft front oil seal – renewal

96 Disconnect the battery earth lead. Remove the radiator and its cowl.
97 Remove the camshaft drivebelt as previously described. If it is oil-soaked it must be renewed.
98 Using two screwdrivers as levers, prise the sprocket from the crankshaft. Remove the Woodruff key.
99 Punch or drill a small hole in the metal face of the oil seal and screw in a self-tapping screw. Use the head of the screw to lever out the seal.

100 Fill the lips of the new seal with grease and tape the step on the crankshaft as previously described (paragraph 80).

101 Using a piece of tubing, tap the oil seal into position. Refit the Woodruff key.

102 Refit the remaining components in the reverse order to removal.

Crankshaft rear oil seal – renewal

103 Remove the flywheel.

104 Punch or drill a small hole in the metal face of the oil seal and screw in a self-tapping screw. Grasp the screw head with pliers and pull the seal out, having first noted its fitted position.

105 Lightly grease the lips and outer periphery of the new seal. Press the seal carefully into its location as far as it will go, using finger pressure and keeping it square to the housing. Place a piece of flat wood across the seal and tap it fully home to its previously noted position.

106 Refit the flywheel.

Engine/transmission mountings – renewal

107 Take the weight of the engine/transmission on a hoist, or jack and a wooden block used as an insulator.

108 Unbolt the mounting brackets from the crankcase or transmission casing and the body frame member and separate the brackets from the flexible member.

109 Refit the mountings with the new flexible components, but have the bolts only 'nipped up' initially.

110 Once the hoist or jack has been removed, tighten all bolts to the specified torque with the weight of the engine/transmission on the mountings.

Part B: Total dismantling and reassembly

Engine – methods of removal

1 Refer to Section 4 of Chapter 1.

Engine – removal

2 The procedure for removing the 1.8 ohc engine (with or without transmission) is similar to that given for the 2.0 CIH engine in Chapter 1.

3 During removal, exercise a degree of common sense. If slight discrepancies in design between the car being worked on and that shown exist, then take care to label or note the position of mating components; do not rely on memory. Double check before lifting the engine out to ensure that all necessary components have been disconnected.

Engine dismantling – general

4 Before attempting to dismantle the engine, read Section 7 of Chapter 1, ignoring paragraph 10.

Engine ancillary components – removal

5 The following ancillary components should be removed before engine dismantling begins. Refer to the appropriate sub-Sections of this Chapter and to the main Chapters of the manual for the necessary procedures.

    (a) *Alternator*
    (b) *Fuel pump*
    (c) *Thermostat*
    (d) *Inlet manifold*
    (e) *Carburettor*
    (f) *Distributor*
    (g) *Coolant pump*
    (h) *Exhaust manifold*

Engine – complete dismantling

6 With the engine removed from the vehicle and suitably positioned on a solid working surface, remove the following:

    (a) *Camshaft drivebelt*
    (b) *Cylinder head*
    (c) *Sump*
    (d) *Oil pump and oil pick-up pipe*
    (e) *Pistons/connecting rods*
    (f) *Clutch and flywheel*

7 Invert the engine so that it is standing on the top surface of the cylinder block.

8 The main bearing caps are numbered 1 to 4 from the drivebelt end of the engine. The rear cap is not marked. To ensure that the caps are refitted the correct way round, note that the numbers are read from the coolant pump side when the crankcase is inverted (photo).

9 Unscrew and remove the main bearing cap bolts and tap off the caps. If the bearing shells are to be used again, keep them with their respective caps. The original shells are colour-coded and if used again must be returned to their original locations.

10 Note that the centre bearing shell incorporates thrust flanges to control crankshaft endfloat.

11 Lift the crankshaft from the crankcase. Extract the upper half shells and again identify their position in the crankcase if they are to be used again.

12 Unbolt and remove the drivebelt cover backing plate.

13 The rubber plug located adjacent to the bellhousing flange on the crankcase covers the aperture for installation of a TDC sensor. This sensor when connected to a suitable monitoring unit, indicates TDC from the position of the contact pins set in the crankshaft counterbalance weight.

Lubrication and crankcase ventilation systems – description and maintenance

14 Oil pressure for all moving components is provided by a gear type oil pump which is driven from the front end of the crankshaft. The crankshaft has flats for this purpose.

15 The pump draws oil from the sump through a pick-up pipe and strainer and pumps it through the oil filter and oil galleries to the engine friction surfaces.

16 A pressure regulator valve is screwed into the body of the oil pump. A relief valve, located in the oil filter mounting base, opens should the

6B.8 Main bearing cap marking

6B.20 Crankcase ventilation system oil separator

6B.22 Loosening the oil pump rear cover screws

filter block due to clogging caused by neglected servicing. An oil pressure switch is screwed into the pump casing.

17 The cylinder bores are lubricated by oil splash from the sump.

18 The hydraulic valve lifters are pressurised with oil to maintain optimum valve clearance at all times.

19 The crankcase ventilation system is designed to draw oil fumes and blow-by gas (combustion gas which has passed the piston rings) from the crankcase into the air cleaner, whence they are drawn into the engine and burnt during the normal combustion cycle.

20 The oil separator can be unbolted from the crankcase, washed out with paraffin and shaken dry. Clean out the connecting pipes at the same time (photo).

21 On fuel injection engines, a flexible oil extraction hose runs between the neck of the oil filler opening and the throttle housing.

Oil pump – overhaul

22 With the oil pump removed from the vehicle, withdraw the rear cover. The cross-head fixing screws are very tight and an impact driver will be required to remove them (photo).

23 Check the clearance between the inner and outer gear teeth (photo).

24 Using a straight-edge across the pump cover flange, measure the gear endfloat (photo).

25 If any of the clearances are outside the specified tolerance, renew the components as necessary. Note that the outer gear face is marked for position (photo).

26 The pressure regulator valve can be unscrewed from the oil pump housing and the components cleaned and examined (photo).

27 Renew the oil seal as a matter of course. Carefully lever it from position with the flat of a screwdriver. Use a socket of the appropriate diameter to tap the new seal into position.

Cylinder head – dismantling, examination, renovation and decarbonising

28 With the cylinder head removed, clean away external dirt.

29 Remove the rocker arms and thrust pads from the cylinder head. Withdraw the hydraulic valve lifters and immerse them in a container of clean engine oil to avoid any possibility of them draining. Keep all components in their original order if they are to be refitted.

30 Using a method similar to that given in Section 12 of Chapter 1, remove the valves.

31 If worn valve guides are evident, have them renewed professionally.

32 Refer to Section 33 of Chapter 1 and decarbonise the cylinder head and piston crowns. Bear in mind that the cylinder head is of light alloy construction and can be easily damaged.

33 Refer to Section 32 of Chapter 1 and examine the valves and valve seats.

34 Check that all valve springs are intact. If any one is broken, all should be renewed. Check the free height of the springs against new ones. Springs suffer from fatigue and it is a good idea to renew them even if they look serviceable.

35 The cylinder head can be checked for warping either by placing it on a piece of plate glass or using a straight-edge and feeler blades. If there is any doubt or if its block face is corroded, have it re-faced by your dealer or motor engineering works.

6B.23 Check oil pump gear tooth clearance

Engine – examination and renovation, general

36 Refer to Section 23 of Chapter 1.

Crankshaft – examination and renovation

37 Refer to Section 24 of Chapter 1 and to the Specifications at the beginning of this Chapter.

Big-end main bearing shells – examination and renovation

38 Refer to Section 25 of Chapter 1.

Cylinder bores – examination and renovation

39 Refer to Section 26 of Chapter 1 and to the Specifications given at the beginning of this Chapter.

Pistons and piston rings – examination and renovation

40 Refer to Section 27 of Chapter 1 and to the Specifications in this Chapter.

41 When removing the rings, keep them in order so that they may be refitted in their original location. The second ring has its upper surface marked TOP.

42 Before checking for piston ring groove wear, check each groove using a section of old piston ring ground to a suitable width as a scraper. Take care to remove only the carbon deposits and not to remove metal or score the piston lands. Protect your fingers – piston rings are sharp!

43 If new rings (or pistons and rings) are to be fitted to an existing bore the top ring must be stepped to clear the wear ridge at the top of the bore, or the bore must be de-ridged.

6B.24 Checking oil pump gear endfloat

6B.25 Oil pump gear positioning mark (arrowed)

6B.26 Oil pump pressure regulator valve components

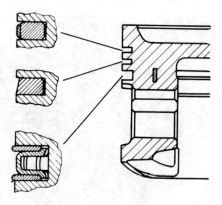

Fig. 13.5 Piston ring details (Sec 6)

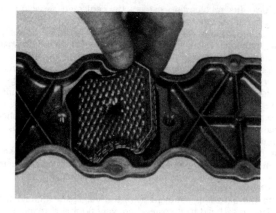

Fig. 13.6 Camshaft housing filter (Sec 6)

44 Check the clearance and end gap of any new rings as previously described. If a ring is slightly tight in its groove it may be rubbed down using an oilstone or a sheet of carborundum paper laid on a sheet of glass. If the end gap is inadequate, the ring can be carefully ground until the specified clearance is achieved.

45 If new pistons are to be installed they will be selected from the grades available after measuring the bores. Normally the appropriate oversize pistons are supplied by the repairer when the block is rebored. Whenever new piston rings are being installed, the glaze on original cylinder bores should be 'broken' using either abrasive paper or a glaze removing tool in an electric drill. If abrasive paper is used, use strokes at 60° to the bore centre line to create a cross-hatching effect.

Connecting rods – examination and renovation
46 Refer to Section 28 of Chapter 1.
47 The gudgeon pins are an interference fit in the connecting rod small end. Removal and refitting of pistons to rods is a job for your dealer, as would be any remedial action required if the gudgeon pin is no longer an interference fit in the rod.

Flywheel – examination and renovation
48 Details of flywheel ring gear examination and renewal are given in Section 37 of Chapter 1.
49 Inspect the machine face of the flywheel as described in Chapter 5, Section 5.

Driveplate (automatic transmission) – examination and renovation
50 Should the starter ring gear on the driveplate require renewal, renew the driveplate complete.

Crankshaft spigot bearing – renewal
51 If the needle bearing in the centre of the crankshaft flange is worn, fill it with grease and tap in a close-fitting rod. Hydraulic pressure will remove it. Alternatively, a very small extractor having a claw type leg may be used. When tapping the new bearing into position, make sure that the chamfered side of the bearing enters first.
52 A spigot bearing may not be fitted to later engines.

Camshaft – examination and renovation
53 With the camshaft removed, examine the bearings for signs of obvious wear and pitting. If evident, a new camshaft housing will probably be required.
54 The camshaft itself should show no marks or scoring on the journal or cam lobe surfaces. If evident, renew the camshaft. See Section 7 of this Chapter.
55 The camshaft retaining plate should appear unworn and without grooves. In any event, check the camshaft endfloat and fit a new plate where necessary.
56 The housing front oil seal should always be renewed at major overhaul. A filter is incorporated in the camshaft housing cover. Remove it and wash thoroughly in petrol and allow to dry.

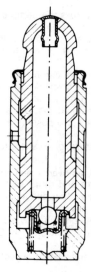

Fig. 13.7 Sectional view of hydraulic valve lifter (Sec 6)

Camshaft drivebelt – examination and renovation
57 Closely inspect the belt for cracking, fraying, oil contamination or tooth deformation. Where evident, renew the belt.
58 If the belt has been in use for 30 000 miles (48 000 km) or more, it is recommended that it is renewed even if it appears in good condition.
59 Whenever the original belt is to be removed but is going to be used again, always note its running direction before removing it. It is even worthwhile marking the tooth engagement points on each sprocket. As the belt will have worn in a set position, refitting it in exactly the same way will prevent any increase in noise which might otherwise occur when the engine is running.

Valve lifters, rockers and thrust pads – examination and renovation
60 Any signs of wear in a hydraulic lifter can only be rectified by renewal, the unit cannot be dismantled.
61 Inspect the rockers and thrust pads for wear or grooving. Again, renew if evident.

Engine reassembly – general
62 Refer to Section 38 of Chapter 1.
63 To ensure maximum life with minimum trouble from a rebuilt engine, not only must everything be correctly assembled, but everything must be spotlessly clean, all the oilways must be clear, locking washers and spring washers must always be fitted where indicated and all bearing and other working surfaces must be thoroughly lubricated during assembly.
64 Before assembly begins renew any bolts or studs, the threads of which are in any way damaged, and whenever possible use new spring washers.

Crankshaft and main bearings – reassembly

65 Read paragraphs 1 to 3 of Section 39, Chapter 1.

66 The central bearing shell takes up the crankshaft endfloat. Note that the half-shells fitted to the cylinder block all have oil duct holes, while only the centre main bearing cap half-shell has an oil duct hole (photos).

67 When the shells are fully located in the crankcase and bearing caps, lubricate them with clean engine oil.

68 Fill the lip of a new crankshaft oil seal with grease and fit it to the end of the crankshaft (photo).

69 Carefully install the crankshaft into position in the crankcase.

70 Lubricate the crankshaft main bearing journals and then refit the centre and intermediate main bearing caps. Tighten the retaining bolts to the specified torque.

71 Clean the grooves of the rear main bearing cap free from old sealant and thinly coat its mating surfaces with sealing compound. Fit the cap and tighten the bolts to the specified torque (photos). Now fill the grooves in the bearing cap with RTV type gasket compound. Inject straight from the tube until the material is seen to exude from the cap joints to prove that any trapped air has been expelled.

72 Fit the front main bearing cap but before fitting the retaining bolts, smear them with sealant, and then tighten to the specified torque wrench setting. Check that the bearing cap is exactly flush with the end face of the crankcase as it is tightened.

73 Now rotate the crankshaft and check that it turns freely, and shows no signs of binding or tight spots. Check that the crankshaft endfloat is within the limits specified. Alternative centre bearing shells are available if necessary to adjust the endfloat. The endfloat can be checked using a dial gauge or with feeler blades inserted between the flange of the centre bearing shell and the machined surface of the crankshaft. Before measuring, make sure that the crankshaft has been forced fully towards one end of the crankcase to give the widest gap at the measuring location (photo).

Piston rings – reassembly

74 Read paragraphs 1 to 5 of Section 41, Chapter 1.

75 Follow the manufacturer's instructions carefully when fitting rings to ensure that they are correctly fitted. Several variations of compression and oil control rings are available and it is of the utmost importance that they be located correctly in their grooves.

76 When the rings are in position check that the compression rings are free to expand and contract in their grooves. Certain types of multi-segment oil control rings are a light interference fit in their grooves and this may not therefore apply to them. When all rings are in position on the pistons move them around to bring each ring gap to be 180° away from the gap on the adjacent ring. With the original type of oil control ring, ensure that the gap of the upper rail is offset by 25 to 50 mm (1 to 2 in) to the left of the spacer gap. Offset the gap of the lower rail the same distance to the right.

Pistons and connecting rods – refitting

77 Refer to Sections 42 and 43 of Chapter 1, ignoring the instructions on rod and bearing alignment. Check that the rod markings are towards the side of the engine as noted before dismantling. This is very important as the piston crowns do not have front directional marks.

Oil pump and sump – refitting

78 Refit the oil pump as described in Part A, paragraphs 80 to 82 (photos).

79 Refit the oil pick-up pipe and strainer.

80 Refit the sump, using a new gasket.

81 Stand the engine on the sump and fit the Woodruff key to the crankshaft.

Flywheel – refitting

82 Offer the flywheel to the crankshaft rear mounting flange.

83 Apply thread locking compound to the bolt threads and screw in the bolts.

84 Jam the starter ring gear teeth and tighten the bolts to the specified torque.

6B.66A Centre main bearing shell showing thrust flange

6B.66B Centre main bearing shell showing locating notch

6B.68 Crankshaft rear oil seal

6B.71A Fitting the rear main bearing cap

6B.71B Injecting sealant into rear main bearing cap grooves

6B.73 Checking crankshaft endfloat

6B.78A Crankshaft step taped

6B.78B Fitting the oil pump

6B.86 Fitting a valve stem oil seal

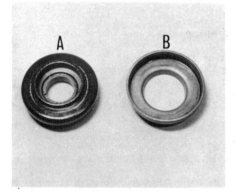

6B.88A Exhaust valve rotator (A) and inlet valve spring seat (B)

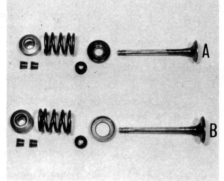

6B.88B Valve components – exhaust (A) and inlet (B)

6B.89 Fitting a valve spring and cap

6B.91 Fitting a hydraulic valve lifter to the cylinder head

6B.92A Fitting a thrust pad

6B.92B Fitting a rocker

Cylinder head and camshaft housing – reassembly and refitting

85 Ensure that all valves and springs are clean and free from carbon deposits and that the ports and valve guides in the cylinder head have no carbon dust or valve grinding paste left in them.

86 Starting at one end of the cylinder head, fit new valve stem oil seals to the ends of the valve guides (photo). Refer also to Section 7.

87 Oil the stem of the first valve and insert it into its guide. The valves must be installed into the seats into which they have been ground, which in the case of the original valves will mean that their original sequence of fitting is retained.

88 With inlet valves, fit the spring seat. With exhaust valves fit the valve rotator. Fit the valve spring (photos).

89 Place the cap over the spring with the recessed part inside the coil of the spring (photo).

90 Using a method similar to that given in Section 46, Chapter 1, fit the valve stem cotters.

91 Lubricate the hydraulic valve lifters and insert them into their bores in the cylinder head (photo). If new hydraulic valve lifters are being used, initially immerse each one in a container of clean engine oil and compress it (by hand) several times to charge it.

92 Fit the rockers and the thrust pads, also new spark plugs of the specified type (photos).

93 Fit the thermostat into its seat, use a new sealing ring and fit the thermostat housing cover. Tighten the bolts to the specified torque.

94 Refit the camshaft to its housing as described in Part A, paragraphs 63 to 65 (photos).

95 Set the engine with Nos 1 and 4 pistons at TDC.

96 Refit and secure the cylinder head as described in Part A, paragraphs 41 to 45.

97 Fit the coolant pump (Section 9), but leave the bolts loose pending drivebelt adjustment.

6B.94A Camshaft retaining plate

6B.94B Checking camshaft endfloat

98 Fit the camshaft drivebelt backplate.
99 Fit the drivebelt sprocket to the crankshaft nose.
100 Fit and tension the camshaft drivebelt as described in Part A, paragraphs 15 to 17.
101 Fit the camshaft housing cover using a new gasket.
102 Fit the camshaft drivebelt front cover.
103 Fit the inlet and exhaust manifolds, using new gaskets.
104 Refit all ancillary components.

Engine – refitting
105 The procedure is similar to that described in Chapter 1, Section 53.
106 Do not rush engine refitting but take time to ensure every component is properly reconnected and that connections are made in a logical order. Recheck connections for security before attempting to start the engine.

Engine – initial start-up after overhaul
107 Refer to Section 54 of Chapter 1, ignoring the reference to hydraulic tappet adjustment. If a new camshaft has been fitted, refer to the running-in procedure given in Section 7 of this Chapter. It is normal for a considerable amount of noise to come from hydraulic valve lifters on initial start-up after overhaul. This should only continue until the valve lifters are properly pressurized with oil.

7   Engine – 1.8 litre ohc, modifications

Valve stem oil seals
1   From late 1983 GM have fitted improved valve stem oil seals. Fig. 13.8 shows the difference between the old and modified seals.
2   When fitting a modified seal, slide it carefully over the valve stem, taking care not to damage the seal lip. Using gentle thumb pressure, push the seal over the valve guide until the seal bead locates in the guide groove. Do not push the seal bead beyond the groove, otherwise the seal is ineffective.

Camshaft – renewal
3   If a camshaft wears excessively and has to be renewed it should only be renewed with a wear-resistant (TIG) type available from GM dealers.
4   After renewal of a camshaft, it is imperative that the following running-in procedure is followed.
5   Coat all bearing surfaces of the camshaft with MoS_2 (molybdenum disulphide) paste (obtainable from your GM dealer) during fitting.
6   Upon starting the engine, do not allow it to run for long periods at idling speed but run it for 4 minutes at the following engine speeds:

    1 minute at 2000 rpm   1 minute at 3000 rpm
    1 minute at 1500 rpm   1 minute at 2000 rpm

7   The engine oil (but not the filter) must be renewed at the first 600 mile (1000 km) interval after camshaft renewal.

Valve lifters and rockers – removal and refitting (using special tool)
8   GM have now introduced a tool which allows removal of the valve lifters and rockers without the need for prior removal of the camshaft. The tool No is KM565.

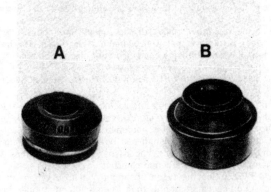

Fig. 13.8 Valve stem oil seals (Sec 7)

A   Old type   *B   New type*

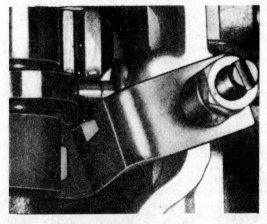

Fig. 13.9 Special tool (KM 565) being used to remove valve lifters and rockers (Sec 7)

9   If it is possible to borrow or hire the tool from a GM dealer, then fit it as follows.

10 Position the appropriate piston at BDC. Locate the tool with the valve spring cap and tighten down on the tool until the rocker, thrust pad and valve lifter can be removed.

11 Refit all components by reversing the removal operation.

8   Engine – 2.0 and 2.2 litre CIH

Cylinder head – modifications

1   From 1981, 20S engines from engine No 0645261 have an improved lubrication system for the camshaft and tappets.

2   Oil seals are now fitted to the stems of both inlet and exhaust valves and the valve guides have been machined to accommodate the seals. The seals are colour-coded red (exhaust) and black (inlet).

3   The exhaust valve spring upper seat (shroud) is no longer fitted. The exhaust valve springs are now identical to those fitted to the inlet valve and the valve rotators have been modified.

4   The oil drain bore situated at the rear of the cylinder head now has a pressed-in tube. This has the effect of raising the oil level which improves camshaft lubrication.

5   Fig. 13.10 shows the difference between earlier and later camshafts. The earlier camshaft can be fitted to both modified and unmodified cylinder heads. **Note:** *Under no circumstances fit a later camshaft (without a journal groove) to an unmodified cylinder head.* This will result in overheating and possible seizure of the camshaft.

Camshaft – renewal

6   If the camshaft is damaged, GM recommend that the following preparation be carried out before a new item is fitted.

7   Thoroughly clean the cylinder head and camshaft housing, drying each component with compresed air.

8   Renew the engine oil, the oil filter element and the hydraulic tappets.

9   Smear the bearing surfaces of the rockers and tappets with a molybdenum disulphide paste (obtainable from your GM dealer) during assembly and lubricate each cam with clean engine oil.

Chilled cast iron camshaft – identification and compatibility

10 From late 1983, GM started replacing the induction hardened camshaft with a chilled cast iron component. To match this change, the hydraulic tappets have induction hardened bottoms.

11 The chilled cast iron camshaft can be identified by the lug cast between the exhaust cams of cylinder Nos 2 and 3. It also has wider cams than the induction hardened camshaft.

12 Fig. 13.12 shows the types of tappet available. When fitting a chilled cast iron camshaft, fit only the tappets with induction hardened bottoms. When an induction hardened camshaft is fitted, fit any type of tappet.

13 Chilled cast iron camshafts are supplied with or without a groove in the front bearing journal. Refer to the rest of this Section before selecting or fitting a new camshaft.

Oil pump sealing (2.2 CIH)

14 As from December 1984 a liquid sealant is applied to the oil pump cover-to-body joint instead of a paper gasket.

15 Always apply the sealant to clean mating surfaces and never be tempted to use a paper gasket, or low oil pressure may result.

9   Cooling system

2.2 CIH – description and maintenance

1   The cooling system on this engine is of sealed 'no loss' type and incorporates an expansion tank.

2   The need for topping-up should rarely occur but check the coolant level regularly when the engine is cold.

3   The coolant should be 30 mm (1.2 in) below the upper edge of the filler neck (cap removed) and slightly above the 'KALT' mark on the expansion tank.

4   Top up if necessary using coolant mixed in similar proportions to the original mixture.

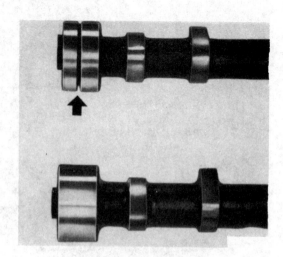

Fig. 13.10 Old type camshaft with oil groove (arrowed). Later type below (Sec 8)

Fig. 13.11 Chilled cast-iron camshaft identified by cast lug – arrowed (Sec 8)

Fig. 13.12 Alternative types of hydraulic valve lifters (Sec 8)

A   Earlier type   *B   Later (induction hardened) type*

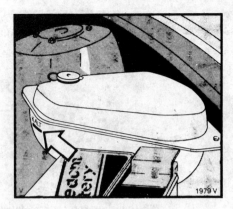

Fig. 13.13 Cooling system expansion tank and level mark (Sec 9)

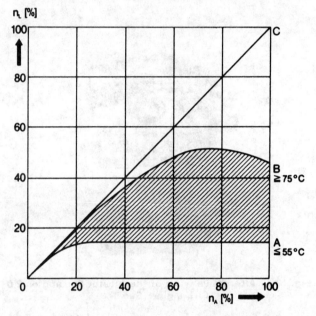

Fig. 13.14 Fan and engine speed comparison chart (Sec 9)

A   Visco fan disengaged
B   Visco fan engaged
C   Directly driven type fan

n_L Fan speed
n_A Engine speed

5   When the engine is at normal operating temperature the level in the expansion tank will rise but drop again as it cools.

Temperature-controlled visco fan (all models) – operation, removal and refitting

6   Later models are fitted with a temperature-controlled viscous coupled cooling fan. The viscous coupling slips at low temperature, so reducing power loss and noise. At high temperatures the coupling slip is reduced and the fan speed rises.
7   The fan and coupling cannot be repaired and if defective or leaking must be renewed.
8   Before attempting removal of the visco fan, obtain an open-ended spanner which will fit closely over the flats of the fan carrier whilst clearing the fan holding nut. A spanner which is too thick can be modified by grinding a chamfer of the necessary width on one side of both of its flats.
9   Gain access to the fan by removing the cowling and radiator. **Note:** *The fan holding nut has a left-hand thread.* Whilst holding the fan carrier steady, remove the holding nut and withdraw the fan assembly. Avoid placing the fan on its face as this can damage the moving pin.

V-belt (all models) – renewal

10   Where a new V-belt has been fitted, start the engine and allow it to idle. Over a five minute period, accelerate the engine several times before allowing it to return to idle.
11   After five minutes, the new belt will have adapted to the pulley profiles and stretched slightly. Stop the engine and recheck the belt tension.

Thermostat (1.8 ohc) – removal, testing and refitting

12   Refer to Section 3 of Chapter 2 and drain the cooling system.
13   Detach the hose from the thermostat housing and unbolt the housing. Withdraw the thermostat.
14   The procedure for testing a thermostat is given in Section 8 of Chapter 2.
15   Renew the thermostat seal and the housing gasket. Ensure all mating surfaces are clean, locate the thermostat and its housing and tighten the securing bolts evenly to prevent distortion. Secure the hose and replenish the cooling system.

Water pump (1.8 ohc) – removal and refitting

16   Disconnect the battery earth cable.
17   Refer to Section 6 of Chapter 2 and remove the fan cowl and radiator. Begin this operation by unclipping the power cable from the cowl and disconnecting it from the battery positive terminal.
18   Remove the camshaft drivebelt (see Section 6). Unless the drivebelt is to be renewed it can be left on the camshaft sprocket.
19   Remove the drivebelt backplate.

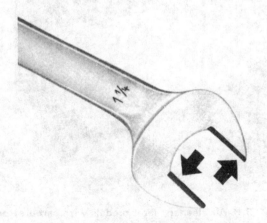

Fig. 13.15 Modified spanner to fit fan carrier Chamfers – arrowed (Sec 9)

Fig. 13.16 Thermostat housing – 1.8 ohc (Sec 9)

9.20 Removing coolant pump

9.22A Coolant pump O-ring seal

9.22B Coolant pump correctly fitted.
Rotational stops (timing belt tension)
arrowed

20 Unbolt the pump and remove it from the block (photo).
21 Although the pump can be dismantled and reassembled, a press
and several special tools are necessary and it is considered that the
work is outside the scope of the home mechanic. For this reason a
defective pump should be renewed.
22 Before fitting the pump, clean its mounting in the engine block and
fit a new O-ring seal to the pump body (photo). Install the pump in the
block and fit the three retaining bolts and washers, but only hand
tighten them at this stage (photo). The cut-out in the pump flange
must be positioned as shown to act as the timing belt adjustment limit
stop when the pump is rotated to tension the timing belt. Refit the belt
cover backplate.
23 Refit and tension the camshaft drivebelt.
24 Refit the remaining components in the reverse order to removal.
25 Refill the cooling system, run the engine and check for leaks.

Thermostat (2.0 and 2.2 CIH) – removal and refitting

26 Post-1981 vehicles will have a redesigned type of thermostat
housing fitted.
27 Providing the correct hoses are fitted, the two types of housing are
interchangeable. On the later one-piece unit, the thermostat is held in
position by a circlip.

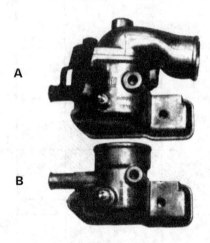

Fig. 13.17 Alternative types of thermostat housing on 2.0
CIH engine (Sec 9)

A   Earlier type   B   Later type

10 Fuel and exhaust systems

Air cleaner (later models) – element renewal
Carburettor models
1   The later type of cleaner assembly is secured to the carburettor by a
single screw. To renew the element, remove the screw and lift the
housing from the carburettor. Release the clips and separate the two
sections of housing to expose the element. Carefully remove the
element.
2   Examine the element as instructed in Section 4 of Chapter 3 and
renew it if necessary.
3   When refitting the element, ensure that it is the correct type and is
pointing in the right direction, see Fig. 13.18. Check that the element is
properly seated before clipping the cover in place.
4   Before reattaching the housing to the carburettor, check that its
mounting aligns correctly with the bracket slot. Check that any
disturbed hoses have been reconnected before refitting the housing
retaining screw.
Fuel injection models
5   The air cleaner housing is located on the wheel arch to the
right-hand side of the radiator. Unplug the airflow sensor electrical
connector and release the hose securing clip, then unclip the housing.
6   Examine the element as instructed in Section 4 of Chapter 3 and
renew it if necessary.
7   When refitting the element, position it in the upper half of the
housing, pushing it firmly into place around its edges so that a good
seal is formed. Press the two halves of the housing together and secure
the clips. Retighten the hose clip. Check the terminals of the electrical
connector for cleanliness before reconnecting it (photos).

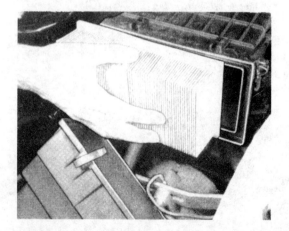

Fig. 13.18 Air cleaner – later models with carburettor
(Sec 10)

10.7A Air cleaner element (fuel injection models)

10.7B Reconnecting the airflow meter plug

10.12 Fuel pump and damper location (fuel injection models)

Fuel pump (later models) – removal, servicing and refitting

1.8 litre ohc carburettor models

8   The pump is mounted on the camshaft housing and actuated by a pushrod from an eccentric cam on the camshaft. The pump is of the semi-sealed type; no repairs are possible.

9   Refer to Section 6 of Chapter 3, paragraph 3 onwards, for details of pump servicing.

10 Pump removal is simply a matter of disconnecting the fuel pipes, plugging the pipe ends, unscrewing the two securing nuts and carefully withdrawing the pump from the camshaft housing.

11 Before refitting the pump, check that both mating surfaces are clean and then renew the base gasket. Push the pump into position and prevent it from tilting when the securing nuts are tightened. Reconnect the fuel pipes and after starting the engine, check for leaks.

Fuel injection models

12 The fuel pump and damper diaphragm unit are located just forward of the fuel tank (photo).

13 Clamp the fuel hoses on either side of the pump to prevent loss of fuel when they are disconnected. Self-locking grips are useful for this. Disconnect the hoses.

14 Unscrew the pump mounting clamp bolts and withdraw the pump from its flexible insulator (photo). Disconnect the electrical plug as the pump is withdrawn.

15 Alternatively, the pump can be removed complete with filter and damper diaphragm unit if the mounting strap nuts are unscrewed and the assembly removed from its flexible mountings.

16 The pump is a sealed unit, no repairs are possible.

10.14 Fuel pump clamp bolt

Fig. 13.19 Fuel pump location – 1.8 ohc (Sec 10)

Zenith 35/40 INAT carburettor

Removal and refitting

17 Removal and refitting are essentially as described in Chapter 3, Section 19. Take note of the fuel, vacuum and electrical connections for reference when refitting.

Setting and adjustment (general)

18 There is very little in the way of mixture adjustment that may be carried out on fixed choke carburettors.

19 One or more of the adjustment screws may be sealed with a 'tamperproof' cap. The purpose of this cap is to discourage (and to detect) amateur adjustment. Satisfy yourself that you are not breaking anti-pollution regulations before removing a tamperproof device.

Idling adjustment

20 When the idling speed is adjusted during manufacture, the stop screw setting of the primary barrel throttle flap is adjusted relative to the ignition vacuum advance connection. The screw is then sealed with a plastic cap and should not be disturbed, because incorrect positioning of the throttle flap at idling speed can affect the ignition timing and the carburettor progression system.

21 Idling speed may be varied by the idle speed adjusting screw (Fig. 13.20) without this having any appreciable effect on the idling air/fuel mixture. The smaller screw is the mixture control screw and should not be tampered with unless a CO meter is available. Adjustment of this screw is only necessary when the carbon monoxide (CO) content is outside the specified limits.

Fast idling adjustment

22 Ensure that the engine is at normal operating temperature and that the idling speed is correct.

23 Open the throttle and close the choke flap to place the fast idle screw on the highest step of the cam (Fig. 13.21). The choke flap may be closed by raising the choke connecting rod to its fullest extent.

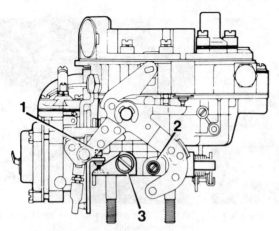

Fig. 13.20 Idle adjustment screws – Zenith 35/40 INAT carburettor (Sec 10)

1   Throttle stop screw (do not   2   Mixture control screw
     touch)   3   Idle speed adjusting screw

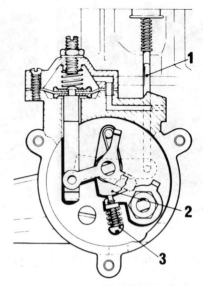

Fig. 13.21 Fast idle adjustment – Zenith 35/40 INAT carburettor (Sec 10)

1   Choke link rod   3   Fast idle screw
2   Cam

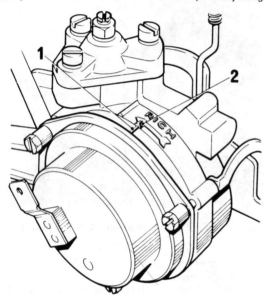

Fig. 13.22 Automatic choke adjustment marks – Zenith 35/40 INAT carburettor (Sec 10)

1   Choke cover mark   2   Choke housing cover

Fig. 13.23 Checking vacuum override travel stop setting. Adjustment screw arrowed (Sec 10)

24 Start the engine without depressing the accelerator pedal and the engine should run at 2700 rpm.
25 To adjust the fast idling speed, stop the engine and open the throttle fully to expose the stop screw through a hole in the automatic choke housing. Turn the screw a small amount in a clockwise direction and again check the fast idling speed. If the alteration is in the wrong direction, stop the engine and turn the screw anti-clockwise a small amount before re-checking. Continue making small changes to the stop screw position until the engine runs at 2700 rpm.

Automatic choke adjustment

26 The setting of the automatic choke cover controls the time which the choke takes to open. To set the cover, check that the mark on its outer edge is aligned with the pointer of the inner cover, see Fig. 13.22. At this setting, the choke flap should open fully within 3 to 5 minutes of the ignition being switched on.
27 To adjust choke operation, slacken the three cover screws slightly and rotate the cover clockwise to weaken choke effectiveness or anti-clockwise to strengthen it. Upon achieving the required setting, retighten the cover screws and make a new alignment mark on the cover edge.
28 To check the travel stop setting of the vacuum controlled override unit, close the choke flap and attach a rubber band to the choke

intermediate lever to hold the flap closed (Fig. 13.23). Lift the vacuum diaphragm to the full extent of its travel and check that a gap of 2.7 to 2.9 mm (0.106 to 0.114 in) exists between the edge of the choke flap and the barrel bore.
29 To check the choke flap rod linkage setting, hold the choke flap closed and check that the distance between the intermediate lever and the vacuum diaphragm pulled boss (dimension 'A' in Fig. 13.24) is 0.2 to 1.0 mm (0.008 to 0.040 in).
30 To adjust the setting, remove the plastic cap from the carburettor cover, slacken the choke rod clamp screw, adjust the rod to give the correct setting and then tighten the clamp.

Secondary barrel throttle flap setting

31 To prevent the secondary barrel throttle flap (Fig. 13.25) from jamming in the closed position, the throttle flap stop screw should be adjusted to give a gap of 0.05 mm (0.002 in) between the edge of the flap and the barrel bore. This clearance is about a quarter of a turn of the stop screw from the flap closed position.
32 An excessive clearance of the secondary throttle flap can make it impossible to obtain correct engine idling speed.

Throttle flap link roller

33 To ensure correct roller contact on the primary barrel throttle flap lever, the link lever screw (Fig. 13.27) should be adjusted to give a gap

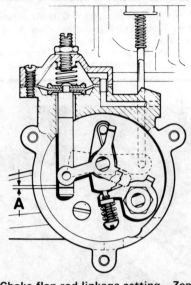

Fig. 13.24 Choke flap rod linkage setting – Zenith 35/40 INAT carburettor (Sec 10)

A = 0.2 to 1.0 mm (0.008 to 0.040 in)

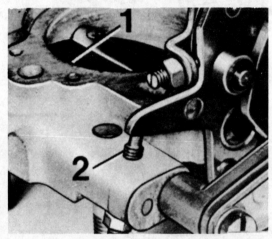

Fig. 13.25 Secondary throttle valve flap (1) and stop screw (2) (Sec 10)

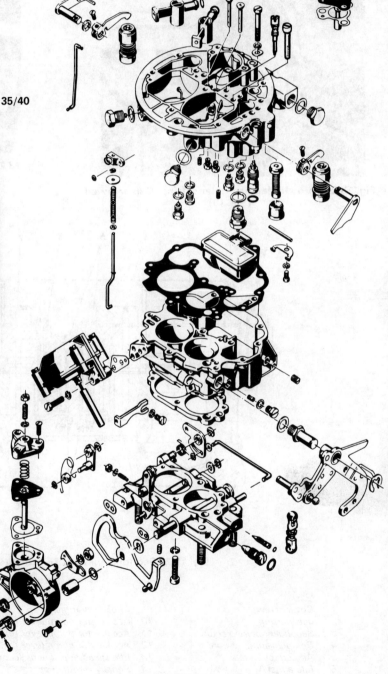

Fig. 13.26 Exploded view of Zenith 35/40 INAT (Sec 10)

of 0.1 to 0.2 mm (0.004 to 0.008 in) between the end of the screw and the secondary barrel throttle flap lever with the primary barrel throttle flap closed.

Float chamber vent valve setting

34 The float chamber vent valve setting (Fig. 13.28) is correct when

there is a gap of 1.5 to 1.8 mm (0.06 to 0.07 in) between the throttle stop screw and its abutment when the vent lever is just touching the base of the vent valve.

35 To alter the setting, adjust the length of the intermediate link. Do not alter the setting of the throttle stop screw.

Fig. 13.27 Throttle flap link roller setting. Gap arrowed (Sec 10)

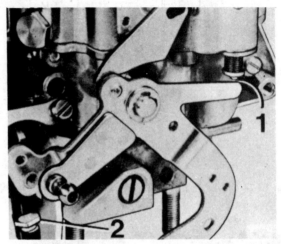

Fig. 13.28 Float chamber vent valve setting – Zenith 35/40 INAT carburettor (Sec 10)

1   Vent lever and valve   2   Intermediate link and adjustment

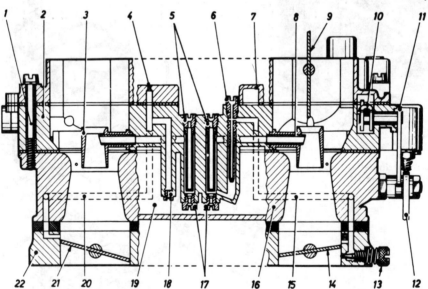

Fig. 13.29 Sectional view of Zenith 35/40 INAT carburettor (Sec 10)

1 Cover screw	9 Choke (strangler) flap	17 Main jets
2 Jet housing	10 Accelerator pump lever (internal)	18 Progression jet
3 Secondary barrel venturi	11 Accelerator pump lever (external)	19 Float chamber
4 Compensating air bore	12 Accelerator pump lever (actuating)	20 Progression passage
5 Air correction jets	13 Idle speed adjustment screw	21 Secondary throttle flap
6 Idle air jet	14 Primary throttle flap	22 Throttle body
7 Cover	15 Idle mixture passage	
8 Primary discharge tube	16 Float chamber housing	

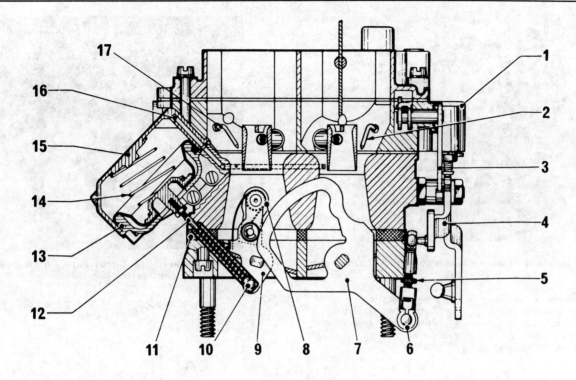

Fig. 13.30 Cross-sectional view of Zenith 35/40 INAT carburettor (Sec 10)

1	Float chamber vent housing	7	Primary throttle flap lever
2	Primary injection tube	8	Throttle flap link lever
3	Accelerator pump lever (actuating)	9	Secondary throttle flap lever
4	Throttle lever	10	Ball
5	Vent valve adjusting screw	11	Insulator
6	Connecting rod	12	Connecting rod

13 Diaphragm
14 Spring
15 Vacuum housing
16 Vacuum passage
17 Secondary injection tube

Automatic transmission throttle damper
36 Refer to Chapter 3, Section 12.
Dismantling, inspection and reassembly
37 Clean all exterior dirt off the carburettor before dismantling begins.
38 Place the carburettor on a clean sheet of paper so that the components can be laid out in order of removal.
39 Remove the plastic plug at the side of the top section of the carburettor and slacken the screw which secures the automatic choke rod.
40 Remove the ten screws which secure the top section. One screw is inside the air filter securing screw recess.
41 Carefully lift off the top section.
42 Disconnect the accelerator pump linkage.
43 Remove the three retaining screws and lift off the jet housing assembly.
44 Lift out the primary accelerator pump piston past the operating lever.
45 To remove the secondary pump piston, first remove the screw securing the operating lever to the shaft and remove piston and lever.
46 The two air correction jets can be unscrewed from the jet housing, but keep them in the right order as they are different sizes.
47 The emulsion tubes can now be lifted out, but make a careful note of their position to ensure correct installation.
48 The various jets can be removed from the jet housing assembly as

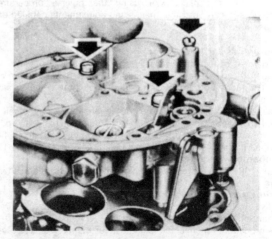

Fig. 13.31 Jet housing securing screws (arrowed) – Zenith 35/40 INAT carburettor (Sec 10)

Fig. 13.32 Jet identification – Zenith 35/40 INAT carburettor (Sec 10)

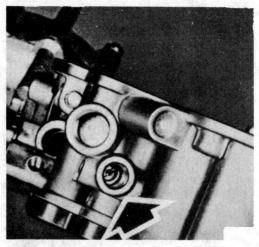

Fig. 13.33 Additional idle jet (arrowed) – Zenith 35/40 INAT carburettor (Sec 10)

1	Pump outlet (primary)	6	Progression jet
2	Pump intake (primary)	7	Pump intake (secondary)
3	Enrichment valve	8	Pump outlet (secondary)
4	Main jet (primary)	9	Idle air vent
5	Main jet (secondary)	10	Idle jet

required (Fig. 13.32). Clean the jets using clean petrol and an air line, if available.

49 The float assembly can be removed by undoing the single screw retaining the bracket.

50 To remove the vacuum control unit, release the control rod from the secondary barrel throttle flap, remove the three securing screws and lift away the vacuum unit.

51 Remove the three screws securing the automatic choke override cover and examine the diaphragm beneath it for damage.

52 The throttle lever can be removed by detaching the spring clip from the end of the shaft and lifting off the lever and two nylon bushes.

53 To gain access to the idling jet inside the float chamber housing, undo the plug from the side of the housing and then unscrew the jet (Fig. 13.33).

54 Clean the parts in petrol and blow dry with compressed air. Blow the carburettor barrel and float chamber passages in the direction of fuel flow.

55 Operate the float chamber vent valve by hand and inspect the valve and seating.

56 Check that all jet inserts are according to the carburettor specification.

57 Renew all gaskets and sealing rings.

58 Reassemble the carburettor using the reverse procedure to dismantling and carry out the checks and adjustments detailed earlier in this Section.

GM Varajet II carburettor
Cover gasket modification
59 From 1981, GM have introduced a modified carburettor cover gasket. The modified gasket has an idle circuit hole which is slotted instead of round.

60 Positive identification can be made by reference to the small hole punched in the gasket periphery. It is permissible to fit a modified gasket to earlier carburettors, but under no circumstances fit an unmodified gasket to carburettors manufactured after date code 17LO.

Float chamber opening screen
61 From 1981, a wire mesh screen is fitted over the float chamber opening.

Fast idle cam modification
62 A five step fast idle cam will be found fitted to carburettors manufactured after 1981.

63 The procedure for checking fast idle adjustment remains as given in Section 18 of Chapter 3, except that the regulating screw should now rest on the fourth step (second highest) of the cam when the throttle flap is released.

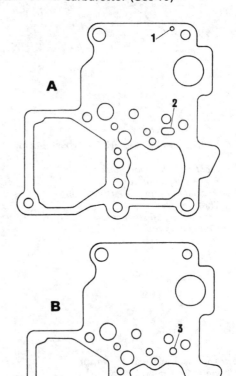

Fig. 13.34 Alternative types of Varajet carburettor gaskets (Sec 10)

A	Later type	2	Elongated hole
B	Earlier type	3	Circular hole
1	Small hole		

Automatic choke adjustment
64 The procedure in Chapter 3, Section 23, has been superseded by that given here. The adjustment is carried out with the carburettor in place and the air cleaner removed. A vacuum source (modified bicycle pump or similar) will be required.

65 Make sure that the choke flap and its connecting rod are free to move.

Fig. 13.35 Checking the choke flap gap – Varajet carburettor
(Sec 10)

Fig. 13.36 Tag (G) on fast idle cam disc (Sec 10)

66 Position the fast idle screw on the highest step of the cam. The choke flap should close completely – if not (eg because the engine is warm) hold it closed with a rubber band.

67 Apply vacuum to the choke vacuum unit. The choke flap should open to the extent that a drill of diameter 'A' (see Specifications) fits snugly between the choke flap and the carburettor wall. If adjustment is necessary, turn the adjusting screw on the vacuum unit. Bend the linkage if necessary to maintain clearance between the stop and the vacuum unit cover. Release the vacuum.

68 Reposition the fast idle screw on the second highest cam step. Open and release the choke flap by hand and allow it to take up its position; a drill of diameter 'B' (see Specifications) should fit snugly between the flap and the carburettor wall.

69 If adjustment of gap 'B' is required, remove the carburttor and the choke cover. Bend the rod which connects the cam disc to the choke flap lever until the gap is correct. Refit the carburettor and recheck gap 'A' (paragraph 67).

70 Using the rubber band to apply closing force to the choke flap, open the throttle wide and check that the choke flap opens to gap 'C' (see Specifications). Adjust if necessary by bending the tag on the fast idle cam disc (Fig. 13.36).

71 With all the above adjustments correct, check that the choke cover is aligned with the correct reference mark (see Specifications). The specified mark has changed several times: if trouble is experienced with over-choking (choke stays on too long), move the cover up to two marks towards 'L' (leaner). If the reverse trouble is the case, move the cover up to two marks towards 'R' (richer).

72 With the engine and carburettor cold (ambient temperature 20°C/68°F nominal) switch on the ignition and observe the movement of the choke flap. It should open fully within 3 to 4 minutes.

73 If the choke flap does not open within 4 minutes, the choke cover must be renewed.

74 Owners who are not convinced of the merits of the automatic choke may wish to fit a proprietary manual choke conversion kit. Such kits are commonly advertised in the DIY motoring magazines.

Vacuum unit damping valve

75 On later versions of the automatic choke carburettor, a damping valve was introduced in order to overcome a tendency to misfire during hard acceleration between 2700 to 3500 rpm. This valve may be fitted to earlier model carburettors.

Part load regulator screw adjustment

76 Problems such as jerking or hesitation at light throttle openings, or excessive fuel consumption despite moderate driving habits, may be due to incorrect adjustment of the part load regulator screw.

77 It is emphasised that this adjustment should not be attempted until all other possible causes of the problems mentioned have been investigated.

78 Remove the carburettor from the vehicle.

79 Prise out the metal plug covering the part load regulator screw (adjacent to the fuel inlet union).

Fig. 13.37 Vacuum unit damping valve – arrowed (Sec 10)

Fig. 13.38 Part load regulator screw (arrowed) with
tamperproof plug removed (Sec 10)

80 If stalling or hesitation is the reason for adjustment – ie the mixture is too weak – turn the screw one-quarter turn anti-clockwise.

81 If excessive fuel consumption is the problem – ie the mixture is too rich – turn the screw one-quarter turn clockwise.

82 Refit the carburettor and test drive the vehicle to see if any improvement has occurred. If necessary a further adjustment can be made, but **do not** deviate from the original setting by more than half a turn of the screw.

83 Fit a new metal plug on completion, where this is required by law.

Idle speed increase system

84 An idle speed increase system has been fitted to vehicles equipped with power steering and/or air conditioning after chassis No 01216702.

85 This system prevents lowering of the engine idle speed during the warm-up time when the steering or air conditioning is operated.

86 Fig. 13.40 shows the component parts of the system connected to

and around the carburettor. Idle speed increase is achieved through advancing the ignition timing.

87 Fig. 13.41 shows the additional items connected to the fuel injection system. A secondary air supply causes an increase in engine idle speed.

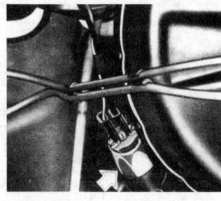

Fig. 13.39 Idle speed increase system switch (arrowed) used in conjunction with power-assisted steering (Sec 10)

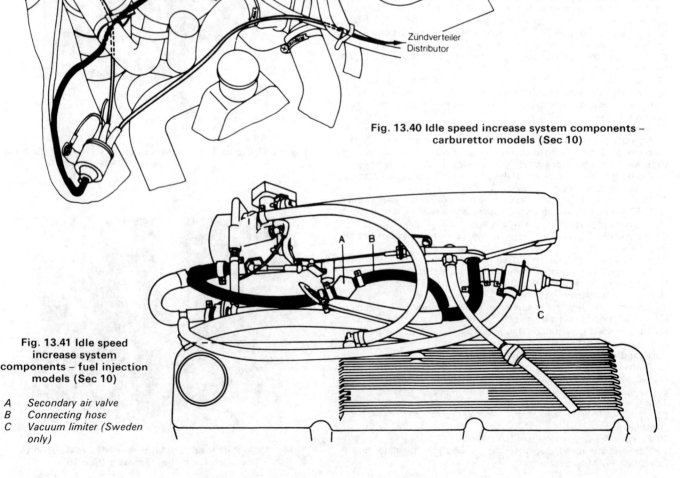

Zündverteiler
Distributor

Fig. 13.40 Idle speed increase system components – carburettor models (Sec 10)

Fig. 13.41 Idle speed increase system components – fuel injection models (Sec 10)

A   Secondary air valve
B   Connecting hose
C   Vacuum limiter (Sweden only)

10.93 Idle speed adjusting screw and locknut (fuel injection models)

10.95 Adjusting the idle mixture with an Allen key (fuel injection models)

10.101 Throttle valve switch

Fuel injection system (all models)
Description
88 The Bosch LE Jetronic fuel injection system is designed to ensure minimum exhaust emission levels throughout the engine speed range, as the fuel is metered precisely according to engine speed and load.
89 The main components of the system are:

    (a) *A control unit which incorporates an electronic fuel cut-off, triggered by the throttle valve switch. The device further reduces fuel consumption. A cold start booster eliminates the need for a separate cold start valve and a thermotime switch*
    (b) *Injection valves, one to each cylinder, ensure precise metering of the fuel*
    (c) *Airflow meter. This incorporates the air temperature sensor*
    (d) *Control relay. This comprises an electronic timing element and a switch relay which cuts off the fuel supply immediately after the engine stops*
    (e) *An electrically-operated fuel pump*

90 In addition and essential to the system are a fuel filter, a throttle valve switch, an auxiliary air valve, a pressure regulator, and temperature sensors to monitor both inlet air and coolant.
Precautions
91 Although the fuel system is virtually trouble-free, observing the following essential requirements will keep it operating efficiently:

    (a) *Never attempt to start the engine unless the battery terminals are securely connected*
    (b) *Never disconnect the batttery as a means of stopping the engine*
    (c) *Never pull out the wiring harness plug from the control unit if the ignition is switched on*
    (d) *If you are testing cylinder compression, first pull the plug from the control relay to interrupt the power supply*

Idle speed and mixture adjustment
92 With the engine at normal operating temperature, connect a tachometer to it if one is not already fitted as standard equipment.
93 Check the idle speed against that given in the Specifications. If necessary, correct it by turning the regulating screw on the throttle connecting piece (photo).
94 To check the mixture (CO level), connect an exhaust gas analyser in accordance with its maker's instructions. Again the engine must be at normal operating temperature, and the ignition system must be correctly adjusted.
95 If the CO content deviates from that specified, remove the cap from the bypass screw on the airflow sensor (photo). Turn the screw in a clockwise direction to enrich the mixture or anti-clockwise to weaken it.
96 On completion of the adjustment, fit a new cap to the bypass screw.
97 Failure to bring the CO content within the specified tolerance will indicate a fault in the system, or a well worn engine.
Throttle valve adjustment
98 Make sure that the throttle valve plate is closed. Refer to Fig. 13.42 or 13.43 as appropriate.
99 Unscrew both the throttle valve stop screw and locknut until they are clear of their cam, then screw the screw in again until it just

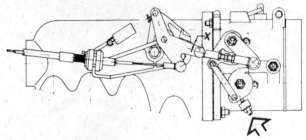

Fig. 13.42 Throttle valve linkage (manual transmission). Stop screw arrowed (Sec 10)

X = 0.5 mm (0.002 in)

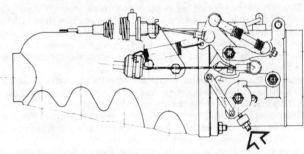

Fig. 13.43 Throttle valve linkage (automatic transmission). Stop screw arrowed (Sec 10)

contacts the cam. Now give it a further quarter of a turn and tighten its locknut.
100 On manual transmission models, release the locknuts on the connecting rod and adjust its length by rotating it so that dimension X is as shown in Fig. 13.42.
Throttle valve switch adjustment
101 Release the switch mounting screws (photo) and rotate the switch in an anti-clockwise direction until resistance is felt. Tighten the screws.
102 Have an assistant open the throttle valve slightly by depressing the accelerator pedal. A click should be heard from the switch. A click should also be heard when the pedal is released.

Fuel injection system components – removal and refitting
103 It is not possible to repair the main components of the fuel injection system. In the event of a fault occurring, it is best to have the fault isolated by your GM dealer or a fuel system specialist as special equipment will be necessary. However, once the problem has been diagnosed, there is no reason why the defective component cannot be renewed by carrying out the following instructions.

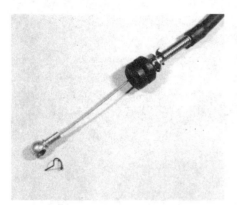

10.110A Throttle cable (ball end fitting)

10.110B Throttle cable end fitting (nipple and quadrant)

10.112 Throttle housing removed

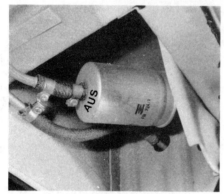

10.121 Fuel filter (fuel injection models)

10.132 Fuel injection control unit

Throttle valve housing
104 Release the securing clips and disconnect the flexible ducting which connects the throttle valve housing with the airflow sensor
105 Disconnect the coolant hoses from the throttle control housing. If the ends of the hoses are retained in their highest position there will be no loss of coolant. If the engine is still warm when this work is being carried out then the system pressure must be released before disconnecting the hoses. Do this by gently unscrewing the expansion bottle cap.
106 Pull the distributor vacuum hose from the throttle valve housing.
107 Disconnect the brake servo vacuum hose and the crankcase ventilation system hose from the throttle valve housing.
108 Disconnect and plug the fuel hoses from the distribution tube pipe stubs. Note that the hose with the white band is located nearer the alternator. Do not connect these hoses incorrectly.
109 Release the wiring harness by disconnecting all the plugs and the earth connections. Mark all the connections for identification so that they can be refitted in their correct positions. Disconnect the following:

  (a) Airflow sensor plug
  (b) Coolant temperature sensor
  (c) Fuel injectors
  (d) Throttle valve switch
  (e) Auxiliary air valve
  (f) Cam cover earth screw

110 Disconnect the throttle cable from the throttle valve housing. Where the cable has a ball end, release it by removing the wire clip (photo). The end fitting of the cable outer can be released from its bracket by removing the E-clip. Where the cable has a cylindrical end and passes over a pulley arrangement, put slack in the cable inner by rotating the pulley against spring pressure and detach the cable end. Release the cable outer from its retaining bracket (photo).
111 Unscrew the throttle valve housing fixing nuts. The lower ones are difficult to reach, but present no problem to remove if a small socket or ring spanner is used.
112 Lift the throttle housing away (photo).
113 Peel off the flange gasket; renew it on reassembly.
114 Refitting is a reversal of removal, but ensure that the harness connections are re-connected in their correct positions, as noted during removal.

Throttle valve switch
115 Disconnect the three-pin wiring plug.
116 Unscrew the two mounting screws and pull the switch from the throttle valve spindle.
117 Refitting is a reversal of removal, but adjust the switch as described previously.

Fuel pump
118 Refer to paragraphs 12 to 16 of this Section.

Fuel filter
119 The fuel filter is adjacent to the fuel pump.
120 Clamp the fuel hoses to prevent loss of fuel when they are disconnected. Self-locking grips are useful for this. Disconnect the hoses and remove the filter.
121 Refitting is a reversal of removal. Observe the AUS (out) marking on the filter showing the direction of fuel flow (photo).

Fuel injectors
122 Ensure that the engine is cool to eliminate the danger of fuel igniting. Do not smoke, and guard against external sources of ignition.
123 Release the hose clamps and pull the fuel distribution pipe from the hoses of the injectors. Catch as much fuel as possible.
124 Disconnect the wiring plug.
125 Unscrew the retaining bolts and withdraw the injector from its holder, taking care not to damage the needle valve.
126 Refitting is a reversal of removal, but renew the sealing rings if there is any doubt about their condition.

Airflow sensor
127 The airflow sensor is attached to the inboard side of the air cleaner housing.
128 Pull the wiring harness plug from the airflow sensor. Release the securing band and remove the rubber trunking.
129 Release the toggle locks and remove the airflow sensor with the upper part of the air cleaner housing.
130 Unbolt the airflow sensor from the air cleaner housing.
131 Check the airflow sensor flap valve for free movement, without any jerkiness.

Control unit
132 The control unit is attached to the side of the front footwell (right-hand side for UK models) behind the trim (photo).
133 With the trim detached, pull the plug from the unit top after

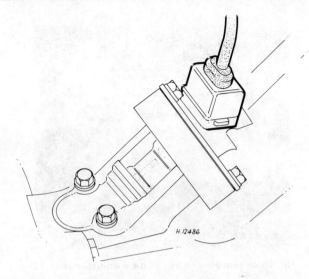

Fig. 13.44 Fuel injector and electrical connector (Sec 10)

10.136 Coolant temperature sensor (fuel injection models)

pressing aside its retaining spring. Remove the retaining screws and remove the unit.

134 Refitting is a reversal of removal. Check that the plug terminals are free from moisture before reconnecting.

Coolant temperature sensor

135 Partially drain the cooling system, about 3 litres (5 pints) should be sufficient.

136 Disconnect the electrical lead and unscrew the sensor (photo).

137 Refitting is a reversal of removal.

138 Top up and bleed the cooling system as described in Chapter 2.

Auxiliary air valve

139 This valve is located on the side of the camshaft housing/cylinder head (photo).

140 Pull the connecting plug from the valve.

141 Disconnect the hoses. Unscrew the two mounting bolts and remove the valve.

142 A check can be made on the serviceability of the valve by observing the regulator disc. With the valve cold, the disc should be open; with the valve hot (by connection to a 12V battery) the disc should be closed.

143 Refitting is a reversal of removal.

Control relay

144 This relay may be located on the front suspension strut turret or the engine bay rear bulkhead (photo).

145 Pull the wiring plug from the relay and unclip the relay from its mounting.

146 Refitting is a reversal of removal.

Fuel pressure regulator

147 The fuel pressure regulator is located between injectors 3 and 4 (photo).

148 Clamp the fuel hoses to prevent loss of fuel. Self-locking grips are useful for this.

149 Disconnect the fuel hoses and the vacuum hose from the pressure regulator.

150 Refitting is a reversal of removal.

Fuel injection system (2.2 CIH)

151 An idle air control system is fitted in conjunction with the LE jetronic fuel injection system on these models.

152 The purpose of the idle air control system is to provide the following advantages:

(a) *Reduction in fuel consumption due to lower idle speed*
(b) *Constant idle speed under all conditions*
(c) *Idle speed adjustment not required*
(d) *Auxiliary air valve no longer required for power-assisted steering or air conditioning*

153 The main components of the system are:

(a) *An idle control unit which is located behind the right-hand footwell trim panel*
(b) *An idle adjuster located within the engine compartment*
(c) *A throttle valve switch*
(d) *A temperature sensor*
(e) *A control relay located under the seal between the engine compartment rear bulkhead and the facia panel*

10.139 Auxiliary air valve

10.144 Fuel injection system control relay

10.147 Fuel pressure regulator

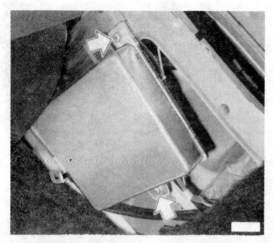

Fig. 13.45 Idle air control unit (Sec 10)

Securing screws arrowed

Fig. 13.46 Idle air control system adjuster (Sec 10)

Securing points arrowed

Idle speed adjuster – checking(2.2 CIH)
154 It is possible to check the opening angle (idle speed) in the following way.
155 Have the engine at normal operating temperature.
156 All electrical accessories switched off and radiator fan not running.
157 Throttle valve switch correctly adjusted (see paragraphs 101 and 102).
158 An ignition dwell angle measuring meter should now be connected in one of the two following ways.
159 If the meter is of the type which connects between the ignition coil (+) and (–) LT terminals then it should be connected for the idle speed check as shown in Fig. 13.49.
160 If the meter is of the type which connects between the ignition coil (–) LT terminal and a good clean earth then it should be connected for the idle speed check between the green cable (B) and the vehicle earth.
161 With the engine idling at the specified speed, the dwell angle indicated on the meter should be between 26 and 28° (29 and 31%).
162 Any adjustment required should be made by turning the throttle valve bypass screw (Fig. 13.50).

Fig. 13.47 Idle air control system relay (Sec 10)

Multi-plug arrowed

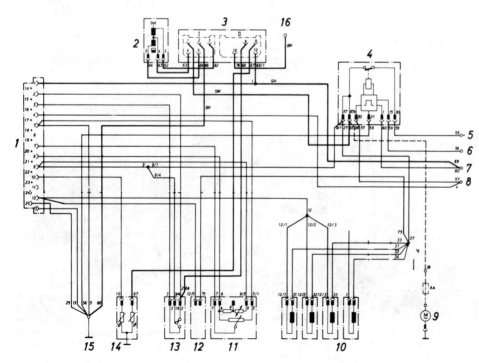

Fig. 13.48 Wiring diagram –
LE Jetronic fuel injection system
with idle air control
system (Sec 10)

1   Plug strip
2   Idle adjuster
3   Idle control unit
4   Engine speed relay
5   Connection B+
6   Connection terminal 15
7   Connection terminal 1
8   Connection terminal 50
9   Fuel pump
10 Fuel injectors
11 Airflow sensor
12 Trip computer
13 Throttle valve switch
14 Temperature sensor
15 Common earth
16 Earth cable for idle speed
    checking

Fig. 13.49 Typical rig for idle speed check (Sec 10)

A   Yellow (lead 63, terminal 4) to dwell angle tester – terminal 15+
B   Green (lead 64, terminal 5) to dwell angle tester terminal 1 –

C   Connection – adapter to idle speed adjuster
D   Connection – adapter to wiring harness plug

Unleaded fuel

163 All engines may be operated on high octane unleaded fuel, but subject to the following conditions.

1.8 litre ohc engines

164 Unleaded fuel may be freely used in these engines.

165 If using unleaded fuel in a carburettor engine it will be necessary to retard the ignition timing if pinking occurs. On fuel injection engines, the ignition timing **must** be retarded (see next Section).

2.0 and 2.2 litre CIH engines (pre March 1985)

166 High octane unleaded fuel may be used in these engines as part of a cycle with full leaded fuel. Five tanks of unleaded petrol should always be followed by one full tank of leaded petrol.

167 The ignition timing may also need adjustment; see paragraph 165.

2.0 and 2.2 litre CIH engines (from March 1985)

168 Modified valve seats were introduced in approximately March 1985. Engines from the following serial numbers may be run exclusively on high octane unleaded fuel.

    20S – 0 844 000
    20E – 0 355 000
    22E – 0 021 000

169 The ignition timing may also need adjustment; see paragraph 165.

11 Ignition system

Electronic ignition system (all models)
Description

1 The electronic (breakerless) ignition system fitted to later models will be one of two types, either AC Delco or Bosch. Both systems are similar in that they require virtually no maintenance or adjustment.

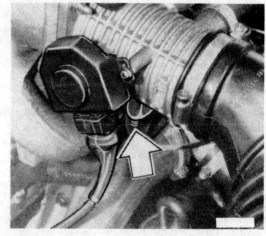

Fig. 13.50 Throttle valve bypass screw arrowed (Sec 10)

2 The main components are a control unit, an ignition coil and a camshaft-driven distributor.

3 Instead of the reluctor and pick-up on the AC Delco induction system, the Bosch system incorporates a permanent magnet, a detector/amplifier, and four vanes. When a vane is masking the detector/amplifier no voltage is induced in the detector, and under these conditions the control unit passes through the low tension windings of the coil.

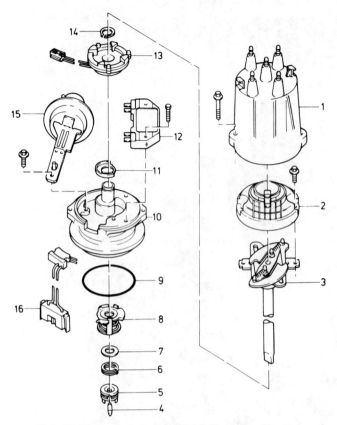

Figh. 13.51 Exploded view of AC Delco breakerless distributor (Sec 11)

1	Distributor cap	9	O-ring
2	Rotor	10	Body
3	Shaft	11	Seal
4	Pin	12	Module
5	Drive dog	13	Induction sensor
6	Spring	14	Circlip
7	Washer	15	Vacuum unit
8	Spring	16	Plug

4 Rotation of the distributor will uncover the detector and cause it to be influenced by the magnetic field of the permanent magnet. The Hall effect induces a small voltage in the detector plate which is then amplified and triggers the control unit to interrupt the low tension current in the coil.

5 The control unit in the Bosch system incorporates a circuit which switches off the low tension circuit if the time between consecutive signals exceeds 1.5 seconds. The coil and internal circuits are therefore protected if the ignition is left switched on inadvertently.

6 It is not recommended that this type of distributor is dismantled beyond the limits of the operations described in this Section.

Precautions

7 In view of the high voltage used in this system, care must be used when handling wiring or components with the ignition switched on. This is particularly important to anyone equipped with a cardiac pacemaker.

8 When cranking the engine with the HT leads disconnected – for example, when making a compression test – either disconnect the plug from the ignition control unit, or securely earth the coil HT terminal. If the coil is energised with the HT leads 'floating' there is a risk of insulation damage.

9 If it is wished to connect an independent tachometer to the breakerless ignition system, an adaptor cable may be needed in order to make contact with the ignition coil negative terminal (terminal 1, green lead). This is necessary if a completely insulated multiple plug is used to connect the coil into the ignition system.

10 When using such an adaptor cable, remember that dangerous voltages may be present at terminal 1. Always switch the ignition off before connecting or disconnecting equipment.

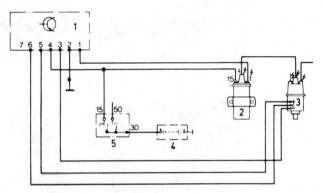

Fig. 13.52 Schematic diagram of electronic ignition system. High voltage at points indicated by lightning symbols (Sec 11)

1	Control unit	4	Battery
2	Ignition coil	5	Ignition switch
3	Distributor		

Ignition timing

11 Stroboscopic timing should be carried out as described in Chapter 4 (2.0 and 2.2 CIH) or later in this Section (1.8 ohc).

12 Static timing as described in Chapter 4 is not possible with breakerless ignition. The position of the rotor arm stud when No 1 piston is firing is denoted by a mark on the rim of the distributor body.

13 Checking and adjusting the dwell angle is not required with breakerless distributors. The ignition timing itself should rarely need adjusting, except after overhaul or renewal of the distributor or related engine components.

Distributor removal and refitting

14 This procedure is as described in Chapter 4 (2.0 and 2.2 CIH) or later in this Section (1.8 ohc).

Distributor dismantling and reassembly

15 Depending on the type of distributor, it will be obvious to what extent and by which method the distributor can be dismantled.

16 Detach the distributor cap, either by releasing its securing clips or by removing the Allen-headed screws.

17 Remove the rotor, after having removed its retaining screws or circlip.

18 Detach the wiring from the module.

19 Detach the vacuum unit by releasing its retaining screws. Remove the module.

20 Renew any defective components.

21 If a new module is being fitted, apply the silicone grease supplied with it between the module mounting base and the distributor body. Reassemble the distributor in conditions of utmost cleanliness.

Fault diagnosis

22 Total ignition failure or misfiring may be due to loose or disconnected wires or plugs, or to component malfunction. Misfiring may also be due to the same faults on the HT side as those described in Chapter 4, Section 12.

23 **Do not** remove plug caps whilst the engine is running in an attempt to locate a misfire. Personal electric shock and/or damage to the coil insulation may result.

24 Testing of the ignition system units should be left to a GM dealer or automobile electrician. Beware of haphazard testing by substitution – a fault in one component may damage other units.

25 If sealing compound is observed to have spilled from the coil cap, displacing the sealing plug, both the coil and the control unit should be renewed.

26 It is possible for the ignition system to malfunction when in close proximity to certain types of VHF radio transmitters. Consult your GM dealer if this is a problem.

Electronic idle speed control (ISC) system (2.0 CIH)
Description

27 From late 1982, GM have incorporated an ISC system in the electronic ignition system of vehicles fitted with the 2.0 CIH engine. The ISC allows the engine to operate at its most efficient minimum idle speed whilst keeping the speed stable as electrical components are switched on.

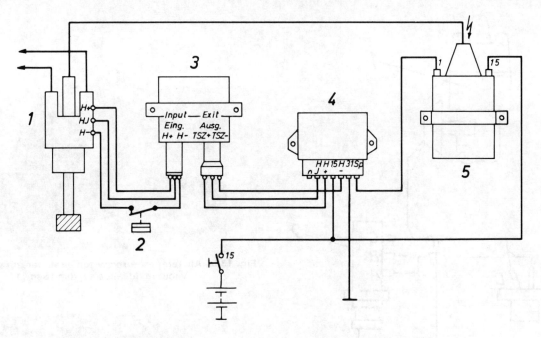

Fig. 13.53 Idle speed control system (ISC) – 2.0 CIH (Sec 11)

| 1 | Distributor | 3 | ISC unit | 5 | Ignition coil |
| 2 | Vacuum switch | 4 | Ignition control unit | | |

28 Fig. 13.53 shows the layout of the ISC system. It operates as follows.

29 The signal emitted by the distributor is evaluated by the ISC which if necessary alters ignition timing to control engine speed. When engine load is increased, causing engine speed to drop, the ISC returns the engine speed to its previous setting.

30 It is possible to isolate the ISC from the ignition system so that in the event of component malfunction, the ISC can be prevented from adversely affecting ignition performance. To do this, simply unplug the two wiring connectors from the ISC unit and join them together.

31 On vehicles fitted with manual transmission and air conditioning, a vacuum switch in the ignition vacuum line isolates the ISC if the ignition vacuum rises beyond a certain level.

Idle speed adjustment

32 Before commencing adjustment, ensure that the ignition timing is correctly set and then run the engine until it reaches normal operating temperature.

33 On vehicles equipped with manual transmission, disconnect both wiring connectors from the ISC unit with the engine turned off. Join the connectors together and restart the engine. Adjust the idle speed to 700 and 750 rpm. Turn off the engine, reconnect both wiring connectors to the ISC and restart the engine. The ISC will automatically reset the idle speed to the correct value.

34 On vehicles equipped with automatic transmission, do not disconnect the ISC. Simply adjust the idle speed to the specified value.

ISC unit test

35 Obtain a timing light equipped with a timing indicator and connect it to the vehicle in accordance with the manufacturer's instructions.

36 Where the vehicle is equipped with manual transmission, check the ignition timing at idle speed. The timing must be seen to advance as electrical components such as the heated rear screen and headlights are switched on. If no timing change is apparent, fit a new ISC unit and retest.

37 Where the vehicle has automatic transmission, chock the wheels and apply the parking brake. Start the engine, allowing it to run at idle speed. Place the selector lever in 'D' and check the ignition timing, which must be more advanced than 5° BTDC. Select 'N' and check that the ignition timing has returned to 5° BTDC. If the test results do not correspond with those stated, renew the ISC unit and retest.

Vacuum switch test

38 In order to carry out this test, it is necessary to obtain a vacuum hand pump. If possible, hire or borrow this tool (no KM-J-23994-01) from your local GM dealer.

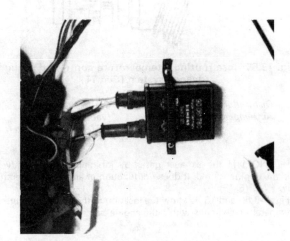

Fig. 13.54 ISC unit mounted on left-hand front suspension strut turret (Sec 11)

39 Disconnect the vacuum hose from the distributor and connect it to the vacuum pump. This hose must be in good condition and firmly connected to the carburerttor stub. If in doubt, renew the hose before testing.

40 Fit a timing light equipped with a timing indicator. Start the engine and allow it to reach normal operating temperature. With the engine at idle, check the ignition timing which should be more advanced than 5° BTDC.

41 Operate the vacuum pump and apply approximately 150 mbar to the vacuum switch. The ignition timing should now return 5° BTDC. If the test results do not indicate correct switch operation, substitute a new vacuum switch and retest.

Temperature-controlled vacuum advance cut-out (2.0 CIH)

42 From mid 1983, GM have introduced a temperature-controlled vacuum advance cut-out system to vehicles fitted with the 2.0 CIH engine and automatic transmission. This system reduces the nitrogen

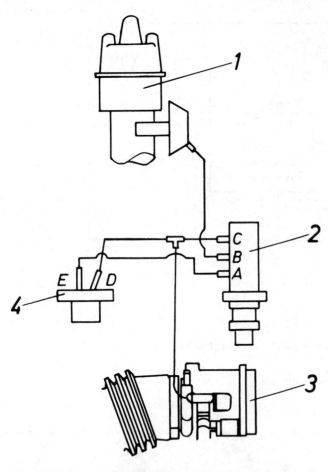

Fig. 13.55 Hose routing – temperature controlled vacuum
advance system (Sec 11)

1	Distributor	3	Carburettor/throttle valve
2	Air temperature switch		(vacuum source)
		4	Oil temperature switch

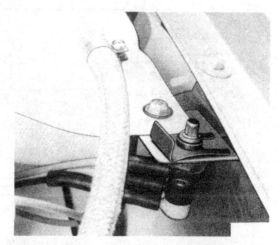

Fig. 13.56 Air temperature switch – temperature controlled
vacuum advance system (Sec 11)

Fig. 13.57 Oil temperature switch – temperature controlled
vacuum advance system (Sec 11)

oxides (NOx) in the exhaust gases by inhibiting vacuum advance
while the engine is cold. It does not function at ambient temperatures
below 17°C (63°F).
43 Figs. 13.56 and 13.57 show the location of the air temperature and
oil temperature switches within the engine bay.

Distributor – removal and refitting (1.8 ohc)
44 The distributor is mounted on the left-hand side of the cylinder
head and is belt-driven from the front of the camshaft.
45 Gain access to the distributor drive cover securing bolts by
removing the appropriate cooling system components (fan cowl, etc).
Remove the cover. Mark the distributor body-to-engine alignment.
46 Refer to Fig. 13.58 and ensure the marks on the distributor gear
and camshaft sprocket align with those on the housing, as shown.
These marks must remain aligned during the removal and refitting
procedure.
47 Detach the distributor cap.
48 Unbolt the distributor body steady strut from the cylinder head.
Disconnect the feed pipe from the vacuum advance unit.
49 Remove the two distributor securing nuts and the steady strut. Pull
the distributor carefully away from its mounting so that its drivegear
slips free of the toothed belt. Remove the distributor.
50 Refitting the distributor is a reversal of the removal procedure.
Ensure that the distributor gear and camshaft sprocket are correctly
aligned and that the distributor body is placed in its previously noted
position before nipping tight the two securing nuts and fully tightening
the steady strut-to-cylinder head bolt.
51 On completion of refitting, check the ignition timing as follows.

Fig. 13.58 Camshaft sprocket (A) and distributor drivegear
(B) alignment marks (Sec 11)

11.52 Ignition timing marks (1.8 ohc)

Ignition timing – checking (1.8 ohc)

52 Obtain a strobe light and connect it into the No 1 cylinder HT circuit, following the manufacturer's instructions. Dab a spot of white paint on the notch in the crankshaft pulley and on the corresponding pointer (photo).

53 Run the engine at idling speed and point the strobe light at the timing marks. At idling speed the white paint marks should appear to be immediately opposite each other; open the throttle slightly and check that as the engine revolutions rise the spot on the crankshaft will move away from the pointer. This indicates the centrifugal advance mechanism is operating correctly.

54 If timing marks do not line up under the strobe light, slightly slacken the distributor clamp nuts and carefully turn the distributor in its location to bring the marks into line. Retighten the clamp nuts.

Ignition timing – adjustment (unleaded fuel)

55 If using high octane unleaded fuel (see Section 10) GM recommend the ignition timing is retarded as follows:

Carburettor engines: retard by up to 5° if pinking (detonation) occurs
Fuel injected engines: retard by 5°

56 Turn the engine by means of the crankshaft pulley bolt, or by engaging top gear and pulling the car forward, until No 1 piston is at TDC on the firing stroke. This can be set by removing No 1 spark plug and feeling for compression with your fingers as the engine is turned.

57 Make a mark on the flywheel (CIH engine) or crankshaft pulley (ohc engine) in alignment with the timing pointer on the engine.

58 The original mark on the flywheel or pulley indicates the initial ignition advance (see Specifications), and the new mark TDC.

59 The new ignition timing setting mark is now either mid-way between the 2 marks (1.8 and 2.2) or at TDC (2.0). Make a suitable mark on the flywheel or pulley and adjust the timing, as described in Chapter 4, Section 11 (CIH), or this Section (ohc).

60 GM recommend the ignition timing on fuel injection engines be retarded by exactly 5° when using unleaded high octane petrol. For carburettor engines, the recommendation is up to 5° if detonation occurs; some experimentation may be worthwhile to achieve satisfactory running.

Electronic advance ignition (2.2 CIH)

61 The electronic (breakerless) ignition system was further improved on 22E engined models after October 1985 by the addition of a spark advance control unit and other components shown in Fig. 13.59.

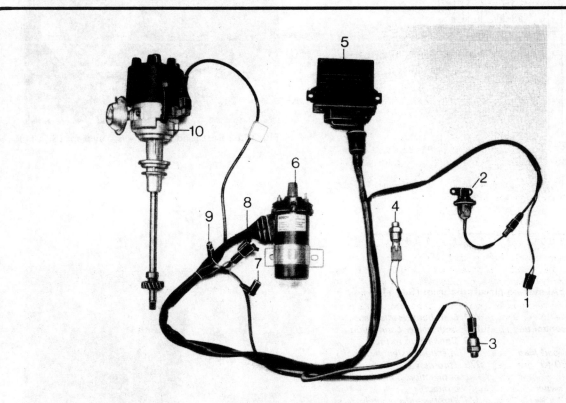

Fig. 13.59 Components of the EAI system (Sec 11)

1	Connection to throttle valve switch	5	Electronic spark advance control unit	8	Connection to vehicle wiring harness, terminal 15, terminal 1 and earth
2	Part load switch	6	Ignition coil with trigger box and baseplate	9	Connection terminal 15
3	Air temperature switch	7	Connection terminal 1	10	Distributor
4	Oil temperature switch				

62 By comparing the information received from the engine speed
sensor, temperature switches, intake manifold vacuum sensor and
throttle valve switch with the ignition settings stored in the control unit
memory, the ignition timing is constantly adjusted to suit all engine
operating conditions.

Electronic advance ignition components – renewal
63 If a component is found to be in need of renewal, disconnect the
wiring plug and extract the mounting screws. The locations of the
components are shown in Figs. 13.61, 13.62, 13.63 and 13.64.

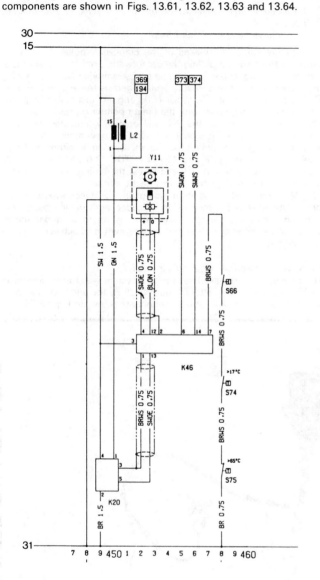

Fig. 13.60 EAI system circuit diagram (Sec 11)

K20 Trigger box
K46 Spark advance control unit
L2   Ignition coil
S66 Vacuum switch (part load
     switch opens at 0.13
     lbf/in²)
S74 Air temperature switch
     (closes at 17°C – 63°F)
S75 Oil temperature switch
     (opens at 65°C – 149°F)

Y11 Distributor Hall sensor
194 Tachometer connection
369 Connection to fuel
     injection system terminal 1
373 Throttle valve switch
     connection (idle speed
     contact)
374 Throttle valve switch
     connection (full load
     contact)

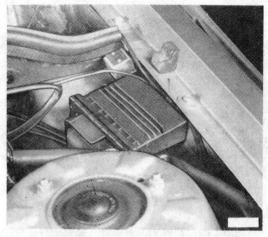

Fig. 13.61 EAI control unit (Sec 11)

Fig. 13.62 Part load switch – EAI system (Sec 11)

Fig. 13.63 Air temperature switch – EAI system (Sec 11)

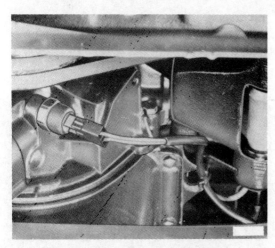

Fig. 13.64 Oil temperature switch – EAI system (Sec 11)

Fig. 13.65 Plastic thrust ring being fitted to clutch diaphragm spring (Sec 12)
Hooks arrowed

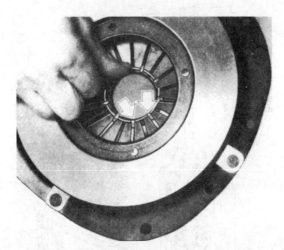

Fig. 13.66 Clutch plastic thrust ring secured by retaining clip (Sec 12)
Hooks arrowed

Fig. 13.67 Clutch setting tool (KM 330) (Sec 12)

12 Clutch

Belleville spring thrust ring (2.0 and 2.2 CIH)
1   From 1983, GM have fitted a plastic thrust ring to the centre of the clutch spring. This prevents whirring noises emitting from the thrust bearing during clutch operation.
2   Fitting of the thrust ring will also reduce wear on the spring lugs, so it is a good idea to include its fitting as part of the clutch overhaul on pre-1983 vehicles.
3   When fitting a thrust ring, refer to Figs. 13.65 and 13.66 and fit the ring from the outside of the spring as shown, making sure that its retaining ring is correctly seated beneath the hooks.

Adjustment
4   The adjustment procedure for all models is essentially as described in Chapter 5.
5   For fuel injected models the setting dimension (release fork to bellhousing) is as follows:

2OE (8.5 in clutch disc) 111.5 mm (4.39 in)
22E (9.0 in clutch disc) 122.5 mm (4.82 in)

6   A special tool (KM 330) is available, and incorporates setting measurements in the form of cut-outs and can be used on all models.
7   To check the clutch pedal, measure the height of the pedal pad above the floor. This should be 155.0 mm (6.1 in). If adjustment is required, do so at the cable end fitting ball nut of the release lever. The clutch pedal should be slightly higher than the brake pedal when correctly adjusted.

13 Overdrive unit

General description
1   An overdrive unit is fitted as an optional extra to 1982 models equipped with a 4-speed manual gearbox. It is attached to the rear of the gearbox and takes the form of an hydraulically operated epicyclic gear. Overdrive operates on top gear only to provide fast cruising at lower engine revolutions. The overdrive is engaged or disengaged by a driver-controlled switch which controls an electric solenoid mounted on the overdrive unit. A further switch called an inhibitor switch is included in the electrical circuit to prevent accidental engagement of overdrive in reverse, first, second or third gears.
2   The overdrive unit is designed to be engaged or disengaged when engine power is being transmittedd through the power line and also without the use of the clutch pedal at any throttle opening or road speed. It is important that the overdrive is not disengaged at high road speeds as this will cause excessively high engine speeds.
3   To avoid the engine labouring, GM recommend that the overdrive ony be engaged at road speeds over 50 mph (80 kph).
4   The overdrive unit is lubricated by oil from the gearbox.

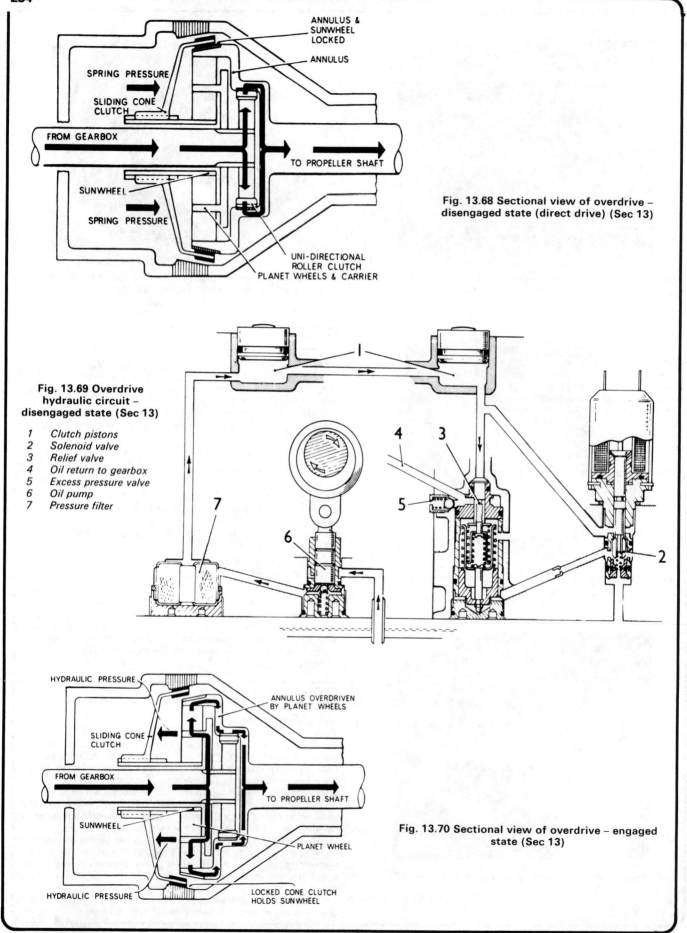

ANNULUS &
SUNWHEEL
LOCKED

ANNULUS

SPRING PRESSURE

SLIDING CONE
CLUTCH

FROM GEARBOX

TO PROPELLER SHAFT

SUNWHEEL

SPRING PRESSURE

UNI-DIRECTIONAL
ROLLER CLUTCH
PLANET WHEELS & CARRIER

Fig. 13.68 Sectional view of overdrive –
disengaged state (direct drive) (Sec 13)

Fig. 13.69 Overdrive
hydraulic circuit –
disengaged state (Sec 13)

1   Clutch pistons
2   Solenoid valve
3   Relief valve
4   Oil return to gearbox
5   Excess pressure valve
6   Oil pump
7   Pressure filter

HYDRAULIC PRESSURE

ANNULUS OVERDRIVEN
BY PLANET WHEELS

SLIDING CONE
CLUTCH

FROM GEARBOX

TO PROPELLER SHAFT

SUNWHEEL

PLANET WHEEL

HYDRAULIC PRESSURE

LOCKED CONE CLUTCH
HOLDS SUNWHEEL

Fig. 13.70 Sectional view of overdrive – engaged
state (Sec 13)

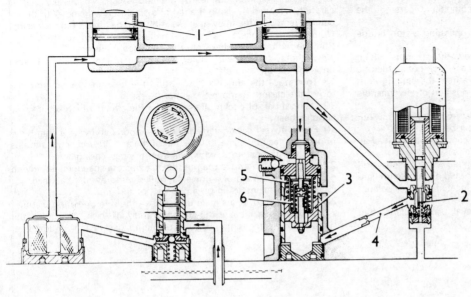

**Fig. 13.71 Overdrive hydraulic circuit –
engaged state (Sec 13)**

1   *Clutch pistons*
2   *Solenoid valve*
3   *Dashpot piston*
4   *Oil channel*
5   *Spring*
6   *Spring*

Removal and refitting

5   It should not be necessary to remove the overdrive unit from the vehicle to attend to the following: solenoid and operating valve, relief and low pressure valve, pump and non-return valve.

6   If the unit as a whole requires overhaul, it must be removed from the vehicle together with the gearbox, details of which will be found in Section 2 of Chapter 6. It should, however, be pointed out that several special tools are required to correctly dismantle and reassemble the overdrive unit, so before work commences make sure that the tools can

be hired or borrowed from your local GM dealer. Otherwise return the unit to the dealer for servicing.

7   Before beginning the sequence to remove the gearbox and overdrive unit it is necessary to drive the vehicle and engage overdrive and then disengage with the clutch depressed. This will release the spline loading between the planet carrier and uni-directional clutch which can make removal difficult.

8   Refitting is a reversal of the removal procedure.

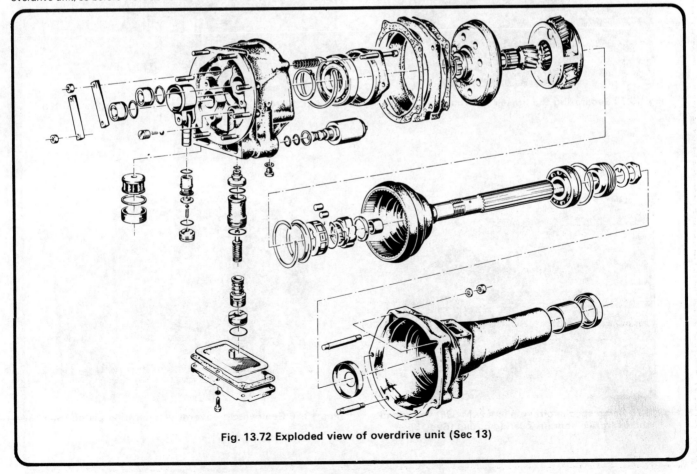

Fig. 13.72 Exploded view of overdrive unit (Sec 13)

Dismantling, overhaul and reassembly

9 Refer to Fig. 13.72 which shows the component parts of the overdrive unit.

10 Remove the locknuts which secure each operating piston bridge piece. Remove the two bridge pieces.

11 Working in a diagonal sequence, unscrew the six nuts which secure the main casing to the rear casing. Release each nut a little at a time as the two casings will be under pressure from the clutch return springs. Remove the nuts and note the fitted position of any washers beneath them.

12 Separate the main casing and brake ring from the rear casing. Remove the four clutch springs. Suport the rear casing.

13 Separate the brake ring from the casing by carefully tapping it away from the mating surface with a soft metal drift.

14 Lift out the sliding member assembly complete with the sunwheel followed by the planet carrier assembly. This should be done with care as it is easy to damage the oil catcher which is located under the planet carrier assembly.

15 If the clutch lining sticks, preventing removal, use a puller to free the clutch disc, see Fig. 13.74.

16 The oil catcher is retained by a circlip which, if necessary, can be carefully removed by using the flat of a small screwdriver. With the oil catcher removed, the freewheel assembly can be lifted from the casing. Note that the rollers are not permanently attached to their cage. Remove the thrust washer from the freewheel housing.

17 Withdraw the speedometer driven gear and housing, having unbolted its retaining plate.

18 To remove the annulus, first unbolt the bearing support from the top of the casing. Remove the support seal.

19 Using a pair of circlip pliers, expand the circlip which secures the annulus bearing.

20 Place the rear casing vertically over supports and with a light blow from a soft-faced hammer on the end of the annulus, drive the annulus complete with bearing downwards from the rear casing.

21 Unscrew and remove the nut that secures the speedometer driving gear and with the aid of a universal puller withdraw the ball race.

22 Place the main casing on a clean work surface.

23 Using a pair of pliers, carefully remove the two operating pistons.

24 Unscrew and remove the six bolts and lockwashers securing the sump to the main casing. Lift away the sump, gasket and suction filter.

Fig. 13.73 Separating the brake ring from the casing
(Sec 3)

Fig. 13.74 Using a puller to free the overdrive clutch
(Sec 13)

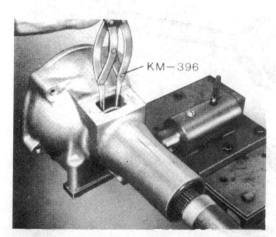

Fig. 13.75 Using special circlip pliers (KM 396) to expand
the overdrive annulus bearing circlip (Sec 13)

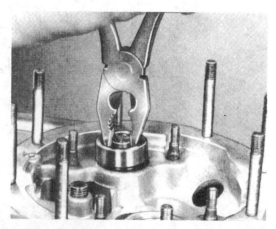

Fig. 13.76 Removing an overdrive operating piston (Sec 13)

25 Special tools Nos KM-492 and KM-496 are now required for removal of the relief valve and dashpot assembly. Use tool No KM-492 to remove the dashpot plug and then withdraw the dashpot piston complete with its component springs and cap, followed by the residual pressure spring. It should be noted that this spring is the only loose spring in the general assembly.

26 The relief valve piston assembly can now be withdrawn by pulling down carefully using a pair of pliers.

27 Using tool No KM-496 inserted into the now exposed relief valve bore, withdraw the relief valve together with the dashpot sleeve. Take great care not to damage these parts during removal.

28 Using tool No KM-492 undo and remove the pump plug, taking care not to lose the non-return valve spring and ball bearing.

29 The pump valve seat can now be withdrawn. The pump body will be held in position by its O-ring, so hook a piece of wire into the inlet port and draw the assembly downwards.

30 To remove the pressure filter, use tool No KM-492 and unscrew the pressure filter base plug. The filter element will be released with the plug. Note the aluminium washer which locates on the shoulder in the filter bore.

31 Remove the pump plunger assembly from the centre of the casing. Unscrew the relief valve plug and remove the valve spring and ball.

32 Using tool No KM-494 or a thin open-ended spanner, unscrew the solenoid control valve. Do not attempt to use a strap wrench or similar tool on the valve body as it will be irreparably damaged.

33 Carefully inspect the dismantled unit. It is advisable to err on the side of safety and renew any components when in doubt. Inspect the unit methodically, as follows.

34 Inspect the teeth and cone surfaces of the annulus for wear. Check that the freewheel rollers are not chipped and that the inner and outer members are free from damage.

35 Examine the spring and cage for distortion. Check the lubrication port at the rear of the annulus is clear.

36 Inspect the rear casing bush and oil seal for wear or damage.

37 Examine the clutch linings on the sliding member for signs of excessive wear or overheating. Should there be signs of these conditions the whole sliding member assembly must be renewed. It is not possible to fit new linings as these are precision machined after bonding.

38 Make sure that the ball-race rotates smoothly as this can be a source of noise when in direct gear.

39 Inspect the clutch return springs for any signs of distortion, damage or loss of springiness.

40 Check the sunwheel teeth for signs of wear or damage.

41 Inspect the main casing for cracks or damage. Examine the operating cylinder bores for scores or wear. Check the operating pistons for wear and renew the sealing rings if there is any sign of damage.

42 Check the pump plunger assembly and ensure that the strap is a good fit on the mainshaft cam and that there is no excess play between the plunger and strap.

Fig. 13.77 Removing the relief valve and dashpot sleeve (Sec 13)

Fig. 13.78 Unscrewing the pump plug (Sec 13)

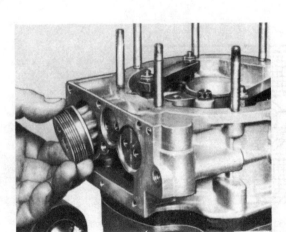

Fig. 13.79 Removing the filter plug and filter (Sec 13)

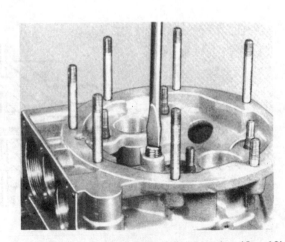

Fig. 13.80 Unscrewing the relief valve plug (Sec 13)

43 Should the pump plunger assembly be worn or damaged this must be renewed as a complete assembly.

44 With the non-return valve assembly clean, inspect the ball and valve seat and also the O-rings for signs of damage.

45 Check the relief valve and dashpot assembly for wear. The pistons must move freely in their respective housings. Ensure that the rings are in good order.

46 Do not dismantle the dashpot and relief valve piston assemblies, otherwise the pre-determined spring pressures will be disturbed.

47 Finally examine the O-rings on the solenoid valve for damage; if evident they should be renewed together with sealing washers.

48 Clean the sump filter in petrol and if any particles are stuck in the gauze, rub with an old toothbrush. Wipe the magnetic plug free of any metallic particles.

49 Reassembly of the unit can commence after any damaged or worn parts have been exchanged and new gaskets and seals obtained. Do not use jonting compound during assembly, and observe scrupulous cleanliness.

50 Fit a new annulus ball race and then position the speedometer driving gear so that the plain portion is facing the ball race. Secure with the nut and new locking washer. Tighten the nut to the specified torque and secure it by bending up the locking washer.

51 Place the ball-race circlip in the rear casing and expand using a pair of circlip pliers.

52 Press the annulus through the circlip and into the casing until the bearing is fully home and the circlip is located in its groove. This must be done with care to avoid damaging the rear bush and oil seal. Protect the seal lip by smearing it with grease.

53 Refit the bearing support to the rear of the casing. Place a new seal beneath the support. Refit the speedometer driven gear and housing, securing it with the plate and bolt.

54 Next position the spring and inner member of the freewheel assembly into the cage, locating the spring so that the cage is spring loaded in an anti-clockwise direction when viewed from the front.

55 Place this assembly onto tool No KM-493 with the open side of the cage uppermost and feed the rollers into place. Refit the bronze thrust washer in the recess in the annulus.

56 Transfer the freewheel assembly from the special assembly tool into its outer member in the annulus.

57 Refit the oil catcher and secure with the circlip. Check that the freewheel rotates in an anti-clockwise direction only.

58 Mount the rear casing assembly vertically in a bench vice and insert the planet carrier assembly over alignment tool No KM-495. The gears may be meshed in any position.

59 Place the sliding member assembly complete with clutch non-return springs onto the cone of the annulus, at the same time engaging the sunwheel with the planet gears. Fit the brake into its spigot in the casing using a new joint washer on both sides.

60 Position the main casing assembly onto the thrust housing pins, at the same time entering the studs in the brake ring.

61 Fit the two operating piston bridge pieces and secure with four new nuts.

62 Fit the six nuts which secure the rear and main casing assemblies, locating any washers in their previously noted positions. Tighten the nuts evenly, a little at a time and in a diagonal sequence against spring pressure.

63 Lightly smear the two operating pistons with gearbox oil and refit them to the main casing, O-ring side first.

64 Refit the pump plunger assembly, having lightly lubricated the plunger. Refit the relief valve ball, spring and plug.

65 Position the main casing so that the sump faces downwards.

66 Before refitting the relief valve and dashpot assembly ensure that all component parts are clean and lightly oiled. Insert the relief body in the bore, and using the relief valve outer sleeve push it fully home. Note the end with the O-ring is nearest to the outside of the casing.

67 Next place the relief valve spring and piston assembly into the dashpot cup, taking care that the ends of the residual pressure spring are correctly located.

68 Place these parts in the relief valve outer sleeve, at the same time engaging the relief valve piston in its housing.

69 Finally fit the base plug and tighten to the specified torque.

70 Place the pump non-return valve spring in the non-return valve plug and then place the ball on the spring.

71 The non-return seat can now be located on the ball and the complete assembly screwed into the main casing using tool No KM-492. Tighten to the specified torque wrench setting.

72 Refit the pressure filter and new aluminium washer. Tighten the plug to the specified torque.

73 Refit the overdrive sump, suction filter and gasket and secure with the six bolts and lockwashers.

74 Refit the solenoid control valve and tighen firmly.

Solenoid control valve – removal, testing and refitting

75 The solenoid and operating valve are a self-contained factory sealed unit.

76 Disconnect the two terminals at the rear of the solenoid, noting which way round the cables are fitted.

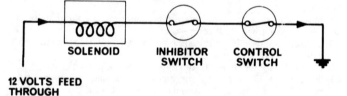

12 VOLTS FEED THROUGH IGNITION SWITCH

Fig. 13.81 Overdrive solenoid theoretical wiring diagram (Sec 13)

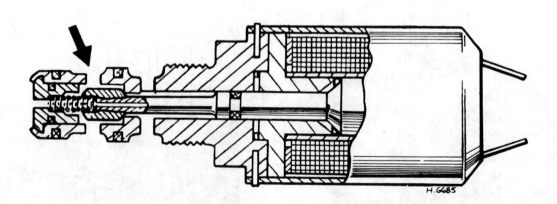

H.6685

Fig. 13.82 Overdrive solenoid and control valve – arrowed (Sec 13)

77 Using special tool No KM-494 or a thin open-ended spanner unscrew the assembly. Do not use a wrench around the cylindrical body of the solenoid valve otherwise it will be severely damaged.

78 To test the solenoid connect it to a 12 volt battery and ammeter. The solenoid should require approximately 2 amps.

79 Check that the plunger in the valve moves forwards when the solenoid is energised and is returned to its direct drive position by spring pressure when de-energised.

80 It should be noted that this type of solenoid does not operate with a 'click' as observed in other types of overdrive.

81 Inspect the O-rings on the solenoid valve for damage and if necessary renew them together with a sealing washer.

82 If it is necessary to clean the operating valve, immerse this part of the solenoid valve only in paraffin until the valve is clean.

83 If the solenoid proves to be faulty it should be renewed as a complete unit.

84 Refitting is the reverse sequence to removal.

Relief valve and dashpot assembly – removal and refitting

85 Before commencing this operation, obtain special tools KM-492 and KM-496. If the vehicle has recently been used, take care to avoid burns from the hot oil which will be released.

86 Unscrew and remove the six bolts and lockwashers which secure the sump plate. Remove the plate, gasket and filter.

87 Using tool No KM-492, remove the dashpot plug. Lift out the dashpot piston complete with its component springs and cup followed by the residual pressure spring.

88 The relief valve piston assembly may now be withdrawn by carefully pulling down with a pair of pliers. The components are shown in Fig. 13.83.

89 Insert tool No KM-496 into the now exposed relief valve bore. Withdraw the relief valve together with the dashpot sleeve, taking extreme care not to damage the valve bore.

90 Do not attempt to dismantle the dashpot and relief valve piston assemblies, otherwise the pre-determined pressures will be disturbed.

91 Inspect the pistons and ensure that they move freely in their respective housings. Make sure the O-rings are not damaged.

92 Before assembly make sure all components are clean and lightly oiled.

93 Insert the relief body in the bore and using the relief valve outer sleeve push fully home. Note that the end with the O-ring is nearest the outside of the main casing.

94 Next position the relief valve spring and piston into the dashpot cup taking care that both ends of the residual pressure spring are correctly located. Carefully position these components in the relief valve outer sleeve, at the same time engaging the relief valve piston in its housing. Fit the base plug and tighten to the specified torque.

95 Refit the filter, gasket and sump and secure with the six bolts and lockwashers.

Pump and non-return valve – removal and refitting

96 For removal a special tool No KM-492 is necessary to remove the pump plug. If the vehicle has been recently used take care to avoid burns from hot oil which will be released.

97 Unscrew and remove the six bolts and lockwashers securing the overdrive sump and gauze filter. Lift away the sump, gasket and gauze filter.

98 Using tool No KM-492 remove the pump plug, taking care not to lose the non-return valve spring and ball. The pump valve seat can now be lifted away.

99 The pump body will be held in position by its O-ring. Should it be necessary to remove this, rotate the propeller shaft until the pump plunger is at the top of its stroke.

100 Next carefully withdraw the pump body by hooking a piece of wire into the now exposed inlet port.

101 Carefully clean and then inspet the non-return valve ball and valve seat and make sure that the O-rings are not damaged. Fit new O-rings if necessary.

102 To refit the non-return valve assembly, first place the spring in the non-return valve plug, then position the ball on the spring.

103 The non-return valve seat can now be located on the ball and the complete assembly screwed into the main case using tool No KM-492. Tighten to the specified torque.

104 Refit the suction filter, sump gasket and sump and secure with the six bolts and lockwashers.

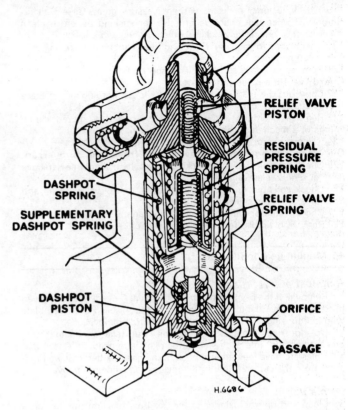

Fig. 13.83 Sectional view of overdrive relief valve and dashpot assembly (Sec 13)

Pressure filter – removal and refitting

105 For removal, a special tool No KM-492 is necessary to remove the box plug. If the vehicle has been used recently take care to avoid burns from hot oil which will be released.

106 Unscrew and remove the six bolts and lockwashers securing the overdrive sump and gauze filter. Lift away the sump, gasket and gauze filter.

107 Using tool No KM-492 remove the pressure filter base plug.

108 The filter element will come away with the plug. Note the aluminium washer which locates on the shoulder in the filter bore.

109 Remove any dirt and thoroughly wash the element in petrol or paraffin.

110 Refitting is the reverse sequence to removal. Always fit a new aluminium washer. Tighten the plug to the specified torque.

Fault diagnosis

111 This is a cumulative diagnosis sequence. There are four faults mentioned. Each fault has a list of checks and remedies listed in order of their likelihood which should be strictly followed. After each check is undertaken, if the fault does not disappear, go on to the next check.

Overdrive does not engage

112 Check oil level. Top up if necessary.

113 Check electrical circuit to solenoid. Rectify break if necessary.

114 Remove the solenoid valve to check operation. Renew if inoperative.

115 Clean the gauze filters and check the pump non-return valve seat for clogging and pitting. Renew if dirty or damaged. If satisfactory check relief valve for sticking piston. Renew assembly if piston will not free.

116 Remove overdrive for specialist inspection.

Overdrive does not disengage

Note: *If in this condition* **do not reverse the vehicle.** *It will damage the overdrive beyond repair.*

117 Check electrical system for closed circuit and correct if necessary.

118 Remove solenoid control valve and check for seized plunger. If seized renew the valve.

119 Check residual pressure with a pressure gauge (see Specifications). If incorrect check relief valve for sticking piston. If clean check control orifice for blocking, otherwise renew parts.
120 Check cone for sticking. If sticking free by tapping brake ring with soft-faced hammer.
121 Remove overdrive for specialist inspection.

Overdrive slips in engagement

122 Carry out the first four checks under 'does not engage'. If these prove satisfactory, carry out the following.
123 Remove overdrive and check for worn and/or glazed clutch linings or a mechanical obstruction of the cone clutch.
124 Remove overdrive for specialist inspection.

Overdrive disengagement slow and/or freewheel on overrun

125 Check the relief valve for sticking piston. If sticking, free defective parts or renew relief valve assembly.
126 Check solenoid for sticking or blocked control valve. Clean and free valve or renew solenoid assembly.
127 Check restrictor orifice for partial blockage. Clean orifice.
128 Remove overdrive for specialist inspection.

14 Manual gearbox (5-speed)

Removal and refitting

1 Removal of the 5-speed gearbox is a similar procedure to that given in Section 2 of Chapter 6 for removal of the 4-speed unit (complete with bellhousing). Drain the gearbox oil before removal.
2 Do not rush removal of the unit, but take adequate safety precautions and note each step in the removal procedure. Check that all cables etc have been moved clear of the gearbox before lowering it away from the vehicle. Refit in the reverse sequence to removal.

Dismantling

3 Clean and dry the exterior of the gearbox. Position the unit on a firm, clean work surface.

4 Examine the rubber mounting bushes for deterioration. Renew any damaged bush. Should a bush seize in its housing, do not attempt to hammer the bush from position, but leave it to soak in releasing fluid for a time and then pull it from position with a tool made from a bolt, sleeve and washers as shown in Fig. 13.85.
5 Before fitting new mounting bushes, clean and lightly grease their housings to aid insertion. Pull them into position with the same tool as used for removal.
6 Remove the speedometer drive assembly retaining plate and nut. Using the flat of a screwdriver, carefully lever the drive assembly out of its location.
7 Unbolt the mounting bracket from the upper rear section of the transmission casing. It may prove difficult to release the bracket retaining bolts because of the locking compound applied to their threads during assembly.
8 Remove the spring sleeve from the end of the selector rod, followed by the retaining pin and joint.
9 Refer to Section 3 of Chapter 5 and remove the clutch release bearing and fork from the bellhousing. Renew the bellhousing gaiters if split or perished.
10 Remove the reverse light switch from the front section of the gearbox casing.
11 Pull the detent plug from the gearbox casing with a pair of pincers as shown in Fig. 13.86. Hook the detent spring and pin from their location.
12 Unbolt the clutch release bearing guide sleeve from the centre of the bellhousing and pull it off the input shaft. Retain the spacer rings(s).
13 Using a pair of circlip pliers, remove the retaining ring from the input shaft, followed by the spacer ring.
14 Release the two halves of the gearbox casing by removing the securing bolts. Note the fitted position of these bolts, making up a cardboard template if necessary. Drive the dowel pins slightly back into the casing front half.
15 Before attempting to separate the casing halves, remove the

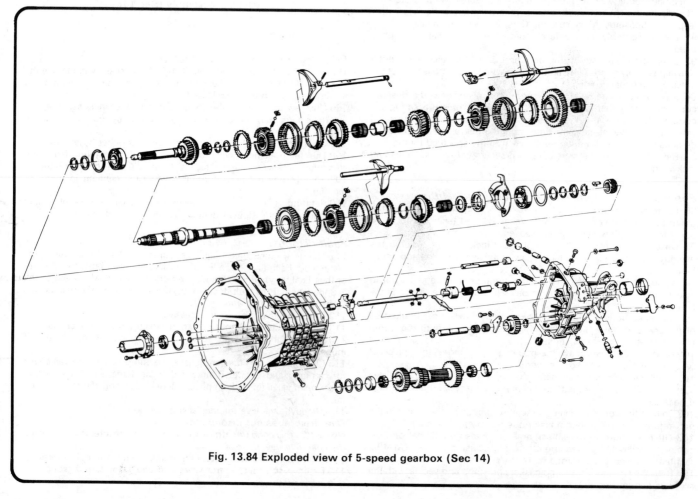

Fig. 13.84 Exploded view of 5-speed gearbox (Sec 14)

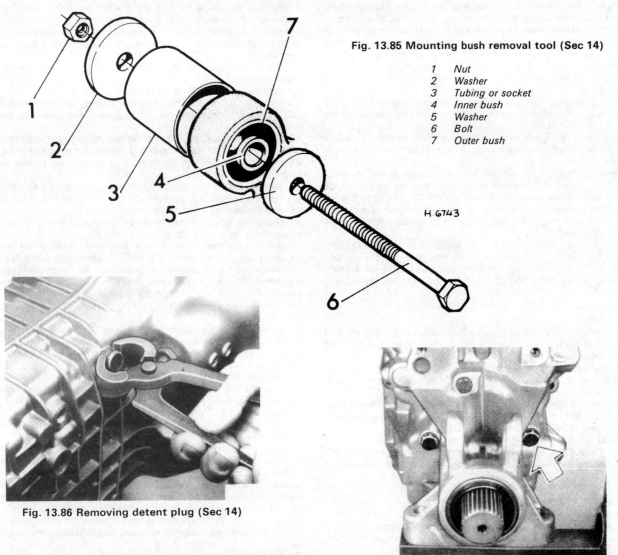

Fig. 13.85 Mounting bush removal tool (Sec 14)

1 Nut
2 Washer
3 Tubing or socket
4 Inner bush
5 Washer
6 Bolt
7 Outer bush

H.6743

Fig. 13.86 Removing detent plug (Sec 14)

Fig. 13.87 Support plate mounting bolts. Bolt arrowed is
65.0 mm in length (Sec 14)

mounting bolts for the reverse idler gear shaft. With the casing rear half held in position, use a soft-faced hammer to separate the front half from it. Strike only on reinforced areas of the casing.

16 Upon separation, all gearbox internals should remain within the casing rear half. Support this casing half on the work surface.

17 Remove the three support plate mounting bolts shown in Fig. 13.87. Note that the bolts are of different lengths and must be refitted in their original locations.

18 Unbolt the reverse idler gear retaining plate. Support the shaft and remove the retaining plate. Remove the reverse idler gear and shaft, noting its fitted position.

19 Support the casing so that the shafts are vertical (open side uppermost). Remove the 5th gear detent retaining screw and the detent spring.

20 Remove the circlip which retains the reverse gear detent plug in position. Push the plug away from the circlip during removal. Spring pressure behind the plug will cause it to be ejected unless care is taken. Remove the plug, spring and detent pin.

21 Withdraw the transfer lever retaining pin. Note the fitted position of the lever and remove it.

22 Pull the selector rail from its end support in the casing. Unscrew the support retaining bolt and remove the support.

23 Support the adjacent selector rod (5th/reverse) with a block of hardwood as shown in Fig. 13.88. Using a parallel pin punch, drive the retaining pin from the selector fork. Check that the fork moves independently of the rod. Detach the rod end support from the casing by removing its retaining bolt. Ease the rod assembly clear of the gearbox, taking care to retain the bearing rollers on the rod end.

24 Carefully release the selector rocker spring tension and withdraw the rocker assembly from the casing.

Fig. 13.88 Driving out selector fork roll pin (Sec 14)

25 Unbolt the detent retaining plate from the casing. This plate will most likely be stuck in position with sealing compound, in which case it should be carefully levered free. The compound may also prevent the detent springs from popping free of the casing, in which case any dried compound must be removed before the springs are hooked free.

26 Place the end of a parallel pin punch against the edge of the 3rd/4th selector rod end cap. Strike the punch so that the cap is tilted through 90°. Remove the cap (photo).

27 Support the free end of the 3rd/4th selector rod and drive the selector fork retaining pin from position. Check the fork is free of the rod.

28 Using a soft metal drift, carefully drive the selector rod forward 20 mm (0.80 in). Doing this will release the detent balls which must be retained.

29 Support the casing so that the shafts are horizontal and the shaft ends readily accessible. GM now recommend that the casing around the mainshaft end be heated to approximately 80°C (176°F) to free the bearing. Place the casing in an oven or immerse it in boiling water. Do not use a naked flame or localised and excessive heat because of the risk of warping the casing.

30 With the casing heated and well supported, use a large soft metal drift and hammer to drive the mainshaft free. Remove the gearbox internals as an assembly and place them on a clean work surface. Retain any detent balls that fall from the casing, also the bearing spacer.

Component examination

31 The principles for component examination are given in Section 4 of Chapter 6. Ignore any specific references to the 4-speed gearbox and note the following points.

32 The methods of measuring selector fork end wear and synchromesh ring wear are shown in the accompanying photographs. Wear limits are given in the Specifications.

33 If the reverse idler gear is not to be removed from the casing, then its clearance with the retaining plate must be checked before the casing halves are rejoined. See paragraph 88.

34 Should it prove necessary to renew bearings or spacers in either casing half, unless the job is obviously straightforward, entrust the task to your GM dealer who will have any special tools and replacement parts needed.

Input shaft – dismantling and reassembly

35 It is not possible to dismantle the input shaft other than to remove the caged roller bearing from its end; this bearing should slip from position quite easily. If any one bearing surface is worn or damaged, renew the shaft complete (photo).

Layshaft – renewal

36 The layshaft is machined as one solid assembly. If damage or excessive wear is apparent then the shaft must be renewed as a whole.

Mainshaft – dismantling and reassembly

37 Using the flat of a small screwdriver, displace the speedometer drivegear retaining clip. Pull the gear off the shaft.

38 With the shaft vertical, place its splined end between the protected jaws of a vice and clamp it in position. Remove the 3rd/4th gear synchromesh bodies retaining circlip.

39 Remove the spacer. Remove the 3rd/4th gear synchromesh bodies, if necessary levering them from position with two screwdrivers positioned opposite to each other. Take care to keep the bodies together during removal, otherwise the springs and balls will be released.

40 Remove the synchromesh ring, 3rd gear and the needle roller bearing assembly.

41 Pull 2nd gear and centre bush off the shaft (photo).

42 Remove the needle roller bearing followed by the synchromesh ring. Do not allow any of the synchromesh rings to become interchanged.

43 Remove the 1st/2nd gear synchromesh bodies retaining circlip and remove the bodies, synchromesh ring, pinion and needle roller bearing.

44 Invert the mainshaft in the vice. Using circlip pliers, remove the first of the two circlips.

45 Remove the lockwasher by carefully levering it from position with the flat of a screwdriver. Remove the second circlip and the spacer.

46 Pull the bearing from the shaft end.

47 Using the flat of a large screwdriver, lever the torsion ring from position, taking care to retain the locating pin.

48 Remove the shaft support plate. Unscrew the thrust nut. Remove the 5th gear/synchromesh ring and the needle roller bearing. Note that this bearing can be separated on one side to allow removal (photo).

49 Remove the 5th/reverse gear synchromesh bodies retaining circlip and carefully lever the bodies from position.

50 Remove the synchromesh ring, the reverse gear and the needle roller bearing.

51 If dismantling the synchromesh bodies, keep each one separate to avoid mixing the component parts. To dismantle each body, carefully slide the outer sleeve off the hub, taking care to retain the springs, balls and slides.

52 Fatigued or broken springs will necessitate renewal. All springs must be of equal length. Renew worn slides or balls as a set (photo).

53 When reassembling a synchromesh body, take care fitting the slides; check that each one moves freely in its location and has its concave (or stepped) side facing outwards. Fit the springs and use one hand to hold all three in position.

54 Align the outer sleeve with the hub so that the recesses between the sleeve splines coincide with those of the hub (photo). Push the sleeve over the hub so that the slides and springs are retained in position. Place the assembly on the work surface and ease the sleeve back just enough for each ball to be fitted. With the balls fitted, fully align the sleeve and hub, checking that each slide is free to move.

55 Reassemble the mainshaft in conditions of absolute cleanliness. Lightly lubricate each bearing surface with the recommended gearbox oil.

56 With the shaft vertical, clamp its splined end between the protected jaws of a vice. Fit the needle roller bearing, 1st gear and synchromesh ring (photos).

57 Fit the 1st/2nd gear synchromesh bodies so that the sleeve flange is uppermost. Fit the retaining circlip so that it is properly located in its groove. If necessary, tap the synchromesh bodies fully home using a length of metal tube of the appropriate diameter (photo).

58 Fit the synchromesh ring and the needle roller bearing. Using a method described earlier, heat 2nd gear and the centre bush. Fit the gear and bush over the shaft, tapping each component into position with a length of metal tube. The bush flange must face the pinion (photos).

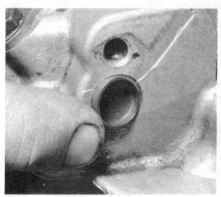
14.26 Selector rod end cap

14.32A Measuring selector fork thickness

14.32B Measuring synchro baulk ring-to-teeth clearance

14.35 Input shaft roller bearing

14.41 Removing 2nd gear and bush from mainshaft

14.48 5th gear needle roller bearing

14.52 Synchro-hub, ball, spring and sliding key

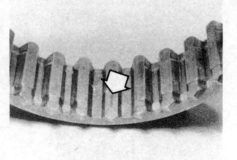

14.54 Synchro sleeve spline recess (arrowed)

14.56A 1st gear needle roller bearing

14.56B 1st gear

14.56C 1st gear synchro ring

14.57 Using tubing to fit 1st/2nd synchro body

14.58A 2nd gear synchro ring

14.58B 2nd gear needle roller bearing

14.58C 2nd gear and bush

59 Fit the needle roller bearing, 3rd grear and the synchromesh ring. Push the 3rd/4th gear synchromesh bodies onto the shaft with the smaller central flange uppermost. Fit the spacer and retaining circlip. Check that the circlip is properly located in its groove (photos).

60 Invert the mainshaft in the vice. Fit the needle roller bearing, reverse gear and the synchromesh ring (photos).

61 Fit the 5th/reverse gear synchromesh bodies, taking care to align it correctly with the ring. Use a length of metal tube to tap the bodies home. Fit the retaining circlip (photos).

62 Fit the split needle roller bearing. Fit the synchromesh ring and 5th gear (photos). Screw the thrust nut onto the shaft finger tight, with the punch mark uppermost.

63 Select a 0.05 to 0.10 mm (0.002 to 0.004 in) feeler gauge and insert it between the underside of the nut and 5th gear. Using finger pressure only, tighten the nut onto the gauge until the gauge can just be slid clear (photo).

64 Taking care not to move the nut, fit the torsion ring and retain it in position with the locating pin. Slight movement of the nut to allow ring

alignment is permitted (photo).

65 Fit the shaft support plate with its centre flange uppermost. Position the bearing on the shaft end with its closed side uppermost. Keeping the bearing square to the shaft, use a length of metal tube of the same diameter as the bearing inner race to tap it into position (photo).

66 Fit the spacer, circlip, lockwasher and second circlip. Slide the speedometer drivegear retaining clip into the shaft groove and push the gear over it (photos). Reassembly of the mainshaft is now complete.

Reassembly

67 Prior to reassembly, measure the total thickness of the mainshaft support plate and bearing. Note the measurement for future reference (photo).

68 Obtain two equal lengths of threaded rod. Each rod must screw securely into the holes provided in the support plate and should be of sufficient length to reach the mainshaft end (photo). GM provide these

14.59A 3rd gear needle roller bearing

14.59B 3rd gear

14.59C 3rd gear synchro ring

14.59D 3rd/4th synchro body

14.59E Spacer and circlip

14.60A Reverse gear needle roller bearing

14.60B Reverse gear and synchro ring

14.61A Using tubing to fit 5th/reverse synchro body

14.61B 5th/reverse synchro secured with circlip

14.62A 5th gear split needle roller bearing

14.62B 5th gear and synchro ring

14.63 Tightening mainshaft nut

14.64 Nut secured with torsion ring and pin

14.65 Fitting mainshaft bearing

14.66A Spacer, circlip and lockwasher

14.66B Second circlip fitted

14.66C Speedometer drivegear clip

14.66D Speedometer drivegear

14.67 Measuring thickness of mainshaft support plate and bearing

14.68 Threaded rods screwed into support plate

rods (known as guide pins) as tool No KM-442.

69 Fit the rods to the mainshaft support plate and then assemble the selector mechanisms to the mainshaft as shown in Fig. 13.89. Place the assembly on a clean piece of rag or paper to avoid contamination. Fit the input shaft to the mainshaft, making sure that the synchro ring and roller bearing are fitted (photo).

70 It is now necessary to determine the amount of mainshaft axial play. Measure the depth of the mainshaft bearing housing in the casing rear half (photo). With this measurement noted, subtract the thickness of support plate and bearing, noted earlier, from it. The resulting measurement will equal the thickness of the bearing spacer required. Spacers are available in thicknesses of 0.3 mm (0.012 in), 0.4 mm (0.016 in) and 0.5 mm (0.020 in).

71 Prepare the rear casing half by removing the selector rod seal (if not already done) with the flat of a screwdriver.

72 The housing for the five detent balls must be checked for cleanliness. Remove any hardened sealing compound. Ensure that each ball can be pressed into position from the outside of the casing. If the holes appear too small, deburr their ends with a large drill (twisting by hand) until the balls enter freely.

73 Heat the casing as previously described around the mainshaft bearing housing. Fit the bearing spacer (photo). Support the casing upright in a vice.

74 Clasping the input shaft/mainshaft/selector mechanism/layshaft assembly in two hands, guide the support plate rods through the casing holes provided. Push the assembly into the casing, checking that the rods remain parallel (photo).

75 Keep a constant check on component alignment when fitting the gearbox internals. If it proves impossible to push the mainshaft bearing home by hand, fit nuts and plain washers to the rod ends and tighten each nut evenly, a little at a time, to pull the bearing into its housing. Ensure the mainshaft remains vertical and do not place excessive force on the nuts. Check for free rotation of both shafts during fitting.

76 With the mainshaft correctly fitted, remove one of the guide rods and replace it with the correct support plate mounting bolt. The bolt threads must be coated with locking compound. Remove the second guide rod and fit the remaining two bolts. Tighten each bolt to the

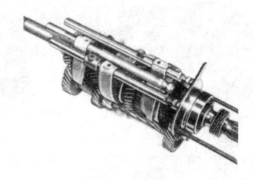

Fig. 13.89 Geartrains and selector components ready for fitting (Sec 14)

specified torque.

77 Refer to Fig. 13.90 and fit the five detent balls as shown, smearing each one with grease so that it remains in position (photo). Use a small screwdriver to insert the middle two balls. Manoeuvre the selector rods as necessary and remember to fit the pin into the centre rod (photo).

78 With all detent balls fitted and selector rods in position, insert the three springs. Coat the mating face of the retaining plate with sealing compound and bolt it in position (photo).

79 Refit the selector rocker assembly into the casing and using a pair of self-locking or flat-nosed pliers, tension the spring so that its end locks into the casing (photos). Push the spring end fully home with a screwdriver.

80 Fit the selector rod end support over the rocker assembly and fit its

14.69 Synchro ring and roller bearing in position prior to fitting input shaft to mainshaft

14.70 Measuring depth of mainshaft bearing housing

14.73 Mainshaft bearing spacer

14.74 Offering geartrains to the rear half casing

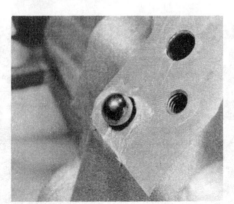

14.77A Detent ball

14.77B Pin in centre selector rod

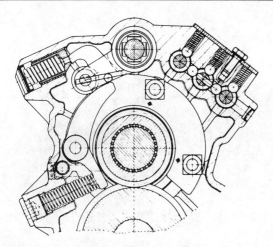

Fig. 13.90 Location of detent balls and springs (Sec 14)

retaining bolt (photo). Coat the ball threads and shank with sealing compound.

81 Fit the selector rod through its end support and fork from the rear of the casing, ensuring that the end bearing rollers are all in position (photo). With the rod pushed fully home, secure the fork to it with the retaining pin, after having checked that the cut-outs in the shaft end are facing away from the group of three selector rods. The retaining pin must be fitted flush to the fork (photo).

82 Check that the other three selector forks are all secured to their rods; again, each retaining pin must be fitted flush to the fork.

83 Fit the selector rail end support into the casing (photo). The support retaining bolt must have its threads and shank coated with sealing compound before fitting. Tighten the bolt to the specified torque.

84 Push the selector rail into its end support, at the same time easing the transfer lever into position with its marked end towards the rail. Fit the lever retaining pin (photo).

85 Fit the reverse gear detent pin, spring and plug. Using a bar to hold the plug down against spring pressure, fit the circlip and ensure that it is fully home in its groove by placing the socket against it and tapping lightly with a hammer (photos).

86 Fit the 5th gear detent spring. Coat the threads of the spring

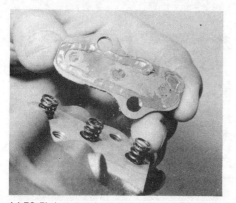

14.78 Fitting the detent spring retaining plate

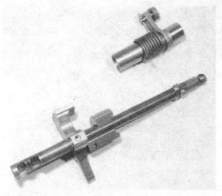

14.79A Selector rocker assembly

14.79B Selector rocker spring in casing

14.80 Tightening the selector rod end support retaining hook

14.81A Fitting the selector rail

14.81B Securing selector fork with roll pin

14.83 Selector rail end support (arrowed)

14.84 Selector rail and transfer lever

14.85A Reverse detent components

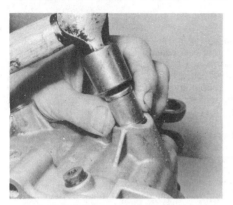

14.85B Settling reverse detent circlip using a socket

14.86 5th gear detent plug and Allen key

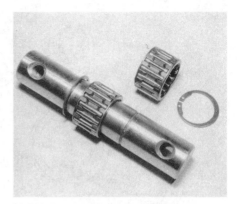

14.87A Reverse idler shaft components

14.87B Fitting reverse idler shaft

14.88 Reverse idler gear retaining plate and narrow feeler blade

14.89 Layshaft roller bearing

retaining plug with sealing compound before fitting (photo). Tighten the plug to the specified torque.
87 Fit the reverse idler gear, tilting it slightly to clear the mainshaft gear. Fit the shaft, complete with needle roller bearings and circlips, into the gear. If fitting the original shaft, place it in its originally noted position (photo). Coat the threads of the shaft-to-casing securing bolt with sealing compound. Align the shaft, fit the bolt and tighten it to the specified torque (photo).
88 Bolt the reverse idler gear retaining plate in position, finger tight. Obtain a narrow feeler gauge of 0.1 mm (0.004 in) thickness and insert it between the plate and groove (photo). With the gauge a good sliding fit, tighten the plate retaining bolt to the specified torque. Recheck the clearance.
89 Fit the caged roller bearing, flanged end uppermost, to the layshaft end (photo).
90 Check the mating surface of each casing half for cleanliness and coat the surface of the assembled half with sealing compound. Make a final check to ensure the gearbox internals are correctly fitted and (where applicable) free to move. Lightly lubricate each bearing surface.
91 Align the casing front half over the shaft ends and push it down onto the rear half until the mating surfaces touch. Do not attempt to force the casing halves together or draw them together with the bolts. If unsuccessful, realign the front half and try again. Fit the casing bolts in their previously noted positions; the topmost right-hand bolt is the largest. Tighten the bolts a little at a time, working diagonally to avoid possible distortion, to the specified torque. Resite the dowel pins so that they are correctly positioned.
92 Fit the second of the reverse idler gear shaft securing bolts, coating its threads with sealing compound and tightening it to the specified torque.
93 If removed, refit the selector rod end covers so that they are flush with the casing (photo). These three covers are within the bellhousing.
94 It is now necessary to fit the spacer and retaining ring to the input shaft so that when fitted, the spacer prevents the ring from rotating. To do this, pull the shaft forward against its bearing, insert the outer edge

of the ring into its groove and insert the spacer between it and the bearing inner race. Spacers are available in thicknesses of 2.3 mm (0.091 in), 2.4 mm (0.094 in), 2.5 mm (0.098 in) and 2.6 mm (0.102 in). Select a spacer which is a good firm fit and slide it over the shaft. Fit the retaining ring into its groove and check that it cannot be rotated (photo).
95 Before fitting the clutch release bearing guide sleeve over the input shaft, determine the spacer ring thickness required. Do this by first measuring the distance between the bearing outer race and the casing-to-sleeve mating face (photo) (value W). Now measure the distance between the bearing surface of the sleeve flange and its lip edge (photo) (value X). Finally, measure the distance between the flange lip and its mating surface with the casing (photo) (value Y). Subtract Y from X and add W to the result to determine the total spacer thickness.
96 Spacer rings are available in thickness of 1.3 mm (0.052 in), 1.4 mm (0.055 in) and 1.5 mm (0.059 in). The maximum permissible axial play is 0.05 mm (0.002 in). Before fitting the selected rings(s), coat each one with grease.
97 Push the spacer rings(s) into the sleeve flange (photo). Coat the flange-to-casing mating surface with sealing compound, also the threads of the retaining bolts. Align the recess in the flange lip with the oilway in the casing and fit the guide sleeve. Tighten the retaining bolts evenly to the specified torque.
98 Fit the detent pin into the casing front half. The end roller of the pin must be parallel to the top surface of the gearbox. Fit the spring and tap the plug home with a soft-faced hammer (photos).
99 Screw the reverse light switch into the casing front half, smearing a little sealing compound around its mating surface with the casing (photo).
100 Move the rear of the gearbox and fit a new selector rail seal. Lightly grease the seal lip and outer edge before fitting and use a length of metal tube of the appropriate diameter to tap it home (photo).
101 Refit the joint, retaining pin and spring sleeve to the selector rail end (photo).

14.93 Selector rod end covers

14.94 Input shaft spacer and circlip

14.95A Measuring from bearing outer track to sleeve mating face

14.95B Measuring from sleeve bearing surface to edge of lip

14.95C Measuring from sleeve mating surface to edge of lip

14.97 Guide sleeve and spacer ring

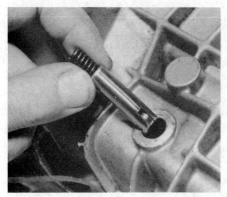
14.98A Fitting front half casing detent pin

14.98B Detent pin plug

14.99 Fitting reverse lamp switch

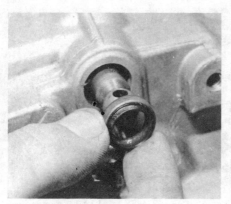
14.100 Fitting the selector rail oil seal

14.101 The selector rail joint

102 Refit the 3rd/4th selector rod end cap so that it is flush with the casing.

103 Bolt the mounting bracket to the upper rear section of gearbox casing. Coat the bolt threads with locking compound before fitting.

104 Renew the O-ring on the speeometer drive housing and smear it lightly with grease. Push the drive assembly into the casing and retain it with the plate and nut.

105 Refit the clutch release bearing and fork, with serviceable gaiters. Smear the bearing guide sleeve and input shaft splines with a molybdenum disulphide based grease.

106 Replenish the gearbox with the specified oil. Reassembly of the gearbox is now complete.

15 Automatic transmission

Selector lever clevis renewal

1   Corrosion or wear of the selector lever clevis may cause difficulty in selecting the various driving ranges. Renew a defective clevis as follows.

2   Move the selector lever to the N position. Jack up the front of the vehicle and support it on firmly based axle stands.

3   Use the flat of a screwdriver to detach the retaining clip from the clevis. Remove the clip and bolt and detach the clevis from the lever. Unscrew the clevis from the rod, having noted its fitted position.

4   Before fitting the new clevis, clean and lubricate the threads of the rod. Fit the clevis in the previously noted position (this will minimise adjustment). Check for correct selector linkage adjustment (see Section 12, Chapter 6) and reconnect the clevis to the lever, checking that the retaining clip is correctly located.

5   Check that all driving ranges can be engaged.

16 Rear axle

Counter-balance weights

1   On some models, counterbalance weights will be found fitted to the rear axle differential casing. These weights damp out vibration and require no maintenance except for the occasional check for damage. Excessive road dirt may cause the weights to 'jam', in which case they should be cleaned. Each weight is bolted to the casing (photo).

17 Braking system

Floating caliper front disc brakes (GMF type)
Pads – inspection and renewal

1   Raise the front of the vehicle. If the roadwheels have been balanced on the vehicle (new vehicles are balanced this way in production) then mark the relative position of the roadwheel to the hub so that it can be aligned correctly when refitting.

2   Inspect the thickness of the friction material on each pad. If any one is at or below the specified minimum, renew the pads as an axle set (four pads) in the following way.

16.1 Rear axle counter balance weights

3   Drive out the pad retaining pins by applying a punch to their inboard ends.

4   Remove the springs.

5   Using a pair of pliers, withdraw the outboard pad.

6   Remove the inboard pad. If it is very tight, move the pad sideways slightly to depress the caliper piston.

7   In order to accommodate the new thicker pads, the caliper piston must be depressed fully into its cylinder using a flat bar of metal such as a tyre lever. The action of depressing the piston will cause the fluid in the reservoir to rise, so anticipate this by syphoning some off using an old (clean) battery hydrometer or similar.

8   Brush out the jaws of the caliper, taking care not to inhale the dust.

9   Insert the pads, making sure that the lining side is against the disc (photo).

10 Locate the spreader springs and drive in the retaining pins (photo).

11 Repeat the operations on the opposite brake.

12 Refit the roadwheels and lower the vehicle.

13 Apply the footbrake hard several times to position the pads against the discs.

14 Top up the fluid reservoir to the correct level.

Caliper – removal, overhaul and refitting

15 Raise the front of the vehicle and remove the roadwheels (see above).

16 Prise off the mounting bolt caps. Do not unscrew the two hexagon-headed bolts, as these connect the caliper body and bracket.

17 Disconnect the fluid line from the caliper and either plug with rubber grommets or allow the fluid to drain into a container.

18 Using an Allen key, unscrew the two socket-headed mounting bolts.

19 Remove the caliper from the vehicle (photo).

17.9 Brake disc pad (GMF caliper)

17.10 Fitting disc pad retaining pins (GMF caliper)

17.19 Removing a GMF type caliper

20 Brush away external dust and remove the disc pads.

21 Using a chisel, release the sliding sleeve inner dust caps from the caliper housing.

22 Prise off the piston dust excluder.

23 Apply pressure to the outboard ends of the sliding sleeves until their dust caps can be disengaged from the sleeve grooves and removed.

24 Press the sliding sleeves from the caliper housing.

25 Place a thin piece of wood or hardboard on the end of the piston and apply air pressure to the fluid pipe connection on the caliper body. Only low air pressure will be required to eject the piston, such as is generated by a tyre foot pump.

26 Once the piston has been removed, pick out the seal from its groove in the cylinder, using a plastic or wooden instrument.

27 Inspect the surfaces of the piston and cylinder bore for scoring or evidence of metal-to-metal rubbing. If evident, renew the caliper complete.

28 If these components are in good condition, discard the rubber seal and dust excluder and obtain a repair kit which will contain all the necessary replacement items.

29 Clean the piston and cylinder bore with brake hydraulic fluid or methylated spirit – nothing else!

30 Commence reassembly by fitting the seal into the cylinder groove.

31 When the piston has been partially inserted, engage the new dust excluder with the groove in the piston.

32 Renew the sealing rings on the sliding sleeves, applying the special grease supplied in the repair kit to the sealing ring grooves. Make sure that the sealing ring is located in the centre groove.

33 Install the sliding sleeves so that the dust cap groove is towards the caliper bracket. Do not push the sleeves fully in at this stage. Install the new dust caps for the sliding sleeves onto their caliper housing collars. Use a piece of tubing to drive them fully home.

34 Depress the piston fully and secure the dust excluder to the housing, driving it fully home with a piece of suitable tubing.

35 Refit the caliper and screw in and tighten the socket-headed mounting bolts, having first cleaned the threads and applied locking compound. Refer to Specifications for the correct torque setting.

36 Fit the bolt caps.

37 Reconnect the fluid hose using new seals.

38 Refit the disc pads.

39 Bleed the hydraulic system as described in Section 3 of Chapter 9 or later in this Section.

40 Fit the roadwheels and lower the vehicle.

Disc – inspection, removal and refitting

41 Raise the front of the vehicle and remove the roadwheel (see paragraph 1).

42 Inspect the braking surface of the disc for deep grooving or tiny cracks. If these conditions are evident, the disc will have to be renewed or refinished. Any refinishing of both faces of the disc must not reduce the thickness of the disc below the minimum specified. Light, shallow scoring is a normal condition for brake discs.

43 If it is thought that the brake disc is distorted, check it for run-out using a dial gauge or using feeler blades between the disc and a fixed point as the disc is rotated.

44 If the run-out exceeds the specified limits, renew the disc.

45 To remove a brake disc for renewal or refinishing, first withdraw the pads as previously described.

46 Extract the small retaining screw and release the disc from the hub. It may be possible to remove the disc with the caliper in position by tilting the disc and easing it clear of the caliper. If not, remove the caliper.

47 It is recommended that both brake discs are refinished or renewed at the same time in order to maintain even braking.

48 Refitting is a reversal of removal.

49 On vehicles which are equipped with light alloy roadwheels, a facing sleeve is mounted on the collar of the brake disc.

Disc shield – renewal

50 Remove the bracket from the caliper body. It is not necessary to disconnect the brake hose from the caliper.

51 Remove the brake disc as previously described. Then, working through the holes in the hub flange, unscrew the disc shield fixing bolts.

52 Rotate the disc shield until its connecting strip can be cut through with metal snips. Remove the shield.

53 Before fitting a new shield, cut off the web. Apply some paint to the cut edge to prevent rusting.

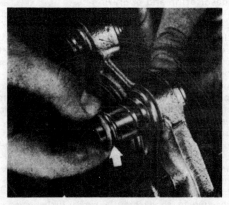

Fig. 13.91 Sliding sleeve dust cap groove correctly located (Sec 17)

54 Locate the shield so that the cut-out is at the topmost position. Screw in the fixing bolts.

55 Refit the disc and caliper.

Twin piston caliper front disc brakes
Disc – removal and refitting

56 From 1981, the disc securing bolts have an 'internal splined' head and are supplied with their threads pre-coated with locking compound.

57 This new type of bolt must be renewed every time the brake disc is removed. Before fitting each bolt, clean its location of hardened locking compound by using an M10 x 1.25 tap. Tighten each bolt to the specified torque.

Rear drum brakes (pre-1984 model year)
Drum – inspection

58 A certain amount of scoring of the brake drum surface is permissible. Drum renewal is only necessary if the depth of scoring is more than 0.4 mm (0.015 in).

Fault diagnosis

59 If the brakes are heard to squeak during operation, this may be due to friction between the brake shoes and flange plate.

60 To cure this problem, refer to Chapter 9 and remove the brake shoes. Clean the flange plate of any grease or rust and apply a thin smear of 'Plastilube' (or similar anti-seize compound) to the areas shown in Fig. 13.92.

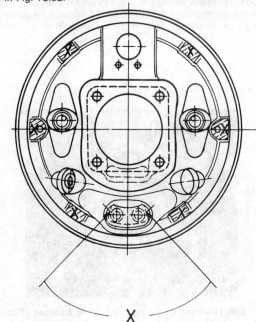

Fig. 13.92 Brake backplate lubrication areas (X) (Sec 17)

Rear drum brakes (1984 model year on)
General description and operation
61 The relay lever fitted to earlier drum brakes is now replaced by an automatic adjuster mechanism which comprises a threaded rod, pushrod sleeve, adjuster pinion and thermoclip.
62 Upon operation of the brake, the lateral movement at the brake shoe arm is converted into rotary movement by the lever on the adjuster pinion, therby compensating for shoe wear.
63 The thermoclip is designed to expand at a preset temperature, thereby compensating for any increase in drum size due to increased temperature. If this were not so, the brakes might lock on when the drum cooled again.
Shoes – removal and refitting
64 During this operation, take care to keep the component parts of each brake assembly separate. The adjuster pinion, lever and return spring bracket will all be colour coded black (left-hand assembly) or silver (right-hand assembly). The threaded rods have left or right-hand threads and are identified by the letter L or R respectively.
65 The procedure for shoe removal is similar to that given in Section 8 of Chapter 9, but with the following differences.
66 To facilitate drum removal, remove the plug from the backplate and, using the flat of a screwdriver, push the handbrake shoe lever back until it contacts the brake shoe arm.
67 After removal of the brake shoe return spring from its bracket, use the flat of a screwdriver to lever the bracket out of its location in the brake shoe.
68 Detach the adjuster lever from the brake shoe and disconnect its return spring.
69 In terms of removal, the automatic adjuster mechanism is the same as the relay lever fitted to earlier models.
70 When lubricating the areas of the backplate with which the shoes make contact, use 'Plastilube' or equivalent instead of the grease recommended in Chapter 9.
71 Refitting the shoes is the reverse sequence to removal, noting the following points.
72 Smear the threaded rod of the adjuster with a thin coat of silicone-based grease. Rotate the adjuster pinion back to its stop. Refit the adjuster mechanism, adjuster lever and return spring. Check that the spring washer fitted over the adjuster lever retaining pin of the brake shoe is not flattened; if so, renew it. Ensure that the thermoclip is fitted correctly, that is, facing upwards.
73 Before refitting the brake drum, ensure that the cam of the handbrake shoe lever contacts the arm of the handbrake shoe. If the cam is allowed to lie on top of the arm, the lever will engage immediately the handbrake is applied. This will result in the brake locking or overheating due to play being lost.
74 With the rear wheels refitted and the car on the ground, depress the brake pedal repeatedly (at least ten times) until it is no longer possible to hear the adjuster lever jumping across to the adjuster pinion. Once the lever ceases operation, adjustment is complete.

Handbrake – adjustment
75 The procedure for handbrake adjustment is similar to that given for the earlier type of brakes in Section 11 of Chapter 9, but with the following exceptions.
76 The handbrake should begin to take effect with the lever pulled up to the second notch on the ratchet.
77 A self-locking nut replaces the two locknuts previously used for cable adjustment.

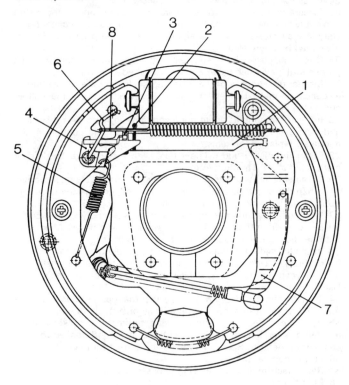

Fig. 13.93 Rear brake components – 1984 on (Sec 17)

1	Adjuster strut	5	Adjuster lever spring
2	Thermoclip	6	Bracket
3	Adjuster pinion	7	Handbrake lever
4	Adjuster lever	8	Shoe return spring

Fig. 13.94 Levering out a return spring bracket (Sec 17)

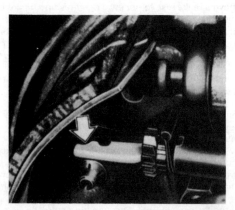

Fig. 13.95 Correctly fitted shoe adjuster strut – arrowed (Sec 17)

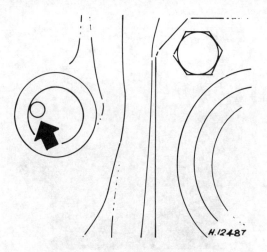

**Fig. 13.96 Checking handbrake adjustment: cam (arrowed)
should be 3.0 mm (0.12 in) from brake shoe arm (Sec 17)**

78 It is possible to check for correct handbrake adjustment by
removing the plug from the brake backplate and observing the
clearance between the cam of the handbrake shoe lever and the arm of
the brake shoe. This clearance should be approximately 3 mm (0.12
in). Refit both plugs on completion.

Anti-lock braking system (ABS) – description
79 An anti-lock braking system is optionally available on all models.
80 This system prevents the roadwheels locking up on slippery
surfaces even though the driver's foot is fully applied to the brake
pedal.
81 The hydraulic pressure on a wheel brake is released immediately
the wheel speed sensor signals the electronic control unit that a
roadwheel has stopped turning (locked). The control unit signals the
hydraulic modulator to release the brake pressure. As soon as the
roadwheel starts to turn again, the braking pressure is reapplied. This is
a continuing process with the front roadwheels being continually
monitored and, in the case of the rear roadwheels, the rear axle
differential is used as the sensor point.
82 When the ignition is switched on, the ABS control indicator
illuminates and goes out after the engine is started. If the indicator
remains illuminated or comes on whilst driving, a fault in the system is
probably the cause.
83 Apart from the simple checks described later a full test of the ABS
can only be carried out by your dealer who will have the necessary
equipment to do the job.

ABS – precautions
84 Before carrying out electric welding on the car, always pull the plug
from the electronic control unit.
85 If a paint oven is being used during body refinishing make sure that
the temperature is limited to 85°C (185°F) for a duration not exceeding
two hours.
86 Never use a rapid type of charger to start the car.
87 Never disconnect or reconnect the multi-plug at the electronic
control unit when the ignition is switched on.
88 The tandem type brake master cylinder fitted in conjunction with
the ABS cannot be overhauled; if faulty, it must be renewed as a
complete assembly.

ABS components – removal and refitting
Hydraulic modulator (1.8 models)
89 The modulator is located on the right-hand side within the engine

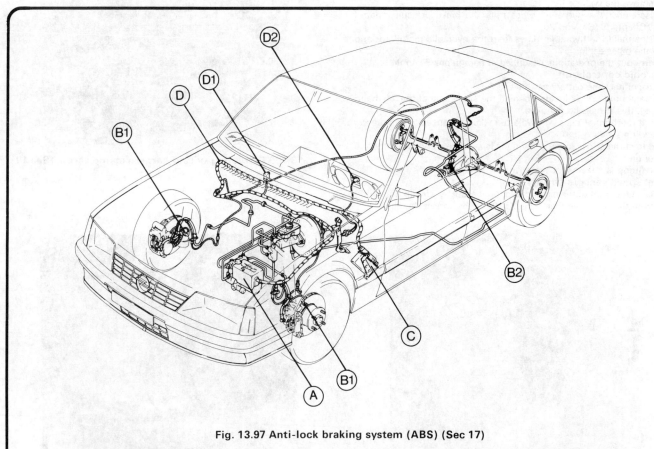

Fig. 13.97 Anti-lock braking system (ABS) (Sec 17)

A Hydraulic modulator	C Electronic control unit	D1 Surge arrestor relay
B1 Wheel speed sensors	D Wiring harness with ABS connectors	D2 ABS warning lamp
B2 Wheel speed sensor (differential)		

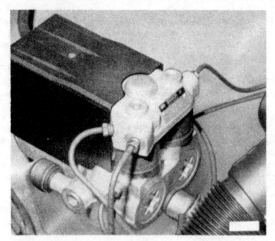

Fig. 13.98 Location of ABS hydraulic modulator on 1.8 ohc models (Sec 17)

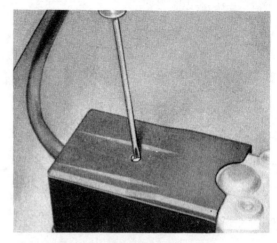

Fig. 13.99 Extracting hydraulic modulator cover screw (Sec 17)

compartment.

90 Disconnect the hydraulic pipes and move them aside.

91 Extract the screw and remove the plastic cover. Disconnect the battery negative lead.

92 Release the wiring harness clamp and pull out the wiring plug.

93 Loosen the front mounting nut, tilt the unit and remove it. No overhaul is possible.

94 Refitting is a reversal of removal. Check the brake hydraulic system.

Hydraulic modulator (2.0 and 2.2 models)

95 Disconnect the battery negative lead.

96 Remove the washer fluid reservoir.

97 Disconnect the hydraulic pipes from the brake pressure control valve (Chapter 9, Section 20).

98 Disconnect the hydraulic pipes from the hydraulic modulator and move the pipes aside.

99 Carry out the operations described in paragraphs 91 to 94.

Electronic control unit

100 Disconnect the battery earth lead.

101 The control unit is located behind the side panel at the left-hand footwell, this should be removed.

102 Pull the bonnet release handle to make clearance for withdrawal of the wiring plug.

103 Extract the upper screw, loosen the lower screw and withdraw the control unit.

104 Refitting is a reversal of removal.

Wheel speed sensors (front)

105 Raise the front of the car and support it securely. Unclip the wiring plug from the body member (Fig. 13.102). Disconnect the plug.

Fig. 13.100 Extracting wiring harness clamp screw (Sec 17)

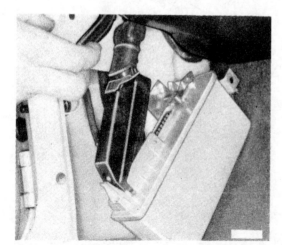

Fig. 13.101 Removing ABS electronic control unit (Sec 17)

Fig. 13.102 Wheel speed sensor wiring connector plug (Sec 17)

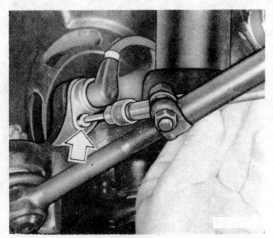

Fig. 13.103 Extracting wheel sensor socket-headed fixing screw – arrowed (Sec 17)

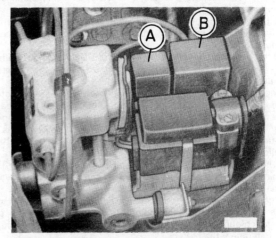

Fig. 13.104 ABS relays (Sec 17)

A   Solenoid valve relay   *B   Return pump motor relay*

106 Unclip the wheel speed sensor lead from its retainers.
107 Extract the socket-headed screws which hold the sensor to the hub carrier.
108 Remove the sensor, if necessary using a screwdriver to prise it out.
109 When fitting the sensor, coat its casing with multi-purpose grease and route the connecting lead correctly.
Speed sensors (rear)
110 Release the wiring plug and disconnect it, and unclip the sensor leads.
111 Extract the socket-headed screw which holds the sensor to the rear axle casing.
112 Withdraw the sensor, noting the sealing ring.
113 When refitting, smear the sensor casing with multi-purpose grease and route the connecting lead correctly.
Relays
114 The relays are generally located under the plastic cover of the hydraulic modulator. Access to them is described earlier in this sub-section.
115 The surge arrestor relay is located on the engine compartment rear bulkhead.
116 Disconnect the battery earth lead and disconnect the wiring plug before releasing the relay mounting screw.
Impulse sensors
117 Removal and refitting of the impulse sensor on the front wheel hub or drive pinion is carried out using a standard two-legged puller. Dismantling of the front hub is fully described in Chapter 11.

Hydraulic system – bleeding
118 Apart from the method described in Chapter 9, Section 3, one of the following additional methods of bleeding the brakes may be used.
119 If the master cylinder or the pressure regulating valve has been disconnected and reconnected then the complete system (both circuits) must be bled.
120 If a component of one circuit has been disturbed then only that particular circuit need be bled.
121 Bleed one rear brake and its diagonally opposite front brake. Repeat in this sequence on the remaining circuit if the complete system is to be bled.
122 Unless the pressure bleeding method is being used, do not forget to keep the fluid level in the master cylinder reservoir topped up to prevent air from being drawn into the system which would make any work done worthless.
123 Before commencing operations, check that all system hoses and pipes are in good condition with all unions tight and free from leaks.
124 Take great care not to allow hydraulic fluid to come into contact with the vehicle paintwork as it is an effective paint stripper. Wash off any spilled fluid immediately with cold water.
125 As the system incorporates a vacuum servo, destroy the vacuum by giving several applications of the brake pedal in quick succession.
Bleeding – using one way valve kit
126 There is a number of one-man, one-way brake bleeding kits available from motor accessory shops. It is recommended that one of

these kits is used wherever possible as it will greatly simplify the bleeding operation and also reduce the risk of air or fluid being drawn back into the system quite apart from being able to do the work without the help of an assistant.
127 To use the kit, connect the tube to the bleed screw and open the screw one half a turn.
128 Depress the brake pedal fully and slowly release it. The one-way valve in the kit will prevent expelled air from returning at the end of each pedal downstroke. Repeat this operation several times to be sure of ejecting all air from the system. Some kits include a translucent container which can be positioned so that the air bubbles can actually be seen being ejected from the system.
129 Tighten the bleed screw, remove the tube and repeat the operations on the remaining brakes.
130 On completion, depress the brake pedal. If it still feels spongy repeat the bleeding operations as air must still be trapped in the system.
Bleeding – using a pressure bleeding kit
131 These kits too are available from motor accessory shops and are usually operated by air pressure from the spare tyre.
132 By connecting a pressurised container to the master cylinder fluid reservoir, bleeding is then carried out by simply opening each bleed screw in turn and allowing the fluid to run out, rather like turning on a tap, until no air is visible in the expelled fluid.
133 By using this method, the large reserve of hydraulic fluid provides a safeguard against air being drawn into the master cylinder during bleeding which often occurs if the fluid level in the reservoir is not maintained.
134 Pressure bleeding is particularly effective when bleeding 'difficult' systems or when bleeding the complete system at time of routine fluid renewal.
All methods
135 When bleeding is completed, check and top up the fluid level in the master cylinder reservoir.
136 Check the feel of the brake pedal. If it feels at all spongy, air must still be present in the system and further bleeding is indicated. Failure to bleed satisfactorily after a reasonable period of the bleeding operation may be due to worn master cylinder seals.
137 Discard brake fluid which has been expelled. It is almost certain to be contaminated with moisture, air and dirt making it unsuitable for further use. Clean fluid should always be stored in an airtight container as it absorbs moisture readily (hygroscopic) which lowers its boiling point and and could affect braking perfromance under severe conditions.

18 Electrical system

Maintenance-free battery
1   On later models a sealed type, maintenance-free battery may be fitted.

2   Apart from keeping the terminals clean and the leads secure, nothing else is required.

3   A battery condition indicator is built into the top surface of the battery casing, which will show normally as a dark background with or without a green dot at its centre (photo).

4   If the indicator appears a light or bright yellow colour without a green dot, do not attempt to jump-start or charge the battery, but consult your dealer or a battery specialist.

5   Trickle charging of a maintenance-free battery (at a rate not exceeding one-tenth of the nominal amp-hour capacity) can be done in the normal way. Rapid or 'boost' charging should only be done by a dealer or battery specialist under carefully controlled conditions.

6   Check that the battery vent is not blocked before charging. If gas is not allowed to escape, there is a risk of bursting.

7   Where electrolyte is seen to spew through the vent during charging, stop or reduce the charge immediately. Wipe up and neutralise any spilled electrolyte.

8   Charging should cease as soon as the indicator shows green. Shake the battery a little every hour during charging and check the indicator colour. If no green indication appears after adequate charging time then renew the battery.

Alternator (2.0 CIH) – modification

9   From 1982, 'machine sensed' alternators are fitted to some vehicles. This has led to a change in the main wiring loom and alternator connections when compared with the 'battery sensed' alternator also fitted.

10 Fig. 13.105 shows the difference between alternator connections.

11 Machine sensed alternators can be fitted in place of the battery

18.3 Battery condition indicator (maintenance-free battery)

sensed type, as long as the wiring is modified to suit. To do this, mask off the connector with black and blue/white wires. Connect the remaining blue/white wire to the spade terminal (D+). Connect the other wires to their respective positive and negative terminals.

Alternator (1.8 ohc) – removal, overhaul and refitting

12 The Bosch or Delco-Remy alternators fitted to the 1.8 ohc engine are similar to those shown in Chapter 10. The procedures for removing, overhauling and refitting the units are therefore also similar, but note the information given in Section 9 of this Chapter when tensioning the drivebelt.

Starter motor (1.8 ohc) – removal, overhaul and refitting

13 The procedures for removing, overhauling and refitting the Bosch or Delco-Remy starter motor fitted to the 1.8 ohc engine are similar to those given in Chapter 10.

Windscreen wipers and washers
Wash/wipe delay relay – location and testing

14 The wash/wipe delay relay is shown in photo 37.2 (top left-hand corner) of Chapter 10.

15 If the relay is thought to have failed, test by substitution with a relay that is known to be serviceable.

16 On fuel injection models, the relay will be mounted above the control unit (photo).

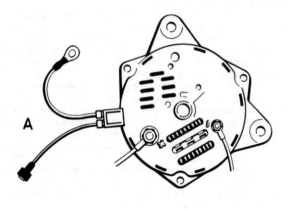

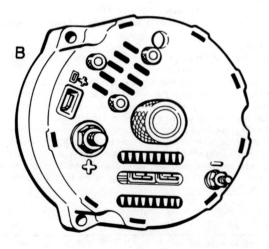

Fig. 13.105 Different types of alternator (Sec 18)

   A   Battery sensed   *B   Machine sensed*

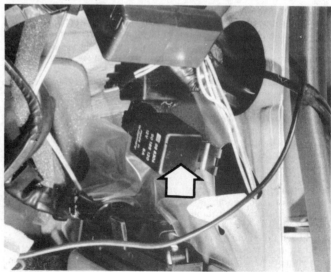

18.16 Wash/wipe delay relay (arrowed) on fuel injection models

Fault diagnosis

17 On models with a wash/wipe delay facility, it is not unknown for the wiper motor to start spontaneously. This is caused by a voltage 'spike' accidentally triggering the wiper motor control relay.

18 Various items of electrical equipment may produce these spikes. Some known causes are:

    (a) *Coil secondary (HT) winding defective (open-circuit)*
    (b) *Alternator voltage regulator defective*
    (c) *Washer pump wires to close to HT leads*
    (d) *Carburettor solenoid cut-off valve loose or defective*
    (e) *Poor earth connections in associated wiring*

19 Consult your GM dealer before embarking on an expensive and haphazard course of component substitution. The coil secondary winding may be checked with an ohmmeter: a small break in the winding will show up as infinite resistance on an ohmmeter, even though the ignition system may function normally as the HT voltage can jump the break.

20 Fitting a suppression capacitor to the alternator is the first line of attack if this is the source of the problem. Failing this, it may be necessary to renew the voltage regulator.

Washer fluid

21 It is recommended that only additives specially prepared for washer systems are used in the fluid reservoir. The use of household detergent or other cleaning agents is likely to damage the pump and rubber components of the system.

22 Never use cooling system antifreeze in a washer system or the paintwork will be damaged. In very cold weather, a small quantity of methylated spirit may be poured into the fluid to prevent freezing.

Headlamp wash/wipe system

23 Where this system is fitted, a combined windscreen and headlamp washer fluid reservoir will be found in the engine bay.

24 To remove a wiper arm, flip up the protective cap at the arm pivot and remove the arm retaining nut. Ease the arm off its splined spindle, having noted its fitted position. If necessary, use the flat of a screwdriver to lever the arm free. Retain the spindle spring.

25 Refit the arm in its previously noted position, using a reversal of the removal sequence (photo).

26 The washer jet assembly is fitted over the wiper motor spindle beneath the wiper arm. This unit can be slid off the spindle after removal of the arm and disconnection of its hose (photo). Upon refitting, use a pin to adjust the washer jet so that the water strikes the headlamp glass.

27 It is necessary to remove the front bumper, radiator grille and, on air conditioned models, the horn to gain access to the wiper motor securing bolts. Remove these bolts and the wiper arm. Ease the motor away from its mounting points within the front wheel before disconnecting the electrical connection.

28 Wiper motors are handed and are marked accordingly (L for left-hand, R for right-hand). Use a reversal of the removal procedure when fitting a motor.

Ignition switch – fault diagnosis

29 If the starter motor has been renewed because of failure of its piston to disengage from the flywheel ring gear, then GM recommend renewal of the ignition switch barrel also.

30 It is possible for the barrel to become stuck in the switch housing, which leads to the above fault.

Headlights (1983 on)

31 Although the headlight units have been modified, the various procedures for bulb renewal are still similar to those given in Chapter 10.

32 From 1983, some headlight units have an integral long range headlight fitted. Renewal of the bulb can be achieved by unclipping and removing the cover from the rear of the light housing, unclipping the bulb and lifting it from its holder (photos).

33 Both the main and long range headlight bulbs are halogen types. Do not touch the glass of these bulbs with the naked hand but use a clean, dry piece of paper if touching the glass cannot be avoided. If contaminated, clean the bulb glass with a cloth moistened in methylated spirit.

Long range headlights – adjustment

34 Beam adjustment is effected by turning the two nylon bolts which protrude from the top of the light housing (photo). These are accessible with the bonnet open. Refer to Section 27 of Chapter 10.

18.25 Fitting a headlamp wiper arm

18.26 Headlamp washer jet

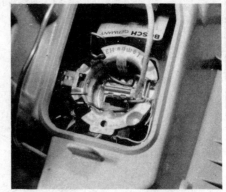

18.32A Long range headlamp bulb holder

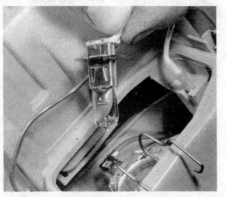

18.32B Long range headlamp bulb

18.34 Long range headlamp beam adjustment screws (arrowed)

Instrument panel – removal and refitting

35 Because of the various design changes which have taken place, the procedure given in Section 39 of Chapter 10 can no longer by relied on as an accurate guide.

36 If it is decided to remove any part of the instrument panel, exercise a degree of caution and common sense. Work in a logical order, noting the fitted position of each component before removal and labelling it if necessary to avoid confusion during reassembly. Do not use excessive force to remove a component but look for a hidden fastener; plastic components are easily broken and can be expensive to replace.

37 Do not forget to disconnect the battery before starting work. Shorting between electrical connections can cause fire, damage and personal injury.

Fuses (later models)

38 With the introduction of new electrical components, fuse locations for later vehicles are likely to differ from those shown in Chapter 10. Refer to Fig. 13.106.

Sunroof fuse rating

39 If the fuse serving the electrically-operated sunroof blows, replace it with a 25 amp rated fuse (as opposed to the 20 amp fuse originally fitted).

Power-operated exterior mirrors

40 Where fitted, the power-operated exterior mirrors are controlled by a four-way switch mounted in the tray of the driver's door. This switch controls both passenger's and driver's mirror according to switch setting.

41 A button in the switch centre will switch on mirror heating (where fitted) for 15 minutes; the button will indicate green when heating is on.

42 To remove the switch, carefully lever it from the tray by using the flat of a screwdriver inserted in the slot provided. Once released, pull the switch upwards to expose its electrical connector (photo). The switch is a sealed unit and must be renewed if unserviceable.

43 Each mirror can be removed by first detaching the small triangular trim from the inside of the door to expose the securing screws. Remove the screws to release the mirror and then separate the electrical connections (photo).

Power-operated windows

44 Where fitted, the power-operated windows are controlled by rocker switches mounted in the centre console. There is one switch to operate each window and a button to render all switches inoperative (child safety device). Where power-operated windows are fitted to the

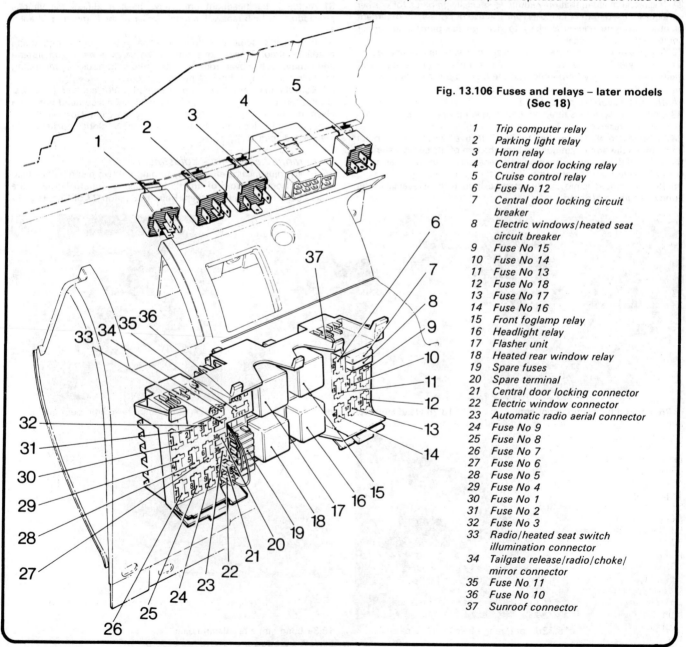

Fig. 13.106 Fuses and relays – later models (Sec 18)

1   Trip computer relay
2   Parking light relay
3   Horn relay
4   Central door locking relay
5   Cruise control relay
6   Fuse No 12
7   Central door locking circuit breaker
8   Electric windows/heated seat circuit breaker
9   Fuse No 15
10 Fuse No 14
11 Fuse No 13
12 Fuse No 18
13 Fuse No 17
14 Fuse No 16
15 Front foglamp relay
16 Headlight relay
17 Flasher unit
18 Heated rear window relay
19 Spare fuses
20 Spare terminal
21 Central door locking connector
22 Electric window connector
23 Automatic radio aerial connector
24 Fuse No 9
25 Fuse No 8
26 Fuse No 7
27 Fuse No 6
28 Fuse No 5
29 Fuse No 4
30 Fuse No 1
31 Fuse No 2
32 Fuse No 3
33 Radio/heated seat switch illumination connector
34 Tailgate release/radio/choke/mirror connector
35 Fuse No 11
36 Fuse No 10
37 Sunroof connector

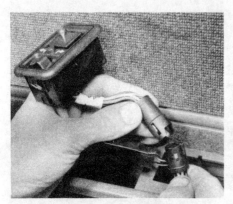

18.42 Removing exterior mirror control switch

18.43 Exterior mirror fixing screws

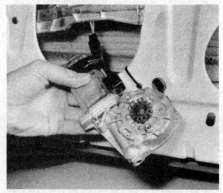

18.47 Removing an electric window winder motor

rear doors, there is also a rocker switch fitted to each door.

45 In the event of a fault occurring, first check the circuit fuse and then the wiring connections for cleanliness and security.

46 Each switch is a sealed unit and must be renewed if suspected of failure.

47 Refer to Section 10 of Chapter 12 and remove the door interior trim to gain access to the motor retaining bolts. Remove these bolts and manoeuvre the motor clear of the door (photo). With the battery disconnected, unplug the motor electrical connection.

48 The motor is a sealed unit and should be renewed if unserviceable. After refitting, test motor operation before fitting the door trim.

Central door locking system – fault diagnosis

49 If the system operates spontaneously, suspect moisture entering the pull-switch of the front passenger door and causing the system relay to earth.

50 A temporary cure is to disconnect the white plug from the pull-switch. Fit a new switch for a permanent cure.

51 The overload circuit breaker, fitted to systems after early 1983, is designed to interrupt power to the door lock motors if the system is operated quickly several times. After a short time the breaker will reactivate the system automatically. The circuit breaker is located inside the fuse box.

Trip computer

52 A trip computer is fitted to certain models which displays the following information digitally by pressing a button.

> Time
> Fuel consumption
> Average speed
> Range
> Stopwatch facility
> Outside temperature

53 Commencing with model year 1986, a modified trip computer is fitted, having round instead of square pushbuttons – but the setting and display change procedure for all models is contained in the driver's handbook supplied by the vehicle manufacturers.

54 Calibration or repair of the trip computer is not within the scope of the home mechanic but should be entrusted to your dealer. However, once a fault is diagnosed, removal and refitting of the individual components of the system may be carried out in the following way.

Trip computer

55 Extract the two upper and the two lower instrument trim panel fixing screws.

56 Remove the instrument panel cowl.

57 Press the trip computer out of its panel and disconnect the wiring multi-plug.

58 Fitting the trip computer is a reversal of removal but if a new unit is being purchased, make sure that it has been calibrated by your dealer.

Odometer frequency sensor

59 This sensor is screwed into the transmission. Disconnect the wiring multi-plug and unscrew the sensor. Be prepared for oil loss.

60 Refitting is a reversal of removal. Check and top up the transmission oil.

Fig. 13.107 Trip computer withdrawn (Sec 18)

Multi-plug arrowed

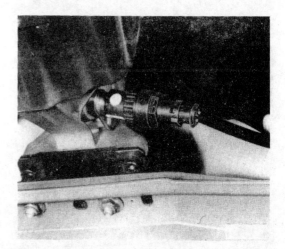

Fig. 13.108 Odometer frequency sensor (Sec 18)

Trip computer relay (fuel injection engine)

61 Prise out the lighting switch from the facia panel and then disconnect the wiring multi-plug.

62 Extract the screws and remove the facia panel under cover.

63 Remove the steering column lower shroud.

64 Extract the screws and remove the facia left-hand trim panel.

65 Pull the relay from the facia panel crossmember.

66 Refitting is a reversal of removal.

Fuel flow meter (carburettor engine)

67 The fuel flow meter is located at the side of the engine compartment.

68 Disconnect the wiring multi-plug and all the fuel hoses and unscrew the flow meter fixing screws.

69 Refit by reversing the removal operations.

Display bulb – renewal

70 With the trip computer withdrawn as previously described, grip the bulbholder with a pair of pliers and twist it and withdraw it. Fit the new bulb to the holder and then fit the holder.

Temperature sensor

71 The outside air temperature sensor is located on the left-hand front wing valance. Disconnect the multi-plug and then pull the sensor from the air deflector plate.

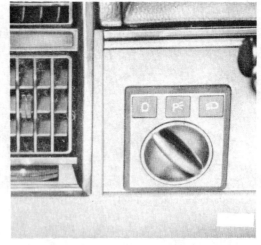

Fig. 13.109 Facia panel lighting switch (Sec 18)

Fig. 13.110 Facia left-hand trim panel screws – arrowed (Sec 18)

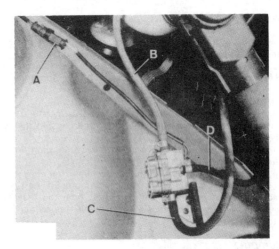

Fig. 13.111 Fuel flowmeter, carburettor engines (Sec 18)

A Multi-plug   C Carburettor hose
B Pump hose   D Return hose

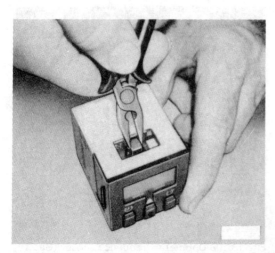

Fig. 13.112 Removing trip computer display bulb (Sec 18)

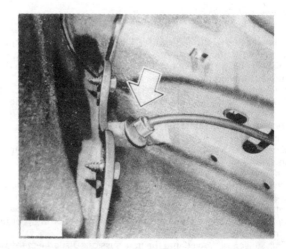

Fig. 13.113 Temperature sensor – arrowed (Sec 18)

Electrically-operated boot lid lock

72 Top of the range models are fitted with a solenoid-operated boot lock. With the ignition switched on, the boot lid can be opened by pressing the switch button under the lower edge of the facia panel.

73 The boot is closed manually in the normal way.

Wiring diagrams – explanatory note

74 The wiring diagrams are laid out to show the circuit of a given component by the shortest possible route. The bottom line of the diagram is the earth track; the numbers along the bottom line are known as track numbers and serve to locate an item using the key.

75 Where a number in a box is found, this indicates that the circuit continues in the track number(s) given in the box.

76 Using Fig. 13.115 as an example, following track 82 (on the first sheet) gives the horn circuit. Starting at the bottom, the circuit is via the horn switch (S5.5) and the horn itself (H2) to fuse F5. The fuse is connected to rail 15 (live with igition on). The four boxes in track 81 give the other track numbers supplied by the same fuse.

77 Many of the systems and components shown in the wiring diagrams are not fitted to vehicles intended for the UK market. References to 'right-hand' and 'left-hand' may not always be correct for RHD vehicles.

Key to Fig. 13.114

No	Track	Component	No	Track	Component
E20	134	Front foglamp (LH)	P6	98, 99	Fuel gauge sender (Diesel)
E21	135	Front foglamp (RH)	P7	194, 195	Tachometer
E22	131	Front spotlight (LH)	P8	197	Oil pressure gauge
E23	132	Front spotlight (RH)	P9	196	Voltmeter
E24	138	Rear foglamp	P10	197	Oil pressure sender
E25	157	Seat heating mat	P11	178 to 183,	Airflow meter
E26	201	Light switch illumination	P12	190,191	Temperature sensor
E27	203,204	Interior lamp (LH rear)	R4	95,96	Glow plugs (Diesel)
E28	205,206	Interior lamp (RH rear)	R5	95,96	Glow plugs (Diesel)
F3 to			R8	150	Air conditioning blower resistor
F14	Various	Fuses in fusebox	R7	200	Carburettor preheating
F15	146	Fuse (air conditioning)	R8	187 to 189	Fuel injector series resistors
F16	167	Fuse (towing socket)	R9	184	Fuel injector series resistors
F17	223	Circuit breaker	S5.6	101, 103,	Windscreen wiper switch
F18	240	Circuit breaker		115 to 117	
G3	86	Battery, RH (Diesel)	S5.7	105,111	Wiper motor contact switch
G4	88	Battery, LH (Diesel)	S8	247	Stop-light switch
G5	250	Frequency sensor	S19	94,95	Starter switch (Diesel)
H15	98	Low fuel warning light (Diesel)	S20	125,127	Rear wiper switch
H16	96	Glow plug light (Diesel)	S21	133,134	Front foglamp switch
H17	159	Trailer direction indicator repeater	S22	138,139	Rear foglamp switch
H18	199	Horn	S23	142	Tailgate/boot lid release switch
K3	93,94	Starter relay (Diesel)	S24	147 to 150	Air conditioning blower switch
K4	130,131	Spotlight relay	S25	152	Air conditioning function switch
K5	134,135	Front foglamp relay	S26	152	Evaporator inlet control (a/c)
K6	145,146	Air conditioning relay	S27	152	Pressure switch (a/c)
K7	146,147	Air conditioning blower relay	S28	152	Compressor cut-out (a/c)
K8	102,104	Wiper delay relay	S29	154	Temperature switch (a/c)
K9	109, 115	Washer delay relay	S30	156,157	Seat heater switch
K10	160	Trailer flasher unit	S31	203	Door switch (LH rear)
K11	175 to 180	Double relay	S32	205	Door switch (RH rear)
K12	237 to 239	Central locking relay	S33	211,212	Sunroof switch (open/close)
K13	242 to 244	Central locking relay	S34	215,216	Sunroof switch (tilt)
K14	248 to 254	Cruise control	S35	212	Microswitch
K15	173 to 190	Timing control (fuel injection)	S36	216	Microswitch
M4	101 to 104	Windscreen wiper motor	S37	220 to 230	Window motor switches
M5	103, 111	Washer pump	S38	220	Isolator switch
M6	108,110,		S39	225,226	Window switch (LH rear)
	111	Headlight wiper motor (LH)	S40	227,228	Window switch (RH rear)
M7	116,118,		S41	236,237	Door locking switch
	119	Headlight wiper motor (RH)	S42	239	Door locking switch
M8	122 to 124	Rear window wiper motor	S43	252,254	Cruise control switch
M9	126	Washer pump (rear)	S44	172,173	Throttle valve switch
M10	146	Air conditioning blower motor	S45	248	Clutch switch (cruise control)
M11	154	Auxiliary blower motor	X1	162,169	Trailer socket
M12	91 to 93	Starter motor (Diesel)	X2	47,67,81	Accessory terminal
M13	214	Sunroof motor	Y1	152	Air conditioning compressor
M14	223,224	Window motor (LH front)	Y2	149	Idle speed increse solenoid
M15	230,231	Window motor (RH front)	Y3	142	Boot release solenoid
M16	225,226	Window motor (LH rear)	Y4	113	Headlight washer valve
M17	227,228	Window motor (RH rear)	Y5	97	Fuel cut-off solenoid (Diesel)
M18	243	Door lock actuator (RH front)	Y6	172,173	Auxiliary air valve
M19	237,238	Door lock actuator (LH rear)	Y7	190	Fuel injectors
M20	243,244	Door lock actuator (RH rear)	Y8	249	Actuator (cruise control)
M21	175	Fuel pump			

Colour code

BL	Blue
HLB	Light Blue
BR	Brown
LI	Violet
GE	Yellow
GR	Grey
GN	Green
RT	Red
WS	White
SW	Black

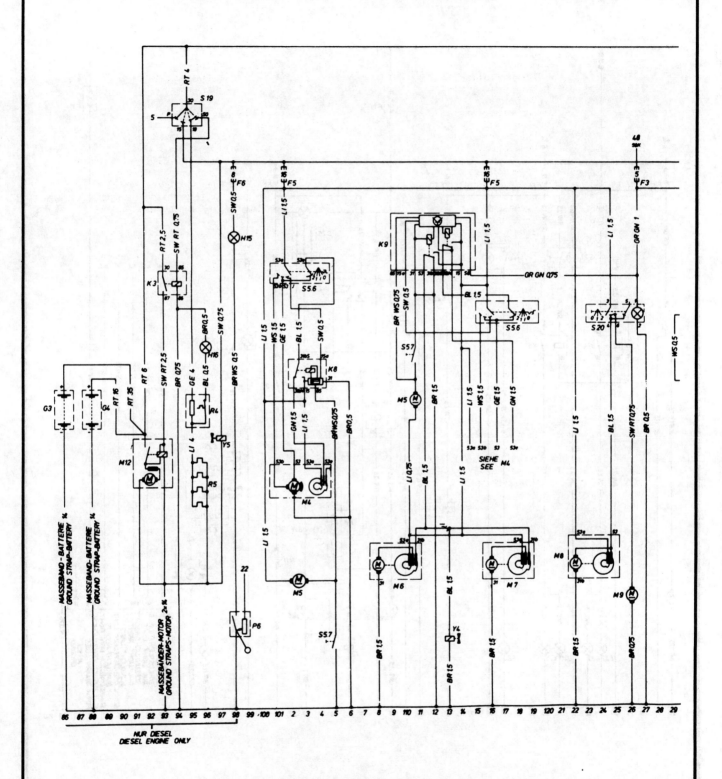

Fig. 13.114 Wiring diagram (schematic) – all models 1978 to 1982

Continued from Chapter 10

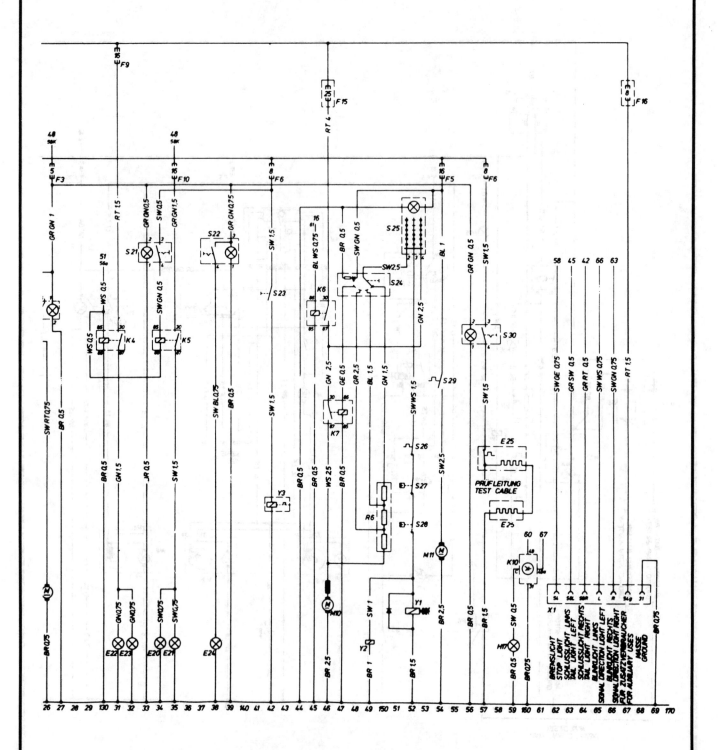

Fig. 13.114 Wiring diagram (schematic) – all models 1978 to 1982 (continued)

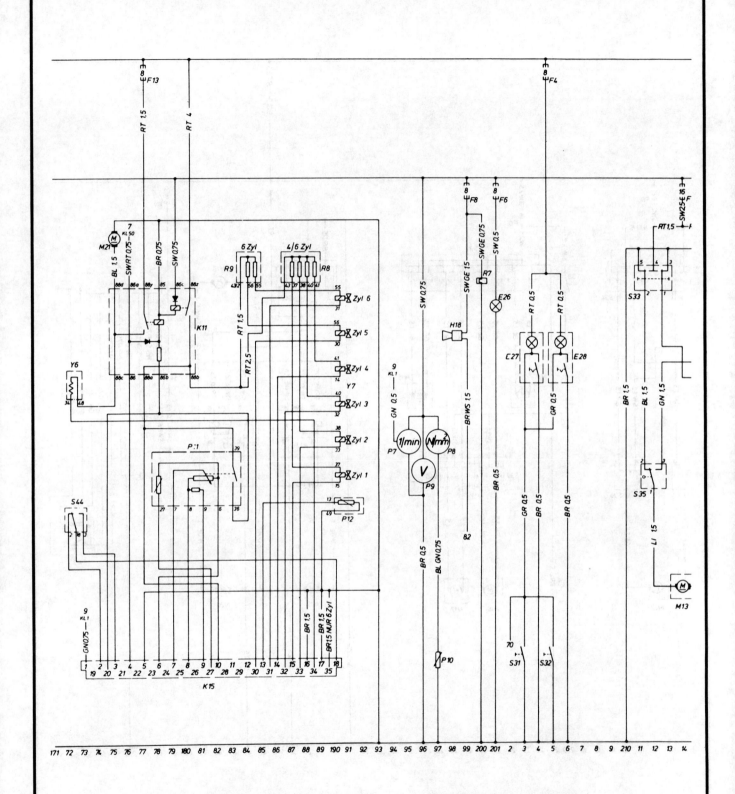

Fig. 13.114 Wiring diagram (schematic) – all models 1978 to 1982 (continued)

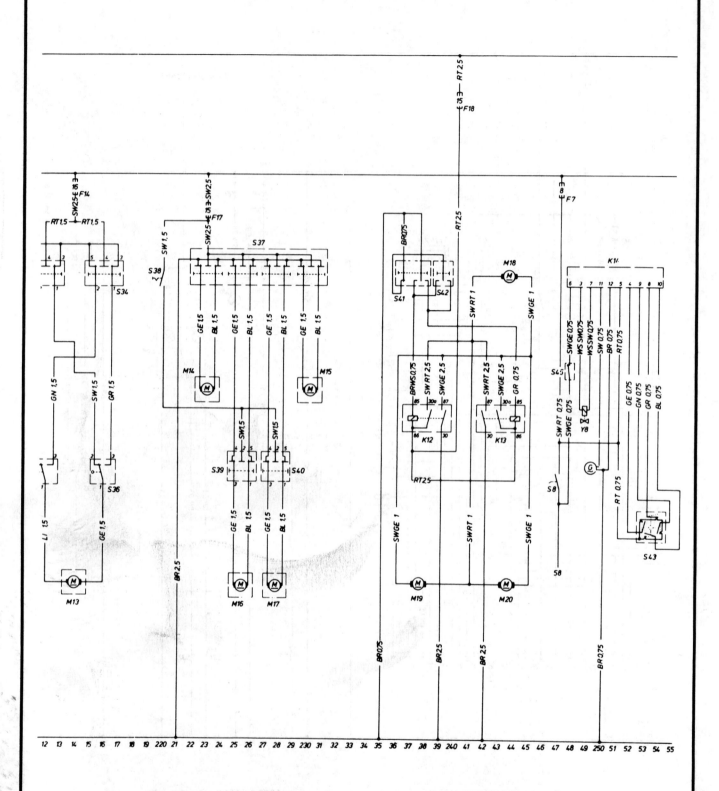

Fig. 13.114 Wiring diagram (schematic) – all models 1978 to 1982 (continued)

Key to Fig. 13.115

No	Track	Component	No	Track	Component
E1	41	Parking light (RH)	H16	96	Glow plug light (Diesel)
E2	42	Tail light (RH)	H17	159	Trailer direction indicator repeater
E3	43	Number plate light	H19	278,279	Buzzer (headlights on)
E4	44	Parking light (LH)	H20	75	Choke warning light
E5	45	Tail light (LH)	H23	401,402	Radio receiver
E6	49	Engine bay light	K1	17,18	Heated rear window relay
E7	51	Main beam (RH)	K2	60	Flasher unit
E8	52	Main beam (LH)	K4	130,131	Spotlight relay
E9	54	Dipped beam (RH)	K5	134,135	Foglamp relay
E10	55	Dipped beam (LH)	K6	145,146	Air conditioning relay
E11	46,48	Instrument lighting	K7	146,147	Blower relay (a/c)
E12	50	Automatic transmission selector light	K8	102 to 104	Wiper delay relay
E13	68	Luggage area light	K9	111,112	Washer relay
E14	70	Interior light	K10	160	Trailer flasher unit
E15	78	Glovebox light	K14	246 to 254	Cruise control unit
E16	77	Cigarette lighter light	K15	346 to 356	Fuel injection unit
E17	79	Reversing lamp (RH)	K16	275,276	Seat heater relay
E18	80	Reversing lamp (LH)	K17	284,285	Parking lamp relay
E19	18	Heated rear window	K18	287,288	Horn relay
E20	134	Front foglamp (LH)	K19	267,268	Level control relay
E21	135	Front foglamp (RH)	K20	8,10,29,33	Ignition module
E22	131	Spotlamp (LH)	K21	264 to 267	Level control sensor
E23	132	Spotlamp (RH)	K22	314 to 322	Taxi alarm timer
E24	138	Rear foglamp (LH)	K23	247,248	Cruise control relay (auto)
E25	157,272 to 275	Heated seat mat (LH)	K24	397,398	Radiator blower relay
E29	330	Taxi roof sign	K25	94 to 97	Preheater relay (Diesel)
E30	272 to 275	Heated seat mat (RH)	K28	308,309	Day running lights relay
E32	74	Clock light	K31	342 to 344	Fuel pump relay
E37	384	Vanity mirror light	K33	407,408	Idle speed increase relay
E38	219	Computer illumination	K34	32 to 35	Idle stabilization unit
E39	137	Rear foglamp (RH)	K35	189 to 192	Mirror heater timer
F1 to			K36	223 to 225	Computer relay
F18	Various	Fuses in fusebox	K37	195 to 202	Central locking relay
F19	202	Circuit breaker	K38	373,374	Converter clutch relay
F20	198	Circuit breaker	L2	9,30	Ignition coil
F21	146	Air conditioning fuse	M1	5 to 7	Starter motor
F24	268	Level control fuse	M3	37 to 40	Heater blower motor
F25	19	Voltage stabiliser	M4	101 to 104	Windscreen wiper motor
G1	1	Battery	M4	397	Radiator blower motor
G2	13 to 15	Alternator	M5	103	Washer pump
G3	86	Battery, RH (Diesel)	M6	108 to 112	Headlight wiper motor (LH)
G4	88	Battery, LH (Diesel)	M7	114 to 117	Headlight wiper motor (RH)
G5	250	Frequency sensor	M8	122 to 124	Rear wiper motor
H1	72	Radio receiver	M9	126	Rear washer pump
H2	82,223	Horn	M10	146	Air conditioning blower motor
H3	64	Direction indicator repeater	M11	154	Auxiliary blower motor
H4	27	Oil pressure warning light	M12	91 to 93	Starter motor (Diesel)
H5	25	Braking system warning light	M13	240	Sunroof motor
H6	23	Hazard warning repeater	M14	205	Window motor (LH front)
H7	15	Charging system warning light	M15	212	Window motor (RH front)
H8	53	Main beam pilot light	M16	207	Window motor (LH rear)
H9	57	Stop-lamp (RH)	M17	210	Window motor (RH rear)
H10	58	Stop-lamp (LH)	M18	201	Lock actuator (RH front)
H11	62	Direction indicator (RH front)	M19	201	Lock actuator (LH rear)
H12	63	Direction indicator (RH rear)	M20	201	Lock actuator (RH rear)
H13	65	Direction indicator (LH front)	M21	342	Fuel pump (fuel injection)
H14	66	Direction indicator (LH rear)	M22	268	Level control compressor
H15	98	Low fuel warning light (Diesel)	M26	402,403	Radio aerial motor

268

Key to Fig. 13.115 (continued)

No	Track	Component	No	Track	Component
M28	172 to 174	Mirror adjustment	S27	152,408	Pressure switch (a/c)
M30	179 to 183	Mirror adjustment and heating (LH)	S28	152,408	Compressor cut-off switch (a/c)
M31	186 to 190	Mirror adjustment and heating (RH)	S29	154,398	Radiator blower switch (a/c)
M32	201	Lock actuator (LH front)	S30	156,157	Seat heater switch
P1	22	Fuel gauge	S31	72	Door switch (LH rear)
P2	20	Temperature gauge	S32	68	Door switch (RH rear)
P3	73	Clock	S35	238,239	Sunroof limit switch (open/close)
P4	21,221	Fuel gauge sender	S36	241,242	Sunroof limit switch (tilt)
P5	20	Temperature gauge sender	S37	205 to 213	Window switches (master)
P7	233	Tachometer	S38	204	Window isolator switch
P8	235	Oil pressure gauge	S39	207,208	Window switch (LH rear)
P9	234	Voltmeter	S40	209,210	Window switch (RH rear)
P10	235	Oil pressure sender	S41	195,196	Locking switch (LH front)
P11	366,367	Airflow meter (fuel injection)	S42	197,198	Locking switch (RH front)
P12	366,367	Temperature sensor (fuel injection)	S43	251 to 254	Cruise control switch
P13	223	Temperature sensor (outside air)	S44	366,367	Throttle valve switch (fuel injection)
P14	215,216	Distance sensor (trip computer)	S45	245,246	Clutch switch (cruise control)
P15	217,218	Fuel meter (trip computer)	S46	271,272	Seat heater switch
P16	196	Release sensor (central locking)	S47	280,281	Contact switch (headlight buzzer)
R2	83	Automatic starting device	S48	327,328	Taxi sign switch
R3	76	Cigarette lighter	S49	321	Alarm switch (taxi)
R5	95 to 97	Glow plugs	S50	75	Choke light switch
R6	150	Blower resistor (a/c)	S51	152,408	Temperature switch (Diesel)
R11	46	Instrument lighting rheostat	S61	405,407	Pressure switch (PAS)
S1	6,7,94,96	Starter switch	S62	366,367	Thermotime switch (fuel injection)
S2	46,313,314	Lighting switch	S66	35	Vacuum switch
S2.1	71	Interior light switch	S67	171 to 174	Mirror switch (adjust only)
S3	36 to 39	Heater blower switch	S68	177 to 185	Mirror switch (adjust and heat)
S4	16,17	Heated rear window switch	S70	374	Vacuum switch
S5	Various	Steering column multi-function switch	S71	374	Engine temperature switch
S5.2	50,51,297,299,319,320	Dipswitch	S72	374	Oil pressure switch (auto)
			U1	389 to 394	Voltage converter
S5.3	62,63,65,289,296	Direction indicator/hazard warning switch	U3	216 to 224	Trip computer
			U3.1	222	Switch – priority clock
S5.4	36,37,301 to 303	Parking light switch	U3.2	222	Switch – function select
			U3.3	222	Switch – function reset
S5.5	82,288	Horn	V2	111	Headlight washer diode
S5.6	101 to 103	Windscreen wiper switch	X1	162 to 169	Trailer socket
S5.7	105	Wiper contact switch	X2	48,72,75,142,167,196,198,204,240	Auxiliary connector
S7	80	Reversing lamp switch			
S8	58,244,373	Stop-lamp switch	X3	319	Radio telephone connector
			Y1	152,408	Compressor clutch (a/c)
S10	7	Starter inhibitor switch (auto)	Y2	149,405,410	Idle speed increase solenoid
S11	24	Brake fluid level warning switch			
S12	25	Clutch travel switch	Y3	142	Boot lid release solenoid
S13	26	Handbrake switch	Y4	114	Headlight washer solenoid
S14	27	Oil pressure switch	Y5	99	Fuel cut-off solenoid (Diesel)
S15	67	Load area light switch	Y6	366	Auxiliary air valve (fuel injection)
S16	69	Door switch (RH front)	Y7	366	Fuel injectors
S17	70	Door switch (LH front)	Y8	247 to 250	Cruise control actuator
S18	78	Glovebox light switch	Y9	266	Level control solenoid valve
S20	125 to 127	Rear wiper switch	Y10	11,12,33,34	Distributor
S21	133,134	Front foglamp switch			
S22	138,139	Rear foglamp switch	Y11	8,10,31,32	Hall sensor
S23	142	Boot lid release switch	Y13	366	Cold start (fuel injection)
S24	147 to 150	Air conditioning blower switch	Y16	374	Converter clutch valve (auto)
S25	152	Air conditioning function switch	Y17	85	Idle cut-off solenoid
S26	152,408	Evaporator inlet control (a/c)			

Wiring colour code as Fig. 13.114

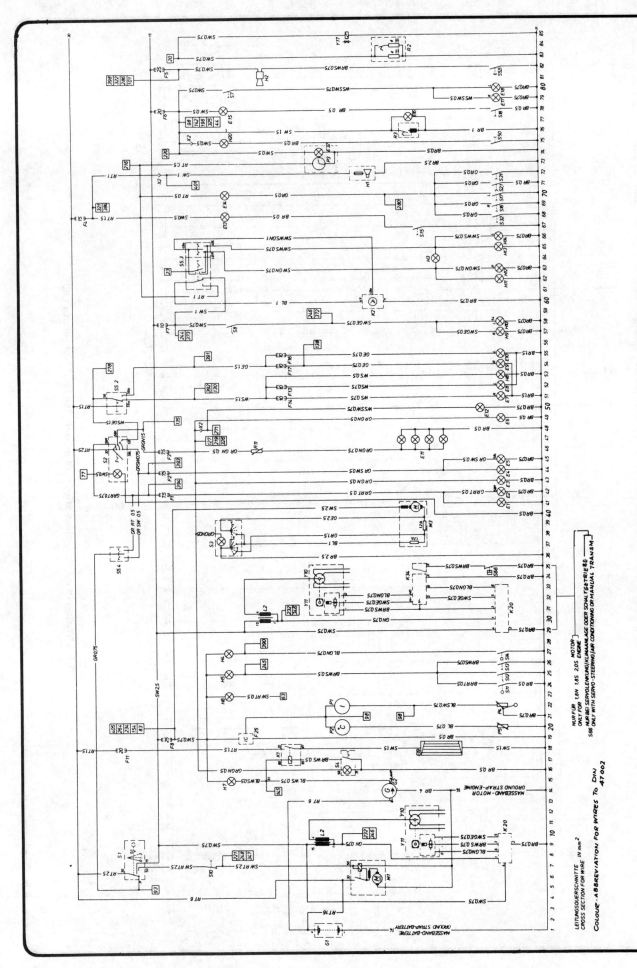

Fig. 13.115 Wiring diagram (schematic) – all models 1983 to 1984

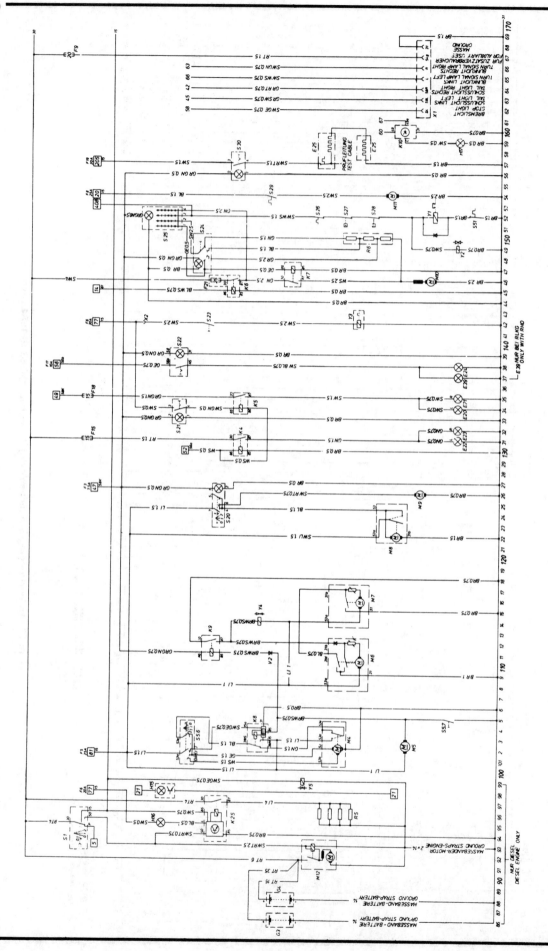

Fig. 13.115 Wiring diagram (schematic) – all models 1983 to 1984 (continued)

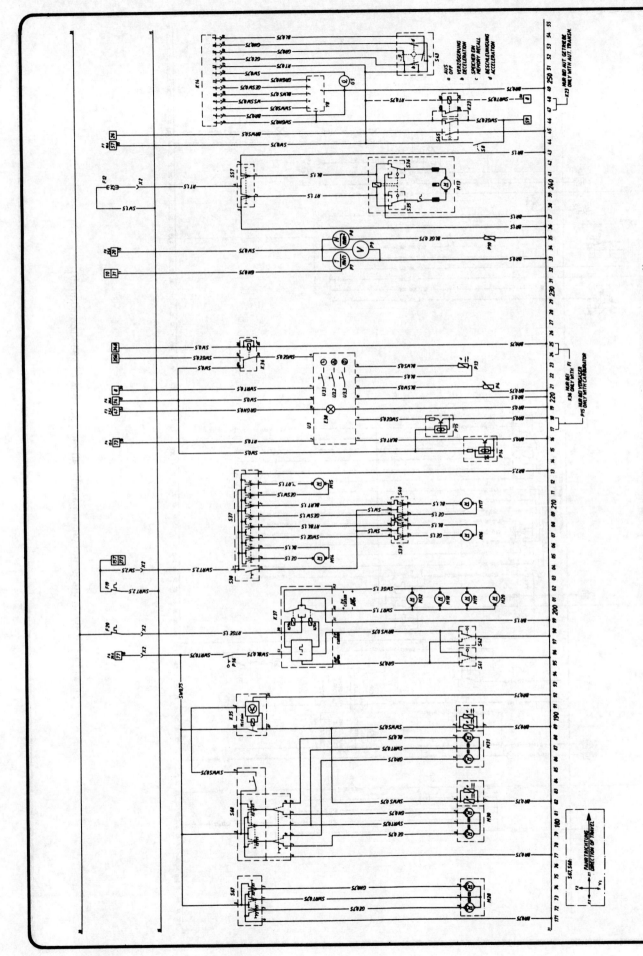

Fig. 13.115 Wiring diagram (schematic) – all models 1983 to 1984 (continued)

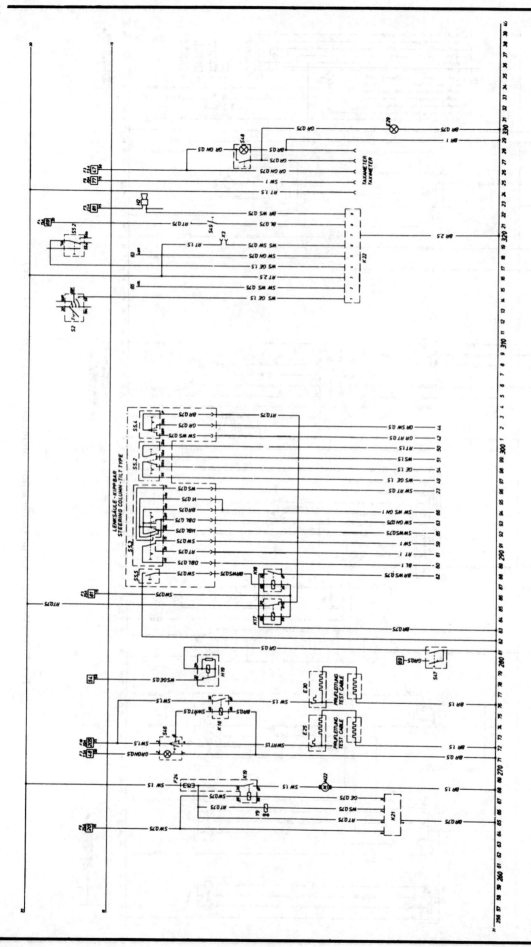

Fig. 13.115 Wiring diagram (schematic) – all models 1983 to 1984 (continued)

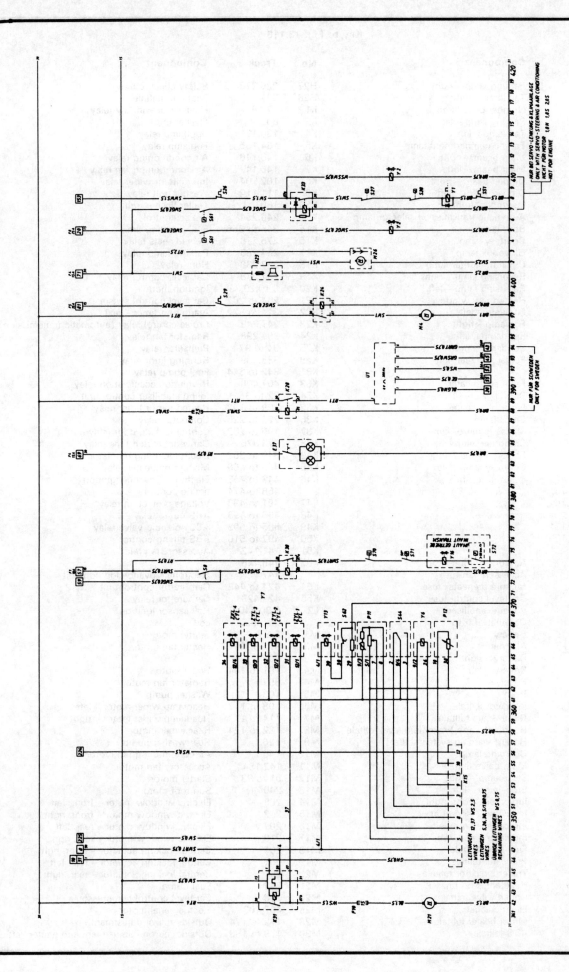

Fig. 13.115 Wiring diagram (schematic) – all models 1983 to 1984 (continued)

Key to Fig. 13.116

No	Track	Component	No	Track	Component
E1	41	Parking lamp – right	H27	226,228	Safety check buzzer
E2	42	Tail lamp – right	H28	227	Seat belt telltale
E3	43	Number plate lamp	K1	17,18	Heater rear window relay
E4	44	Parking lamp – left	K2	60	Flasher unit
E5	45	Tail lamp – left	K4	130,131	Spotlamp relay
E6	49	Engine compartment lamp	K5	134,135	Foglamp relay
E7	51	Main beam – right	K6	145,146	Air conditioning relay
E8	52	Main beam – left	K7	146,147	Air conditioning fan relay
E9	54	Dipped beam – right	K8	102,104	Intermittent wiper relay
E10	55	Dipped beam – left	K9	111,112	Washer unit relay
E11	46,48	Instrument lighting	K10	160	Trailer flasher unit
E12	50	Automatic transmission selector lamp	K14	246,254	Cruise control
E13	68	Boot lamp	K15	346 to 356	Fuel injection timer
E14	71	Courtesy lamp	K16	275,276	Heated seats relay
E15	78	Glovebox lamp	K17	284,285	Parking lamp relay
E16	77	Cigarette lighter lamp	K18	287,288	Horn relay
E17	79	Reversing lamp – right	K19	267,268	Car level control relay
E18	80	Reversing lamp – left	K20	8,10,29,33	Ignition module
E19	18	Heated rear window	K21	264 to 267	Car level control sensor
E20	134	Foglamp – left	K22	314 to 322	Alarm unit timer – taxi
E21	135	Foglamp – right	K23	247,248	Cruise control relay (automatic transmission)
E22	131	Spotlamp – left	K24	397,298	Radiator fan relay
E23	132	Spotlamp – right	K25	94 to 97	Preheater relay
E24	138	Foglamp – rear, left	K28	388,389	Running light relay
F25	157,272 to 275	Front seat heater	K31	342 to 344	Fuel pump relay
E29	330	Roof sign (taxi)	K33	407,408	Revolution acceleration relay
E30	276 to 279	Front seat heater	K34	32 to 35	Idling stabiliser control unit
E32	74	Clock lamp	K35	189 to 192	Heated mirror timer relay
E37	384	Make-up mirror lamp	K36	223 to 225	Computer relay
E38	219	Computer lamp	K37	195 to 202	Central locking door relay
E39	137	Foglamp – rear, right	K38	373,375	Converter clutch time relay
E41	68,70	Courtesy lamp delay	K40	349 to 353	Electronic idling regulator
F1 to	42,44,45,	Fuses in fusebox	K45	459 to 460	Mixture preheater relay
F20	68,82,78,		K46	448 to 453,	Electronic advance ignition
	58,19,167,			468 to 474	timing control
	342,18,240,		K47	491 to 493	Voltage protection relay
	52,51,131,		K48	496 to 499	ABS pump relay
	55,54,135,		K49	505 to 508	ABS solenoid valve relay
	202,198		K50	497 to 510	ABS timing control
F21	146	Air conditioning fuse	K51	141,142	Accessory fan relay
F22	142	Accessory fan fuse	K52	445,446,	
F23	460	Mixture preheater fuse		447	Electronic advance ignition coil
F24	268	Car level control fuse	K54	424 to 442	Carburettor control unit
F25	19	Voltage stabiliser	K55	422,423	Carburettor relay
F26	422	Carburettor fuse	L2	9,30,446,	Hall sensor ignition
G1	1	Battery		467,468	coil
G2	13 to 15	Alternator	M1	5,6,7	Starter motor
G3	86	Battery – right	M3	37,38,39,	Heater fan motor
G4	88	Battery – left		40	
H1	72	Receiver	M4	101 to 104	Wiper motor
H2	82,223	Horn	M4	397	Radiator fan motor
H3	64	Indicator telltale	M5	103	Washer pump
H4	27	Oil pressure telltale	M6	108 to 112	Headlamp wiper motor – left
H5	25	Handbrake and brake fluid level telltale	M7	114 to 117	Headlamp wiper motor – right
H6	23	Hazard warning system telltale	M8	122 to 124	Rear wiper motor
H7	15	Charging lamp	M9	126	Rear washer pump
H8	53	Main beam telltale	M10	146	Air conditioning fan motor
H9	57	Stop-lamp – right	M11	142,154	Accessory fan motor
H10	58	Stop-lamp – left	M12	91 to 93	Starter motor
H11	62	Indicator – front, right	M13	240	Sun roof motor
H12	63	Indicator – rear, right	M14	205	Electric window motor – front, left
H13	65	Indicator – front, left	M15	212	Electric window motor – front, right
H14	66	Indicator – rear, left	M16	207	Electric window motor – rear, left
H15	58	Fuel level telltale	M17	210	Electric window motor – rear, right
H16	96	Preheater telltale	M18	201	Central locking actuator – front, right
H17	159	Trailer indicator telltale	M19	201	Central locking actuator – rear, left
H19	278,279	Headlamps on buzzer	M20	201	Central locking actuator – rear, right
H20	75	Choke valve telltale	M21	342	Fuel pump
H23	401,402	Electric aerial	M22	268	Car level control compressor
H25	184	Mirror heater telltale	M26	402,403	Electric aerial motor
H26	505	ABS telltale	M28	172 to 174	Outside mirror adjustment
			M30	179 to 183	Outside mirror – adjustment and heater, left

Key to Fig. 13.116 (continued)
Colour code as Fig. 13.114

No	Track	Component	No	Track	Component
M31	186 to 190	Outside mirror – adjustment and heater, right	S31	72	Courtesy light switch – rear, left
M32	201	Central locking actuator – front, left	S32	68	Courtesy light switch – rear, right
M33	367	Idling power unit	S35	238,239	Sunroof switch
M34	494	Hydroaggregate pump	S36	241,242	Sunroof switch
P1	22	Fuel gauge	S37	205 to 213	Electric window switch
P2	20	Temperature gauge	S38	204	Children safety switch
P3	73	Clock	S39	207,208	Electric window switch – rear, left
P4	20,221	Fuel sensor	S40	209,210	Electric window switch – rear, right
P5	20	Temperature sensor	S41	195,196	Central locking switch – front, left
P7	233	Tachometer	S42	197,198	Central locking switch – front, right
P8	235	Oil pressure gauge	S43	251 to 254	Cruise control switch
P9	234	Voltmeter	S44	366,367	Throttle valve switch
P10	235	Oil pressure sensor	S45	245,246	Cruise control clutch switch
P11	366,367	Airflow meter	S46	271,272	Heated seat switch
P12	366,367	Temperature probe	S47	280,281	Courtesy light and headlamps on switch
P13	223	Temperature sensor (outside air)	S48	327,328	Roof sign switch (taxi)
P15	217,218	Fuel flow meter	S49	321	Alarm switch
P16	196	Central locking release sensor	S50	75	Choke switch
P17	502	ABS sensor – front, left	S51	152,408	Temperature switch
P18	504	ABS sensor – front, right	S57	239,241	Sunroof switch
P21	230,231	Optical frequency sensor	S61	407	Power steering pressure switch
P22	504	ABS sensor – rear	S62	366,367	Thermotime switch
P29	429	Intake manifold temperature sensor	S66	34,474	Vacuum switch
P30	431	Water temperature sensor	S67	171 to 174	Outside mirror adjustment switch
P31	430 to 432	Throttle potentiometer	S68	177 to 185	Outside mirror adjustment and heater switch
R2	456	Carburettor preheater	S69	374,378	Vacuum switch (low)
R3	76	Cigarette lighter	S70	374	Vacuum switch (high)
R5	95,96,97	Glow plugs	S71	374	Engine temperature switch
R6	150	Air conditioning fan resistor	S72	374	Converter oil pressure switch
R7	459 to 461	Mixture preheater	S73	459	Temperature switch
R11	46	Instrument control switch	S74	474	Air temperature switch
R12	83	Automatic choke	S75	474	Oil temperature switch
S1	6 to 7, 94 to 96	Starter switch	S76	140	Compressor pressure switch
			S83	436	Idling switch
S2	46,313,314	Light switch	S84	380	Converter oil pressure switch
S2.1	71	Courtesy light switch	S89	228	Seat belt switch
S3	36,37,38,39	Heater fan switch	U1	389 to 394	Voltage transformer
S4	16,17	Heated rear window switch	U3		Computer
S5		Indicator switch	U3.1		Clock switch
S5.2	50,51,297, 299,319, 320	Main beam switch	U3.2		Priority select switch
			U3.3		Function reset switch
S5.3	62,63,65, 289,296	Indicator and hazard warning switch	U4	494 to 508	ABS hydroaggregate
			V2	111	Headlamp washer diode
			V3	506,507	ABS diode
S5.4	36,37, 301,303	Parking light switch	X1	162,169	Trailer socket
			X2	48,72,75, 128,167, 388	Connectors
S5.5	82,288	Horn switch			
S5.6	101 to 103	Intermittent wiper switch			
S5.7	105	Wiper contact switch	X3	319	Radiophone connector
S7	80	Reversing lamp switch	Y1	152,408	Air conditioning compressor clutch
S8	58,244,373	Stop-lamp switch	Y2	149,410	Revolution accelerator lifting magnet
S10	7	Automatic transmission switch	Y3	128	Boot lid release solenoid
S11	24	Brake fluid level switch	Y4	114	Headlamp washer solenoid
S12	25	Clutch control switch	Y5	99	Diesel solenoid valve
S13	26	Handbrake telltale switch	Y6	366	Auxiliary air valve
S14	27	Oil pressure switch	Y7	366	Solenoid valves
S15	61	Boot light switch	Y8		Actuator
S16	69	Courtesy light switch – right	Y9	266	Car level control solenoid
S17	70	Courtesy light switch – left	Y10	11,12,33,34	Distributor
S18	78	Glovebox lamp switch	Y11	8,10,31, 32,448 to 450,469 to 471	Hall sensor
S20	125 to 127	Rear wiper switch			
S21	133,134	Foglamp switch			
S22	138,139	Rear foglamp switch			
S23	128	Boot lid release switch	Y13	366	Cold start valve
S24	147 to 150	Air conditioning fan switch	Y16	374,378	Converter clutch solenoid
S25	152	Air conditioning switch	Y17	85	Idle cut-off solenoid
S26	152,408	Evaporator inlet control	Y19	501	Solenoid valve – front, left
S27	152,408	Pressure switch	Y20	503	Solenoid valve – front, right
S28	152,408	Compressor cut-off switch	Y21	502	Solenoid valve – rear
S29	142,154, 398	Radiator fan switch	Y22	452,473	Distributor (EAI)
			Y26	422 to 428	Throttle valve positioner
S30	156,157	Heated seat switch	Y27	434,435	Pre-throttle valve

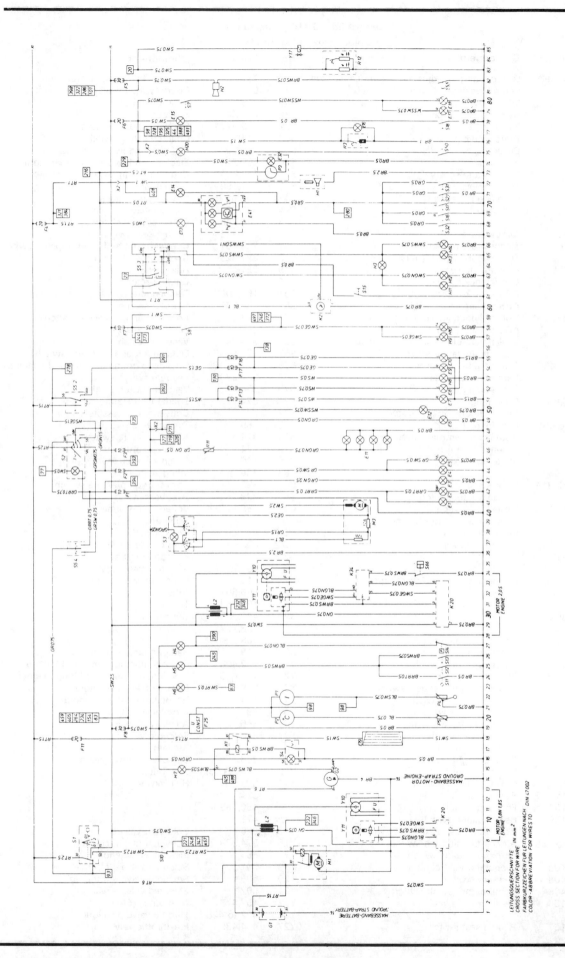

Fig. 13.116 Wiring diagram (schematic) – all models 1985 to 1986

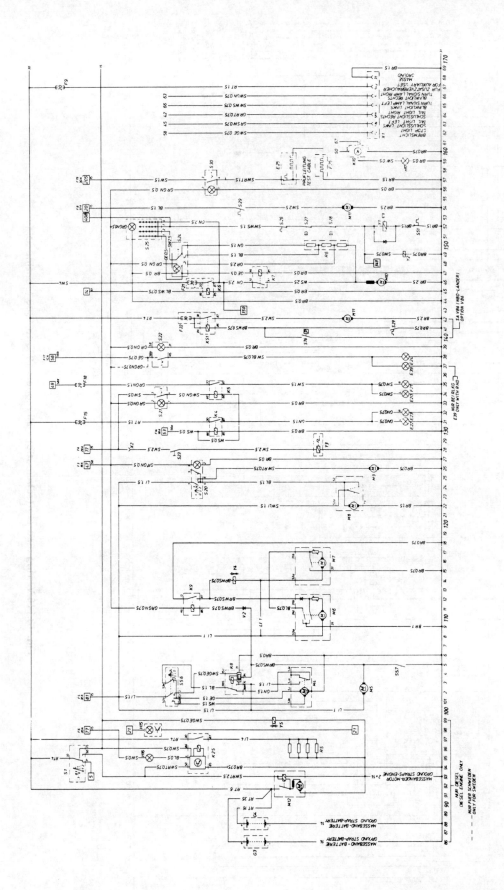

Fig. 13.116 Wiring diagram (schematic) – all models 1985 to 1986 (continued)

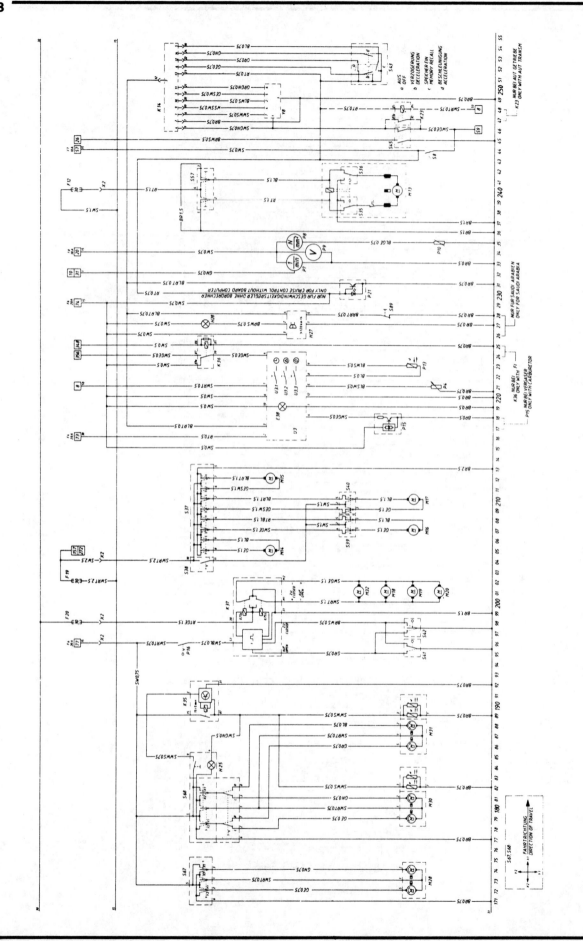

Fig. 13.116 Wiring diagram (schematic) – all models 1985 to 1986 (continued)

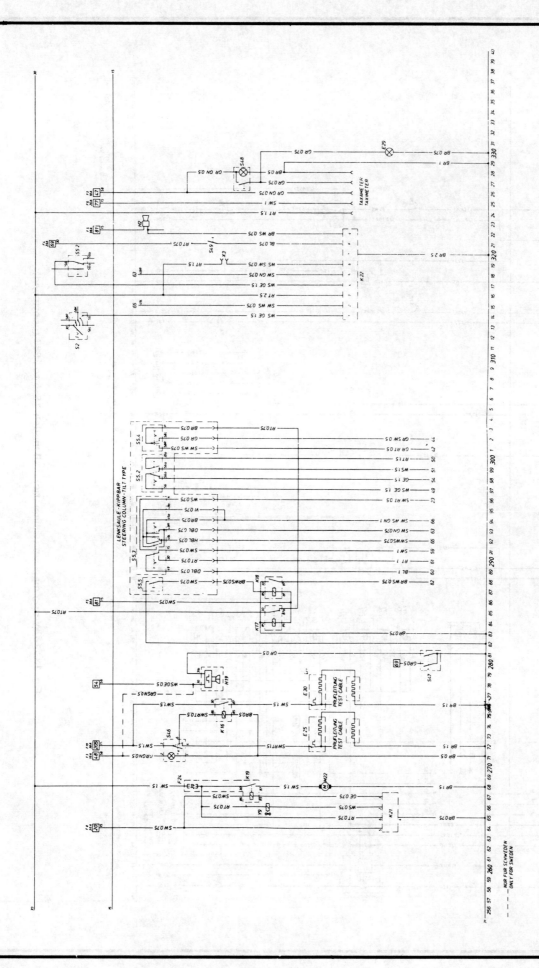

Fig. 13.116 Wiring diagram (schematic) — all models 1985 to 1986 (continued)

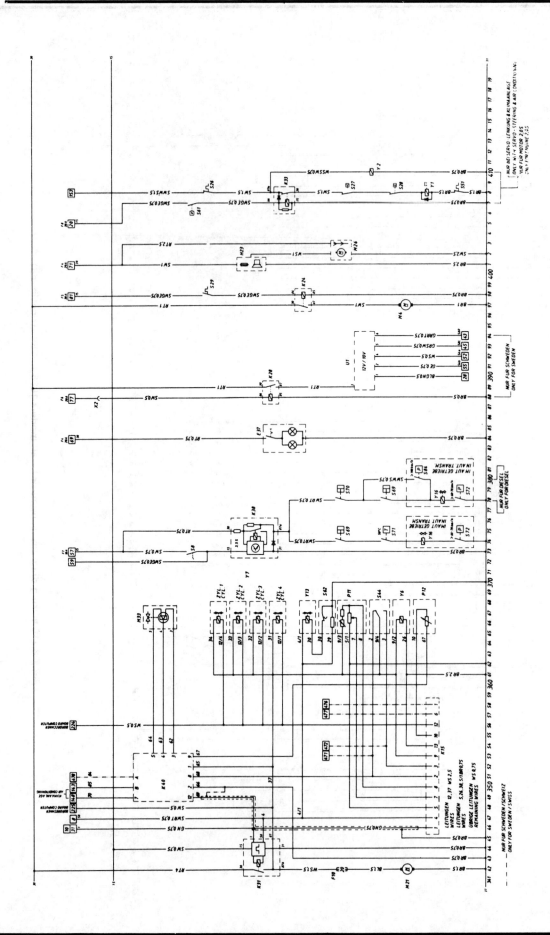

Fig. 13.116 Wiring diagram (schematic) – all models 1985 to 1986 (continued)

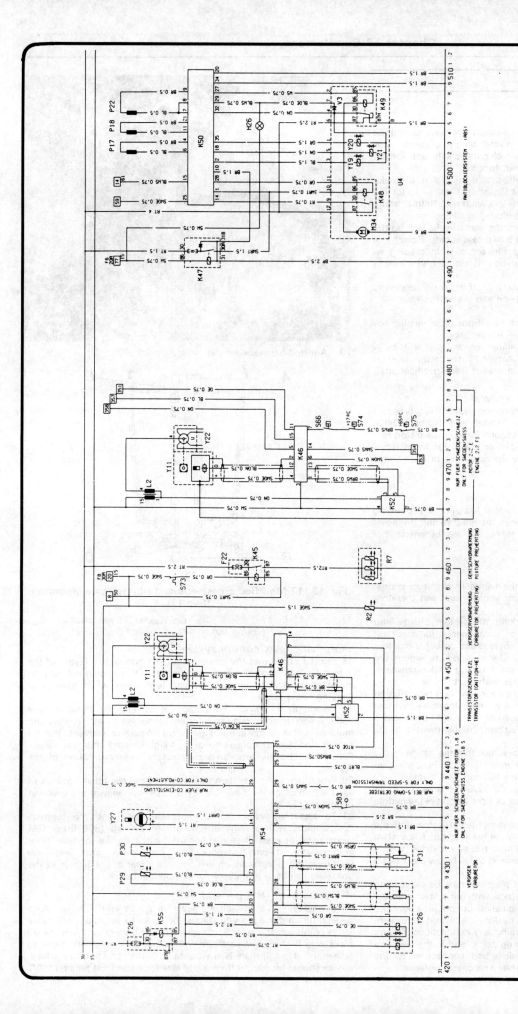

Fig. 13.116 Wiring diagram (schematic) – all models 1985 to 1986 (continued)

19 Suspension and steering

Front suspension modifications

Anti-roll bar and stabiliser rods

1 The stabiliser system of the front suspension has been redesigned for greater efficiency. The rubber-supported mount of each track control arm has been replaced by a rod which connects the anti-roll bar end to a bracket on the MacPherson strut (photo).

2 Removal and refitting of the modified anti-roll bar is a similar procedure to that given in Section 9 of Chapter 11, allowing for the differences in end fitting explained in the following text. Before fitting, each chassis-mounting bush should be dipped in silicone oil.

3 To remove a stabiliser rod, first chock the rear wheels, jack up the front of the car and support it on firmly based axle stands. Detach the rod from the anti-roll bar end and MacPherson strut by placing an open-ended spanner over the flats of the rod and removing its securing nut.

4 Before fitting a rod, renew its securing nuts. If flattened, renew the lockwasher which fits between the rod end and the anti-roll bar.

Front crossmember

5 From 1981, GM have modified the four front crossmember-to-body side-member mountings to give greater security.

6 Although the procedure for crossmember removal and refitting is similar to that given in Section 13 of Chapter 11, the torque wrench setting for each securing bolt has been increased (see Specifications).

Front shock absorber cartridge – renewal

7 Care must be taken not to mix cartridge types. Two types of cartridge are available, 'Delco' and 'Fichtel and Sachs'. Delco cartridges have 'BA' stamped on the hexagonal head of the piston rod; Fitchel and Sachs types have 'TA' stamped on the piston rod end.

8 It is not strictly necessary to renew the cartridges of both shock absorbers if only one is defective.

Rear suspension modification

9 The anti-roll bar fitted to later models has its ends pointing forwards. The upper control arm has been modified to suit. Removal and refitting procedures given in Chapter 11 are otherwise not affected.

Manual level control system

10 Where fitted and correctly charged, the manual level control system will help to maintain an almost constant vehicle level and therefore improve handling when towing.

11 Maintenance is confined to checking the system charge and carrying out a regular examination of components for signs of impending failure. Pressure loss will be obvious and probably due to a valve, pipeline or connection failure. Check at points where the pipelines pass through the bodyshell to see if fretting is taking place. If necessary, protect these areas of pipelines with plastic tube.

12 The system can be charged by using garage forecourt tyre inflation equipment connected to the charge point which is located either just above the left-hand rear light unit (Saloon) or to the right of the same light unit (Estate). In both cases the luggage compartment must be opened to expose the charge point.

13 The following charging procedure assumes that the gauge of the inflation equipment being used is accurate. If in doubt, obtain an accurate tyre gauge. Park the vehicle on a flat and level surface.

14 With the vehicle unladen, check that the system charge is 0.8 bar (11.6 lbf/in²) and then measure the distance from a point at the middle of the rear bumper to the ground.

15 Load the vehicle as required and then recharge the system until the rear bumper attains its height measured before loading. The system maximum pressure of 5 bar (71 lbf/in²) must not be exceeded. With a full load, system pressure must not be allowed to fall below 3 bar (43.5 lbf/in²) when in use on the road.

16 After unloading the vehicle, system pressure must be reduced to compensate. Never drive an unladen vehicle with full system pressue.

17 Do not attempt to repair a fractured pipeline, but obtain a new line with end connections from your GM dealer. Check that all system pressure has been released before undoing any connections. During removal, take note of the pipeline securing points and fit the new line in the same manner. Tighten each disturbed connection to the specified torque. Finally, charge the system and check for leaks.

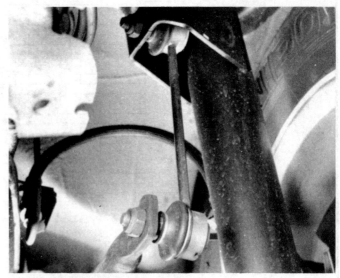

19.1 Anti-roll bar stabiliser rod

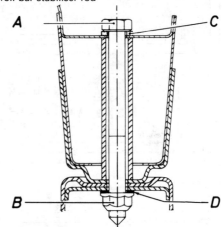

Fig. 13.117 Modified crossmember-to-bodyframe mounting (Sec 19)

A Bolt   C Washer 3.5 mm thick
B Self-locking nut   D Washer 1.0 mm thick

Automatic level control system

18 Fig. 13.118 shows the component parts and system layout of the automatic level control system. Where fitted, this system will help to maintain an almost constant vehicle level even when towing or carrying heavy loads.

19 Paragraph 11 gives the details of system maintenance. The compressor, electrical relay and system sensor are all sealed units and must be renewed complete if defective. Where convenient, test by substitution. Component removal is straightforward after disconnection of the battery and, where necessary, depressurisation of the system.

20 When removing a system component, note the fitted position of each electrical connection. Details of pipeline renewal are given in paragraph 17.

21 To test the system for correct operation, load the luggage compartment with a minimum weight of 140 kg (308 lb) – GM recommend at least three mechanics! Switch on the ignition. After approximately twenty seconds, the compressor must begin to pressurise the system, which will return the rear of the vehicle to the unloaded height. If not, check for component failure.

Alloy roadwheels – general

22 Periodically examine alloy wheels for cracks and chipping. As a general rule a damaged wheel must be renewed as cracks will cause stress points which may lead to sudden failure under heavy load. Small nicks may be radiused carefully with a fine file and emery paper to relieve the stress. If there is any doubt as to the condition of a wheel, advice should be sought from a GM dealer or specialist repairer.

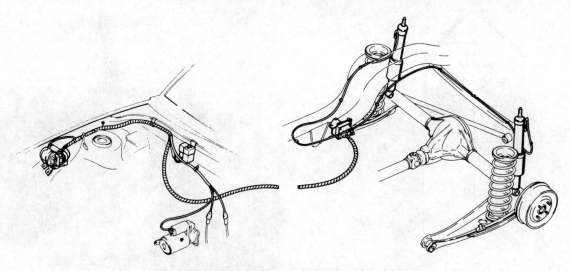

Fig. 13.118 Automatic level control system (Sec 19)

23 Each wheel is covered with a protective coating to prevent corrosion. If damage occurs to the wheel and the finish is penetrated, the bared aluminium alloy will soon start to corrode. A whitish grey oxide will form over the damaged area, which in itself is a protective coating. This deposit however, should be removed carefully as soon as possible and a new protective coating applied.

24 Note that serious corrosion or impact damage will affect tyre seating, leading to a loss of air pressure. If pressure loss is experienced, renew the wheel or seek specialist advice.

Wheel trim removal

25 Where fitted, the plastic wheel trims can easily be damaged during removal if care is not taken. Grasp each trim as shown (photo) and pull the valve hole area out to remove.

Tilt steering wheel

26 A tiltable steering wheel is fitted to some models. The wheel is unlocked and then locked after adjustment by moving a lever on the left-hand side of the upper column.

27 Removal of the steering column is as described in Chapter 11, Section 23, but dismantling should be limited to removing the steering wheel, column switch and lock.

28 Wear should be rectified by replacement with a new assembly.

Rear shock absorber mountings

29 In order to avoid noise from the rear suspension, which may be due to the shock absorbers, it is essential that their mountings are tightened

in the following way.

30 Tighten the lower mounting bolt to 45 Nm (33 lbf ft). The upper mounting nuts must be tightened to give a dimension in accordance with the appropriate illustration dependent upon the type of rear suspension – see Figs. 13.119, 13.120 and 13.121.

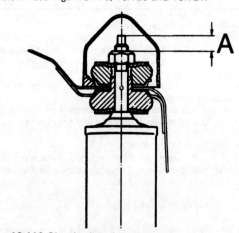

Fig. 13.119 Shock absorber upper mounting – standard suspension (Sec 19)
A = 8.5 to 9.5 mm (0.33 to 0.37 in)

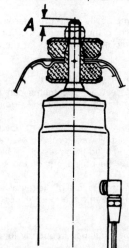

Fig. 13.120 Shock absorber upper mounting – suspension with load levelling (Sec 19)
A = 5.5 to 6.5 mm (0.22 to 0.26 in)

19.25 Wheel trim correctly gripped for removal

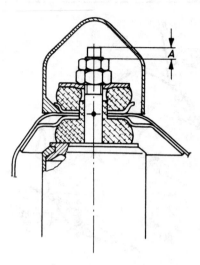

Fig. 13.121 Shock absorber upper mounting stud fitted with two locknuts (Sec 19)

A = 5.5 to 6.5 mm (0.22 to 0.26 in)

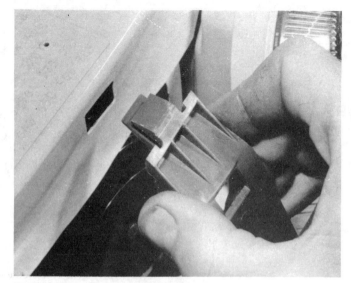

20.1 Radiator grille securing clip

20 Bodywork and fittings

Radiator grille – removal and refitting

1   To remove the radiator grille, first open the bonnet and detach the grille upper securing clips. Each clip is a firm fit in its location and should be carefully eased from position by pressing the flat of a screwdriver against its top edge (photo).
2   Pull the top of the grille slightly forwards and then up to clear its bottom locating pegs (photo).
3   Refitting the grille is a reversal of the removal procedure. Use a tommy bar or similar tool to tap the upper clips fully home.

Front seats – removal and refitting

4   The seat runners are bolted to the floorpan. To unscrew the bolts, first push the seat fully forwards and unscrew the rear bolts then push it rearwards and unscrew the front bolts.

Rear seats – removal and refititng
Saloon
5   Pull the two loops under the front edge of the seat cushion, the cushion can then be withdrawn.
6   The seat back can be removed if the lower fixings are released and the seat back then lifted upwards off its retaining clips.
Estate
7   The rear seat (assymmetrically split on later models) may be removed by folding it down to the maximum load position and then disconnecting the pivot brackets at the sides of the cushion or seat back.

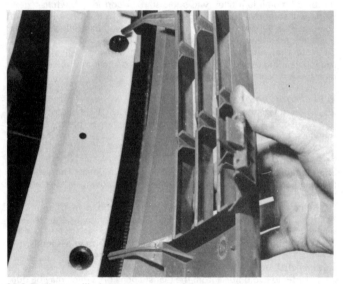

20.2 Radiator grille lower mountings

Head restraints – removal and refitting

8   Where fitted, the front seat head restraints can be removed for cleaning or repair. As shown in Fig. 13.122 it will require two people to do this.
9   With one person pressing the head restraint down onto the seat backrest, the other person should feel for the pressure points of both head restraint retaining springs and then press them hard into the seat. The head restraint can now be pulled out of the seat by jolting it sharply upwards.
10 Refitting a head restraint is a reversal of the removal procedure. The retaining springs should engage into the rod notches.

Seat belts

11 The seat belts should be examined frequently for signs of fraying and, if evident, renewed.
12 If the belts require cleaning, wipe them with a damp cloth moistened with liquid detergent. Never use a solvent of any description.

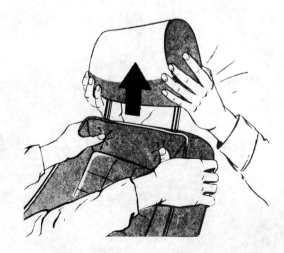

Fig. 13.122 Front seat head restraint removal (Sec 20)

13 If the car has been in a front end collision and the belts have already been strained by the impact, they should be renewed.

14 If a seat belt is removed and refitted always make sure that the sequence of the anchor plate components (spacer, wave washer and anchor plate) is maintained.

15 1986 models have rear seat belts fitted as standard.

Door window operating mechanism (power-operated) – removal and refitting

16 The procedure for removing the operating mechanism from doors equipped with power-operated windows is similar to that given in Sections 12 and 13 of Chapter 12. Any references to window winder handles can be ignored.

17 The motor can either be removed with the mechanism or beforehand as described in Section 18. Disconnect the battery before unplugging the motor. It is advisable to mark the fitted position of all components before removal as doing this will avoid alignment problems when refitting.

Plastic components

18 With the use of more and more plastic body components by the vehicle manufacturers (eg bumpers, spoilers, and in some cases major body panels), rectification of damage to such items has become a matter of either entrusting repair work to a specialist in this field, or renewing complete components. Repair by the DIY owner is not really feasible owing to the cost of the equipment and materials required for effecting such repairs. The basic technique involves making a groove along the line of the crack in the plastic using a rotary burr in a power drill. The damaged part is then welded back together by using a hot air gun to heat up and fuse a plastic filler rod into the groove. Any excess plastic is then removed and the area rubbed down to a smooth finish. It is important that a filler rod of the correct plastic is used, as body components can be made of a variety of different types (eg polycarbonate, ABS, polypropylene).

19 If the owner is renewing a complete component himself, he will be left with the problem of finding a suitable paint for finishing which is compatible with the type of plastic used. At one time the use of a universal paint was not possible owing to the complex range of plastics encountered in body component applications. Standard paints, generally speaking, will not bond to plastic or rubber satisfactorily. However, it is now possible to obtain a plastic body parts finishing kit which consists of a pre-primer treatment, a primer and coloured top coat. Full instructions are normally supplied with a kit, but basically the method of use is to first apply the pre-primer to the component concerned and allow it to dry for up to 30 minutes. Then the primer is applied and left to dry for about an hour before finally applying the special coloured top coat. The result is a correctly coloured component where the paint will flex with the plastic or rubber, a property that standard paint does not normally possess.

ABS – fault diagnosis

Symptom	Cause
System indicator light comes on at roadspeed of 20 mph (30 km/h)	Faulty wheel sensor Poor connection at 35 pin wiring harness plug

System indicator light stays on after starting	Poor earth connection at one of the following points:
	    Hydraulic modulator to ignition coil bracket
	    Alternator mounting bracket
	    Wiring harness intake manifold
	    Engine to body sidemember

System indicator light flickers after engine start-up	Alternator voltage drop

Fault diagnosis

Introduction

The vehicle owner who does his or her own maintenance according to the recommended schedules should not have to use this section of the manual very often. Modern component reliability is such that, provided those items subject to wear or deterioration are inspected or renewed at the specified intervals, sudden failure is comparatively rare. Faults do not usually just happen as a result of sudden failure, but develop over a period of time. Major mechanical failures in particular are usually preceded by characteristic symptoms over hundreds or even thousands of miles. Those components which do occasionally fail without warning are often small and easily carried in the vehicle.

With any fault finding, the first step is to decide where to begin investigations. Sometimes this is obvious, but on other occasions a little detective work will be necessary. The owner who makes half a dozen haphazard adjustments or replacements may be successful in curing a fault (or its symptoms), but he will be none the wiser if the fault recurs and he may well have spent more time and money than was necessary. A calm and logical approach will be found to be more satisfactory in the long run. Always take into account any warning signs or abnormalities that may have been noticed in the period preceding the fault – power loss, high or low gauge readings, unusual noises or smells, etc – and remember that failure of components such as fuses or spark plugs may only be pointers to some underlying fault.

The pages which follow here are intended to help in cases of failure to start or breakdown on the road. There is also a Fault Diagnosis Section at the end of each Chapter which should be consulted if the preliminary checks prove unfruitful. Whatever the fault, certain basic principles apply. These are as follows:

Verify the fault. This is simply a matter of being sure that you know what the symptoms are before starting work. This is particularly important if you are investigating a fault for someone else who may not have described it very accurately.

Don't overlook the obvious. For example, if the vehicle won't start, is there petrol in the tank? (Don't take anyone else's word on this particular point, and don't trust the fuel gauge either!) If an electrical fault is indicated, look for loose or broken wires before digging out the test gear.

Cure the disease, not the symptom. Substituting a flat battery with a fully charged one will get you off the hard shoulder, but if the underlying cause is not attended to, the new battery will go the same way. Similarly, changing oil-fouled spark plugs for a new set will get you moving again, but remember that the reason for the fouling (if it wasn't simply an incorrect grade of plug) will have to be established and corrected.

Don't take anything for granted. Particularly, don't forget that a 'new' component may itself be defective (especially if it's been rattling round in the boot for months), and don't leave components out of a fault diagnosis sequence just because they are new or recently fitted. When you do finally diagnose a difficult fault, you'll probably realise that all the evidence was there from the start.

Electrical faults

Electrical faults can be more puzzling than straightforward mechanical failures, but they are no less susceptible to logical analysis if the basic principles of operation are understood. Vehicle electrical wiring exists in extremely unfavourable conditions – heat, vibration and chemical attack – and the first things to look for are loose or corroded connections and broken or chafed wires, especially where the wires pass through holes in the bodywork or are subject to vibration.

All metal-bodied vehicles in current production have one pole of the battery 'earthed', ie connected to the vehicle bodywork, and in nearly all modern vehicles it is the negative (–) terminal. The various electrical components – motors, bulb holders etc – are also connected to earth, either by means of a lead or directly by their mountings. Electric current flows through the component and then back to the battery via the bodywork. If the component mounting is loose or corroded, or if a good path back to the battery is not available, the circuit will be incomplete and malfunction will result. The engine and/or gearbox are also earthed by means of flexible metal straps to the body or subframe; if these straps are loose or missing, starter motor, generator and ignition trouble may result.

Assuming the earth return to be satisfactory, electrical faults will be due either to component malfunction or to defects in the current supply. Individual components are dealt with in Chapter 10. If supply wires are broken or cracked internally this results in an open-circuit, and the easiest way to check for this is to bypass the suspect wire temporarily with a length of wire having a crocodile clip or suitable connector at each end. Alternatively, a 12V test lamp can be used to verify the presence of supply voltage at various points along the wire and the break can be thus isolated.

If a bare portion of a live wire touches the bodywork or other earthed metal part, the electricity will take the low-resistance path thus formed back to the battery: this is known as a short-circuit. Hopefully a short-circuit will blow a fuse, but otherwise it may cause burning of the insulation (and possibly further short-circuits) or even a fire. This is why it is inadvisable to bypass persistently blowing fuses with silver foil or wire.

Spares and tool kit

Most vehicles are supplied only with sufficient tools for wheel changing; the *Maintenance and minor repair* tool kit detailed in *Tools and working facilities*, with the addition of a hammer, is probably sufficient for those repairs that most motorists would consider attempting at the roadside. In addition a few items which can be fitted without too much trouble in the event of a breakdown should be carried. Experience and available space will modify the list below, but the following may save having to call on professional assistance:

Spark plugs, clean and correctly gapped
HT lead and plug cap – long enough to reach the plug furthest from the distributor
Distributor rotor, condenser and contact breaker points (as applicable)
Drivebelt(s) – emergency type may suffice
Spare fuses

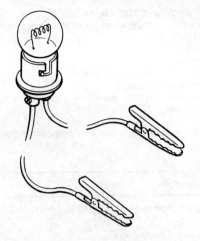

A simple test lamp is useful for tracing electrical faults

Set of principal light bulbs
Tin of radiator sealer and hose bandage
Exhaust bandage
Roll of insulating tape
Length of soft iron wire
Length of electrical flex
Torch or inspection lamp (can double as test lamp)
Battery jump leads
Tow-rope
Ignition water dispersing aerosol
Litre of engine oil
Sealed can of hydraulic fluid
Emergency windscreen
Worm drive clips

If spare fuel is carried, a can designed for the purpose should be used to minimise risks of leakage and collision damage. A first aid kit and a warning triangle, whilst not at present compulsory in the UK, are obviously sensible items to carry in addition to the above.

When touring abroad it may be advisable to carry additional spares which, even if you cannot fit them yourself, could save having to wait while parts are obtained. The items below may be worth considering:

Throttle cables
Cylinder head gasket
Alternator brushes
Fuel pump repair kit
Tyre valve core

One of the motoring organisations will be able to advise on availability of fuel etc in foreign countries.

Engine will not start

Engine fails to turn when starter operated
Flat battery (recharge, use jump leads, or push start)
Battery terminals loose or corroded
Battery earth to body defective
Engine earth strap loose or broken
Starter motor (or solenoid) wiring loose or broken
Automatic transmission selector in wrong position, or inhibitor switch faulty
Ignition/starter switch faulty
Major mechanical failure (seizure)
Starter or solenoid internal fault (see Chapter 10)

Starter motor turns engine slowly
Partially discharged battery (recharge, use jump leads, or push start)
Battery terminals loose or corroded
Battery earth to body defective

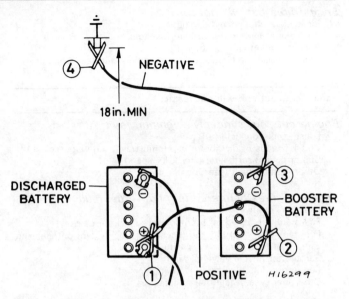

Jump start lead connections for negative earth vehicles – connect leads in order shown

Engine earth strap loose
Starter motor (or solenoid) wiring loose
Starter motor internal fault (see Chapter 10)

Starter motor spins without turning engine
Flat battery
Starter motor pinion sticking on sleeve
Flywheel gear teeth damaged or worn
Starter motor mounting bolts loose

Checking for a spark – note use of insulated tool

Engine turns normally but fails to start
Damp or dirty HT leads and distributor cap (crank engine and check for spark) (photo) – try moisture dispersant such as Holts Wet Start
Dirty or incorrectly gapped distributor points (if applicable)
No fuel in tank (check for delivery at carburettor)
Excessive choke (hot engine) or insufficient choke (cold engine)
Fouled or incorrectly gapped spark plugs (remove, clean and regap)
Other ignition system fault (see Chapter 4)
Other fuel system fault (see Chapter 3)
Poor compression (see Chapter 1)
Major mechanical failure (eg camshaft drive)

Engine fires but will not run
Insufficient choke (cold engine)
Air leaks at carburettor or inlet manifold
Fuel starvation (see Chapter 3)
Ballast resistor defective, or other ignition fault (see Chapter 4)

Engine cuts out and will not restart

Engine cuts out suddenly – ignition fault
Loose or disconnected LT wires
Wet HT leads or distributor cap (after traversing water splash)
Coil or condenser failure (check for spark)
Other ignition fault (see Chapter 4)

Engine misfires before cutting out – fuel fault
Fuel tank empty
Fuel pump defective or filter blocked (check for delivery)
Fuel tank filler vent blocked (suction will be evident on releasing cap) – not N. American cars with sealed cap
Carburettor needle valve sticking
Carburettor jets blocked (fuel contaminated)
Other fuel system fault (see Chapter 3)

Engine cuts out – other causes
Serious overheating
Major mechanical failure (eg camshaft drive)

Engine overheats

Ignition (no-charge) warning light illuminated
Slack or broken drivebelt – retension or renew (Chapter 2) (photo)

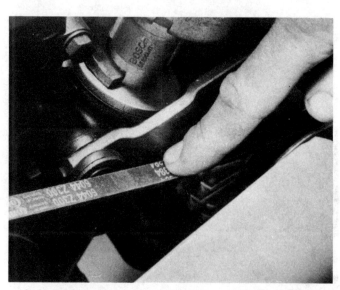

A slack drivebelt can cause overheating and battery charging problems

Ignition warning light not illuminated
Coolant loss due to internal or external leakage (see Chapter 2)
Thermostat defective
Low oil level
Brakes binding
Radiator clogged externally or internally
Engine waterways clogged
Ignition timing incorrect or automatic advance malfunctioning
Mixture too weak

Note: *Do not add cold water to an overheated engine or damage may result*

Low engine oil pressure

Gauge reads low or warning light illuminated with engine running
Oil level low or incorrect grade
Defective gauge or sender unit
Wire to sender unit earthed
Engine overheating
Oil filter clogged or bypass valve defective
Oil pressure relief valve defective
Oil pick-up strainer clogged
Oil pump worn or mountings loose
Worn main or big-end bearings

Note: *Low oil pressure in a high-mileage engine at tickover is not necessarily a cause for concern. Sudden pressure loss at speed is far more significant. In any event, check the gauge or warning light sender before condemning the engine.*

Engine noises

Pre-ignition (pinking) on acceleration
Incorrect grade of fuel
Ignition timing incorrect
Distributor faulty or worn
Worn or maladjusted carburettor
Excessive carbon build-up in engine

Whistling or wheezing noises
Leaking vacuum hose
Leaking carburettor or manifold gasket
Blowing head gasket

Tapping or rattling
Incorrect valve clearances
Worn valve gear
Worn timing belt
Broken piston ring (ticking noise)

Knocking or thumping
Unintentional mechanical contact (eg fan blades)
Worn drivebelt
Peripheral component fault (generator, water pump etc)
Worn big-end bearings (regular heavy knocking, perhaps less under load)
Worn main bearings (rumbling and knocking, perhaps worsening under load)
Piston slap (most noticeable when cold)

General repair procedures

Whenever servicing, repair or overhaul work is carried out on the car or its components, it is necessary to observe the following procedures and instructions. This will assist in carrying out the operation efficiently and to a professional standard of workmanship.

Joint mating faces and gaskets

Where a gasket is used between the mating faces of two components, ensure that it is renewed on reassembly, and fit it dry unless otherwise stated in the repair procedure. Make sure that the mating faces are clean and dry with all traces of old gasket removed. When cleaning a joint face, use a tool which is not likely to score or damage the face, and remove any burrs or nicks with an oilstone or fine file.

Make sure that tapped holes are cleaned, and keep them free of jointing compound if this is being used unless specifically instructed otherwise.

Ensure that all orifices, channels or pipes are clear and blow through them, preferably using compressed air.

Oil seals

Whenever an oil seal is removed from its working location, either individually or as part of an assembly, it should be renewed.

The very fine sealing lip of the seal is easily damaged and will not seal if the surface it contacts is not completely clean and free from scratches, nicks or grooves. If the original sealing surface of the component cannot be restored, the component should be renewed.

Protect the lips of the seal from any surface which may damage them in the course of fitting. Use tape or a conical sleeve where possible. Lubricate the seal lips with oil before fitting and, on dual lipped seals, fill the space between the lips with grease.

Unless otherwise stated, oil seals must be fitted with their sealing lips toward the lubricant to be sealed.

Use a tubular drift or block of wood of the appropriate size to install the seal and, if the seal housing is shouldered, drive the seal down to the shoulder. If the seal housing is unshouldered, the seal should be fitted with its face flush with the housing top face.

Screw threads and fastenings

Always ensure that a blind tapped hole is completely free from oil, grease, water or other fluid before installing the bolt or stud. Failure to do this could cause the housing to crack due to the hydraulic action of the bolt or stud as it is screwed in.

When tightening a castellated nut to accept a split pin, tighten the nut to the specified torque, where applicable, and then tighten further to the next split pin hole. Never slacken the nut to align a split pin hole unless stated in the repair procedure.

When checking or retightening a nut or bolt to a specified torque setting, slacken the nut or bolt by a quarter of a turn, and then retighten to the specified setting.

Locknuts, locktabs and washers

Any fastening which will rotate against a component or housing in the course of tightening should always have a washer between it and the relevant component or housing.

Spring or split washers should always be renewed when they are used to lock a critical component such as a big-end bearing retaining nut or bolt.

Locktabs which are folded over to retain a nut or bolt should always be renewed.

Self-locking nuts can be reused in non-critical areas, providing resistance can be felt when the locking portion passes over the bolt or stud thread.

Split pins must always be replaced with new ones of the correct size for the hole.

Special tools

Some repair procedures in this manual entail the use of special tools such as a press, two or three-legged pullers, spring compressors etc. Wherever possible, suitable readily available alternatives to the manufacturer's special tools are described, and are shown in use. In some instances, where no alternative is possible, it has been necessary to resort to the use of a manufacturer's tool and this has been done for reasons of safety as well as the efficient completion of the repair operation. Unless you are highly skilled and have a thorough understanding of the procedure described, never attempt to bypass the use of any special tool when the procedure described specifies its use. Not only is there a very great risk of personal injury, but expensive damage could be caused to the components involved.

Conversion factors

Length (distance)

Inches (in)	X	25.4	= Millimetres (mm)	X 0.0394	= Inches (in)
Feet (ft)	X	0.305	= Metres (m)	X 3.281	= Feet (ft)
Miles	X	1.609	= Kilometres (km)	X 0.621	= Miles

Volume (capacity)

Cubic inches (cu in; in³)	X	16.387	= Cubic centimetres (cc; cm³)	X 0.061	= Cubic inches (cu in; in³)
Imperial pints (Imp pt)	X	0.568	= Litres (l)	X 1.76	= Imperial pints (Imp pt)
Imperial quarts (Imp qt)	X	1.137	= Litres (l)	X 0.88	= Imperial quarts (Imp qt)
Imperial quarts (Imp qt)	X	1.201	= US quarts (US qt)	X 0.833	= Imperial quarts (Imp qt)
US quarts (US qt)	X	0.946	− Litres (l)	X 1.057	− US quarts (US qt)
Imperial gallons (Imp gal)	X	4.546	= Litres (l)	X 0.22	= Imperial gallons (Imp gal)
Imperial gallons (Imp gal)	X	1.201	= US gallons (US gal)	X 0.833	= Imperial gallons (Imp gal)
US gallons (US gal)	X	3.785	= Litres (l)	X 0.264	= US gallons (US gal)

Mass (weight)

Ounces (oz)	X	28.35	= Grams (g)	X 0.035	= Ounces (oz)
Pounds (lb)	X	0.454	= Kilograms (kg)	X 2.205	= Pounds (lb)

Force

Ounces-force (ozf; oz)	X	0.278	= Newtons (N)	X 3.6	= Ounces-force (ozf; oz)
Pounds-force (lbf; lb)	X	4.448	= Newtons (N)	X 0.225	= Pounds-force (lbf; lb)
Newtons (N)	X	0.1	= Kilograms-force (kgf; kg)	X 9.81	= Newtons (N)

Pressure

Pounds-force per square inch (psi; lbf/in²; lb/in²)	X	0.070	= Kilograms-force per square centimetre (kgf/cm²; kg/cm²)	X 14.223	= Pounds-force per square inch (psi; lbf/in²; lb/in²)
Pounds-force per square inch (psi; lbf/in²; lb/in²)	X	0.068	= Atmospheres (atm)	X 14.696	= Pounds-force per square inch (psi; lbf/in²; lb/in²)
Pounds-force per square inch (psi; lbf/in²; lb/in²)	X	0.069	= Bars	X 14.5	= Pounds-force per square inch (psi; lbf/in²; lb/in²)
Pounds-force per square inch (psi; lbf/in²; lb/in²)	X	6.895	= Kilopascals (kPa)	X 0.145	= Pounds-force per square inch (psi; lbf/in²; lb/in²)
Kilopascals (kPa)	X	0.01	= Kilograms-force per square centimetre (kgf/cm²; kg/cm²)	X 98.1	= Kilopascals (kPa)
Millibar (mbar)	X	100	= Pascals (Pa)	X 0.01	= Millibar (mbar)
Millibar (mbar)	X	0.0145	= Pounds-force per square inch (psi; lbf/in²; lb/in²)	X 68.947	= Millibar (mbar)
Millibar (mbar)	X	0.75	= Millimetres of mercury (mmHg)	X 1.333	= Millibar (mbar)
Millibar (mbar)	X	0.401	= Inches of water (inH₂O)	X 2.491	= Millibar (mbar)
Millimetres of mercury (mmHg)	X	0.535	= Inches of water (inH₂O)	X 1.868	= Millimetres of mercury (mmHg)
Inches of water (inH₂O)	X	0.036	= Pounds-force per square inch (psi; lbf/in²; lb/in²)	X 27.68	= Inches of water (inH₂O)

Torque (moment of force)

Pounds-force inches (lbf in; lb in)	X	1.152	= Kilograms-force centimetre (kgf cm; kg cm)	X 0.868	= Pounds-force inches (lbf in; lb in)
Pounds-force inches (lbf in; lb in)	X	0.113	= Newton metres (Nm)	X 8.85	= Pounds-force inches (lbf in; lb in)
Pounds-force inches (lbf in; lb in)	X	0.083	= Pounds-force feet (lbf ft; lb ft)	X 12	= Pounds-force inches (lbf in; lb in)
Pounds-force feet (lbf ft; lb ft)	X	0.138	= Kilograms-force metres (kgf m; kg m)	X 7.233	= Pounds-force feet (lbf ft; lb ft)
Pounds-force feet (lbf ft; lb ft)	X	1.356	= Newton metres (Nm)	X 0.738	= Pounds-force feet (lbf ft; lb ft)
Newton metres (Nm)	X	0.102	= Kilograms-force metres (kgf m; kg m)	X 9.804	= Newton metres (Nm)

Power

Horsepower (hp)	X	745.7	= Watts (W)	X 0.0013	= Horsepower (hp)

Velocity (speed)

Miles per hour (miles/hr; mph)	X	1.609	= Kilometres per hour (km/hr; kph)	X 0.621	= Miles per hour (miles/hr; mph)

Fuel consumption*

Miles per gallon, Imperial (mpg)	X	0.354	= Kilometres per litre (km/l)	X 2.825	= Miles per gallon, Imperial (mpg)
Miles per gallon, US (mpg)	X	0.425	= Kilometres per litre (km/l)	X 2.352	= Miles per gallon, US (mpg)

Temperature

Degrees Fahrenheit = (°C x 1.8) + 32   Degrees Celsius (Degrees Centigrade; °C) = (°F - 32) x 0.56

It is common practice to convert from miles per gallon (mpg) to litres/100 kilometres (l/100km), where mpg (Imperial) x l/100 km = 282 and mpg (US) x l/100 km = 235

Index